Client/Server Communications Services

AF332916

Other McGraw-Hill Books of Interest

ALLEN/BAMBARA/BAMBARA • *Informix: Client/Server Application Development,* 0-07-913056-9

ANDERSON • *Client/Server Database Design with Sybase,* 0-07-001697-6

BAMBARA/ALLEN • *Power Builder: A Guide for Developing Client/Server Applications,* 0-07-005413-4

BERSON • *Client/Server Architecture, 2/e,* 0-07-005664-1

BERSON/ANDERSON • *Sybase and Client/Server Computing, Featuring System 11, 2/e,* 0-07-006080-0

CLIFFORD • *Mastering Sybase SQL Server 11,* 0-07-011662-8

CLIFFORD • *Sybase Replication Server Primer,* 0-07-011515-X

GREEN/BROWN • *PowerBuilder 5: Object-Oriented Design and Development,* 0-07-024469-3

JONES • *Developing Client/Server Applications with Microsoft Access,* 0-07-912982-X

JONES • *Ready-Made PowerBuilder Applications,* 0-07-912062-8

NEMZOW • *Visual Basic Developer's Toolkit,* 0-07-912309-0

ROSEEN • *InfoMaker 5: A Guide to Developing Client/Server Applications,* 0-07-053999-5

SANDERS • *Developer's Guide to DB2 for Common Servers,* 0-07-057725-0

To order or receive additional information on these or any other
McGraw-Hill titles, in the the United States please call 1-800-722-4726.
In other countries, contact your local McGraw-Hill representative.

Client/Server Communications Services

A Guide for the Applications Developer

Thomas S. Ligon

McGraw-Hill

New York San Francisco Washington, D.C. Auckland Bogotá
Caracas Lisbon London Madrid Mexico City Milan
Montreal New Delhi San Juan Singapore
Sydney Tokyo Toronto

Library of Congress Cataloging-in-Publication Data

Ligon, Thomas S.
    Client/server communications services : a guide for the
applications developer / Thomas S. Ligon.
        p.   cm.
    Includes bibliographical references and index.
    ISBN 0-07-038118-6
    1. Client/server computing.   2. Application software—Development.
3. Electronic data processing—Distributed processing.   I. Title.
QA76.9.C55L55   1997
005.7′1376—dc21   97-10723
                                                         CIP

McGraw-Hill

A Division of The McGraw·Hill Companies

Copyright © 1997 by The McGraw-Hill Companies, Inc. All rights reserved. Printed
in the United States of America. Except as permitted under the United States
Copyright Act of 1976, no part of this publication may be reproduced or distributed in
any form or by any means, or stored in a data base or retrieval system, without the
prior written permission of the publisher.

1 2 3 4 5 6 7 8 9 0   FGR/FGR   9 0 2 1 0 9 8 7

ISBN 0-07-038118-6

*The sponsoring editor for this book was John Wyzalek, the editing supervisor was
Stephen M. Smith, and the production supervisor was Pamela A. Pelton.*

Printed and bound by Quebecor/Fairfield.

McGraw-Hill books are available at special quantity discounts to use as premiums and
sales promotions, or for use in corporate training programs. For more information,
please write to the Director of Special Sales, McGraw-Hill, 11 West 19th Street, New
York, NY 10011. Or contact your local bookstore.

 This book is printed on recycled, acid-free paper containing a minimum of
50% recycled, de-inked fiber.

Information contained in this work has been obtained by The McGraw-Hill
Companies, Inc. ("McGraw-Hill") from sources believed to be reliable.
However, neither McGraw-Hill nor its authors guarantee the accuracy or completeness of any information published herein and neither McGraw-Hill nor its
authors shall be responsible for any errors, omissions, or damages arising out
of use of this information. This work is published with the understanding that
McGraw-Hill and its authors are supplying information but are not attempting
to render engineering or other professional services. If such services are
required, the assistance of an appropriate professional should be sought.

Contents

Contents

Contents

Preface

This is a book on distributed computing, with the main emphasis on what communications services are available and how they can be used by applications. Since the book covers a broad range of distributed computing situations, it could just as well be called "distributed systems", "distributed processing", "cooperative processing", or even "client/server architecture". However, in most of the book, we have used the term "client/server" as a special case of distributed computing.

The primary content of the book is the technical basis for distributed computing, especially as it applies to applications programming. This has been treated thoroughly, including an explanation and comparison of the methods available for implementing distributed systems, instead of being restricted to a presentation of a specific technique, such as client/server architectures or distributed transaction processing.

Particular emphasis has been given to communications, since it is the primary technical basis for distributed systems. However, this is not a book on how to implement communications subsystems; it is a book on how to use them, and on what the applications programmer needs to understand about the differences between various communications methods in order to make good applications.

The origin of the book is my work in the Softlab communications department, which has included projects for a number of large organizations. During this work, my colleagues and customers have often come to me with questions and remarks about which communications protocols to use, and how. Here are some typical examples:

- "My customer has the following configuration… Our application will do this… Can I solve the problem with APPC? Should I use APPN instead?"
- "Do I have to learn all of that? Why can't I just send the messages and forget about them?"
- "How can I know if the messages get to the partner? Do I need to implement a response and a time-out mechanism to check up?"
- "We want to make our applications independent of the communications protocols used, so we plan to add a layer that hides the differences. That way, it shouldn't matter whether we use APPC, RPC, or something else. Why doesn't the vendor sell this as a standard part of the operating system?"
- "We are writing a distributed application on UNIX which needs to coordinate multiple databases. We have implemented a two-phase commit protocol on top of the Sockets interface. Are you saying that there was another way of doing it?"
- "One application is the sender, the other is the receiver. All we need is a one-way pipe that gets the data across the line. That's the way we have always done it. Why should we change?"

- "Most of our applications need an asynchronous interface with guaranteed delivery. That is why we have developed our own communications package, which has been established as a standard within the company. Do you want to help us sell it to other companies?"

These examples show some important things about what applications programmers need:

- They need to know which communications protocols are suited to their applications.
- They need to know how communications will affect the structure of their applications.
- They do not need to know how the protocols work, and often don't have time to learn it.

There are a number of good communications books on the market. Most of them describe how the protocols work, but say little about how they affect the application. In fact, this is also the case with many other aspects of distributed computing: These books describe how a network-management system is constructed, how the elements of DCE Security exchange keys, or how an encryption algorithm works, but they don't help the applications programmer decide which one to use, or how to use it to full advantage.

This is the motivation for writing a book on communications services for applications. The goal is to help applications programmers (and managers) understand which subsystems they need, which ones are best suited to their applications, and how to use them adequately.

In order to achieve this goal, this book stresses the concept of services. The services of a subsystem (for communication, network management, security, etc.) help you answer the following questions:

- What does it do for me?
- What makes it different from other choices?
- How does it affect the behavior and architecture of my application?

"Part 1. Introduction" presents the major issues involved in distributed computing. The first chapter also introduces you to APE (Animal Proliferation Enterprises), an organization which provides a lot of good and bad examples of distributed computing. APE is fictitious: None of the animals quoted here are among our customers. At the same time, the examples are very real, and I hope you will find a number of cases that apply to your organization or to other aspects of your real-life situation. This part also includes a general discussion of services and standards. The chapter on processing models is very important for this book, because it explains the meaning of the basic models (client/server, distributed transactions, queuing, etc.), thus providing the basis for discussing how these models are supported by various systems and how they affect the applications that use them.

"Part 2. Systems" reveals my liking for a bottom-up approach to explaining how things work. (Other topics, such as systems management and security, are treated in a more top-down fashion.) The chapters on hardware and operating systems provide a basis for discussing how the relevant services are implemented in a distributed environment, and what the major trends are. This is followed by a number of chapters on specific systems, including OSF DCE, which can be considered as "middleware", or as an add-on part of an NOS (Network Operating System).

"Part 3. Communications" begins with a general discussion of services offered by communications and of the basic structure of networks, thus explaining some of the most important communications concepts from the point of view of the application. The following chapters present a number of the most important lower layers of communication for local and wide area networks.

"Part 4. Middleware" covers the middle ground between traditional communications services and application-support systems, including RPC (Remote Procedure Calls), distributed transaction processing, distributed objects, distributed SQL, and message-oriented middleware. These are the most important upper-layer communications protocols used today, and the stress is again on the services provided for the application.

"Part 5. Systems Management" begins with an explanation of the major concepts involved in managing networks, systems, security, and applications. This is followed by a discussion of the systems and products used for implementing these functions. The part closes with a chapter on security which presents the major concepts and goals of security in distributed systems, followed by a discussion of the methods used for implementing and managing security.

Finally, "Part 6. Applications" explains some of the major issues and design decisions involved in creating distributed applications. There is also a chapter on the question of how to migrate existing applications to the new environment. All of it is based on examples. This is also where you will find a chapter on the Internet.

Most chapters list services, standards, and some products relevant to the topic discussed. The list of products is intended to help the reader connect the technology with product names; it is not complete, nor is any attempt made to evaluate or compare the products. The appendix contains an extensive glossary of all abbreviations and technical terms used in the book, a bibliography covering all sources, and an index.

The book is best understood when read sequentially, but it should be possible to start anywhere and refer to the other sections as necessary. In fact, some parts could be skipped and then used only as reference material. When the book is used this way, it would still be valuable to begin with one piece of the fundamentals, "Chapter 4. Processing Models".

Acknowledgments

I would like to thank my colleagues at Softlab for providing an interesting and productive working environment. In particular, thanks are due to Elisabeth Schieblich, who read parts of this book and provided useful suggestions.

My thanks also go to Alex Berson, the editor of this series, for reviewing the manuscript in various stages of its completion, and the editors of McGraw-Hill, especially Jennifer Holt DiGiovanna and many unnamed people, such as those who did the proofreading.

Thomas S. Ligon

Trademarks

The following pages list the trademarked products mentioned in this book, their companies, and the conpanies' URLs (Uniform Resource Locators, i.e., Internet addresses).

Action Technologies, http://www.actiontech.com
      ActionWorkFlow Manager

ADB Incorporated
      M.A.T.I.S.S.E.

American Telephone and Telegraph, http://www.att.com
      AT&T, EasyLink, and Tuxedo.

Andyne, http://www.andyne.on.ca
      Andyne GQL

Apertus Technologies Incorporated (formerly Systems Strategies Incorporated),
      http://www.apertus.com
      ezBRIDGE, SSI, and Transact.

Apollo Computer, Inc., a subsidiary of Hewlett-Packard Company
      Apollo, NetLS, Network License System, and NCS.

Apple Computer Incorporated, http://www.apple.com
      Appletalk and Macintosh.

Asset Software International, http://www.assetpro.ca
      AssetPro

Attachmate, http://www.attachmate.com
      OpenMind

BanTec (formerly Recognition International), http://www.plx.com
      Plexus FloWare

Banyan Systems Incorporated, http://www.banyan.com
      Banyan Vines, ENS, Enterprise Network Services, Network Event Logger, and
      StreetTalk.

BMC, http://www.bmc.com
      Patrol

Boole & Babbage, http://www.boole.com
      Command/Post

Borland International, http://www.borland.com
      dBase and Interbase.

Brio, http://www.brio.com
> Brio DataPrism

Bull, http://www.bull.com
> Unikix

Bull, Olivetti and Siemens Nixdorf
> BOSX

Cabletron systems, http://www.cabletron.com

Candle, http://www.candle.com
> Candle Command Center

Carnegie Mellon University, http://www.cmu.edu
> AFS and Andrew File System.

Cisco Systems, http://www.cisco.com
> CiscoFusion

Collabra Software, http://www.collabra.com
> Collabra Share

Component Integration Lab
> CIL and OpenDoc.

CompuServe, http://www.compuserve.com
> CompuServe

Computer Associates, http://www.cai.com
> CA, CA-Unicenter and CA-Unicenter/TNG.

Covia Technologies, http://www.covia.com,
> http://www.tandem.com/TAG/COVIA.HTM
> CI and Communications Integrator.

Digital Equipment Corporation, http://www.dec.com
> ACA (Application Control Architecture), ACMS, All-In-1, Alpha AXP, CMA, DEC, DECmessageQ, DECNET, DEC ObjectBroker, dns, dts, LinkWorks, Object/DB, OpenVMS, Polycenter, Polycenter AssetWorks, Polycenter NetView, ULTRIX, and VMS.

Fairfield Software
> Clear Access

FileNet, http://www.filenet.com
> Visual Workflow and WorkFlo.

Gradient Technologies, http://www.gradient.com
> NetLS

Trademarks

Gupta Technologies Incorporated (now Centura Software Corporation),
        http://www.centurasoft.com, http://www.gupta.com
        Gupta

Hewlett-Packard, http://www.hp.com
        HP, HP Distributed Smalltalk, HP ORB Plus, HP-UX, OpenODB, OpenView,
        MPE/iX, NetMetrix, Omniback, OpenView Network Node Manager,
        OpenView Software Distributor, OpenMail, OpenView Traffic Monitor, PA-
        RISC, PerfView, and Postmaster.

Hewlett-Packard & SunSoft
        DOMF (Distributed Object Management Facility)

Horizon Strategies Incorporated (formerly Momentum Software Corporation)
        Extended IPC, Message Exchange, MX, and X-IPC.

Horizons Technology, http://www.horizons.com
        LANauditor

Hyperdesk
        DOMS (Distributed Object Management System)

Information Builders Incorporated, http://www.ibi.com
        EDA/SQL

Informix Incorporated, http://www.informix.com
        Informix

Ingres Corporation (now part of Computer Associates), http://www.ingres.com
        Ingres

Insignia Solutions, http://www.insignia.com
        SoftPC and SoftWindows.

Institute of Electrical and Electronics Engineers, http://stdsbbs.ieee.org.
        IEEE and POSIX.

Intel Corporation, http://www.intel.com
        LANDesk Manager

Intermetrics, http://www.intermetrics.com
        Intermetrics

International Business Machines Corporation, http://www.ibm.com
ADSTAR Distributed Storage Manager, AIX, APPC, APPN, Bookmaster, CICS, CMVC (Configuration Management Version Control), CPI-C, DB2, DDCS, DFSMS, DRDA, DSOM (Distributed System Object Model), ESA, FlowMark, IBM, IMS, LAN Network Manager, MQI, MQSeries, MVS, NetView, NetView Distribution Manager, NetView Performance Monitor, NWays, OS/2, OS/2 LAN Server, OS/400, PowerPC, Profs, RISC System/6000, SAA, SNA, SOM (System Object Model), SOMobjects, TPF, Trouble Ticket/6000, TSO, Ultimedia Mail/2, VSE, WorkGroup, and Workplace OS.

Intersolv, http://www.intersolv.com
Intersolv Q+E and PVCS.

Iona, http://www.iona.com
Orbix

Itasca Systems, smtp://sales@itasca.com
Itasca ODBMS

Janus Technologies
Argis

Keyfile Corporation, http://www.keyfile.com
Keyfile and Keyflow.

Legent Corporation, now a part of Computer Associates
Endevor and Paradigm/XP.

Lotus Development Division of IBM, http://www.lotus.com
Approach, cc:Mail, Lotus, Lotus Forms, Lotus IPS (Image Processing Server), Lotus Notes, and Lotus Organizer.

MAK Software Consultants
Object Skipjack

Massachusetts Institute of Technology, http://www.mit.edu
Athena, Palladium, X Window System, and X11.

MAXM Systems, http://www.maxm.com
MAX/Enterprise

Mesa Group
Conference+

Microsoft Corporation, http://www.microsoft.com
COM, DDE, Exchange, MS-DOS, Internet Explorer, Internet Information Server, Microsoft Query, Schedule+, SourceSafe, Microsoft SQL Server, ODBC, OLE, Visual Basic, Windows, Windows NT, Windows NT Server, Win32, and WOSA.

Trademarks

Mips Technologies Incorporated, http://www.mips.com
     Mips

Momentum Software Corporation, http://www.momsoft.com
     Extended IPC, Message Exchange, MX, and X-IPC.

Mortice Kern Systems, http://www.mks.com
     InterOpen

Motorola Incorporated, http://www.mot.com
     Motorola

NCR, http://www.ncr.com
     Top End, NCR, and ProcessIT.

Netscape, http://www.netscape.com
     Communicator and Navigator

New Dimension Software (previously 4th Dimension Software),
     http://www.ddddf.com
     Control-M

Next, http://www.next.com
     NextStep

Novadigm, http://www.novadigm.com.

Novell Incorporated, http://www.novell.com
     AppWare, CMS (Collaborative Message Server), GroupWise, LANalyzer,
     ManageWise, NetWare, NetWare Global MHS, NMS (NetWare Management
     System), NetWare Navigator, SoftSolutions, and UnixWare.

O_2 Technology, Incorporated, http://www.o2tech.com
     O_2

Object Design Incorporated, http://www.odi.com
     ObjectStore and ODI.

Object Management Group, Incorporated, http://www.omg.org.
     CORBA, COSS, Object Request Broker, OMG, and ORB.

Objectivity Incorporated, http://www.objectivity.com
     Objectivity/DB

Ontos, Incorporated, http://www.ontos.com
     Ontos DB

Open Software Foundation, http://www.osf.org.
     DCE, DME, Motif, OSF, and OSF/1.

Open Horizon, http://www.openhorizon.com
   Connection

OpenVision Technologies, http://www.ov.com
   AXXiON

Oracle Corporation, http://www.oracle.com
   Oracle Database, Oracle Transparent Gateway, SQL*NET, and WebServer.

O'Reilly & Associates Inc.. http://www.software.ora.com
   Website Professional

PaperClip Software Incorporated, http://www.paperclip.com
   PaperClip Workflow

Peerlogic Incorporated, http://www.peerlogic.com
   Peerlogic Pipes

Persistent Data Systems
   IDB Object Database

Platinum, http://www.platinum.com
   POEMS and Platinum Open Enterprise Management System.

Poet Software Company, http://www.poet.com
   Poet

PowerBroker (formerly Expersoft), http://www.expersoft.com
   XShell ORB

PowerOpen Association
   PowerOpen

Powersoft (now a part ov Sybase), http://www.powersoft.com
   PowerBuilder

QNX Software, http://www.qnx.com
   QNX

Raima Corporation, http://www.raima.com
   Raima Object Manager

Reach Software
   WorkMAN

Remedy Corporation, http://www.remedy.com
   Action Request System

Rocket Software, Incorporated, http://www.rocketsoftware.com

Trademarks

RSA Data Security, Inc., http://www.rsa.com
        S/WAN (with TimeStep)

Santa Cruz Operations
        Open Desktop and SCO.

Seagate Enterprise Management Software, a subsidiary of Seagate Technology,
        http://www.seagate.com
        AssetManager (previously from NetLabs), LANAlert, and Frye LAN Directory
        for Windows.

Seer Technologies, http://www.seer.com
        NetEssential

Servio Corporation
        GemStone

Siemens Nixdorf Informationssysteme AG, http://www.sni.com
        BS2000, DIR-X, Sinix, and SNI.

Soft-Switch Incorporated
        Enterprise Message Exchange and EMX.

Spry, http://www.spry.com
        Mosaic

Staffware, http://www.staffware.com
        Staffware

Standard Performance Evaluation Corporation
        SPEC

StarQuest Software, Incorporated, http://starweb.starware.com

Stratus, http://www.stratus.com
        System/88

Sun Microsystems, http://www.sun.com
        DOE (Distributed Objects Everywhere), HotJava, Network File System, NFS,
        Open Look, Solaris, SunOS, SUN SPARC, and Wabi.

Sybase Incorporated, http://www.sybase.com
        Sybase

Symantic, http://www.symantic.com
        Norton Administrator for Networks.

Systems Strategies Incorporated
        ezBRIDGE, SSI, and Transact.

Tally Systems, http://www.tallysys.com
    Cenergy

Tandem, http://www.tandem.com
    Guardian and Pathway.

Tensegrity
    Tensegrity OO Database for Smalltalk

Texas Instruments
    TI

TimeStep Corporation, http://www.timestep.com
    S/WAN (with RSA Data Security)

Tivoli Systems, now a part of IBM, http://www.tivoli.com
    AMS, Application Management System, HUGS, Tivoli, TME (Tivoli
    Management Environment), and WisDOM.

Transarc Corporation, http://www.transarc.com
    Encina and Transarc.

UB Networks, http://ub.com
    Empower

UniSQL, Incorporated
    UniSQL/X Database Management System

Unisys, http://www.unisys.com
    CTOS

University of California at Berkeley
    Berkeley Software Distribution and BSD.

VC Software, Incorporated
    ODBMS 2.0

Versant Object Technology Corporation, http://www.versant.com
    Versant

ViewStar
    ViewStar System

Wang, http://www.wang.com
    OPEN/Workflow

Watcom (now a part of Sybase), http://www.watcom.com

WordPerfect Incorporated
    WordPerfect

Trademarks

X/Open Corporation, http://www.xopen.org
    UNIX and X/Open.

Xsoft, http://www.xsoft.com
    InConcert

Client/Server Communications Services

Part 1. Introduction

Introduction to Part 1

Why is distributed processing so important now? How is it being driven by technological development, and how does it provide the basis for other applications? What are the most fundamental, or general, aspects to be thought of when developing distributed applications? These are the questions addressed in this part.

"Chapter 1. Our Habitat" presents the major issues involved in distributed processing, including the motivation for the technology and the repercussions of it on society. It also includes some remarks about the human aspects of how the technology is developed. It also introduces you to APE (Animal Proliferation Enterprises), an organization which provides a lot of good and bad examples of distributed processing.

"Chapter 2. Services" defines some very general services which can be offered by almost any system and discusses their importance. These, along with the specific services presented in the subsequent chapters, can also be used as a checklist for evaluating products.

"Chapter 3. Standards" discusses standards and open systems in the same generality, and introduces the major standardizing organizations relevant to distributed processing.

"Chapter 4. Processing Models" is very important for this book, because it explains the meaning of the basic models (client/server, distributed transactions, queuing, etc.), thus providing the basis for discussing how these models are supported by various systems, and how they affect the applications that use them.

Chapter 1. Our Habitat

Before digging into the technical details of distributed processing, we would like to take a look at some of the general developments which are related to this technological endeavor. On the one hand, technology is changing the way we live and think: We are constantly moving closer to one another in a "global village", being influenced by the mass media, and changing our business practices and structures to adapt to these changes. On the other hand, the way we think and feel has a profound effect on our work: We may be looking at the big picture, be lost in detail, or be in constant search of beauty or of a holy grail such as the ultimate way of using computers. And finally, all of the very technical and mechanical aspects of computing, from hardware architecture to programming style, very clearly reflect the personalities of the people who created them.

The Global Village

The global village is becoming reality fast. Different parts of your enterprise are networking with one another and connecting to outside sources such as customers and suppliers faster than ever before. This presents you with a number of potential advantages, such as improved efficiency, shorter time to market, and completely new business opportunities.

It also contains a number of possible risks. Things are happening faster than anyone can possibly plan for. If you don't take part in this, you will lose an important competitive advantage. If you do take part in it, you will have to work hard at keeping the networks and distributed applications working the way they should.

The term "global village" was coined by Marshall McLuhan in his book *Understanding Media: The Extensions of Man* [McLuhan] to describe the social effects of the electronic media, including telephone, radio, and television. Since then, immediate, global news coverage by television has become commonplace, and the effects of it on the outcome of history have been dramatic, as in the Vietnam war, the fall of Communism, and the war in Iraq.

Developments in the use of communications technology within the information-processing industry, the proliferation of personal computers, and the mixing of computer technology with entertainment have added to the reality of the global village. Now, the vision of a global village includes two-way global communication and even access to all of the information of the world [Stix 1993]. The recent book *Paradigm Shift* discusses the business aspects of this development, and includes a large number of current and potential ways of using the new technology [Tapscott and Caston]. It also makes it clear that the trend towards increased takeovers, mergers, and cooperation increases the need for flexible ways of communication between diverse groups on both an intra- and interenterprise scale.

This whole book is basically about how the technical infrastructure for the global village is being built. It is a matter of distributed processing in various forms, some very loosely coupled and uncoordinated, others closely coupled and working together, but all over some kind of communication medium.

The Medium Is the Message

Another statement from Marshall McLuhan, "the medium is the message", is perhaps more important than the dream of a global village. This tells us that the medium, whether it be phonetic writing, printing technology, telephone, or television, has a profound effect on our society as a whole, and on the way we live. The medium shapes our thinking and our social interactions more than its content does. Thirty years after his famous book on the subject was written, it still makes very stimulating reading.

Isn't this already true for computers? Isn't the hacker subculture or the way people interact via electronic mail networks a good example of how the medium shapes its users?

And there is much more to come. Information at your fingertips, global, interactive multimedia communications, virtual reality, cyberspace—all this is here in its infancy, and growing fast. The marriage of computer technology and the entertainment business, the birth of infotainment as a literary genre, the use of the Internet for cyberpunk games—it's all here now.

Even if you consider computing as pure business, and have no intention of making games out of it, you will be affected by the influence of entertainment on computing. According to Dennis Allen, editor-in-chief of *Byte* magazine, "Developments in the entertainment industry are strong indicators of just what lies ahead for the enterprise-computing world" [Allen].

In this book, we have tried to take account of this influence where possible. But we have also tried to take a step back, and look at things from a distance where possible. This has been done by stressing the services (i.e., the content) offered by technologies such as communication, instead of their inner workings (i.e., the medium itself).

The Network Is the Computer

Today's local area networks, consisting of client workstations and dedicated servers for such things as file storage and printing, are to a large degree the analog of yesterday's mainframes, with specialized processors for CPU, I/O, and disk controllers, all connected by some internal bus or channels.

This observation, on a purely technical level, sometimes helps us to understand the structure of the "total system" made up of LAN, workstations, and servers. On the level of metaphors, it is another insight into what makes up the fascination of such systems. This is especially true if we consider the whole Internet, or any other global network, together with all its stored knowledge and potential for interaction of man and machine.

As a biological analogy, the anthill or beehive is sometimes thought of as being a single intelligent organism, exposing a character completely different from that which any individual ant or bee could offer. Or think of the strange planet in

Stanislaw Lem's *Solaris* [Lem], where it was discovered that the pulsating ocean covering it formed the basis of a global intelligence, analogous to our gray matter. Seen from this perspective, the emerging global super network is much more than a way of sending electronic junk mail or downloading games; it is an electronic incarnation of the universal cosmic consciousness.

Networks are treated extensively (see "Part 3. Communications" on page 96), and we conclude that the best network is one which is not directly visible to the user. However, the idea of the network as computer is perhaps better seen in systems which offer a layer of functionality on top of a (hidden) network (see "Chapter 7. Middleware" on page 81, especially "Network Operating Systems" on page 82).

No Islands

"No man is an island entire of himself; every man is a piece of the continent, a part of the main. ... and therefore never send to know for whom the bell tolls; it tolls for thee" [Donne].

In mathematics, it has become clear that the relationships between entities are more important than the entities themselves. For example, the very concept of number, i.e., the cardinality of a set, is defined as that property shared by all sets which are isomorphic to each other, i.e., have a one-to-one mapping to each other.

In modern computer programming, objects are characterized less and less by their internal structure, and more and more by the operations they admit. This development also affects distributed processing (see "Object Orientation" on page 70 and "Chapter 16. Distributed Objects" on page 175).

Even home PCs today are connected to networks, such as CompuServe, fax machines, and the Internet, and corporate networks often support many more external connections than the network managers are aware of (see "Internet Services" on page 350 and "ISPs and On-line Services" on page 360).

Power to the User

According to McLuhan, the printed word "created individualism and nationalism in the sixteenth century", and "the typographical extension of man brought in nationalism, industrialism, mass markets, and universal literacy and education" [McLuhan, pages 19 and 172]. What will be the effect of global networked computing, of immediate access and exchange of unlimited information?

The primary effect is more enablement and empowerment of individuals to act on their own, independent of centralized control. "It is not feasible to exercise delegated authority by telephone" [McLuhan, page 271]. "Individual employees and work groups are empowered to act and create value" [Tapscott and Caston, page 209].

On the technical side, this is reflected by a move away from host-based, centrally controlled networks to distributed systems where the initiative and control comes from the client, or user. In fact, this is the basic characteristic, or definition, of client/server computing (see "Client/Server Computing" on page 27). It is also an important facet in understanding how to build and manage tomorrow's distributed systems. And it is just as important in understanding how to plan, or not to plan, these systems: Centrally controlled five-year plans are rapidly becoming impossible in the light of innovation cycles of twelve to eighteen months and users who choose their systems without waiting for central approval.

The Law of Change

It has often been observed that change is a very important aspect of our business: "The only constant throughout history has been change" [IBM GC31-7057-00]; "the only constancy is change itself" [Brooks, page 117].

The idea of change as a basic element of life certainly goes back a long way, at least to the first Confucian classic, the Book of Changes (I Ching), and to the classic of the Way and Power (Tao Te Ching), attributed to Lao Tzu in the sixth century B.C. In the spirit of Taoism, we should accept the fact that our environment is continuously changing, and try to find the right Way to live in harmony with it.

In fact, along with metabolism, growth, and reproduction, the ability to adapt to change is also an important characteristic of living things, irrespective of whether they are individual biological organisms or the organizations we work for. So it should not be surprising that the technical basis for the organization's activities needs to adapt, or be adapted, just as much as does the organization itself.

Interestingly enough, even the emptiest and most inanimate of all things, the physical vacuum, is in a constant state of change, characterized by the continuous and spontaneous creation and destruction of virtual particle–antiparticle pairs. This observation is the basis for an extensive and interesting comparison between Eastern mysticism and Western physics [Capra].

So it should be no surprise that the technological basis for the development of distributed processing is also changing fast. As soon as you get those machines installed and running the applications you need, they are outdated. And if you plan for full compatibility first, it will be outdated before you even install it.

The result is a mixture of different hardware platforms, different operating systems, different networking technologies, and, you guessed it, different methods for implementing distributed processing. It is impossible to design a uniform system when things are changing so fast. The only chance you have is to try to understand the issues involved, and prepare yourself to adapt to a rapidly changing environment.

Part of the solution is to use standards wherever possible; that will reduce the complexity of the total system, improve interoperability and portability, and reduce your dependence on individual vendors (see "Chapter 2. Services" on page 13). But you will keep some old proprietary systems (legacy systems) because it is too hard or too expensive to change them. And you will get new ones, because new technology is being developed faster than the standards are.

A good example of this can be seen in the structure of APE (Animal Proliferation Enterprises). APE was originally founded by a small group of innovative animals for the purpose of proliferating their own species, but since then, the organization itself has proliferated at unexpected speed to become one of the leading intergalactic enterprises. Growth and diversification have included such activities as gene pools, housing projects (lairs, nests, dens, ...), and a specialized transportation infrastructure over air, land, and water.

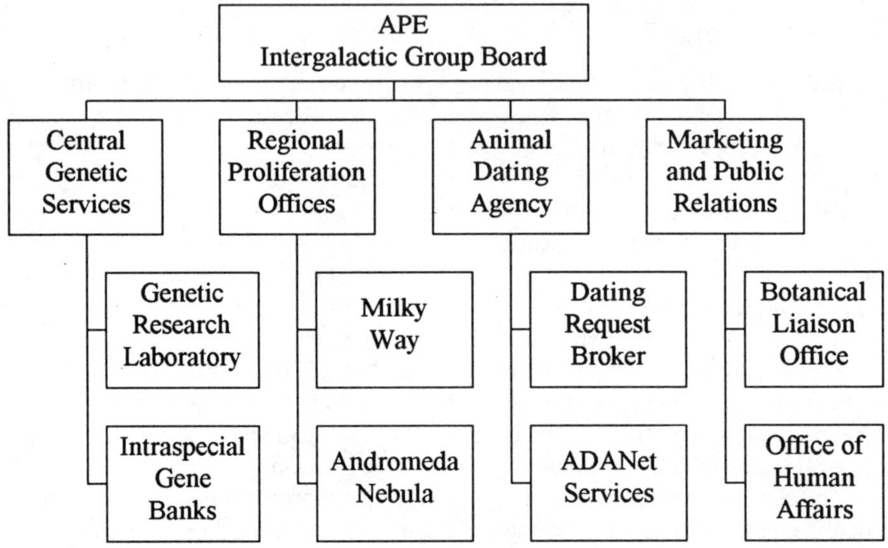

Figure 1. APE (Animal Proliferation Enterprises) Organization Chart

Did I just catch you looking at the organization chart, planning your next move, thinking about your next career step, where to apply next, or how to get that big project in distributed processing? Don't bother! By the time you finish reading this book, the company will have reorganized! The organizational structure will be just as obsolete as the technical basis of its computer systems. In fact, to be honest, the organization chart was not accurate even when it was drawn: Some groups are more progressive than hierarchical, and others succeed in obscuring their structure from anyone except the best informed.

The fact that things are changing so rapidly has an important effect on how we implement information technology, both centralized and distributed. Very often, the classical, top-down, plan-first-then-implement approach is simply not feasible, because the business is changing faster than the systems can be planned or designed, and because new people in the organization are more concerned with their basic business activities than with planning a new technical infrastructure. This was stressed by Apple as part of its architectural framework [VITAL, page 5]. Besides choosing the right kind and right amount of planning, we can also improve this situation by using accepted standards and proven, reusable components, for example (see "Chapter 8. DCE" on page 86).

Conway's Law

This whole discussion of organization charts is also reflected in Conway's Law: "Organizations which design systems are constrained to produce systems which are copies of the communication structures of these organizations" [Conway], as discussed in [Brooks, page 111]. As Conway also observed, this can work both ways, so that the organization ends up looking like the design of the system it was set up to develop.

The classical examples of Conway's Law are operating systems, where the various utilities such as editors, compilers, and file systems may all use different formats, because their developers all worked independently. In fact, one famous test for consistency within an operating system is to write a FORTRAN program that creates a file containing a FORTRAN program that the compiler will understand. One of my favorite examples is to be found in the centrally controlled structure of classical (subarea) SNA, as opposed to the Internet suite or the newer APPN version of SNA.

The relevant examples here are the distributed-computing systems being operated by today's large enterprises. The individual parts, such as graphical user interfaces on a PC client or database transactions on a server or host, are often developed by different teams, who need to communicate with one another just as much as their software counterparts do (see "Chapter 27. Distribution Models" on page 318).

Murphy's Law

"If something can go wrong, it will." This, or something similar, is often referred to as Murphy's Law, and cited in a humorous way. But in the business of computers and networks, it is not a joke, but everyday reality! There are many reasons for this, from the inherent complexity of digital systems, or the myriad of possible disturbances in public telephone lines, to the constant business pressure of budgets and deadlines.

Suppose you are writing a program that requests a service from a remote machine. What happens if the partner is not available: Will the program be notified, or will it hang? Or what happens if the request is sent, but the response never comes back? Should you set a timer and retry when it runs out? What happens if the response arrives after you quit trying? Or could you get two responses after retrying?

Or maybe your program needs to accept input from a human user. What happens if the user goes to lunch in the middle of a session? Or hits the break key? Or leans on the keyboard while talking on the phone? And how do you coordinate these actions with requests to remote machines which just might go off line at the most embarrassing point for your application logic?

All of these examples show how important error handling is to creating robust applications. And experience shows that thorough error handling can easily account for more work and more lines of code than the "normal" cases, where everything runs as expected.

The first examples are cases where problems may arise because the communications may be less than 100% reliable. They also show how much the logic of the application depends on the nature of the communications protocols used, i.e., whether they are connection-oriented or connectionless, whether they guarantee delivery or nonduplication. So, whereas applications programmers do not need to know how the communications protocols work, they do need to know what services the subsystem provides (see "Chapter 9. Services" on page 98).

The other examples are more a case of protecting a program from unexpected input or other surprises. They may make the difference between a program which is "working as designed" and one which satisfies the needs of its users.

Records Are There to Be Broken

Not only records, such as those set in athletic competition, are there to be broken; all assumptions made by computer programmers and hardware designers about limits that won't ever be reached have one main purpose: To come back and haunt those who made them.

Every new generation of microprocessor, from 8-bit to 16-, 32-, and 64-bit technology, requires a whole new set of software. Do those addresses really have to have a fixed length? Either they end up being too small, or they use up a lot of unnecessary space, or both. And how often has the software depended on those fixed lengths? Examples include the 24-bit addressing on the IBM 370 architecture and the 640-KB limit of MS-DOS: How long did it take for all parts of MVS to be converted to true XA? How many programs are unable to use memory above 640 KB?

Of course, we shouldn't forget more commonplace things like zip codes that can only be 5 digits long, or dates that will not work after the year 2000.

The Rising Level of Abstraction

Progress in computing technology has always been accompanied by a movement of the level of abstraction of programming upward from machine-oriented to more user-oriented methods. This is visible in the change from machine-language programming, to assembly language, to high-level languages, and on to the use of tools which either generate the necessary code or allegedly make programming unnecessary.

Another example of this is the increasing use and reuse of finished parts. For example, the runtime library supplied with C compilers contains very useful routines, such as "printf", which raise the level of abstraction well above that of the language itself. A more recent development is object-oriented programming, together with the use of class libraries. Much hope has been placed in the object-oriented method as the basis for reuse, for example by Brad Cox [Cox 1987 and Cox 1990] and Grady Booch [Booch, page 77]. The idea is that the development endeavor should become a "software parts industry" [Tapscott and Caston, pages 179 and 305].

While this development has freed us from machine-language programming and made much more sophisticated applications possible, it hasn't made life easier for the programmer. For example, as long as PC screens were handled in character mode, systems such as CP/M or MS-DOS had only one system call for console output, with very few possibilities for formatting it, such as the ANSI escape sequences. As an alternative, the program could write directly into the screen buffer, a technique which required only knowledge of how to address rows and columns or set the attribute bits. In contrast, OS/2 contains about 500 Presentation Manager function calls [Petzold, page 11], and the IBM C++ User Interface Class Library contains over 260 classes and over 2600 member functions [IBM S82G-3743-00, page 15]. This situation clearly cries out for something that makes this inverted pyramid come back together at the top, such as one of the tools available for defining screens and controls with little or no programming. This is just what Jon Udell is doing when he says, "Object technology failed to deliver on the promise of reuse. Visual Basic's custom controls succeeded" in his article "Componentware" [Udell 5/94].

This same trend also applies to the technological basis for distributed systems, and especially to communications. The results have often been referred to as middleware, distributed-computing platforms, or network operating systems. A knowledge of the current state of this development is important to the applications developer, in order to make full use of today's technology (see "Network Operating Systems" on page 82).

For example, the developer should think very seriously before implementing a response mechanism, sequence number, retry, or time-out at the applications level. If these methods are necessary, they should be part of a communications protocol which provides the application with services such as reliable transport and protection against loss or duplication of messages. However, this does not mean that these mechanisms should be implemented only at the lowest possible level, or only at one level. For example, today's high-speed communications technology, such as FR (Frame Relay) and ATM (Asynchronous Transfer Mode), takes error correction out of the link layer and puts it completely into the transport layer (see "ATM" on page 127). A discussion of the relative merits of implementing services in lower vs. higher layers can be found in [Saltzer et al.].

For the same reason, it is becoming increasingly inappropriate for application programs to make use of transport-level interfaces such as Berkeley Sockets; higher-level interfaces provide additional functions, such as data conversion, transaction control, and directory or security services. In many cases, the correct level of abstraction to use is an important aspect of choosing the right communications method (see "Part 3. Communications" on page 96).

Paradigms

Does the use of object-oriented methods represent a major paradigm shift for the computing industry? Is the client/server model the most adequate paradigm for distributed processing? And is the word "paradigm" itself just a popular buzzword, or does it mean something for us?

The term "paradigm" was introduced to the study of the history and philosophy of science by Thomas Kuhn [Kuhn]. He describes scientific advancement as phases of relative stability and consensus interrupted by scientific "revolutions".

During the stable phases, researchers are able to continuously solve new problems on the basis of accepted theories and methods. In order to do this, they often learn by examples (paradigms) and work by analogy with known problems. The term "paradigm" thus refers to simple examples or exemplary problems and exercises, but can also be extended to mean accepted methods and theories.

At the end of a phase of stability, the inability to solve certain problems culminates in a crisis, which is resolved by the introduction of a new method. This new method, or discovery, is so different from the established methods that it requires the textbooks to be rewritten, not simply amended, and Kuhn refers to it as a "scientific revolution".

In this context, it may well be appropriate to use the word "paradigm" for the methods used in our field, but the real question is whether any of these represent a revolution, or "paradigm shift", as many people now call it. As we will see, client/server computing and the other models used for distributed processing are nothing new: They are useful (networked) extensions of well-known methods of nondistributed computing (see "Chapter 4. Processing Models" on page 27). Even object-oriented technology, which is a very significant advance, is more evolutionary than revolutionary, in that it builds on older techniques, such as information hiding, abstract data types, and simulation.

Tools

The real issue here is a matter of choosing the best tools for the job to be done, as has often been observed, e.g., [Brooks, Chapter 12].

To be sure, the task of choosing the right tools for distributed processing is the central theme of this book. Just as you can write practically any program in almost any programming language, you can also use just about any communications protocol as the basis for your distributed system. But choosing the method which is best suited to your problem will save work and reduce risks.

In order to help you choose the right method for your problem, this book begins with a comparison of the basic models used for distributed processing. Then, each topic is oriented around the services which that particular method provides for the application (see "Chapter 4. Processing Models" on page 27).

Truth and Beauty

It has often been claimed that physicists and other scientists doing basic research are engaged in a search for truth and beauty. What are the people working in the computing and telecommunications fields searching for?

What is it that makes some people such great fans of UNIX, while others say it is just a toy? Why is the PC world polarized into MS-DOS/Windows versus Macintosh? Or, more in the line of distributed systems: Why are some people so enthusiastic about the Internet? Is it the dream of a global village?

In his recent book *Dreams of a Final Theory,* Steven Weinberg notes: "The important thing for the progress of physics is not the decision that a theory is true, but the decision that it is worth taking seriously—worth teaching to graduate students, worth writing textbooks about, above all, worth incorporating into one's own research" [Weinberg, page 81]. He goes on to discuss examples of this and comes to the conclusion that beauty in theoretical physics has a lot to do with simplicity and inevitability. A beautiful theory is one which is based on only a few fundamental principles, with the rest following from these principles without room for, or need for, arbitrary assumptions.

Simplicity is certainly a part of good computer programs, as has often been reiterated in the admonition KISS (keep it simple and straightforward). A system design which consistently uses a few basic principles to achieve a comprehensive functionality may not be inevitable, but it is certainly more convincing and more practical than a hodgepodge of unrelated concepts. Most computer professionals have a clear idea of what an "elegant" solution is: A clear, consistent concept, free of arbitrary, "quick and dirty" workarounds and kludges.

If truth in computing is a program that works, then truth is only skin deep, as anyone who has seen the insides of some successful programs knows. Beauty, on the other hand, goes much deeper; it is a matter of form, of structure, of architecture. (Unless, of course, what turns you on is the "look and feel" of your software.)

What are we searching for? In our business, the economic factor is certainly important, and so is software that works, but these things are not everything. Success is often determined by that "something extra" that motivates people, that makes them feel they are working on something worthwhile, something new and exciting. Some of the things which many of us are enthusiastic about (because each one has its own special kind of "beauty") are the Internet (see "Chapter 31. The Internet" on page 349), DCE (see "Chapter 8. DCE" on page 86), and CORBA (see "CORBA" on page 175).

The Culture Clash

In today's world, it is increasingly common for people of different cultures to meet and work together. For example, during APE's international airline reservation project, a Dane and a Spaniard were assigned to the same team. Both were experienced, well trained, and highly motivated, and each had his own style. When confronted with a difficult problem, the Dane would close his door, sit at his desk, and put his full concentration on his work. In order to solve the same problem, the Spaniard would walk around the office and discuss it with numerous colleagues. Unfortunately, during the course of the project, the two became increasingly alienated: The Dane accused the Spaniard of spending most of his time socializing, and the Spaniard claimed that the Dane was secretive and uncooperative.

Such problems are often observed in international projects. In addition to this, distributed computing has a number of its own typical culture clashes, which are almost certain to occur when various components of the big system are brought together. These include:

Part 1. Introduction

- users versus programmers
- PC versus mainframe programmers
- application versus systems programmers
- UNIX programmers versus the rest of the world

In each case, the culture clash causes some basic problems in understanding, just like those between the Dane and the Spaniard. The team assigned to such a project will need a way of bringing these different views together. This becomes particularly evident when we look at the different parts that make up distributed applications (see "Chapter 27. Distribution Models" on page 318).

Think Big, Start Small

Traditional software engineering wisdom tells us that it is important to analyze the requirements and design the system before implementing it. Design changes made during a late phase, or errors found late, cost much more to accommodate than those taken care of early. "A stitch in time saves nine."

At the same time, we have seen (and will continue to see) a number of factors that make it impossible to plan the implementation of distributed systems thoroughly, if at all:

- The technology is changing rapidly.
- The business use of technology is changing rapidly.
- The users are increasingly autonomous in their choice of technology and applications.

The solution to this problem is to think big, but start with small steps. This can also be referred to as establishing a long-term strategy, but making tactical decisions only as they become necessary. As Grady Booch says, establish a clear architectural vision, and then develop iteratively and incrementally [Booch, pages 230–231]. The architectural framework defines principles, or statements of direction and preferred practice [Tapscott and Caston, pages 236ff.].

The content of the architectural framework will vary, depending on whether you are designing programs, operating a network, or using the technology for your business activities. In any case, it needs to establish the direction, define methods and practices, and present the big picture. It should be visionary and based on well-informed sources. It should not be detailed, dogmatic, cumbersome, or burdensome.

The detailed planning and development should be done in small steps which are manageable and affordable, according to the concept of incremental or evolutionary development. These steps should most often be aimed at bringing the largest gain in the shortest time: They should fill the most urgent needs and provide immediate benefits. At the same time, in order to keep all of these steps going in the right direction, they need to be guided by the "clear architectural vision" mentioned above.

Chapter 2. Services

What good is it? Ask not what you can do for OSI, ask what OSI can do for you!

Services are a central theme of this book. In each chapter, we have listed some of the most important services offered by the technology being discussed. In other words: what it can do for you!

To be completely precise, some of the issues discussed are more accurately defined as properties of the system than as services, but even these uncover the services or potential benefits of the system.

The services provided by a subsystem are what it offers to the application, and they determine how the application can use the subsystem, and what the application needs to do in order to use it. This is why the services are so important in discussing the systems from an application programmer's point of view.

In OSI terminology, the services are what one layer offers to the next higher layer (at the API). The protocol is what the two partners (OSI: peer entities) need in order to understand each other.

Before the description of the individual implementations in a particular area, the services relevant to that area are defined and discussed. The services presented in this chapter are so general that they can apply to any of the technologies discussed in the book.

Vendor Independence

What would happen if your main supplier went bankrupt? Or, suppose the competition offered the same service at a better price. Could you take advantage of it without big losses due to retooling your operations? This is basically what vendor independence is about.

Many people consider it very important to become independent of single vendors, and this has been in the headlines of the industry's publications for some time. In fact some companies have declared vendor independence as a business goal to be pursued by all levels of management.

Some of the advantages of vendor independence are the ability to negotiate and the protection of investment (in case a vendor discontinues a service). And, of course, there are disadvantages, such as losses due to adaptation when moving from one vendor to another.

As an example, consider the experience of Monty Katz, manager of Cheetah, a subsidiary of APE. The business of this company is to operate a VAN, a network which provides specialized communications services for the members of the APE enterprise. Originally, Cheetah based its operations on the technology provided by IBM. In the course of time, the company became more and more convinced that this was a bad choice, and began to install UNIX-based systems from HP. During the transition period, Cheetah was able to pit the two vendors against each other and take advantage of the highly competitive atmosphere. After the company had converted completely from IBM to HP, it not only wanted to avoid dependency on the new vendor, but also looked for ways of applying the same kind of bargaining pressure it had become accustomed to. As a result, it entered a phase of buying only the hardware and operating systems from HP, and the software from some of the larger systems houses. But the same rules applied here. As a final step, Cheetah had a network-management platform developed by one of its clever culinary consultants. After the consultant went on to his next assignment, and the managers involved moved on to their next career steps, the company was left with a system that hardly anyone knew, and that no one was committed to supporting or enhancing.

An opposing point of view can be found in [Walton]. The book describes the method of William Edwards Deming, who was the person who taught SQC (Statistical Quality Control) to the Japanese, starting in 1950. Much later, around 1980, he advised important American companies, including Ford, AT&T, and Honeywell. In many respects, Walton's book stresses the value of quality, long-term goals, and partnership with suppliers instead of constant change based on a lowest-bid policy.

Portability

Once you have everything working on system X, what happens? Of course, one of the departments using it decides to buy its next system from Y, so it's back to the drawing boards. Unless, of course, the software is so portable that this change doesn't pose any problems.

Portability is a property often required of software. It means that the code can be ported, i.e., moved from one machine to another. The need for portability is a matter of cost and of time to deliver a software product, and is particularly important in heterogeneous environments or for vendors who produce software for multiple platforms.

One important aspect of this definition is that portability is not a yes or no question, but a matter of degree, i.e., how much it will cost to port the software. In fact, it should be defined as a comparison of the effort to convert existing software to the new machine with the effort to write it from scratch [Gilb].

There are a number of means for achieving portability, and they have all been discussed extensively in the software engineering literature. Some of these methods are:

- use of high-level languages
- use of high-level APIs
- structuring the software to isolate dependencies on:
    - hardware
    - operating systems
    - communications protocols
    - other subsystems

This discussion should also make it clear that portability is not purely a matter of programming languages. In fact, proper design may in some cases be much more important than the language chosen.

Integration

Suppose you buy software packages from two separate vendors. Can each application use the data generated by the other one? If it can't be used directly, can it at least be converted, or does it have to be entered into the system again? This is one concern related to integration of software.

However, software integration covers more than just this. Here are some important aspects of integration:

- **data:** Can data be passed between applications? Is there a general understanding of its meaning?
- **process:** Can control of the processing flow from one application to another?
- **user interface:** Can the user access all applications via the same interface? Do they all operate in a similar manner?

In the software available today, there are many examples of all of these aspects of integration, but just as many where they do not exist.

Automation

How often do you have to repeat the same task in order to get your job done? Is this something a machine could do better? If so, it is a classic case for automation.

This example shows only one of the most obvious reasons for automating things, i.e., to save effort and with it cost. Another reason is to reduce the number of errors that occur, especially in tasks which are tedious or complex. For example, the space shuttle must be flown by its automatic pilot when it reenters the atmosphere; manual control would be too slow.

At the same time, automation contains its own dangers, due to the fact that the human users are not in direct control and often do not see what is being done. An example of this is the accident at the nuclear power plant at Three Mile Island, where the operators hesitated to take control because they had so little experience doing tasks that were normally automated.

In order to achieve good automation, it is necessary to have effective means of gathering information about the processes involved, and of expressing them in an understandable way which can be easily modified when necessary. Often, it also depends on a good degree of integration of the components involved.

Data processing is full of examples of automation of traditional tasks, but seems to create a new need for automation just as fast. You just have to think of things like scripts for logon sequences or database access, or macros used in word processors, or some more technical applications such as software distribution or system operation.

As a result, existing software systems often show an astounding degree of automation, but at the same time often make it just as clear where further development in this area is necessary.

Scalability

What happens when the size of your operations grows? Can your system be adapted to the change without redoing everything? And just as important, what about those small operations? Can they be accommodated without undue costs, i.e., without buying an oversized, overly expensive system? These questions are concerned with the size, or scale, of the systems involved, and so the ability to adapt to changes of scale is often referred to as scalability.

The question of scalability applies to hardware, which may be upgraded by adding additional processors, or memory, or disks. And it is also important for software, which should be able to handle small jobs inexpensively, and to manage the big ones without running into hidden limits, such as the maximum value for a number or the size of a file.

Some other limitations in scalability are related to performance, and often related to certain bottlenecks. For example, any system that makes use of polling (periodic checking of certain values) cannot exceed a certain size without being flooded by these messages.

In order to achieve scalability, it is not sufficient just to avoid arbitrary limits (which is difficult enough; see "Records Are There to Be Broken" on page 8). The designers must also modularize the system so that it can be adapted to simple tasks as well as complex ones. In addition, there needs to be a way of adding new elements, such as cascading the systems, in order to account for tasks which are simply too big for one system alone.

Extensibility

Even if your system is big enough in scale, it still may be necessary to add some functions to it. For example, the address file doesn't have any size problems, but then you discover that it was written for U.S. addresses (with the zip code after the city name) and can't handle most European addresses (with the postal code before the city name).

This is a matter of extensibility, and the trick is to make it possible to add new functions, without knowing what those functions will be beforehand. An example where this has worked well is the loadable device driver in MS-DOS, which has made it possible for third-party vendors to create many new devices without the need to change the operating system. In many cases, this is not possible, and adding new functions means changing so much of the logic that it may be more feasible to rewrite the whole program.

Achieving extensibility often depends on having a good modular structure, as well as interfaces which are open to other vendors and accepted by the rest of the industry.

Reliability

The question is: Is it there when you need it? Along with that, of course: What happens if it isn't? If your business depends on a system, then reliability is very important. And even if you make do with less, it is often financially important to have things work smoothly.

Even though reliability is a very well known requirement, it is often fulfilled minimally if at all. The reasons for this include the basic complexity of digital logic, insufficient understanding of how to make systems reliable, and the basic difficulty of getting a budget for things which aren't clearly visible to those who make the financial decisions.

The means for attaining reliability have been a major topic in software engineering and are readily available. However, there is an asymptotic aspect to this, meaning that the closer you get to perfection, the more it costs to make the next improvement. Reliability is a question of operations as much as it is of the development of the components involved. In this case, the methods for attaining it include such topics as management, i.e., monitoring and control.

Securability

In order to keep a system working, it is necessary to protect it from intentional and accidental damage. At the same time, some kinds of data need to be kept confidential. These basic requirements are the same for centralized and distributed systems, but are much more difficult to achieve for the latter.

The property of securability means that the system can be set up and operated in such a way that all security requirements are met. This is the topic of a chapter of this book (see "Chapter 25. Security" on page 293).

Distributability

A good piece of advice for users of data-processing systems has always been to buy finished products or components rather than develop their own—assuming that products which meet their requirements are available.

So, suppose you have decided on a particular set of software products, and suppose you have also decided on distributed systems. Can you separate the software into individual components which run on different machines? And, can you move the components from one machine to another as needed? If so, it is appropriate to label the software as "distributable".

Reusability

Any time something can be reused, it usually saves money to reuse it. This certainly applies to software, and has been an important goal of software design for decades. Unfortunately, it doesn't seem to be easy to achieve, even with the use of object-oriented tools.

To be realistic, we should think of reusability in degrees, as with portability. In other words, we shouldn't expect it to be possible to reuse software components with no effort at all. Instead, we need to compare the effort of reusing a component to the effort of writing a new one.

Dynamic Configuration

There is a little joke about the telephone company that requests everyone to hang up on Friday afternoon, so that the company can install a new line. Unfortunately the analogy to many computing systems is all too real.

The goal of dynamic configuration is to make it possible to change whatever needs changing without stopping operations of the system, i.e., without impairing availability. Along with a number of cases where this is possible, there are plenty more where it is a long way from being true.

Ease of Use

Easy-to-use, or "user-friendly", software is more than just a pleasant surprise. It is an important factor in achieving good productivity and economical use.

In some cases, deficiencies in the ease of use of application software may prevent it from being used at all. For example, the author of a novel should be able to use a word processor without learning about CPU caching or bit-mapped video displays. And a physician should be able to analyze data on the effect of his therapy without taking the time to learn how to normalize a relational database.

Even when used by data-processing experts, easy-to-use software may be an important economic factor. For example, user-friendly network-management applications may reduce the time a system is not available to its users. This, in turn, reduces time lost and even damage to the company's core business, such as when customers choose another supplier.

Internationalization

Distributed systems lead quite naturally to the use of the same software packages in different countries. But even without this, the global marketplace has created a need to produce software which is useful for and attractive to people of different nationalities.

There are plenty of things that can (and do) go wrong when this isn't done, such as lost characters, incorrect dates, or addresses that are practically illegible because a piece of software was hard-coded into believing that the zip code comes after the city name, even though the European postal code is written before the city name.

An amusing example occurred during development of the APE airline reservation system, when a Swedish colleague tried to type his first name, Göran, into a ticket request. The "ö" was treated as a "\" (the difference between German and American 7-bit ASCII), and the host computer treated the "\" as a new line (because the original terminal designers had forgotten to make a key for new line, and had decided to use the backslash instead). Of course, the whole exercise was irrelevant anyway, because the airline reservation software accepts only upper-case 7-bit U.S. ASCII characters. So Göran will have to live with being called GORAN or GOERAN or something else, but at least he won't be called G\RAN.

An important contribution to solving this problem is the definition of standards for character sets, such as 8-bit ASCII, which include some of these special national characters. However, for Asian languages such as Chinese, 8 bits aren't sufficient, so we need a DBCS (Double-Byte Character Set) or one which accommodates multibyte (wide) characters which can be 16 or 32 bits long.

The best solution available today is called Unicode, and has been approved by the ISO [ISO/IEC 10646]. It is being promoted by a nonprofit organization, the Unicode Consortium, which was founded in 1991 by Apple, IBM, Microsoft, Novell, Sun, and Xerox. (The Unicode Consortium can be reached on the Internet at unicode-inc@unicode.inc.)

Simply making it possible to code the characters needed isn't always enough, since you still can't expect someone in the U.S. to actually use characters such as the German "ß". Of course, the Germans know that this character can legitimately be replaced by an "ss", and sometimes even call it by that name. So they would write "Straße" (street) as "Strasse", not "Strabe". Should we expect this intelligence to be implemented in the next version of your word processor's "AutoCorrect" software?

This first step in this direction is the adaptation of a piece of software to a particular locale, often referred to as "localization" and abbreviated as "l10n" because there are 10 letters between the "l" and the "n". Similarly, the process of creating software which is usable internationally is referred to as "internationalization" and abbreviated as "i18n".

Here is a list of many of the conventions which must be observed in order to produce truly international software [Miller]:

- **characters:** This may include the Spanish "ñ" and "¿", or Kanji characters which require more than one byte to code.

- **punctuation:** In addition to the Spanish "¿" and "¡", some countries use "«" and "»" as quotation marks, and the Greek question mark looks like our semicolon.

- **sorting:** Those extra characters need to be sorted correctly; for example, "ö" is sorted as "oe" in German and at the end of the alphabet in Swedish.

- **writing direction:** English is written from left to right, and then from top to bottom, while Arabic and Hebrew are written from right to left. The question of whether numerals are written from left to right is a matter of how you think of them: most Westerners are accustomed to thinking of Arabic numerals as being written from left to right, but this is also a convention, as can be seen by the nursery rhyme "Four and twenty blackbirds ..." or the German "vierundzwanzig".

- **numerals:** 3,912.45 is written 3.912,45 in Germany. The British word "billion" means 10^{12}, whereas the American "billion" means 10^9.

- **time:** 8:32 P.M. in the U.S. is 20.32 Uhr in Germany.
- **dates:** June 7, 1994 is 7. Juni 1994 in Germany and is abbreviated 6/7/94 in the U.S., 7/6/94 in Denmark, and 7.6.94 in Germany.
- **calendars:** Most countries use the Gregorian calendar, but Israel also uses the Hebrew calendar, Arab countries also use the Islamic calendar, and Japan also uses the imperial Japanese calendar.
- **currency:** Some countries have different symbols, such as "$", "£", and "¥", and there are different ways of using them.
- **addresses:** American addresses have the street number before the street name and the zip code after the city name. German addresses have the street number after the name, and most European addresses have the postal code before the city name, often prefixed by a country code.
- **measurement:** It may be necessary to convert inches and degrees Fahrenheit to centimeters and degrees Celsius.
- **paper:** Most countries use the metric paper sizes A3, A4, and A5, whereas the U.S. uses letter, legal, and ledger.
- **colors:** The meaning "stop and go" for the colors red and green may not be understood by Chinese users.
- **icons:** American mailboxes and British postal boxes look significantly different. Hand gestures and religious signs may take on a different meaning or even be insulting in a different culture.

Chapter 3. Standards

In order to make distributed systems work, it is certainly necessary to define some common language spoken by various members of the community. This need for standardization has become particularly important in distributed processing, but has also gained much importance in centralized computing as well. This is due at least in part to changes in business practices, such that alliances are made and broken faster than before, and users are no longer willing to be tied to a single vendor.

However, even though the road to distributed processing may be smoothed out by standardization, it is still very bumpy, and every step of the way involves decisions about which standard, if any, to choose. We are confronted with the choice between starting with available building blocks which don't fit together or drawing up a complete architecture and then looking for the right material.

Open Systems

A good definition of the concept of open systems has been provided by the IEEE TCOS (Technical Committee on Operating Systems): "Open Systems consist of a comprehensive and consistent set of international information technology standards and functional standards profiles that specify interfaces, services, and supporting formats to accomplish interoperability and portability of applications, data, and people" [IBM SC28-8135-00, page 4-13]. In a slightly broader, more business-oriented context, open systems foster the interoperability of technology and people (suppliers, consumers, partners) and the portability of software, information, and users.

For the users of information technology, there are a number of benefits of implementing open systems:

- **integration:** It is easier to integrate business activities, organizational units, individual people, and software and hardware components.
- **flexibility:** There are more possibilities for designing a total system consisting of pieces from differing sources.
- **scalability:** There are more chances for moving a component from a small system to a larger one and vice versa.
- **investment protection:** There is a greater chance that technological choices will remain viable in the future, and will be supported by other vendors.

To be precise, we should separate the goals (interoperability and portability) from the means to achieve them (standards). Of course, these goals are based on the need of every business to operate in an economical and efficient manner. The following table lists the basic goals of open systems and the means for achieving them.

Part 1. Introduction

goal	standards
interoperability	communication protocols
portability of applications	APIs (application programming interfaces) and ABIs (application binary interfaces)
reuse of applications	languages, object-oriented technology, ORBs (object request brokers)
portability of data	formats (character codes, file structure, message definitions)
portability of people	user interfaces, including display standards and usage of special keys

Table 1. Goals of Standards

Conformance and Interoperability

When systems, especially communications systems, are tested for being truly open, there are generally two sets of tests. Conformance testing checks to see if the system conforms to the standard, and interoperability testing checks to see which implementations can communicate with each other. Theoretically, conformance alone should be enough, but in the current state of the art of standardization, two systems which have both been proven to comply with the same standard may fail to interoperate. Similarly, systems which can communicate with each other do not necessarily both adhere to the standard.

A good example of de facto standardization can be seen in the activity of the APE's ADA (Animal Dating Agency). ADA was originally founded as a simple inter- and intraspecies dating service, but it has become very popular and has reached true intergalactic dimensions. The technical basis for the ADA activities has been the ADANet, which has been a proving ground for new networking and communication technology. In order to achieve its goals of rapid development and deployment of useful technology, the AETF (ADANet Engineering Task Force) was set up to review and proliferate standards for use within the net.

The designation for ADA was inspired by Ada, Countess of Lovelace, because she had such a nice name. Any relationship she may have had with Charles Babbage is kept in perfect discretion, in compliance with the general statutes of the agency.

One of the most popular services of the ADANet has traditionally been SEX (Software Exchange). Another, more advanced, research project was the interplanetary real-time multimedia interspecies animal-language translation service.

Organizations

Standards of any kind are generally made by organizations, and the type of organization has a lot to do with what kind of standard results. For example, the organization may represent the users, the vendors, or both. In addition, it may be large and general or small and specialized, and it may be formal or informal.

The nature of the organization may also determine how long the consensus process requires and how well the resulting standard is accepted. As a result, the standards may be created fast and disappear almost as quickly, or they may be slow in coming but worth the wait. Of course, in some fortunate cases they arise fast and stay long, and in some less fortunate ones they are nothing other than long and laborious stillbirths.

Of the many different kinds of organizations involved in producing various standards, most belong to one of the two following categories:

- Official organizations, such as government agencies and their international counterparts. They produce official standards, often referred to as "de jure" standards.
- Consortia composed of vendors, users, or both; or single vendors. These groups may publish documents to which they all agree, thus establishing an unofficial, or "de facto", standard. Or they may produce or distribute products or technology which is used so widely as to have a standardizing character.

The following list of organizations includes the official bodies and industry and user consortia which are most important for distributed computing.

ANSI (American National Standards Institute) is the primary standardization body in the United States. Even though ANSI's official jurisdiction is national, many ANSI standards have been accepted and used internationally. Examples include the standards for programming languages such as COBOL and C, and the ASCII (American National Standard Code for Information Interchange) code. http://www.ansi.org.

BSVC (Banking System Vendor Council), a vendor consortium which defines WOSA/XFS, includes Andersen Consulting, DEC, EDS, Microsoft, Olivetti, SNI, Tandem, and Unisys.

CCITT (Comité Consultatif International Télégraphique et Téléphonique = International Consultative Committee for Telegraphy and Telephony) is the previous name of the ITU-TS.

CEN (Comité Européen de Normalisation = European Committee for Standardisation) and CENELEC (Comité Européen de Normalisation Electrique = European Committee for Electrotechnical Standardisation) are associations of national standards bodies from European countries. They are concerned with standardizing equipment.

CIL (Component Integration Lab), a vendor consortium which defines OpenDoc, includes Apple, Borland, Claris, and WordPerfect.

COSE (Common Open Software Environment), a consortium founded in 1992 and including IBM, HP, SCO, Sun, and Univel, is defining a set of specifications to be deployed by all UNIX vendors. The topics covered include graphical user interfaces, object-oriented technology, multimedia, and systems management.

DMTF (Desktop Management Task Force) is a vendor consortium which has defined DMI (Desktop Management Interface) and consists of DEC, HP, IBM, Intel, Microsoft, Novell, Sun, and SynOptics. http://www.dmtf.org.

ECMA (European Computer Manufacturers Association) is composed of both manufacturers and users, and has produced about 250 standards for information processing and telecommunications systems and technical reports, many of which have been endorsed by ISO/IEC, ETSI, and CENELEC. http://www.ecma.ch.

EMA (Electronic Messaging Association) is an interindustry forum with more than 500 members dedicated to the promotion, development, and use of electronic mail (e-mail), voice mail, fax, electronic data interchange (EDI), and other messaging technologies for secure global electronic commerce. Standards include CMC (Common Messaging Calls). http://www.ema.org.

ETSI (European Telecommunications Standards Institute) is a nonprofit organization composed of 289 members from 25 countries, representing government agencies, public network operators, manufacturers, and users. Its purpose is to produce telecommunications standards that will be used in Europe. http://www.etsi.fr.

IAB (Internet Activities Board) is the standardization body for Internet specifications (RFCs). Examples include TCP/IP, FTP, SMTP, and SNMP.

IEC (International Electrotechnical Commission), the worldwide standardization body for electrical and electronics standards, publishes (nonbinding) international standards for the purpose of harmonizing national standardization efforts, and works closely with the ISO through the JTC (Joint Technical Committee— Information Technology).

IEEE (Institute of Electrical and Electronics Engineers) is a professional society with over 300,000 members. The IEEE Standards Board has published standards such as the RS232C serial interface, the 802.X series of LAN protocols, and POSIX (Portable Operating System for Computer Environments). http://stdsbbs.ieee.org.

IETF (Internet Engineering Task Force) is the group charged with standardizing protocols for the Internet, which is the commercial successor to the U.S. Department of Defense's ARPANET (Advanced Research Projects Agency Network). These standards, called RFCs (Requests For Comment), include very widely accepted technology such as TCP/IP (Transmission Control Protocol/Internet Protocol) and SNMP (Simple Network Management Protocol). http://www.ietf.org.

IMA (Interactive Multimedia Association) is a vendor consortium concerned with multimedia. For example, the DSP Technical Working Group of the IMA is working on an API which will encapsulate DSP (Digital Signal Processor) functions. This group includes Apple, AT&T, IBM, Intermetrics, and Microsoft.

IrDA (Infrared Data Association) is an industry consortium which has defined a standard for infrared wireless communication. The first version defines a speed of 115.2 Kbit/s and a maximum distance of 3 meters. The IrDA has 70 members, including HP, DEC, Microsoft, Intel, IBM, and Sun.

ISO (International Standards Organization) is a worldwide federation of national standards bodies from some 90 countries. Its purpose is to promote the development of standardization in many different areas for the whole world. Examples of ISO standards include the OSI protocols and services, such as FTAM. http://www.iso.ch.

ITU-TS (International Telecommunication Union—Telecommunications Sector, formerly CCITT) is an international organization of official standards bodies that studies technical, operating, and tariff questions and issues recommendations for standardizing telecommunications on a worldwide basis. Examples of ITU-TS standards include the X.25 packet-switching network, the X.400 Message Handling System (electronic mail), and the V.-series of standards for modems and related equipment. http://www.itu.ch.

NMF (Network Management Forum) is composed of 125 users and suppliers of computer and communication systems in 25 countries and is dedicated to accelerating the interoperability of network management platforms and systems through the development of the OMNIPoint open interface specification. http://www.nmf.org/new.htm.

ODMG (Object Database Management Group), a part of the OMG, defines standards for object-oriented databases. The members of the ODMG include HP, ODI, Objectivity, Ontos, Servio, TI, and Versant. http://www.odmg.org.

OMG (Object Management Group) is a nonprofit corporation of vendors, users, and developers for promoting object-oriented technology. CORBA (Common Object

Request Broker Architecture) was defined by the OMG and is being implemented by a large number of vendors. http://www.omg.org.

Open Group was formed in 1996 through the merger of OSF and X/Open. http://www.opengroup.org.

OSF (Open Software Foundation Inc.) is an organization that selects and develops technology which is then released to vendors to be implemented in their systems. OSF/1 is a standardized version of UNIX, and OSF Motif is a GUI (Graphical User Interface) based on the X/Open X-Windows standard which has been implemented on a large number of UNIX systems. The OSF DCE (Distributed Computing Environment) has been implemented on a large number of platforms and has already had a large impact. The OSF DME (Distributed Management Environment) is newer and has been less successful than DCE. In 1996, OSF merged with X/Open to form "The Open Group". http://www.osf.org.

SAG (SQL Access Group) was founded in 1989 as an industry consortium, then merged with X/Open, which later merged with OSF. The SAG defined the SQL CLI (Call-Level Interface), which is the basis for ODBC (Open Database Connectivity) and was later submitted to ANSI and ISO.

SPEC (System Performance Evaluation Corporation) defines standards for measuring the performance of hardware, such as SPECfp, SPECint, and SPECmark. SPEC was founded by DEC, HP, IBM, and Intel. info@specbench.org.

W3C (World Wide Web Consortium) is a consortium dedicated to Web technology, with over 40 members. http://www.w3c.org.

WFMC (Workflow Management Coalition) is an industry consortium which defines standards for workflow. http://www.aiai.ed.ac.uk/WFMC.

X/Open Company Ltd. is a nonprofit corporation that has been very influential in UNIX-related standards but has increased its scope to the point where the name, which suggests UNIX, may have to be changed. Examples of X/Open standards are XPG (X/Open Portability Guide), XMP (X/Open Management Protocol), XTI (X/Open Transport Interface), and XTP (X/Open Transaction Processing), including the XA protocol for communication between transaction monitors and databases. In 1996, X/Open merged with OSF to form "The Open Group". http://www.xopen.org.

Chapter 4. Processing Models

A distributed system, just like many large centralized systems, must consist of a number of components which all work together. The behavior of the individual parts, and how they cooperate, is a fundamental part of the overall system design. The basic concepts involved in this are treated in this chapter. As we will see, there are a few basic concepts, or models, which apply to all large systems, both centralized and distributed. They also apply to most levels of processing, from the hardware up through subsystems to the application itself.

The design of a large system requires choosing a processing model for the interaction between the parts. If the system is distributed, the processing model also provides the application designer with the key to choosing the right means of communication between the physically remote parts. In contrast, it would be a mistake to go to the one extreme of digging into the details of communications protocols, or to the other extreme of trying to ignore all aspects of communications. In practice, both of these extremes are quite common, as was mentioned in the preface. Since a good understanding of the processing models is the basis for application design and for adequate use of communications technology, it should be considered as a foundation for the rest of the material in this book.

Client/Server Computing

What does the client/server concept really mean? The simplest, and perhaps most obvious, answer can be found in its name: The application consists of two parts, a client, which initiates the processing, and a server, which supplies services to the client [OSF. Introduction to OSF DCE].

This model is often applied to hardware (e.g., PCs as clients, midrange computers or mainframes as servers). However, it is much more useful when applied to software (e.g., a financial application as a client, a database or naming directory as server).

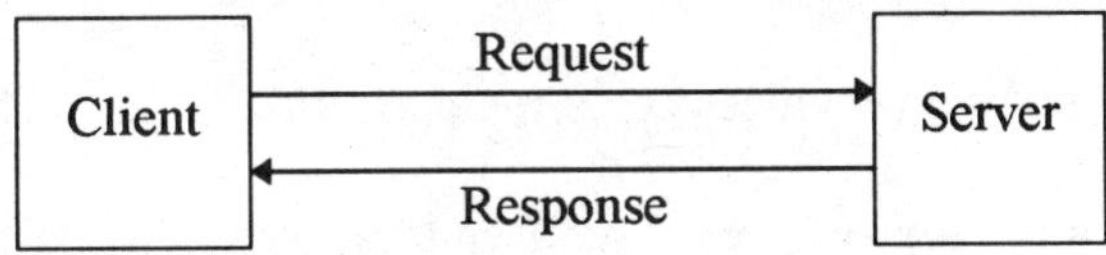

Figure 2. The Client/Server Model

This basic model can be extended in two ways:

- One client uses the services of more than one server.
- The server for one request acts as a client in requesting services from another server.

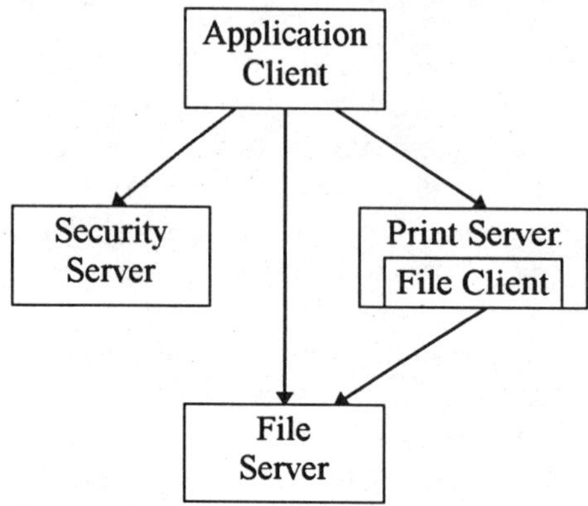

Figure 3. General Client/Server Configuration

The basic concept for communication between client and server is also quite simple: Each interaction consists of a request (client to server) and a response (server to client). One convenient way of implementing this is via an RPC (remote procedure call). However, it is quite feasible to use almost any other communications technique, such as APPC (see "APPC and CPI-C" on page 159), remote SQL (see "Chapter 15. Remote SQL" on page 164), or any transport-level protocol.

In any case, this interaction is always synchronous in nature. In most cases, the API is constructed much like a normal program call, so that the client is blocked until the server finishes its work. Even when a nonblocking API is available, the client is rarely able to do anything else until the server has finished, so it simply waits for the response. Of course, it is possible to write programs which dispatch nonblocking requests and receive responses, all in an asynchronous manner, but this is not the client/server model.

Some examples of servers are:

- **application server:** provides access to application logic, such as existing host transactions.
- **communications server:** serves as a gateway between the clients (e.g., in a LAN) and some other network, such as communications to a host system or facsimile over telephone lines.
- **database server:** sole task is the operation of a database. Most often, clients access the database via a remote SQL, such as Oracle's SQL*Net.
- **directory server** (also referred to as a name server): provides information, such as addresses, for a given name. Example: X.500 or DNS.
- **file server:** typically has a large disk system to store files, such as documents, spreadsheets, and software. One advantage is that the file server can be backed

up centrally, relieving the individual clients of the task. Very often, the clients access the files via a system such as Sun's NFS (Network File System).

- **print server:** controls access to printers, and provides for buffers (temporary storage).
- **security server:** provides such information as password checking or encryption keys.
- **time server:** provides an accurate clock for the purpose of synchronizing clocks of various machines.

The simplicity of the basic client/server model is certainly an advantage, since it helps to produce a simple overall design. On the other hand, this aspect alone doesn't warrant the name "client/server architecture" unless you apply it to a large design that you create based on the client/server model.

Now that we have a simple and convincing concept which has proven to be very useful, and can be implemented on the basis of existing systems, what is all the excitement about? To be sure, it's not about anything like a fundamentally new technology. Rather, it's a question of control: In a client/server system, the control over what is done is in the distributed clients, not in the central system. And (see "Conway's Law" on page 7) this has repercussions on the structure of the organization operating the system, and on the power of the individuals in charge of parts of it. This is what is often referred to as empowerment or enablement of the end users to choose how and what they do with computing technology.

Distributed Transaction Processing

Originally, the term "transaction" was not concisely defined, but was applied very generally to any process which ran for only a brief time. Typically, each message from a terminal would start a transaction program, which would process the input, store its state and context data, and terminate.

An example of a system which provides this kind of transaction processing is IBM's TPF (Transaction Processing Facility) [IBM GH20-2157-00 and IBM GH20-7488-00].

TPF was developed during the early 1960s under the name of PARS (Programmable Airline Reservation System). Later, the application part was separated from the system part, which was named ACP (Airline Control Program). When the system was sold to a number of financial institutions as well as airlines, it was given the name TPF.

One essential aspect of TPF is the fact that it is a transaction monitor and an operating system in one, meaning that there is no redundancy in program management. Also, because of its background, TPF is very simple and has no file system, no DBMS, and no commit protocol. On the other hand, it has been constantly updated in order to support SNA, APPC, and the most modern IBM mainframe hardware. As a result, it is also a very fast system.

Today, the old characterization of transaction processing is still valid for most examples, but the definition of the word "transaction" has been replaced by a much more important concept, the so-called ACID test:

- **atomicity:** Transactions are indivisible, and must run either completely or not at all.
- **consistency:** All data must remain consistent, even when the transaction fails.
- **isolation:** Partial results (before the transaction has completed) must remain invisible to all other transactions.
- **durability:** The final results of the transaction must be permanent.

This definition has been studied thoroughly, and has now been made part of an international standard, OSI TP [ISO/IEC 10026].

The basis for implementing the ACID conditions is to be found in the commit and rollback operations of a database. Before all operations of a transaction are complete, the changes to the data remain invisible to any other users of the database. Then, if everything runs successfully, the changes are committed, making them visible to others and permanent. If any operation is not successful, all other operations are rolled back, thus reinstating the original state of the database.

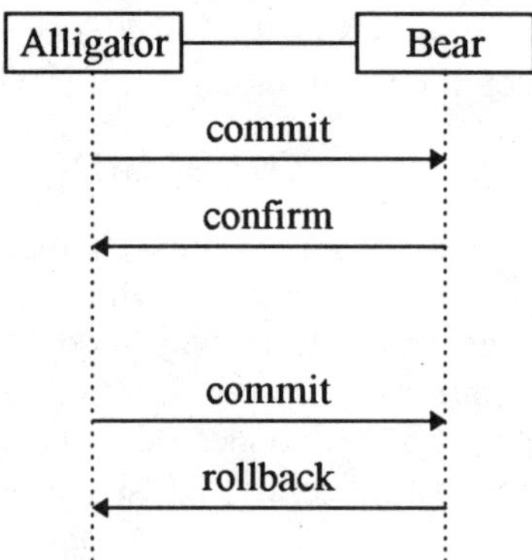

Figure 4. One-Phase Commit

When two programs are involved in a single transaction, they coordinate their processing via a commit protocol: When the operations are complete, one program (Alligator) requests the other (Bear) to commit its operations. If Bear is successful, Alligator commits its changes; otherwise it rolls them back, leaving everything the way it was before the transaction was started. This is called a one-phase commit protocol.

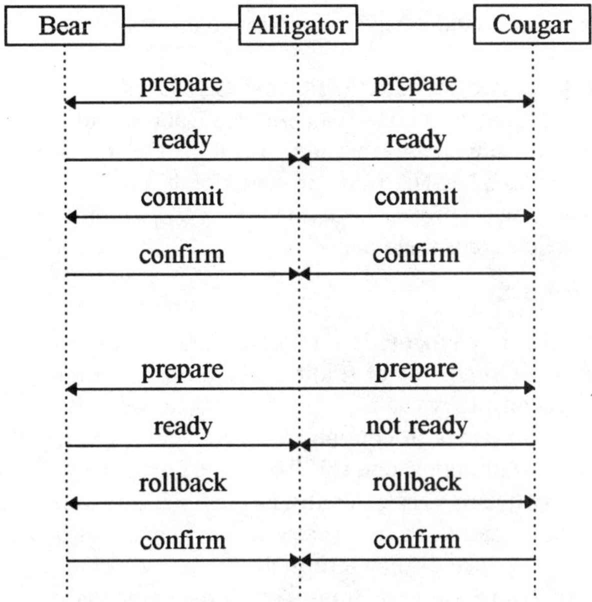

Figure 5. Two-Phase Commit

When three or more programs are involved in a single transaction, more is required of the commit protocol. Suppose Bear's commit succeeds, but Cougar's fails. Then it would be too late to roll Bear's changes back. Therefore, the process runs in two stages. In the first, Alligator requests Bear and Cougar to prepare to commit, i.e., to determine if they are capable of committing. After this, Alligator has the responses from Bear and Cougar. If both are positive, Alligator requests both to commit; otherwise it requests them to roll back. Because of the two steps involved, this is called a two-phase commit.

Examples of communications protocols which support a two-phase commit are:

- APPC
- OSI TP
- TxRPC

The OSI TP protocol was influenced strongly by IBM's LU 6.2, or APPC, and presumably influenced the definition of the SAA API CPI-C. As a result, CPI-C is sufficiently general to be used for either LU 6.2 or OSI TP, and has been included in the X/Open standards.

To be precise, OSI TP contains only transaction control elements, and makes use of OSI CCR (Commitment, Concurrency, and Recovery). Data transfer is done via the OSI protocols RDA (Remote Database Access) and ROS (Remote Operations

Service). On the other hand, APPC contains both transaction control and data transfer.

One other difference between APPC and OSI TP is in data conversion. APPC "mapped conversations" use the GDS (Generalized Data Stream) format, which makes installation-dependent conversion routines possible. On the other hand, OSI TP supports the full services of ASN.1 in its presentation layer.

TxRPC is a newer protocol, defined by X/Open and consisting of RPC, enhanced by transaction-control elements.

Transaction Monitors

Before discussing the implementation of distributed transaction processing, it is important to look at the functions of traditional transaction monitors, in order to see how they are being changed by the new technology. As we will see, these transaction monitors have many functions in common with today's operating systems, but differ in their emphasis on transaction control. To make things more confusing, the term "monitor" has also been used very generally for any piece of software that monitors or controls other processes, and has been used synonymously with the term "operating system" and even with "video display terminal".

Traditionally, OLTP (on-line transaction processing) is done on a mainframe computer which supports a large number of terminals. The application programs run under the control of a transaction monitor, such as IBM's CICS. Transaction monitors are also called "TP monitors", which means "transaction-processing monitor" but originally meant "teleprocessing monitor" [Gray and Edwards]. This name change shows how the importance of the various functions of these systems has changed over time.

The functions of a traditional transaction monitor are:

transaction management	resource management	program–program communication	program management	terminal management
checkpoint, logging, restart	data storage, commit processing	data transport, data conversion, commit synchronization	subtasking, serialization, memory management	dialogue control, format control

Table 2. Traditional Transaction Monitor Functions

The table shows a slightly simplified picture of the functions of a traditional transaction monitor, but with a functional grouping and naming that corresponds to the modern approach.

The most important function is transaction management. Checkpoint and logging provide the basis for commit, rollback, and restart/recovery.

Resource management is concerned with data storage. In order to provide a commit protocol for file systems that don't support it natively, the resource manager keeps "before" and "after" images of all changes to the files. Today, this function is normally provided by database managers, and sometimes provided by file systems.

Program–program communication is an important part of traditional transaction monitors, which often supply a number of methods, depending on whether the communication is between programs running under the same monitor, on separate monitors, or on separate machines. This context also makes it clear why LU 6.1 and LU 6.2 were developed within the CICS environment. Today, most operating systems offer communications subsystems with these functions.

Program management is concerned with multitasking, serialization of programs, and storage management. Today, multitasking is provided by most operating systems, but the overhead of task switching is often too large to make this a good basis for transaction processing. Because of this, the POSIX 1003.4 standard and OSF DCE define lightweight processes called threads. Program serialization is no longer necessary, now that compilers are capable of producing reentrant code. Storage management is provided by operating systems and by the runtime environments of many compilers.

For traditional transaction monitors, managing a large number of terminals was a very important task, including dialogue control, communications protocols, and terminal formatting. Today, some parts of this are contained in communications subsystems. Format control is done in the PC or workstation, which provides a modern graphical user interface and makes it unnecessary to transfer screen formats via the communication line.

The prime example of a traditional transaction monitor is IBM's CICS (Customer Information and Control System) for MVS. It was developed in the early 1970s, has been continually enhanced since then, and is probably the most widely used transaction monitor on the market. CICS supports all the functions discussed above, including resource management for a large number of file systems and support for a number of programming languages.

CICS is a large, monolithic transaction monitor with support for a large functionality and high performance. The APIs are not standard, and it is not possible to replace individual components. Some of the traditional transaction monitors are:

- DEC ACMS
- IBM CICS
- IBM IMS
- Tandem Pathway

More recently, a standardized model for transaction processing has been developed, as shown in Figure 6.

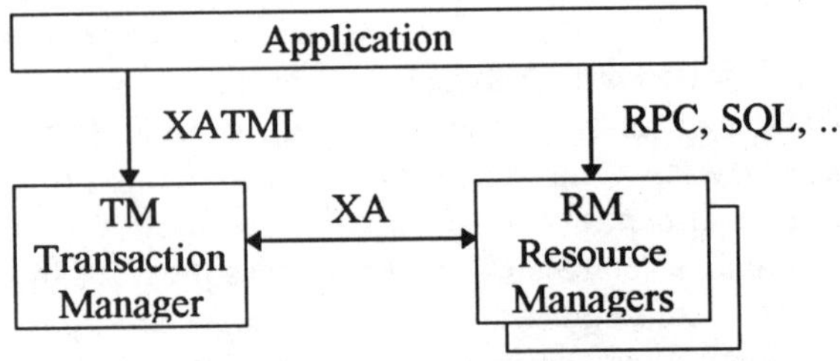

Figure 6. X/Open Transaction Processing Model

The X/Open Transaction Processing Model is a standard that defines how to implement transaction processing using a number of standardized components instead of one large, monolithic transaction monitor [X/Open G504]. This standard is important, and has been implemented by a number of vendors.

The components of such a system are the application program, a TM (Transaction Manager), and any number of RMs (Resource Managers). The task of the TM is to control transactions involving multiple RMs. The RMs provide such services as files, databases, printers, and remote communications. The application communicates with the TM and any number of RMs via standardized APIs.

The API between the application and the TM is called XATMI (X/Open Application Transaction Manager Interface), and was motivated by the ATMI of Tuxedo [X/Open C506].

For the communication between the application and the RMs, there are a number of APIs, depending on the function of the RM:

- X/Open ISAM
- SQL
- RPC

The interface between the TM and the RMs is called XA. This protocol makes it possible for the TM to control and coordinate global transactions involving multiple RMs [X/Open C193]. The application does not need to use this interface, but it is very important to know if a commercially available RM, such as a database server, supports XA.

Program–program communication in the X/Open Transaction Processing Model is done via specialized communications Resource Managers. The API chosen by X/Open is called CPI-C, which was developed by IBM and can be used with either LU 6.2 or the OSI Transaction Processing protocol.

Examples of transaction monitors which run on UNIX and support the X/Open model, at least in part, are:

- AT&T Tuxedo
- Transarc Encina

- IBM CICS/6000
- NCR Top End

Tuxedo was developed by USL (UNIX System Laboratories) and runs on a large number of different hardware and operating system platforms. The databases supported include Oracle, Informix, Ingres, and Sybase, and both LU 6.2 and OSI TP program–program communications are supported.

Encina was developed by Transarc and is relatively new and modern. IBM's CICS/6000 is based at least in part on Transarc technology and, in order to make it easy to port old applications, also supports the traditional CICS API, as do its other relatives, CICS/400 and CICS/2.

AT&T's Top End is based on the NCR product Multi-Tran. It is also migrating towards the X/Open Transaction Processing Model.

Going further down the scale of sizes, we should mention another group of products which could be considered as miniature transaction monitors. Most APPC implementations can start a transaction program when a request to begin a new conversation (an attach or allocate command) comes in. Along with the multitasking support of the underlying operating system, and combined with a database or file system that supports a commit protocol, this is the basic function we need in order to implement distributed transactions. Examples of such implementations are:

- APPC/VM
- APPC/MVS
- Communication Manager/2

Messages, Queues, and Pipes

Messages

The basic concept of messaging systems is quite simple: The sending application sends a message to the receiving application, which can retrieve it at any time it chooses. In some systems, there is a notification method for receipt of messages, e.g., in the form of a pop-up window, a call-back routine, or an interrupt.

Messaging can be done at different layers of communication, and with greatly varying levels of service offered to the application.

At the transport level, messaging often exists in the form of a datagram protocol. This means that messages are sent directly to the partner, normally without guarantee of delivery. Added features, such as transparent routing or security, are also missing at this level.

The best-known datagram protocol is probably the UDP (user datagram protocol) of the Internet suite. Since it runs on top of IP (as an alternative to TCP), it is also referred to as UDP/IP. Even though this is a very simple protocol, without guaranteed delivery, it can be very useful. For example, it is used by SNMP (Simple Network Management Protocol), also from the Internet suite, and by NFS (Network File System).

At the application level, messaging offers much more in the way of services, such as guaranteed delivery, robustness, and so forth. One example of messaging at the application level is to be found in IBM's MQI, which is discussed below, in the section on Queues, and in a later chapter (see "Chapter 17. Messaging and File Transfer" on page 191).

Mail systems are another example of messaging systems. Most such systems, based on the X.400 standard or on proprietary standards such as Microsoft Mail, include an API. This makes it possible to write applications whose communication is based on the services of a mail system, including, e.g., worldwide connectivity, distribution lists, registered mail, etc. Among the things they do not offer are a guarantee that the messages will be received in the same order they were sent, and high-performance data transfer.

For example, a messaging API such as Microsoft's MAPI [Hansen, page 161] could be used for the following purposes:

- group calendars
- integration of voice mail
- workflow management
- central archives
- computer conferencing
- bulletin boards

Queues

Queues, also called FIFO (first-in–first-out) lists, are a very common method of IPC (interprocess communication), i.e., communication within a single system. They are the basis for most real-time systems, including communications subsystems, are very important for IMS applications, and are even used in the transaction-oriented CICS (e.g., Transient Data Queues).

Even though transaction processing is by nature synchronous, and cannot tolerate large delays, transaction monitors often need to use queues, at least internally, to transfer requests to a central process. In this case, the queue provides a mechanism for decoupling processes within the framework of a transaction, and should involve relatively small delays.

With this method, the sending application writes a message into the input queue of the receiving application, which reads from this queue when it has time. Since writing to the queue is a simple data transfer, it is a fast operation for the sending application. The receiving application can choose to read in an asynchronous manner (a return code may indicate that the queue is empty) or in a synchronous manner, in which case it may wait until data arrives in an empty queue.

This provides an important decoupling between the applications, meaning that they can operate at different speeds (how long this can go on depends on the size of the queue, which may be in main memory or on disk).

One example of the use of queues can be found in terminal emulation software, i.e., a program which is used to make a PC capable of playing the role of a video terminal attached to a remote host computer.

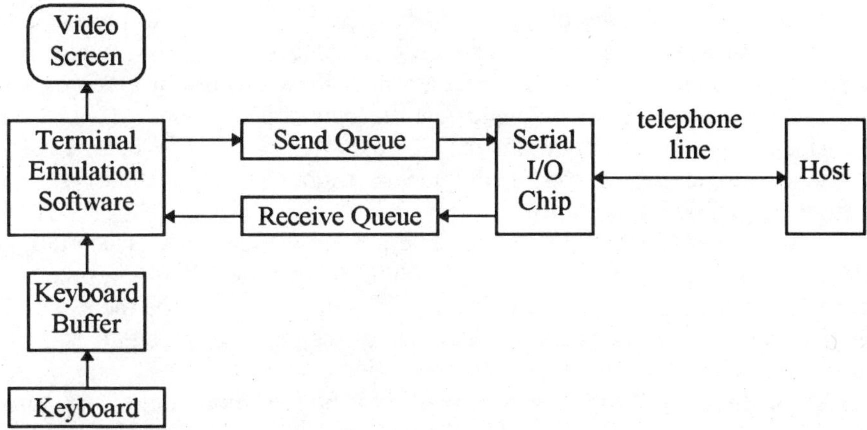

Figure 7. Queues in a Terminal Emulation

The terminal emulation software receives data from the keyboard and from the host computer and sends data both to the host and to the local video screen. Therefore, it provides an example of a process which must communicate with multiple devices, each of which has its own timing requirements.

The serial I/O chip is responsible for sending and receiving bits one at a time (serially) over a telecommunications line. Since the bits are transferred at a fixed rate (baud, or bits per second), the chip must operate at exactly this set speed. When it finishes receiving a byte from the line, it puts it into the receive queue and, depending on other details, may cause an interrupt. When it finishes sending a byte, it removes it from the send queue and tries to read the next data or command. If either of these buffers is not filled or emptied fast enough, the serial I/O chip will work either inefficiently or wrong.

Thus, the send and receive queues are a way of making it possible for the serial I/O chip to operate at an absolutely even rate while the terminal emulation software does its work in irregular pieces. For example, after receiving one byte, it may simply display a character on the screen, and after receiving another, it may have to reformat the whole screen. These queues are also often referred to as buffers or FIFOs.

Similarly, the keyboard buffer makes it possible for the terminal emulation software to do some things at a different speed from the user. For example, the user can hit a few keys very fast, and the results will not be lost, even if they require extensive processing ("type ahead"). This buffer, or queue, is normally part of the PC's operating system or BIOS (Basic Input/Output System).

Finally, the screen is normally controlled by direct calls to the video controller. Since this has a synchronous nature, the terminal emulation software must be written in such a way as not too spend to much time in formatting the screen without allowing for interrupts from the keyboard or the telecommunications line. Video controllers normally don't have output queues, but this would be an improvement in some cases.

Many similar examples of the usage of queues can be found in process control software or embedded real-time systems. All of these systems need some way of decoupling the operation of certain devices, which have to work at a certain speed, from the software processes which implement the logic of the system.

Another interesting example is the way that Windows 3.1, Windows NT, and OS/2 use queues to pass keyboard and mouse actions to applications (see "GUI Queues" on page 74).

In the case of queues, an important question is: What happens when the queue is full? For example, the receiving process might be off-line for a long time, or the queues may be filled faster than they can be emptied. In addition, there may be a significant performance degradation after the queue reaches a certain size, since searching or paging may come into effect.

All of these problems show that there is a limit to how much decoupling is possible: The queue can even out only a limited amount of difference in speed, for a limited time. Planning for this is part of the error handling that belongs to every good piece of software (see "Murphy's Law" on page 7). The solution to the problem may involve a kind of graceful degradation, or slowdown mode, when the queues are almost full, or it may involve some kind of flow control (see "Control Functions" on page 103).

The asynchronous API is an important element of queuing, because it allows the application to continue processing independent of the time required for transmission and for the receiver to respond. This also makes it easier for the sending application to handle high-volume data. It also makes it possible for an application to process high-priority data first, since the data left waiting in the queue is not lost. This is also one way of exploiting parallel processors: Multiple processes can write into or read from the same queue and do the processing work in parallel.

When queues are used for distributed processing (remote queuing), there is normally a sending queue on one end of the network and a receiving queue on the other. There are also programs, or subsystems, called queue managers, which take the messages from the sending queue and transmit them to the receiving queue. All of this is done transparently to the application program, which still has only its read/write API, as with local queues.

Depending on how robust the queuing system needs to be, each step in this process may be made more secure. The read/write API may be made more secure with a transaction-oriented commit protocol, so that the application can back out of the whole unit of work if writing to the queue fails. The communication between the queue managers can also use a commit protocol to synchronize writing to one queue with removing from the other. (This can be a simple response or a one-phase commit.) Also, this protocol can be made so that it protects from loss, duplication, and sequence errors.

Pipes

Pipes are unstructured streams of data passed from one application to another. They are similar to queues in that they operate in a FIFO fashion, but differ by using data streams instead of records. For example, consider the following command-line input:

- dir | sort (on MS-DOS)
- ls -l | sort (on UNIX)

Here the first program reads the directory of a disk and puts the result in its standard output. The pipe takes this and puts it into the standard input of the next program (sort), which processes it and puts the result (a sorted directory list) into its standard output (which will be directed to the screen).

On UNIX, which is a multitasking system, the output of "ls" can be passed directly to "sort". On MS-DOS, which does not support multitasking, the output of "dir" is directed to a (temporary) file, then "sort" is started and given the file as input.

This makes it clear that pipes are a connectionless protocol: The two partners (the one writing and the one reading) can operate independently of each other. However, the communication with the pipe itself, which is done via open/write/close and open/read/close, is connection-oriented (see "Connections" on page 98).

The pipe itself is unstructured in the sense that it has no records. However, the API supplied by the system recognizes new-line characters (UNIX) or carriage return / line feed sequences (MS-DOS), conventions that establish a record structure within the pipe.

The original UNIX pipes, used for redirecting the output of one process to the input of another, were limited to this predefined configuration. The next step, called "named pipes", was introduced in UNIX System V. With this service, it is possible to create new pipes and refer to them by name. In good UNIX tradition, they are treated exactly like files, so that applications can exchange information via files or via named pipes (a form of interprocess communication) with the same API.

Since then, the concept has been extended once more, so that pipes can be used to transfer data between two separate machines. This time, it was the developers of communications software who provided the service of named pipes over LANs. For example, much of Microsoft networking is based on named pipes, which can be run on top of any of the LAN protocols supported by Windows.

Distributed Data Storage

Why should the application program be concerned with communication at all? If it can just access all necessary data as if they were stored locally, then there is no need for communications APIs in the application program.

In fact, this model can be used as the basis for good application design. In effect, it shifts the responsibility for a number of concerns down into the next level of processing, that of a distributed system. This way, standard components can be used for solving a number of the problems involved in distributed systems design.

However, this does not solve all of the problems. The design, or at least the configuration, of the distributed system remains the responsibility of the application design team.

As a first step, we can provide remote access to central data.

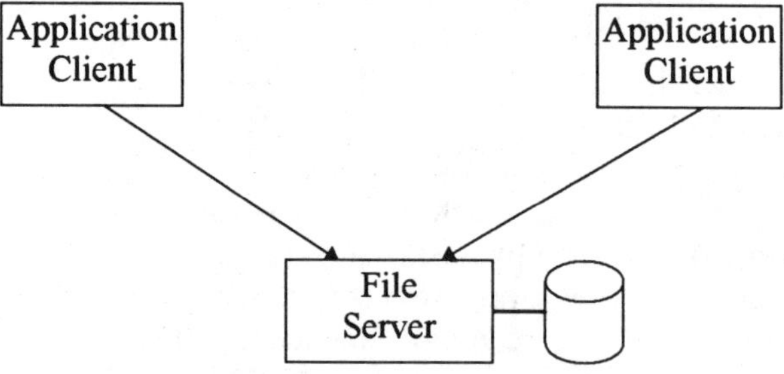

Figure 8. Distributed Access

A typical example of this configuration is a file server within a LAN. A number of workstations access files, such as documents and programs, which are stored on one central machine. Some advantages of this technique are:

- **multiple access:** All clients can access the same files.
- **management:** It is easier to back up and restore data, and to manage software licenses.
- **storage utilization:** Disk space is used more efficiently.

One significant disadvantage of this configuration is the load on the network. This is especially true if the network is a low-speed WAN.

One method of reducing the network load is to put a copy, or replica, of some or all of the central data on the remote machines.

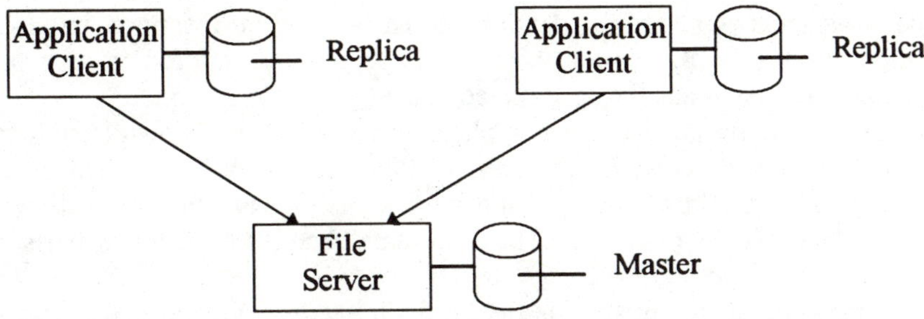

Figure 9. Replicated Data

A typical use of this is to make a read-only copy of a database on a machine used for data analysis. This way, the data is moved only at certain intervals, and the application can perform complex analysis and high-volume access locally without adding load to the network.

The difference between these methods can be summed up in two definitions:

- **operational data:** Data which is the basis for the operations of an organization. Typically, it changes rapidly and is accessed often.
- **informational data:** Data which is the basis for management information and other analysis processes. This data is relatively static in nature and can often be stored in archive form.

The difference between these types of data has been discussed within the framework of IBM's Information Warehouse concept [IBM GC26-4876-02] and Apple's VITAL program (data capture versus data access) [VITAL, page 13]. The concept of a Data Warehouse was introduced by [Inmon].

The final step in this approach is truly distributed data.

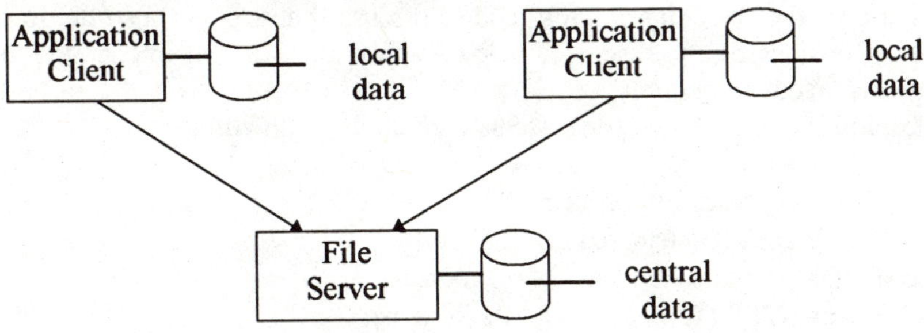

Figure 10. Distributed Data

In this case, different pieces of the data are stored in different locations, but are seen by the application as if they were one. This is sometimes referred to as a "single system image" because it has the appearance of being a single system.

In a relatively simple case, each application has access to its own local data and to data which is stored centrally. In addition, there may be some exchange of data between the local and central systems. In a more complex case, the applications have access to all data, and there is a need to coordinate changes to different parts of the data.

One example of this method is the DCE directory service (see "Directory" on page 87). Here, each cell (an autonomous part of the total network) has its own local directory (cell directory). Most accesses to the directory occur locally within the cell, which is often implemented on a LAN and used by a relatively small group of users. When directory information from another cell is required, the system automatically accesses the global directory and then the directory of the remote cell. This way, the directory appears to the user (or application) as a single system, but really consists of multiple, coordinated pieces.

In summary, the distributed data model can be divided into three groups:

- distributed access
- replicated data
- distributed data

Up to now, we have not said what kind of data we have been discussing. Interestingly enough, all of this can be applied to at least the following types of data:

- files
- databases
- objects

In fact, not only the basic distribution models discussed above, but also the important issues to be considered (and discussed below), apply more or less unchanged to all of these data management systems.

Examples of distributed file systems include the following:

- Sun NFS (Network File System)
- OSF DCE DFS (Distributed File System)
- IBM DDM (Distributed Data Management)
- Microsoft NTFS (Windows NT File System)

NFS and DFS provide distributed access to files, and DFS includes a method for replicating files.

Examples of distributed access to relational databases include the following:

- Oracle SQL*Net
- IBM DRDA (Distributed Relational Database Architecture)
- Microsoft ODBC (Open Database Connectivity)

Examples of distributed access to objects include the following:

- OMG CORBA (Common Object Request Broker Architecture)
- IBM DSOM (Distributed System Object Model)
- Novell AppWare

Examples of higher-level services based on distributed object services include the following:

- Microsoft OLE (Object Linking and Embedding)
- CIL OpenDoc

Issues

What problems can be solved by using distributed data (access)? What new problems will arise because of it?

After deciding what type of data to use (files, databases, object-oriented systems), there are a number of alternatives in designing the system.

- **storage location:** Should data storage be centralized or distributed?
- **replication:** Should some parts be replicated? Will they be used only for read-only access, or do they need to be updated?
- **consistency:** How will the parts be kept consistent?
- **integrity, availability:** What are the requirements for integrity and availability? How will they be guaranteed?
- **reliability:** Is it possible to restore a consistent state after a system crash, for example due to disk failure? What steps are necessary, and how long will it take to repair the damage?
- **administration, backup:** What steps are necessary to manage the data storage systems?
- **query optimization:** Can queries be optimized in order to improve performance and reduce network load? Is this possible for global queries (affecting multiple DBMSs)?
- **concurrency and locking:** Are concurrency methods such as locking necessary? How can excessive locking be prevented? What is the granularity (record, page, table) of the available locking mechanisms? Is there any deadlock detection?

- **Heterogeneous Systems, Data Conversion:** Will the system contain components with different architecture?
- **Security:** What security requirements are there? How will they be enforced and managed?

The following twelve rules proposed by C. J. Date [Date] for judging distributed relational database management systems can be applied to a large degree to all three kinds of distributed data systems discussed here.

1. **Local autonomy:** The systems at each site should be independent of one another. In particular, individual DBMSs should provide their own security, locking, logging, integrity, and recovery.
2. **No reliance on central site:** By avoiding dependence on a single site, there is no single point of failure and no central bottleneck.
3. **Continuous operation:** The system should not require downtime, which means that it should provide on-line backup and recovery, as well as full and incremental archiving.
4. **Location transparency and location independence:** Users (and applications) should not need to know where data is stored. This makes it possible to move data from one location to another without changing applications. It is sometimes implemented with the help of a data dictionary or a directory service.
5. **Fragmentation independence:** In relational databases, this refers to storing parts of a table at different sites. Again, users and applications should not be aware of this.
6. **Replication independence:** This is similar to the last two rules, but applies to replicas. It requires automatic synchronization of the replication process.
7. **Distributed query processing:** The performance of distributed queries should be optimized with respect to data location and the utilization of CPU, I/O, and network resources.
8. **Distributed transaction management:** The distributed system should support atomic transactions.
9. **Hardware independence:** A distributed system should operate consistently on different hardware platforms.
10. **Operating system independence:** A distributed system should also run on different operating systems.
11. **Network independence:** The system should also run over different (and mixed) communications protocols.
12. **DBMS independence:** This means that the individual (and different) DBMSs (or data/object management systems) should interoperate. In contrast with the last rule, this means that there must be some standardized communications protocol and data formats supported by all systems.

Comparison

Which of the processing models is best? Of course, this depends on the requirements of the application. In order to come closer to the answer to this question, the following pages contain a comparison of these models based on some of the major issues involved, such as synchronization, network utilization, and programming complexity.

One of the most important aspects in the design of a distributed system is to decide how actions, such as changes to data, are synchronized between different parts of the system. The following table summarizes the synchronization aspects of each basic method.

model	processing	synchronization
messages, queues, pipes	point-to-point	delayed
client/server	point-to-point	immediate
distributed transactions	multipoint	immediate

Table 3. Data Synchronization

Messages, queues, and pipes are most often used to send data from one program to another, i.e., in a point-to-point configuration. In addition to this, broadcast messages, or mailing lists, involve a one-to-many configuration, and a many-to-one situation occurs when many applications put data into the input queue of one receiver. However, even though these situations are multipoint configurations in terms of data flow, they are not capable of ensuring synchronization of multiple entities.

All of these methods contain some element of delay. In fact, this is their primary use, i.e., to decouple one application from another, allowing them to operate at different speeds. The actual delay may be very small, perhaps a millisecond, in cases such as when pipes are used for interprocess communication. Remote queues (i.e., via a network) often involve slightly longer delays, such as one second, and may also be used to store data for as much as a few hours during a network failure. Messaging systems such as mailboxes used for e-mail often hold messages for a number of days or even longer.

The client/server model, which always involves a request/response mode of communication, is always synchronous in nature. Even when an asynchronous API is used for communications, the client waits for a response before continuing to work. As a result, the actions of the client and the server are always synchronized. However, this synchronization always involves a point-to-point configuration between a client and a server. Even though multiple clients normally access the same server, there is no communication between the clients, and thus no synchronization of their actions.

The only method capable of guaranteeing immediate synchronization of the actions of multiple entities is distributed transaction processing. In fact, this is the primary purpose of the commit protocol used by this method.

The need for synchronization arises most often when data is stored in multiple locations, making it necessary to keep all parts of a complex structure consistent when any changes are made. In fact, when we think of transactions or commit protocols, we often assume that a database is involved. However, the need for synchronization can arise in any situation involving changes to persistent status information. For example, when a telecommunications carrier makes changes to multiple devices within the network, it may be necessary to keep the devices consistent at all times. As a result, work has been done on combining network management protocols with the commit protocol (see "Transaction Synchronization" on page 242).

data storage	synchronization
central	not required
distributed, partitioned	not required
distributed, with overlap	required

Table 4. Data Storage and Synchronization

The simplest case of distributed processing involves distributed access to one central data storage site, so there is no need for synchronizing multiple pieces of information. When the data is stored at multiple sites, it may still be possible to partition it, or divide it into separate pieces which do not need to be coordinated.

For example, an Alligator of the APE organization keeps a database of all swamps, and a Bear maintains another database containing a description of all dry forests. Each animal has read-only access to the other's data, and all aspects of data presentation and communication have been standardized by an interspecies organization. As a result, the data can be used from any location and in any combination, but there is no synchronization problem involved, since each animal updates only its own database.

On the other hand, if there is no way to partition the data according to its meaning, function, ownership, or any other criterion, then it is necessary to synchronize changes to it.

For example, APE's Animal Dating Agency has implemented some very sophisticated methods for matching the dating requests and preferences of its clients. The system not only involves the use of artificial intelligence and fuzzy set algorithms, but is capable of setting up interspecies orgies while taking all cultural nuances into consideration. Once a good match has been found, all calendars of all individuals are updated without any loss of consistency.

When synchronization applies only to data, either this can be done directly in the application, or the task can be delegated to a subsystem, such as a distributed file system or a distributed database. If this is done, the subsystem will most likely use one of the methods discussed here. For example, replication servers can be thought of as a kind of queuing system. Also, the implementation of a true distributed database will most likely be based on distributed transaction processing. In fact, this may be one of the most important uses of distributed transactions: to hide their complexity from the application.

Another very important aspect of distributed processing is the utilization of the network. As we will see, the different processing models put different demands on the bandwidth and availability of the communications subsystem.

model	network utilization
messages, queues, pipes	low
client/server	medium
distributed transactions	high

Table 5. Network Utilization

As far as availability of the network is concerned, the asynchronous method of messages, queues, and pipes is not very demanding. Similarly, since there is no synchronization protocol, there is very little added overhead to use up bandwidth. Of course, large amounts of data may require a lot of capacity, but even here, the method can normally cope with some unexpected transmission delays, as long as the total throughput is sufficient. On the other hand, e-mail packages or message-handling systems may generate overhead of a different nature, due to such things as universal addressing methods or intricate storage systems.

The client/server model is much more demanding with regard to network availability, since access to the server is synchronous. When the network is down, the client must either wait or implement some other way of handling the loss. Also, since there is some logic involved in the correlation of requests and responses, and in formatting parameters for remote procedure calls, this model also adds a bit more to the overhead.

What should a client do when a server it needs is not available? In most cases, it simply displays a message such as "service not available, please try later", passing the problem on to the end user. On the other hand, if the application designer has included an error-handling scheme which temporarily stores the request until the server comes back on line, the logic may be nothing other than a private implementation of a queuing method.

Distributed transactions place the highest demands on the network. By the very nature of the method, no transaction can complete unless all parties involved are available. Since this often involves locking mechanisms in order to prevent inconsistencies, distributed transactions with a high load can tolerate only small delays. In addition, the two-phase commit protocol itself generates a significant amount of overhead. As a result, distributed transaction processing is generally feasible only with a high-speed network which is also very reliable.

Once it has become clear which alternatives for solving a particular problem are available, it is also worthwhile to consider how difficult it will be to program the system. A method which is easy to program will cost less to implement and to maintain, be finished sooner, and be more reliable.

model	programming complexity
messages, queues, pipes	low
client/server	medium
distributed transactions	high

Table 6. Programming Complexity

Of all the methods shown here, messages, queues, and pipes are the simplest to program, since there is very little to do other than specify the name or address of the partner and send the messages, or check if a message has arrived. In special cases, there may be additional complexity due to special features such as transaction-oriented queues.

The client/server model is a very natural and straightforward method for most programmers. However, some additional complexity arises from the necessity to use an interface definition language to define remote procedures, or to define data structures which provide the same function. And of course it is necessary to keep different versions of these things consistent, which requires some administrative work.

Distributed transactions are the most complex to create. This is due partly to the commit protocol itself, and also to the necessity of designing the system in such a way as to avoid problems such as excessive locking. Because of the all-or-nothing nature of transaction processing, there is very little room for problems without compromising the whole system.

The summary of programming complexity shown in the table applies mainly to the communications API, and not to the rest of the application logic. In particular, if the method chosen does not solve the problem well, there may be a significant amount of additional logic, such as error handling, which makes the total system much more complex.

Summary of Part 1

Many forms of distributed processing are important aspects of today's world. This includes informal communication via telephones, fax, and e-mail, now augmented by on-line services and the Internet, as well as complex, highly structured applications used within enterprises, such as order processing or inventory. At the same time, we are experiencing a change in business practices, resulting in more decentralized activity and less central control. The technological side is similar, characterized by rapid change, new opportunities, and increasing decentralization. In order to cope with these changes we need to search for the right mixture of control and freedom, or of planning and ad hoc adaptation.

In order to free ourselves from the internal aspects of technology, we need to look at it from a high level of abstraction whenever possible. This means focusing on the services offered by the technology instead of its internal function.

All types of distributed processing involve many situations where various components need to cooperate: at the interface with the user or with data storage, and in communication both within layers of software (peer communication) and between them (service interface). This is best accomplished by standards, which, however, need to be suitable, available, and accepted by the community which will use them. As a result, countless standards and even more less formal agreements are constantly being developed by many different organizations.

Finally, there are only a few basic models used when multiple processes communicate with each other. These apply equally to systems on both a small and a large scale, and to systems either within a single computer or distributed across the whole world. The most common model, used by client/server applications, involves a synchronous request/response mechanism. A higher degree of coordination of multiple activities can be achieved by using the transaction-processing model. Asynchronous communication, providing a much looser coupling of the partners, can be done with messaging and queuing. Or, any one of these methods can be hidden from the application by using a distributed data model.

Part 2. Systems

Introduction to Part 2

After the discussion of fundamental principles and methods in the first part of this book, this part goes into the basic building blocks of computing systems in general and distributed systems in particular. It begins at a low level, taking a look at hardware and operating systems. Then, by considering distributed or network operating systems, we arrive at a layer that actually encompasses communication, overlapping and anticipating the material of the next part. In addition, it also gives a preview of "Chapter 25. Security".

"Chapter 5. Hardware" is a brief discussion of some trends in hardware systems, and how they affect distributed processing systems. Even though hardware is the layer which is the farthest removed from applications, it should be clear that the basic services and performance aspects of hardware determine whether particular applications are possible at all.

"Chapter 6. Operating Systems" covers the next layer upwards. Here, the basic services of operating systems have been covered in more detail, because they are both the basis for all application development and the basis for their distributed counterparts. At the end of the chapter, a section on GUIs (Graphical User Interfaces) and queues shows one way in which queues are used within operating systems. It provides examples of how queues can be used, how GUI behavior is affected, and how applications should be designed in order to perform well in this situation.

"Chapter 7. Middleware" begins with a short but general discussion of what "middleware" is and why it is important. Then it goes into the topic of NOS (network operating systems), which can be thought of as operating systems which extend over a network, or just as simple service providers.

"Chapter 8. DCE" then goes on to cover a particularly important NOS, the OSF DCE (Distributed Computing Environment). This system is an example of a development which represents the current state of the art in distributed systems. It is a multivendor solution which is standardized to a relatively high degree and is still very realistic. Even if it doesn't become the most widely used architecture in the near future, it is still a good example of what can be done today.

Within APE, the development of systems, including hardware and operating systems, has traditionally been the domain of amphibians. Ironically, it all started with a joke, when one of APE's managers suggested that the lowest of the seven OSI layers could best be handled by animals who could see things from a frog's-eye view. Soon, however, this idea became reality, with thousands of frogs transformed into the princes of chip design. The huge success that has followed is often attributed to the frogs' ability to operate seamlessly at the interface between land and water, which they were able to apply to the shoreline between hardware and software. Often, frogs were instrumental in laying the foundations for complete industries, which were later taken over by other species. In fact, many of the large companies in operation today were started by a few frogs working in a garage or a backyard pond.

Chapter 5. Hardware

Perhaps the one technological advancement that has contributed most to the development of distributed processing is the microprocessor: As the basis for PCs, it has brought computing power directly to the user—and given the user the power to decide what to do with it (see "Power to the User" on page 4). As a result, many aspects of distributed processing are tied closely to the capabilities and limitations of PCs. This chapter presents a few aspects from the rapidly changing field of computer hardware. In particular, it discusses some trends which now give us another chance of buying operating systems which are less dependent on the kind of chips they run on.

Services

The basic service provided by microprocessors is to be found in its "machine language", and in how fast it can understand or perform the elements of its own "native" language and the "foreign" languages of other processors.

Instruction Sets

What does the CPU (Central Processing Unit) do? The most important part of this is the instruction set that it offers. Every compiler then has to help bridge the "semantic gap", i.e., the big difference between what the application really needs to accomplish and the capability of the instructions which are available on the CPU.

This doesn't mean that the best CPU is the one that delivers the most complex instructions. This has been illustrated very well by the big RISC/CISC debate (see "RISC versus CISC" on page 54). In addition, there are many more subtle ways to improve performance, such as reading and processing multiple instructions at once, using an internal cache, etc.

The usefulness of the instruction set also depends on how well suited it is for writing programs. For example, most CPUs seem to love registers, which are special, fast little pieces of memory. If certain instructions, such as arithmetic operations, are defined to deal only with registers, these instructions can be much faster than they would be if they had to deal directly with memory addresses. However, when a program is written in assembly language, or written in a higher-level language and later compiled, it ends up containing a lot of instructions that do nothing other than load, unload, save, and restore registers. Now the question is, What is better, fewer instructions or more and faster ones?

In fact, there are a number of alternatives to using registers. One of them is for all instructions to address memory directly, as was done in the TI 99 microprocessor. Another way, which is very well suited to processing arithmetic expressions, is to have all arithmetic instructions address the stack, as was done in the Lilith system [Wirth]. In addition to these, CPUs have been developed which support higher-level language constructs, such as COBOL or LISP statements, as well as object-oriented methods or special database support.

All of this makes it clear that the art of defining instruction sets which are both efficient to implement and useful for programming is far from complete; there is plenty of room for improvement. Add to this the effects of market presence, company influence, and so forth, and the result is a field which is very interesting, rapidly changing, and sure to bring some more surprises in the future.

Hardware Emulation

Another service related to instruction sets is the ability to emulate the instruction set of another CPU. In general, emulation is a very important technique for keeping things compatible with the old order while still offering something new. Instead of keeping the instruction set of each new version compatible with the last one, CPUs with completely new instruction sets are being developed, but with the added feature of emulation of older CPUs.

For example, in 1964, IBM's new System/360 was able to emulate the older 1401 instruction set. Today, the PowerPC and other RISC processors are being used to provide emulation in a hybrid fashion, partly hardware and partly software [Halfhill 4/94].

From a practical point of view, it is important to know which operating system will run on a particular CPU. Since it is not always feasible or economical for the hardware vendor to port all important operating systems to each new CPU, operating system support is sometimes accomplished by emulation techniques.

Speed

The speed of a processor is clearly an important factor. However, it is not so easy to determine as it may seem.

One way of increasing the speed of a processor is "pipelining", where multiple instructions are lined up in a "pipeline" for simultaneous processing. For example, if instructions require five steps (CPU cycles) to process, the last instruction to be put into the pipeline is in the first step of processing, the next one is in the second step and so forth up to the oldest instruction, which is almost finished. However, if an instruction turns out to be a branch (i.e., "go to" or "jump"), the pipeline has to be emptied and restarted at the address specified in the branch instruction. This problem can be further reduced by a method known as "branch prediction".

Another way of increasing overall speed is the use of a "cache", i.e., a relatively small piece of memory which is much faster than the normal main memory. Whenever it is necessary to transfer data to or from main memory, larger chunks, or "blocks", are transferred to or from the cache. This way, subsequent memory requests have a chance of being satisfied by the cache without going to the slower main memory.

One common measure of speed is simply the clock frequency, given in MHz. However, this is useful only for comparing CPUs with the same instruction set, since different instructions require a different number of CPU cycles. Even then, it has lost much value since the effects of pipelining and caching have made it inaccurate to simply measure the time required for any individual instruction.

Some other measures which come a bit closer to reality are MIPS (Million Instructions per Second) and FLOPS (Floating-Point Operations per Second). At least, these measure the time used for real instructions. But what instructions? And again, they break down under the subtle effects of pipelining, caching, etc.

A number of improved methods, such as SPECfp, SPECint, and SPECmark, have been developed by SPEC (System Performance Evaluation Corporation) (see "Organizations" on page 23). The rapid evolution of these standards (they are renewed every few years) shows that there is still plenty to be done here, too.

Standards

There are many standards for hardware, but most of them are outside the scope of this book. Here are just two examples which have been mentioned in this chapter.

- IEEE Floating Point [IEEE 754].
- Benchmark tests by SPEC.

Trends and Products

Even though it is not specific to distributed computing, the development of new CPUs, both CISC and RISC style, is very important in determining what systems can be used in this area. Something more related to communication, and also to multimedia, is the concept of a DSP (Digital Signal Processor).

RISC versus CISC

The RISC/CISC debate has been given a lot of coverage in the press and advertising, and is used as an argument for both sides, i.e., why RISC or CISC is better. What is really important?

The original idea of RISC (Reduced-Instruction-Set Computer) was to make the instructions so simple that they could be performed much faster than on a conventional chip, which was then given the name CISC (Complex-Instruction-Set Computer); any more complex operations could be done in software. This also had the advantage of making it possible for the instructions to be shorter and of equal length, reducing the time required for fetching and decoding the instructions. In addition to improving performance, it was expected that this simplicity would improve the manufacturing and testing of both CPUs and compilers.

In the meantime, both lines of microprocessors have been developed so much farther that the difference is dwindling. For example, descriptions of "CISC" chips [Halfhill 6/94] use the terminology "RISC-like technology" to denote the following properties:

- long superscalar pipelines
- wider data paths
- on-board instruction/data caches
- a larger number of registers with dynamic renaming
- branch prediction
- speculative execution

Although these techniques may have been used in RISC processors first, they also show that the industry has come a long way from the original idea of "reduced" or "simple" instruction sets. In fact, the technology has moved so far that it is practically meaningless to debate whether so-called RISC or CISC chips are better. Instead, we should look at what the chips offer in terms of processing power for the needs of real software.

CPUs

Some of the CPUs currently competing for the next generation of machines are:

- Intel 80x86
- DEC Alpha AXP
- Sun SPARC
- MIPS R4x00
- HP PA-RISC
- IBM PowerPC

DSPs

The DSP (Digital Signal Processor) is a microprocessor specially designed to process digitized signals. The applications of DSPs include:

- audio (e.g., sound cards, synthesizers, speech compression)
- imaging
- telecommunications (e.g., modem modulation)

The advancements being made in DSP technology will have the following effects on (distributed) computing:

- Multimedia will become cheaper and more common. Applications that do not support multimedia will soon look old and lose acceptance. New applications will become possible.
- Multimedia applications will demand more telecommunications capacity and support for isochronous data transfer.

- Communications technology will improve and be included in more hardware solutions.

Another trend in hardware is the inclusion of DSP logic on CPU chips. In some cases, this may make it unnecessary to install extra hardware for audio or for modems. Also, standardized DSP interfaces are being built into operating systems, which will help make their services more easily available to many applications.

The Next Generation

As a result of these changes, the next generation of PCs should be able to depart from the current hardware architecture and use a completely new design [Halfhill 10/95]. As a part of this development, IBM has chosen to follow in the footsteps of APE's successful system amphibians by displaying a new PC which it has nicknamed "Leapfrog", and which sits on a docking station called the "lily pad".

Chapter 6. Operating Systems

In today's computing environments, the hardware is not (or should not be) accessed directly by the application programs. There is always a fairly large piece of software, the "operating system", between the hardware and the application or the end user. When we move to a distributed environment, we can think of a complex system either as numerous operating systems coupled by communication links, or as one operating system or "single system image" which consists of distributed components. In fact, both today's real and tomorrow's emerging distributed systems often contain some aspects of both views. So, before looking at distributed systems, we will begin by taking a short look at the fundamental tasks of operating systems as such.

Services

The basic function of an operating system can be thought of as the task of running the computer. In order to do this, it needs to manage all hardware resources and schedule and coordinate their activity. And in doing so, it also provides a higher level of service to the application or user (see "The Rising Level of Abstraction" on page 8).

HW and Device Support

Since an operating system is nothing other than a program for managing and allocating resources, it is very important to see what it actually supports. This includes:

- CPUs
- memory
- disks
- terminals
- communications (LAN and WAN)
- multimedia devices
- printers

APIs and ABIs

Most operating-system services are offered to applications programs in the form of an API (Application Programming Interface). This is a set of calls that can be used in the application program, which then must be compiled and linked with a library of subroutines which implement the services. In other words, an API is an interface for use with source code before it is compiled.

In a similar way, the services can also be offered via an ABI (Application Binary Interface). The difference here is that the programs which use the services do not need to be recompiled, because the interface is binary-compatible with some standard. In other words, it is an interface for use with object code, i.e., code which has already been compiled.

The primary reason for offering ABIs to an operating system or similar services is to make it possible to reuse existing programs with a new operating system. For example, WABI (Windows Application Binary Interface) is one of the solutions which make it possible to run existing Windows programs on UNIX operating systems.

File Systems

The basic services of file systems are the standard file operations, such as "open", "close", "read", and "write", that support the basic I/O operations. Locking of whole files or parts of a file is needed for controlling concurrent access. Memory-mapped files (in Windows, VSAM in MVS) provide a faster access method. Auxiliary functions such as searching through a directory make programming file handling more efficient.

Some of the variants of file systems, along with the special services they provide, are:

- **transactional file system:** includes support of a commit protocol
- **object-oriented file system:** provides storage of objects, including data and methods
- **installable file system:** makes it possible to add or remove file systems dynamically
- **recoverable file system:** can be restored after a system crash
- **journaled file system:** keeps a log of all changes, so that they can be restored quickly at system restart.

Databases

More than just a way to store and retrieve complex data, a DBMS (Database Management System) provides the following services:

- persistence
  - storage
  - retrieval
- integrity
- consistency
- reliability

Whereas persistence is the obvious service of any storage system, the storage and retrieval API may be complex in order to provide sufficient support for the data model used. Integrity and consistency are not trivial in environments which support multiple concurrent access, and are guaranteed along with the ACID (atomicity, consistency, isolation, durability) properties of transactions (see "Distributed Transaction

Processing" on page 29). These are guaranteed by the use of a commit protocol and other techniques such as locking and serialization. Reliability refers to the ability to recover from system failures.

Today, the RDBMS (Relational Database Management System) is the most important form of database system. It has its strong points in its ability to guarantee data integrity (by eliminating redundancy), and has achieved good performance in a number of fields of application. Most experts agree that the RDBMS will remain the most important form in many, and perhaps in most, fields of application.

The most common language for accessing relational databases is SQL (Structured Query Language), which was created by IBM but has since been standardized by organizations such as ANSI, X/Open, and ISO/IEC. SQL also exists in various distributed forms (see "Chapter 15. Remote SQL" on page 164).

Along with the general movement toward more and more object-oriented techniques in data processing, it is natural to extend the database concept to cover arbitrary objects. In fact, many people expect that the ODBMS (Object-oriented Database Management System) technology will play a major role in the storage of complex objects in fields of application such as CAD (Computer-Aided Design), engineering, and multimedia [Stein]. These objects are often too complex and interrelated to be stored efficiently in a series of tables of a relational database.

Object databases have recently been standardized by the ODMG (Object Database Management Group) [Cattell; Ben-Natan, Chapter 7]. Some of the components of that standard are:

- OID (Object Identifier): A unique ID assigned to each object when it is created. Internally, this may be converted to an address at runtime, but the OID format can be stored in the database and used as a reference.
- ODM (Object Data Model): A definition of object-oriented data modeling. This is also known as the ODMG/OM (ODMG Object Model), and is an extension of the OMG/OM (OMG Object Model), which is the basis for CORBA.
- ODL (Object-Definition Language): A formal language, analogous to DDL (Data Definition Language), along with a compiler which converts ODL to C++ or Smalltalk.
- OML (Object Manipulation Language): This concept, analogous to DML (Data Manipulation Language), is not supplied by the ODMG standard. Instead, bindings to C++ and Smalltalk are defined, making object manipulation a part of the programming language used.
- OQL (Object Query Language): This is analogous to SQL, but operates directly on objects and their attributes, rather than on tables.

The ODMG standard specifies the storage of the object's attributes (its data) in the database, but not its methods (its procedures).

Remote access to an object database is generally achieved through an ORB (Object Request Broker), which provides a platform-independent mechanism for transparent access to distributed objects. This has been standardized as CORBA (Common Object Request Broker Architecture) by the OMG (Object Management Group) [Ben-Natan].

Examples of commercial ODBMS packages are:

- DEC Object/DB
- Servio GemStone
- Persistent Data Systems IDB Object Database
- Itasca ODBMS
- ADB M.A.T.I.S.S.E.
- O_2 Technology O_2
- Objectivity/DB
- MAK Software Consultants Object Skipjack
- Object Design ObjectStore
- VC Software ODBMS 2.0
- Ontos DB
- HP OpenODB
- Poet Software Poet
- Raima Object Manager
- Tensegrity OO Database for Smalltalk
- UniSQL/X Database Management System
- Versant Object Database Management System

Multiprocessing and Multiuser Systems

Today, most operating systems provide support for multiprocessing or multitasking, meaning that multiple processes can run simultaneously. When the system runs on a single CPU, or processor, this requires a mechanism for switching between processes. One of the early uses of multitasking was as a basis for multiuser systems. Mainframe operating systems such as MVS, and UNIX, which was originally developed on midrange machines, support multiple users simultaneously, in a time-sharing mode.

Today, the trend towards the use of PCs as clients means that each user has a dedicated system, and that other machines provide services such as files and printing. The servers used for this purpose need to handle multiple requests simultaneously, and thus need some kind of multiprocessing. The difference between a multiprocessing system and a multiuser system is actually very small: Multiuser support requires multiprocessing and a bit of logic for user management.

One important difference between multiuser operation and a typical multiprocessing server is the duration of requests: Users normally login for extended periods of time, whereas typical client/server-style requests are very short. This makes server systems similar to traditional transaction monitors, but without the support for user management and screen formatting. This need for fast task switching is one reason for the fact that these transaction monitors often have a program-switching mechanism on top of the multiprocessing operating system.

In more recent developments, the need for fast task switching in server systems has lead to another concept, called the "lightweight process" or "thread". By definition, a process contains a complete user environment, including address space and files. By contrast, a "thread of execution" is just enough to allow another program to run. All threads within the same process share the resources of address space, files, etc. As a result of this, switching between threads is much faster than process switching, and is therefore very useful for servers. On the other hand, processes are a very good way of protecting different applications from one another, since separate processes cannot overwrite one another's code, data, files, etc.

For the application developer, this means that programs written by different people and modified often should be run as separate processes. A complete "server" system, on the other hand, designed and implemented by a single team, and modified less frequently than most client systems, should make use of multiple threads.

Until recently, most PC operating systems, such as MS-DOS, did not support multiprocessing. As a result, programs that required it, such as background communications, often used low-level methods such as interrupt handlers in TSR (Terminate and Stay Resident) programs. This has changed, since OS/2 and the newer versions of Windows all support full multiprocessing capabilities, including threads. Whereas the need for multiprocessing in servers should be clear now, the value of multiprocessing clients is not so obvious. After all, a PC is "personal", i.e. dedicated to a single user. Some of the advantages to be expected from multiprocess or multithread client applications are:

- **better applications:** Multithreaded applications can delegate slow operations (database queries, requests to remote servers) to separate threads, leaving the user interface ready to respond to the user.
- **fault tolerance:** Application errors cannot destroy other applications or the operating system itself.

Parallelism

Instead of just making the CPU faster, we can increase the capacity of a computer by employing multiple CPUs which all work simultaneously. However, in order to make this work, the operating system must coordinate the activity of the CPUs.

Even though the benefit of parallel processors has often been demonstrated in special applications, it has been slow to come to the market in the commercial environment. This is due in part to the fact that CPU capacity is seldom the most important bottleneck for commercial applications, and in part to the difficulty of adapting the large base of existing systems and applications to parallel processors.

Today, this situation is changing rapidly, and most operating systems provide support for SMP (Symmetric Multiprocessing). This advancement will lead to a short-term improvement in the operating system's performance and also establish a basis for more efficient applications on a longer-term basis. Some of the most striking improvements are to be seen in fields with inherent parallelism, such as transaction processing and database queries. In fact, these are also the areas most likely to benefit from massively parallel computing.

Memory Management

When a program requests memory from the operating system, the services available often depend on how the operating system uses the addressing mechanisms of the underlying hardware. For example, it might be possible to get memory blocks only of a certain maximum size, such as 64 KB. Some systems may limit this to the actual memory available in hardware, while others provide access to virtual memory, and support this by paging mechanisms where necessary.

In addition to this, the runtime system of most compilers usually adds on another layer of memory management which makes it possible to attach and release variable-length memory blocks without inducing operating system overhead each time. And, of course, object-oriented class libraries offer another set of memory management tools, and use them extensively for their own "create" and "destroy" operations.

In addition to local memory management, most operating systems provide a method for allocating shared memory blocks. These can be accessed by multiple processes and used as a means of interprocess communication.

In addition to the rudimentary functions of allocating, accessing, and releasing memory in both small and large blocks, there are a number of more subtle issues involved. One of these is a problem of fragmentation: What happens when the available memory has been broken up into a number of small noncontiguous pieces? Another is a matter of cleaning up, or "garbage collection", when memory is released only on an implicit basis and thus needs to be regained by the operating system. And, finally, performance and robustness are important.

Memory Protection

Along with the services of memory management, it is important to have a way of protecting the memory of one program from the errors of another. The size and complexity of today's systems, along with many other factors, make errors a commonplace thing. As a result, the total system can be robust and survive errors in individual parts only if memory is properly protected.

The basic support for memory protection must be part of the hardware: There must at least be a way of marking pieces of memory as protected or read-only, and the CPU must prevent individual instructions from unauthorized access to memory. However, this is valuable only if there is a method for managing these mechanisms, i.e., processes, memory, and access rights. In fact, the task of the operating system consists mostly of managing this type of resource.

As a result, the most immediate and important benefit of multiprocessing operating systems for PC users results from their memory protection and not from their support for parallel processing.

IPC (Interprocess Communication)

Now that we expect our operating system to support multiprocessing, and because we expect the operating system and the applications to make use of this feature, it is also necessary for the operating system to provide ways for separate processes to communicate with each other. This is the basic reason for interprocess communication. But then, when we step back and take a more global view of this, we can see the fundamental similarity between:

- IPC in a traditional operating system
- IPC in a distributed, or network operating system
- communication between applications in a distributed system

Because of this similarity, the basic concepts have been presented in the chapter on processing models (see "Chapter 4. Processing Models" on page 27). Here, we will limit the discussion to IPC within a single system.

One very common method of implementing IPC, shared memory (i.e., a piece of memory accessible by multiple processes), is discussed above. In order to coordinate the access of independent processes, semaphores can be used. These are simply indicators used to lock or unlock access to the shared memory. Since semaphores must be set or cleared in a single, consistent step, the operating system provides an API for this, and prevents the action from being interrupted by other processes. Another name for the same concept is mutex (mutual exclusion lock). When shared memory and semaphores are migrated to a distributed environment, they are often replaced by shared files with a locking mechanism.

Another common method for IPC is pipes (see "Pipes" on page 39). They provide a simple but unstructured way of passing data from one process to another.

The API which an operating system provides for its own services is typically a call-style interface (which is nothing other than the client/server concept, see "Client/Server Computing" on page 27). Internally, the parameters are passed to other processes via mechanisms such as interrupts or SVCs (Supervisor Call, an instruction in the IBM /370 architecture). Unfortunately, most operating systems do not offer this method for application-to-application IPC, unless the user chooses to employ an RPC implementation, which is generally not optimized for performance within a single system.

All of the traditional methods mentioned above are really low-level, because they include no standardized way of passing structured data or method invocations between applications. Some newer methods which go farther in this direction are:

- DDE (Microsoft Dynamic Data Exchange)

- OLE (Microsoft Object Linking and Embedding)
- SOM (IBM System Object Model)

User Interface

Support for some kind of user interface is typically part of the operating system. The user interface is the method for displaying information on a screen, and may be character-based or graphical.

Actually, it is quite possible to separate the formatting of user interfaces from the rest of the operating system. This was done in UNIX, where the kernel provides the basic functions such as multiprocessing and files, and the shell provides the user interface. This has the advantage of keeping the kernel independent of the shell, which can then be changed without disturbing the inner workings of the kernel. In addition, good application design will separate the user interface from the rest of the program, such as database access, in order to achieve a similar independence and make it possible to change or move parts of the application as needed.

On the other hand, another part of user-interface support consists of managing such resources as the terminal, keyboard, and mouse and coordinating their effects on multiple applications. This generally requires some kind of central authority, and is therefore generally a part of the operating system. As a result, graphical user interface support is rarely separated from the operating system.

The terminals in use today on machines ranging from mainframes to PCs can be classified as follows:

- character-based, character-mode
- character-based, block-mode
- graphical

Character-based terminals display predefined characters, such as those in the ASCII set.

Character-mode operation (of a character-based terminal) means that each character is transmitted individually. This is a very flexible mechanism, since applications and screen-formatting services can react to each character differently, and implement any kind of behavior required. Problems with this mode often occur when the terminal is used remotely, since there is sometimes a large amount of overhead for each character transmitted (see "Chapter 26. Editing a File" on page 313). Also, since the operating system must handle each character individually, there is sometimes a bottleneck there as well. A typical example of this terminal is the DEC VT100.

Block-mode operation (of a character-based terminal) means that the characters are transmitted in a group, or block, after a special key (ENTER) is pressed. In order to offer enough comfort, they generally have logic for forms (input fields, insert and delete, etc.) in the terminal itself. These terminals were invented for efficient remote operation over slow WAN connections. A typical example of this terminal is the IBM 3270.

Graphics terminals show anything that can be made of the individual dots, or pixels (picture elements), which they display. Since this requires the manipulation and movement of large amounts of data, much work has been done, and is still being done, on defining good APIs and implementing the low-level routines for graphics displays. A typical example of this terminal is represented by the MIT X Terminal standard. While it is possible to use the X protocol remotely, this is generally feasible only via high-speed connections such as LANs.

Some of the higher-level services used for formatting and managing information on a GUI (Graphical User Interface) are:

- OSF Motif (with X Windows)
- Microsoft Windows
- IBM OS/2 PM (Presentation Manager)

Extensibility

The ability to add new functions to a system (extensibility), or to change its size (scalability) are of general importance (see "Scalability" on page 16). This is also true for the characteristic of dynamic configuration (see "Dynamic Configuration" on page 18).

In operating systems, one of the most important methods for achieving extensibility is the use of loadable device drivers. Since the device driver is the piece of code closest to the hardware, programming it often requires special knowledge about the hardware involved, and this is not generally available, especially for new devices. In addition, programming close to the hardware requires special techniques which, fortunately, not every programmer needs to know.

The ability to add new devices simply by copying the driver to the disk, editing a configuration file, and rebooting have made it possible for UNIX and PC operating systems to support a multitude of new devices that were unknown when the operating system was originally designed. In order to make this configuration mechanism flexible, it is useful to be able to unload device drivers as well.

These techniques are also part of a limited kind of dynamic configuration. Operating systems rarely require the ability to be reconfigured without interruption, so rebooting is acceptable.

Reliability

In operating systems, the degree of reliability, robustness, and fault tolerance is largely a matter of software quality, a topic which would lead us to the large field of software design techniques, coding, and project management. To keep things short, we will mention only a few methods of achieving reliability which are typically used in operating systems.

One important method, which was already described above, is memory protection or, more generally, separation of unrelated components. Even though this principle has been well understood for a long time in the mainframe environment, it has been necessary to "reinvent" it on PCs, and many users have become painfully aware of its necessity.

Some of the techniques used to achieve reliability of disks are mirroring (duplication of data), striping (distribution of data over multiple disks), and parity checking (check sums for data). In RAID (Redundant Arrays of Inexpensive Disks), these techniques can be used individually or combined to implement a level of reliability which makes it possible to replace one whole disk without disrupting service.

Security

Even though we may often be inclined to think of security as a matter of protecting secret or confidential data, it is really much more than that. In fact, security is concerned with ensuring the availability and integrity of all systems, and protecting them from errors is often more important than preventing malicious attacks. In distributed systems, security is just as important as it is in centralized systems, but is more difficult to achieve, so we have dedicated a special part of this book to it (see "Chapter 25. Security" on page 293).

Security of computing systems is concerned with protecting resources, and these are typically exactly those resources that are managed by the operating system. As a result, mechanisms for authentication, such as the login process, or for controlling access to files must be an integral part of the operating system. For example, the basic file operations, such as "read" and "write", must prevent unauthorized access to files, and the operating system must prevent these operations from being circumvented.

Today, most single-user operating systems provide such a poor level of security that the only good ways to protect them are organizational methods (rules and regulations) or physical methods (lock them up). On the other hand, a relatively high degree of security is offered by some multiuser operating systems which have been adapted to this requirement.

In distributed systems, a high level of security is rarely a reality today, but much progress has been made. In order to achieve it, the methods must

- encompass communications as well as operating systems
- be standardized so that they can be applied to all systems of all vendors
- be integrated in the operating systems

Compatibility

Due to today's rapid development of new operating systems and of new hardware, it is often desirable to protect an investment by running existing applications on a new hardware platform, a new operating system, or simply a new version of the old operating system. As a result, operating system design is often in a state of conflict between support for the old way of doing things and support for newer and better technology. Similarly, the marketplace success of an operating system may depend more on its support for old applications than on the basic features it offers. For example, one reason for the early success of MS-DOS was the fact that it was easier to migrate from 8-bit CP/M to MS-DOS than to 16-bit CP/M. On the other hand, today's MS-DOS still contains those old CP/M-style services, even though practically no one uses them.

Some of the compatibility issues important for operating systems are:

- **upward compatibility**: the ability of a new version of the system to run programs written for an older version
- **source compatibility**: the ability to reuse the same application source code (after recompilation)
- **binary compatibility**: the ability to reuse the same application object code (without recompilation)

Standards

A few of the standards which apply to operating systems are listed here. The newest standard in UNIX is called the "X/Open Single UNIX Specification" and is the successor of a consortium specification which defined 1170 API calls and was referred to as the "Spec 1170".

- POSIX 1003.1 (IEEE Portable Operating System Interface, API) [ISO/IEC 9945-1].
- POSIX 1003.2 (IEEE Portable Operating System Interface, Shell) [ISO/IEC 9945-2].
- ODMG-93 [Cattell].
- X/Open Single UNIX Specification
    - System Interface Definitions, Issue 4, Version 2 [X/Open C434].
    - System Interfaces and Headers, Issue 4, Version 2 [X/Open C435].
    - Commands and Utilities, Issue 4, Version 2 [X/Open C436].
    - X/Open Curses, Issue 4, Version 2 [X/Open C610].
    - Networking Services, Issue 4 [X/Open C438].
- Unicode [ISO/IEC 10646].
- XPG4 [X/Open C434, X/Open C435, and X/Open C436].

Trends and Products

At present, operating systems for small and medium-sized systems are changing very rapidly. This is due in part to the evolution of the hardware basis for the systems, but also to changes in software technology, most notably the move to higher-level APIs (see "The Rising Level of Abstraction" on page 8) and object orientation.

The effect of these changes could be a complete reordering of the market for operating systems and hardware during the next few years, since we will soon be faced with a whole new set of choices and more freedom to mix hardware and software in new ways. An overview of some of these trends can be found in [Udell 1/94].

Microkernels

A microkernel is a small piece of code that implements the most fundamental parts of an operating system [Varhol]. Typical functions of microkernels are:

- **memory management:** allocation and freeing of memory, i.e., managing the RAM
- **process (and thread) management:** initiating, activating, and deactivating processes, i.e., managing the CPU
- **interprocess communication:** normally, message passing within one machine
- **input/output:** a limited form of I/O, mainly concerned with interrupt handling and sometimes involving device drivers, i.e., managing peripheral devices
- **security:** mainly a question of memory protection, this also involves checking authorization to use kernel services, i.e., managing access rights
- **objects:** in object-oriented kernels, this is similar to memory and process management, i.e., managing low-level objects

The primary advantage of microkernels is increased portability: When these basic functions are centralized in one small piece of code, it is much easier to port large parts of the system to other platforms.

Another important advantage is improved extensibility: New parts of the system do not need to address the complexity of the hardware. Instead, they make use of a standard set of services defined by the microkernel.

Microkernel technology also improves reliability: Critical functions, such as interrupt handling and process control, and complex hardware-dependent functions are coded only once (in the microkernel), not multiple times in different parts of the system. This code can then be designed and tested much more rigorously than normal applications, and can be run in a protected mode of the CPU.

Even though this technique has been well known for a long time, it was not always used for small systems, because of performance considerations. Now, the hardware and software have reached a state that makes microkernel technology the obvious best choice for system design. On the other hand, the exact definition of what should be in a microkernel varies greatly from one system to another.

Basically, all operating system makers are now moving towards extensive use of the microkernel technique. Some of the more common microkernels today are:

- Mach, developed by Carnegie Mellon University and used by OSF and IBM
- Chorus, developed by Chorus Systems and used by USL
- The kernel of QNX, from QNX Software
- The kernel of CTOS, from Unisys
- The Microsoft Windows NT Executive

Hardware Independence

Traditionally, most operating systems have been tied to a particular hardware platform. As a notable exception, UNIX and variants of it have been implemented on many different platforms. Recently, for PC systems, this has begun to change dramatically.

The reasons for the close tie between hardware and operating system vary:

- **technical difficulties:** The operating system contains complex hardware-dependent code, which is difficult to port.
- **performance:** Hardware-independent layers add to the overhead.
- **company politics:** Sometimes, vendors chose to tie the systems together in an attempt to protect some of their investment.

Examples of this dependency are MS-DOS and Windows 95, which run only on Intel architecture, and Apple MacOS, which runs only on Motorola hardware. Of course, it is possible to emulate each one of these systems on top of the other, by using either additional hardware or additional software. However, the loss in performance due to the added overhead has kept these emulators from being very popular.

In the near future, the next generation of operating systems, such as Windows NT, can be expected to run on any of the next generation of microprocessors. One of the things that has made this possible is the increased power of the hardware, which makes it possible to afford the additional overhead of hardware-neutral software layers and emulation code. Another reason is the fact that the next generation of processors were designed with instruction sets which make it easier (and more efficient) to emulate the instruction sets of other machines [Halfhill 4/94].

But the real reason is the fact that more and more of the processing done for an application is done by the services of higher layers of software, such as GUI presentation services (see "The Rising Level of Abstraction" on page 8). Since these services can be ported or rewritten for the new operating system or hardware platform, this part of the application's processing can run with optimal performance. The remaining part, which must run in emulation mode, is only a small part of the total, and thus is less important than it used to be. For example, Apple has stated that typical Mac applications spend 90% of their time in Mac toolbox routines, and

SunSelect says that Windows applications spend 60% to 80% of their time in the Windows kernel.

The technique of porting subsystems is referred to as "library translation", as opposed to "emulation". Thus, the rising level of APIs means that more of the processing can be supported by (efficient) library translation and less of it needs to be done by emulation.

Multiple Personalities

The term "personality" is now used to refer to the "look and feel" of an operating system [Hayes]. Each system has its own user interface, and sometimes even more than one. Examples of personalities are:

- Apple Macintosh user interface
- Microsoft Windows
- IBM OS/2 Workplace Shell
- OSF/Motif and OpenLook (both based on X Windows)
- Character-based command-line interfaces, such as MS-DOS and UNIX shells

As discussed in the last section, it is becoming increasingly feasible to provide support for more than one set of high-level services in any particular operating system or on any particular hardware platform. As a result, vendors are supporting and announcing future support for increasing numbers of personalities on their operating systems. Examples of this are:

- IBM OS/2: DOS, Windows
- IBM Workplace OS: DOS, Windows, OS/2, AIX
- Microsoft Windows NT: DOS, Windows, Win32, OS/2 POSIX
- PowerOpen: Macintosh, AIX
- UNIX: Windows, using SunSelect's WABI (Windows Application Binary Interface) or Insignia Solutions' SoftWindows
- Windows: Macintosh, using Insignia Solutions SoftPC

Object Orientation

As part of the general trend toward object orientation, all major vendors are working on object-oriented extensions to their operating systems, and some on completely new, totally object-oriented systems [Wayner 1/94].

One of the totally object-oriented systems has the code name Pink and is under development by Taligent, a joint venture of IBM and Apple. Another such system, NextStep from Next, which is perhaps a bit less radical, is available today on Intel and Motorola processors.

For example, even though the first version of Microsoft's Windows NT is not object-oriented in a strict sense, it uses the concept of objects for many resources, such as files, printers, and process. This way, all of these things are treated uniformly and all make use of the same common aspects of these objects, such as creation and deletion, naming, and security checking. In other words, objects are used as a method for achieving code reusability, and this can be applied very well to operating systems, where the main task is to manage many different resources [Custer, pages 21 and 50] .

Many object-oriented extensions take the form of object brokers, and are often compliant with the CORBA standard. A more thorough discussion of CORBA, and a list of compliant implementations, is contained in a later chapter (see "CORBA" on page 175).

One notable object-oriented extension is IBM's SOM (System Object Model), which runs on OS/2 and AIX. SOM is CORBA-compliant (see below) and offers the following services:

- **upward binary compatibility:** Object modification without recompilation.
- **language neutrality:** Objects can be used by different programming languages.
- **replication frameworks:** Copies of a single object are made available to multiple clients.

DSOM (Distributed SOM) includes network support and was developed in cooperation with HP.

Microsoft's counterpart to SOM is COM (Component Object Model), which is based on C++ but is not completely CORBA-compliant, since it does not support inheritance. Instead, the programmer can explicitly use a method called aggregation, which makes it possible to include references from old objects in new ones.

At the same time, Microsoft and DEC have written a specification called COM (Common Object Model), which is intended to ensure interoperability between Microsoft's OLE and DEC's ObjectBroker. In this collaboration, DEC will contribute its UDT (Uniform Data Transfer), which involves some minor extensions to the OSF DCE RPC called ORPC (Object RPC).

Document Orientation

An important step past object-oriented computing applies to the way we use the desktop, and is sometimes referred to as document-oriented computing or as compound documents. In document-oriented computing, instead of starting an application (such as a word processor) and then opening a document (or other object), you activate the document, which causes the proper application to be invoked. This is relatively new to Windows, where it is currently partially supported on the basis of file name extensions. However, it has been the norm for some time in systems such as the Macintosh.

One advantage to this method is that it is a more natural way of thinking of things, i.e., in terms of the objects to be manipulated and not in terms of the applications, which are just the way a computer happens to support the work. A much more important advantage of this method is the ability to construct a single document out of pieces which will be manipulated by different applications (such as word processors, spreadsheets, drawing programs, and databases).

An important step in this direction was the ability to cut pieces from one document and paste them into another. This was supported by such systems as Microsoft's DDE (Dynamic Data Exchange), but it was still necessary to manipulate the separate pieces with separate applications.

The next step is a seamless integration of the pieces which start the corresponding application when activated. This will be supported by:

- OLE (Object Linking and Embedding) Version 2.0, from Microsoft, which is available now on Microsoft Windows and Apple Macintosh.

- OpenDoc, defined by CIL (Component Integration Lab), which should be available for beta test during 1994 and should be supported by a larger number of vendors.

WOSA

WOSA (Windows Open Services Architecture) [WOSA] defines a number of services for Windows and Windows NT platforms. Although WOSA is defined and controlled entirely by one vendor (Microsoft), various parts of it cover almost all of the ground between proprietary specifications and open standards. This is due to the fact that some parts are completely proprietary and not accepted by other vendors, others are proprietary but can be expected to become the dominant architecture and be accepted by many vendors, and yet others are based on formal standards or de facto standards. WOSA includes services for:

- SNA (Systems Network Architecture)
  - LUA (LU API)
    - RUI (Request Unit Interface)
    - SLI (Session Level Interface)
  - APPC (Advanced Program-to-Program Communication)
  - CPI-C (Common Programming Interface Communications)
  - HLLAPI (High-Level Language Application Programming Interface for IBM 3270 emulation)
  - CSV (Common Service Verbs, a NetView API)
- Sockets, for TCP/IP, including Berkeley sockets and Microsoft extensions
- RPC (Remote Procedure Call)
- ODBC (Open Database Connectivity), a call-level SQL
- MAPI (Messaging API), for electronic mail
- License Service
- TAPI (Telephony API)
- XFS (Extensions for Financial Services)

- XRT (Extensions for Real Time Market Data Specification)

The WOSA definition includes APIs, which specify the interface for application programs, and SPIs (Service Provider Interfaces), which specify the interface for the software provided by the vendors of special devices. The SPIs are much like the definition of a device-driver interface in that they make it possible to add devices which were not known when the original design was written.

This makes WOSA extensible, in that service provider code can be added like loadable device drivers in MS-DOS. However, since the data format is passed through to the API, this does not always make it possible to add new devices without changing the applications.

In order to achieve openness, most of the APIs have been made compatible with well-established implementations. For example, the SNA APIs were defined by a large consortium of vendors including IBM and are compatible with the IBM OS/2 CM APIs, RPC is compatible with OSF DCE RPC, and ODBC is compatible with the SAG (SQL Access Group) specification (40 vendors).

ODBC version 2.0 is fully compliant with the SAG standard released in November 1992. The ODBC API is a standard, vendor-independent interface that makes it possible for an application to access any of a number of databases. For example, an Excel spreadsheet can use data directly from an Oracle database. Access to the databases is accomplished with the help of ODBC drivers, which are also available from third-party vendors. Drivers are available for almost all databases on PCs, UNIX, and MVS, including dBase, DB2, IMS, Informix, and Oracle.

WOSA/XFS (Windows Open Services Architecture Extensions for Financial Services) [WOSA/XFS] was created by the BSVC (Banking System Vendor Council), a vendor consortium, and contains basic functions and APIs for the following devices:

- **printers:** receipt, journal, passbook, and document printers
- **magnetic stripe readers and writers:** swipe, dip, motorized, and writeable. Also referred to as IDCU (ID card unit)
- **cash dispensers:** ATMs (automatic teller machines), teller service centers
- **PIN (personal identification number) pads:** with/without display/encryption
- **check readers:** MICR (magnetic ink character recognition) and OCR (optical character recognition)
- **image scanners**

The following extensions to the WOSA/XFS specification are currently being planned:

- financial transaction messaging and management (possibly X/Open specification)
- network and system management
- security
- emerging technologies (object-oriented systems, multimedia)

GUI Queues

In this chapter, we have discussed operating systems and briefly introduced GUIs, which are generally a part of the operating system. In addition, an earlier part of the book handled the used of queues as a basic model for communication between programs (see "Messages, Queues, and Pipes" on page 35). Now, we would like to bring the two together by showing how the GUI part of operating systems uses queues.

This section demonstrates the way queues can be used to loosely couple separate processes, and provides some good examples of how they should and should not be used. It also explains one of the reasons for some problems that GUIs often encounter and then goes into a very important aspect of application design. Even though the queues discussed here are local, the example is especially important in the context of distributed processing, because the problems occur more often when an application makes use of remote resources.

Figure 11 shows a screen on which two windows are displayed:

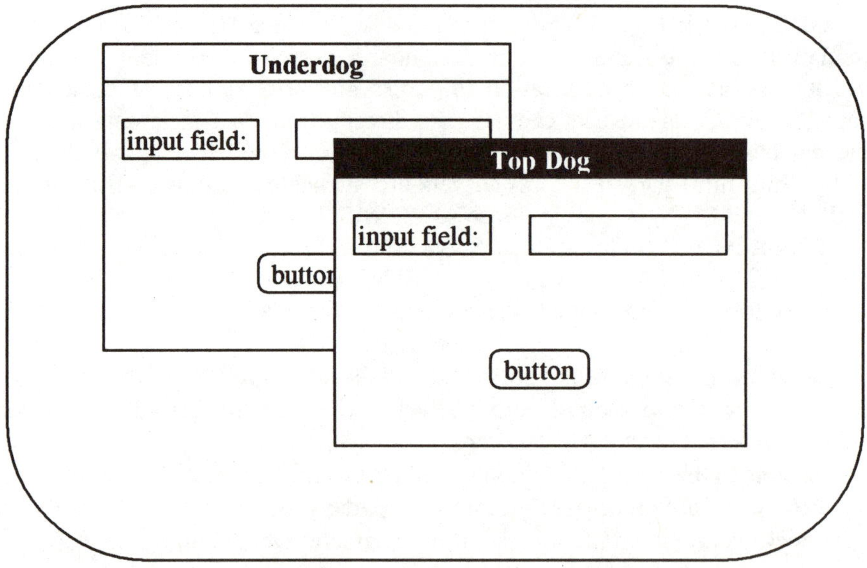

Figure 11. Two Dog Windows

This is a simplified view of a situation which is common to all GUIs, including Windows, Macintosh, OS/2, and Motif. Note that there is an important difference between the windows: Only one of them can be active at any given time. The system makes this visible by putting the active window on top of the others and highlighting the name bar at the top of the window. In this case, the "Top Dog" window is active.

To be more precise, the "Top Dog" window has the "input focus". This means that all keyboard input and all mouse input on the overlapping part of the two windows will be directed to the "Top Dog" and not to the "Underdog". The "Underdog" will not be able to receive this type of input message until it acquires the input focus, for example, as the result of a mouse action within a part of the screen covered only by the "Underdog" window. However, in a preemptive multitasking system, the "Underdog" application can still be active in the sense that it can use the CPU to perform actions that do not require keyboard input. This is similar to the situation where the "Top Dog" application is running in the "foreground" and the "Underdog" in the "background", i.e., without access to the keyboard, mouse, and display screen.

The Queues and Their Problems

Figure 12 shows how Windows 3.1 uses a queue to hold keyboard and mouse messages until they are processed by the applications.

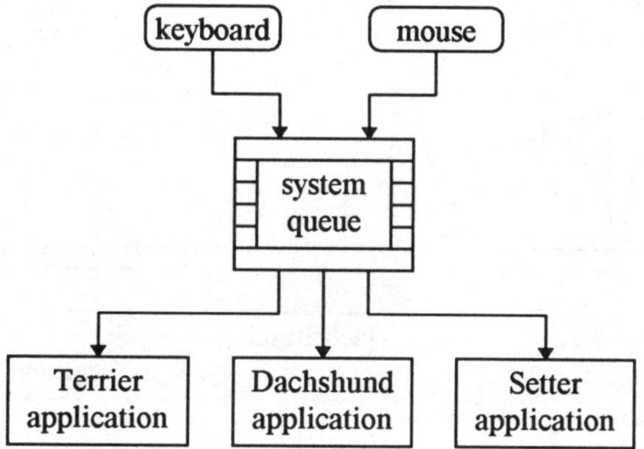

Figure 12. Windows 3.1 Message Queue

In Microsoft Windows version 3.1, all keyboard and mouse events are put into a system queue, and then moved from the queue to each application. This provides an important degree of decoupling between the input devices and the applications, similar to that provided by the keyboard buffer of MS-DOS (see "Queues" on page 36). This way, it is possible, for a limited time, to create input faster than the application can read it. For example, the user can "type ahead" without danger of having the characters lost just because the application needs a little bit longer for some of the formatting involved.

Unfortunately, there is a serious problem in this configuration. Suppose that one application, for example, the Terrier, begins to chase its own tail and goes into an endless loop. As a result, it stops reading messages from the queue. Now, if the Terrier has the input focus, i.e., it is the "Top Dog", then the input messages will be directed to it, so the queue will be blocked and all other applications will have to wait forever, thus blocking the whole system. And even if the Terrier stops chasing its tail and starts reading input messages after a few minutes, the user of the system may have lost patience and restarted the PC. The basic problem here is the fact that all applications share the same queue, in contrast with the traditional design of multiprocessing systems, where every process has one input queue but may write into many other queues. As a result, the Windows 3.1 system queue decouples the software from the hardware, but does not decouple the applications from each other.

In comparison, Figure 13 shows an example of a system which improves this.

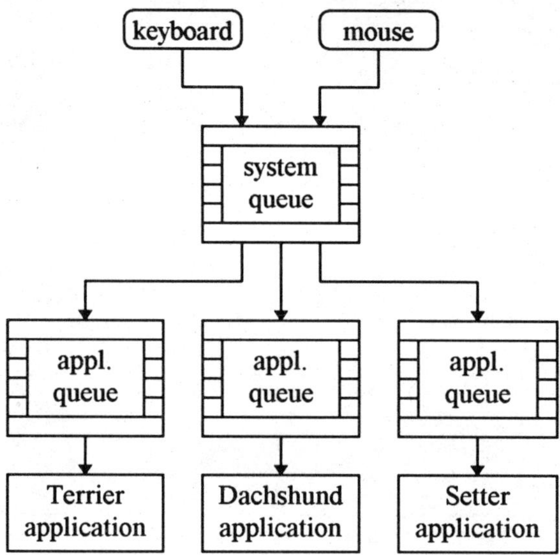

Figure 13. OS/2 PM Message Queues

In the case of the IBM OS/2 PM (Presentation Manager) GUI, there is one system queue and one queue for each application. This way, if an individual application does not read its queue, it doesn't block the other applications.

However, the situation is not as simple as it may seem. Suppose again that the Terrier application has the input focus, i.e., it is the "Top Dog" in "Figure 11. Two Dog Windows" on page 74. And also suppose that the user types ahead, i.e., types faster than the application can work for the moment. Now, if one of the characters typed is Ctrl-X, this may be a way of telling the "Top Dog" application to terminate. The remaining characters then have to be given to the "Underdog" application. At least, this is the way the OS/2 PM sees things [Petzold, page 788].

As a result of this view of things, the OS/2 PM cannot move messages from the system queue to the respective application queue until the previous messages have been processed. And this means that an application which stops reading its input queue will block all other PM applications. And even if the user decides to stop waiting for the Terrier application and clicks the mouse on the window of another application, the other application cannot be given the input focus, because it cannot read the "set focus" message from its input queue.

On the bright side of things, the other applications can still work in background, and they can react to timer messages. Even though the timer messages are also transmitted via the queue, they do not need to be kept in the system queue until keyboard and mouse messages are processed, so they are moved to the application queues earlier.

Yet another example of the OS/2 PM is the case where one of the OS/2 applications is the "Win Box", i.e., a Windows 3.1 running under OS/2. In this case, all Windows applications share the Windows system queue within it. This way, one Windows application can block the others, but without disturbing the OS/2 applications. Figure 14 shows a similar situation, i.e., the queues in Windows 95.

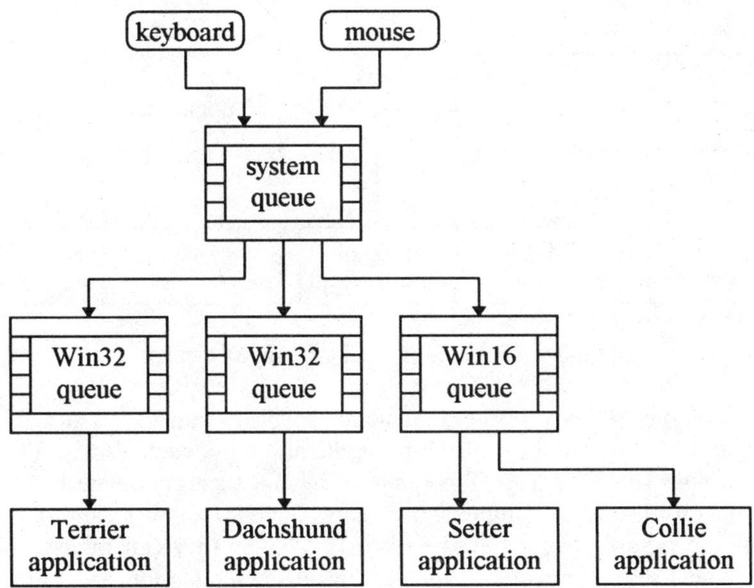

Figure 14. Windows 95 Message Queues

In Microsoft Windows 95, each 32-bit application has its own queue, similar to the situation in OS/2. In addition, all 16-bit applications share one queue, the Win16 VM (virtual machine) queue. This means that 16-bit Windows applications running under Windows 95 still have the same queue-blocking problem that they had under Windows 3.1, but 32-bit applications are better off.

In addition to the queue blocking, there is another problem that has similar effects. Since much of the 16-bit system code was not written in a manner which allows preemptive multiprocessing, its usage must be serialized, similar to the usage of the message queue. Thus, if one application hangs, it may block some of the 16-bit system code, which also blocks all other 16-bit applications [Kennedy]. Figure 15 shows how queues are handled in Windows NT.

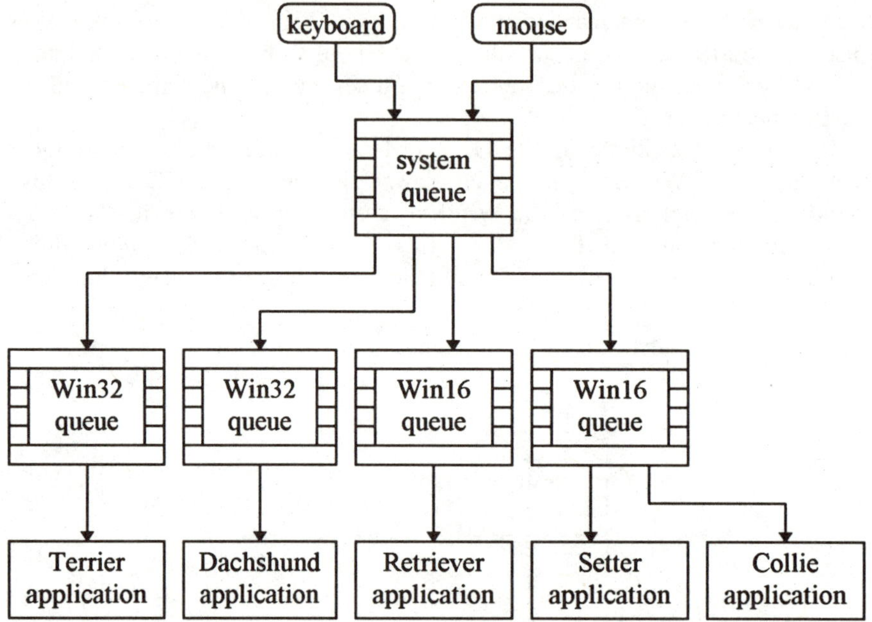

Figure 15. Windows NT Message Queues

Microsoft Windows NT has a system queue for keyboard and mouse messages, and a separate application queue for each 32-bit application and each Win16 VM. Since it can run multiple 16-bit VMs, it is possible to have a separate queue for each 16-bit application as well. In the example shown here, the Setter application and the Collie application are running under the same Win16 VM, so they can interfere with each other. But the Collie application and the Retriever application are running under separate VMs and have separate queues, so they cannot interfere with each other, either by blocking the queue, by blocking the 16-bit system code, or by overwriting each other's memory. This helps make Windows NT very robust, even for 16-bit applications, when they are all run in separate Win16 VMs.

This makes the queue structure of OS/2, Windows 95, and Windows NT almost identical, except for the restriction of only one 16-bit VM in Windows 95. However, there is still one important difference. Both Windows 95 and Windows NT transfer messages from the system (or "raw") queue to the application queue "as soon as they can" [Microsoft NT, page 29]. In other words, the system determines which window has the input focus at the time the keyboard or mouse message is input, and immediately transfers the message to that application's queue.

To see the effect of this, consider the example where the "Top Dog" window is active and the user types "Hush!", Ctrl-X, and "Heads up!". We also assume that the termination processing which is done after the Ctrl-X takes some time, since it may have to move some data from internal memory to disk. As a result, the system immediately moves all characters to the "Top Dog" queue. The "Top Dog" retrieves the characters "Hush!" and Ctrl-X, and terminates. The characters "Heads up!" are then discarded, because they are in the queue of an application which has terminated. The next section shows how some of these problems can be avoided.

A Solution: Application Threads

In all cases discussed in the last section, there is a potential problem whenever a GUI application does a piece of processing which takes either a long time or an unpredictable amount of time. One very good example of this is accessing a database: The access logic itself may involve so much searching that it cannot be fast; or, if the database is remote, it may depend on the load on the database server or on the network. If the application logic is too simple, it will stop reading messages from its input queue until the database request has completed. As a result, it might block other applications or cause input messages to be lost or given to the wrong application.

The solution to this problem is for the application to use threads in order to decouple long-running tasks from its input processing [Petzold, pages 775–821]. Whenever such a task arises, the application will create a separate thread (i.e., lightweight process) and delegate the task to it. The main thread can then continue to accept keyboard and mouse input and produce any necessary reactions on the GUI screen. This way, the application can react to input and, most important, does not block any other applications.

In this solution, the communication between the separate threads can be done using any kind of interprocess communication methods available on the system. However, an elegant solution is to use exactly the same type of queue as for keyboard and mouse messages. In other words, the main thread gives a job to a subordinate thread by putting a message into its queue. This way, each subordinate thread reads requests from its own input queue and writes the responses into the main thread's queue. The main thread does nothing other than read keyboard and mouse (and timer) messages from its input queue, send formatting requests to the GUI system, send requests for long-running tasks to subordinate threads, and read the responses to these requests from the same input queue. Thus, it works exactly like the dispatcher of a traditional real-time system.

This solution, which is generally accepted as the best solution to the problems discussed above, is also a good example of the way that the use of multiprocessing can improve the behavior of applications on a single-user system. Even though only one person is using the system at any one time, individual applications may have to wait for certain things to finish, and multiprocessing makes it possible for the system as a whole to still respond to the user's input.

Summary

The examples discussed above show a number of important aspects of the use of queues and of GUIs and how GUI applications should be designed. They are:

- Whenever queues are used as a communication method, each process should have its own input queue. The fact that Windows 3.1 did not do this can be understood only as a vestige of its single-processing past. This has been improved since.
- GUI systems are event-driven. The application must always be able to respond to input from the user, who has much more influence on the application's behavior than with traditional systems. Queues are a good way of decoupling tasks which do not always run at the same speed.
- GUI systems are not perfect. There is a fundamental ambiguity present whenever "type ahead" is done in connection with a change of focus. OS/2 PM is more likely to ensure that the data is not lost and is given to the right application; Windows NT is more likely to ensure that the system is never blocked.
- GUI applications should use multiprocessing, preferably threads, to defer long-running tasks to the background and prevent the main loop from blocking. This is particularly important for distributed applications.

Chapter 7. Middleware

The term "middleware" has become very popular recently, and has been applied to a lot of different things. When something like that happens, we often have to admit that the term has lost its meaning by becoming too "universal". But at the same time, the fad is a symptom of a very real need.

Clearly, "middleware" must be in the middle of something; and, just as clearly, there must be a need for something like that. In fact, we found three very important gaps which are all filled very well by some kind of middleware. They are:

- the semantic gap
- the communication gap
- the vendor gap

"Semantic gap" used to be a popular term in describing compilers. It referred to the gap between the high-level language and the machine language, i.e., what had to be bridged by the compiler. In any case, the problem always exists—it's the gap between what you want to do and what the available tools can accomplish. And as soon as we get better tools for that job, we think of new jobs that raise the ante again (see "The Rising Level of Abstraction" on page 8). This gives middleware the job of filling the gap between the upper layers (i.e., the application) and the lower layers (i.e., the operating system). In other words, it's the middle layers. For example, if your operating system supports files and databases, but you need distributed transactions, then your middleware might be a transaction monitor.

The "communication gap" is whatever separates the client from the server, or any other two software components from each other. The problems to be solved might involve wires, or radio waves, or error detection, or flow control, or data formats. And it might not be a case of networks as much as a basic matter of speaking the same language (see "The Culture Clash" on page 11). This puts the middleware in between the client and the server, or the PC and the mainframe, or the Macintosh and the OS/2. For example, an application may need to use the services of a procedure on another machine, and both systems are delivered with TCP/IP and Berkeley sockets, but the RPC (Remote Procedure Call) is an add-on, which needs to be bought separately.

The "vendor gap" is the difference between the "same system" made by two different vendors. This gap is sometimes reduced by the use of standards and informal agreements, only to be widened again by technological advancements and competition. It will never disappear, because standards cannot keep pace with technology, and because vendors need to differentiate their products in order to compete. This gives middleware the task of mediating between the systems of two different vendors. For example, if your software accesses databases from two different vendors, then your middleware may be a software component which adapts one flavor of SQL to another; and it might be produced by one of the database vendors or by a third-party software house that makes its living by filling the gap intentionally opened by the vendors.

Another characteristic of middleware is that it should be a short-term investment. As important as it is to fill the three gaps today, each one should disappear as the result of normal progress (but with new gaps opening up somewhere else). The higher level of function and communication service offered by add-on middleware should become an integral part of the operating system. And the methods you wisely choose today should become accepted industry standards tomorrow; if they do not, it might be better to change the methods.

Depending on the gap to be filled, there may be many different types of middleware, but, in practice, one middleware package may span multiple gaps at the same time.

Middleware Services

Some of the most important services offered by middleware are:

- **application support:** This includes the basic operating system services.
- **location transparency:** The user shouldn't need to know where resources are located.
- **migration transparency:** It should be possible to move resources from one location to another without disrupting the applications.
- **communication:** It should be possible to communicate with remote resources using the process model required by the application (see "Chapter 4. Processing Models" on page 27).
- **data translation:** Data should be automatically translated into the format required by the target system.
- **load balancing:** The system should automatically route requests to a server depending on the load on the available systems.
- **heterogeneous systems:** The services should be available on multiple platforms.
- **management:** There should be facilities for efficiently managing the middleware itself and the applications which use it.
- **security:** It should be possible to include all parts of the middleware in a global security mechanism.

Network Operating Systems

The basic purpose of an operating system is to control devices, such as disks, printers, and CPUs, and to provide higher-level interfaces, such as file systems, to these devices. Shouldn't it then be possible to create an operating system that does this same job, but on the basis of devices which are distributed over a network?

In fact, this is the basic idea behind the concept of a NOS (Network Operating System). If this goal can indeed be achieved, then it will solve a lot of problems of distributed computing for application developers, since most services required by application programs are supplied by the operating system.

Services

The ideal NOS, according to this, should supply all operating system services on a distributed platform. This should be transparent to the application program; i.e., the NOS should provide a "single system image". This means that the whole collection of CPUs, disks, etc., appears to the user as if it were one single computer. In order to do this, the NOS must be capable of providing the following services:

- **distributed file system:** It should be possible to store data anywhere on the network, access it from anywhere, and move it from one place to another without disturbing the application.
- **distributed printing:** In order to use any of the available printers from any application, the system needs to manage print spooling and sharing (concurrent access).
- **distributed peripheral device support:** All devices controlled by the operating system should be accessible by all applications, in much the same way printers are.
- **CPU allocation:** When an application is started, the system should choose an appropriate CPU and allocate it, then distribute load and reallocate when necessary.
- **application support:** It should be possible to run applications on different machines, or even distributed over multiple machines, without worrying about hardware or software dependencies or the location of the resources.

Trends and Products

Providing all operating system services over a network may seem like a very difficult task if we think of how complex many traditional operating systems are. However, it looks much easier if we think of an operating system as simply a program for managing resources, and easier yet if all resources can be treated in a uniform way. One of the first steps in this direction was UNIX, which treats most resources (files, printers, terminals) as byte streams. By doing so, it achieves a high degree of flexibility, but its limitations become apparent as soon as we need more complex structures than byte streams.

There have been numerous proposals for accommodating more complex resources while still keeping the basic advantage of uniformity. One of these involves moving from an "everything is a file" motto to "everything is a database" [Balzer]. So far, none of these ideas has made its way to success in the operating system marketplace. Today, the motto for accommodating complexity while preserving uniformity is "everything is an object". In fact, this is the basis for some important operating system projects, including Cairo (Microsoft) and Pink (Taligent, i.e., Apple and IBM).

If, in fact, successful operating systems can be built by treating all resources as objects, then the NOS, or distributed operating system, should result from distributing objects, using techniques such as ORBs (Object Request Brokers).

One UNIX successor which did become successful was an operating system developed and used entirely within APE. Instead of the UNIX "everything is a file" idea, it encompassed all aspects of operating systems under the slogan "everything is a frog". Based on this grand unified amphibian theory of operating systems, it was given the name "toados".

Some of the services of NOS have been implemented in multiprocessor systems on tightly coupled complexes, i.e., machines with multiple CPUs which share memory. They implement the function of CPU allocation, making a multiprocessor machine operate as a single one. However, they do not provide distribution over large networks, or services such as distributed file systems.

In addition, some research projects have produced "distributed operating systems" which address all aspects mentioned above, including the task of CPU allocation on a group of loosely coupled machines [Tanenbaum 1995]. None of them claims to cover all aspects completely, and they are generally not available as products. However, they provide a good example of what is possible today, and parts of them have been used as the basis for products. These systems include:

- **Amoeba** (of the Vrije Universiteit Amsterdam)
- **Mach** (of the University of Rochester)
- **Chorus** (of the French research institute INRIA)

Another group of products implements the distributed file and printing services over a LAN. As such, they are often adequately referred to as "LAN servers". Since they don't cover all operating system services, such as CPU allocation, they are much less than an ideal NOS. Some of these products, often referred to as NOS, are:

- Banyan Vines and ENS (Enterprise Network Services)
- IBM OS/2 LAN Server
- Microsoft Windows NT Server
- Novell NetWare
- NCS (Network Computing System) from Apollo (Hewlett-Packard)
- Sun NFS (Network File System)
- AT&T RFS (Remote File System)
- LAN Manager/X
- OSF DCE (Distributed Computing Environment)

A comparison of Banyan Vines and ENS 6.0, IBM OS/2 LAN Server 4.0, Microsoft Windows NT Server 3.5, and Novell NetWare 4.1 can be found in [Johnson, 5/95] and [Darling, 9/95]. Among other things, the articles show how important two aspects are: operating system services and directories. A NOS can be only as good as the local operating system functions it supports, and such things as good multitasking, memory protection, and robustness are especially important for a server. Also, manageability and flexibility are greatly improved by the use of a global directory service (see "Chapter 18. Directories" on page 204). For example, NetWare 4.1 has its (proprietary) NDS (NetWare Directory Service), which tracks a number of objects, including users, groups, printers, queues, servers, and applications. Banyan Vines' ENS includes a directory called StreetTalk, and Microsoft Cairo (a code name for a future version of Windows NT) is expected to contain a global directory which will be compliant with the X.500 standard.

In summary, NOS products cover most aspects of distributed operating systems. One exception is the service of distributed CPU allocation, which has been proven possible, but is not important for most commercial applications. These systems have recently begun to employ global directories, which has made it possible to manage them much more efficiently.

Chapter 8. DCE

OSF DCE (Distributed Computing Environment) is a platform for supporting open distributed processing [OSF. *Introduction to OSF DCE*]. It was developed by OSF and is delivered in the form of source code to the vendors, who integrate it into their operating systems.

In this sense, DCE is technology and not standards. However, since DCE is supported by a large number of vendors, it has the effect of establishing a "de facto" standard of its own. And since large parts of DCE are based on standards, it has the effect of defining the usage of these standards, such as standards profiles do.

Services

The basic services offered by DCE are listed here more or less in a bottom-up fashion. The "higher-level" services, RPC and DFS, are those most likely to be used directly by an application.

Cells

DCE systems are organized in a set of cells. The boundaries of the cells can be defined independently of the underlying network, but often correspond to the organization of the network in individual LANs or groups of LANs.

Each cell contains its own set of basic services, including time, directory, and security. Normally, an application makes use of the services within its cell. When necessary, these local services communicate with the services of other cells. This gives the user a single interface for services which are distributed throughout the system. One advantage of this structure is performance: Most access to the basic services is within the local cell. Another advantage is flexibility: Global services can be moved without changing the application's interface to them.

This structure also facilitates administration: Managing such things as names and security within each relatively small group of systems and users is often more efficient than doing it globally for the whole enterprise.

DTS (Distributed Time Service)

The purpose of DTS is to keep the clocks of all systems within the DCE network synchronized.

One reason a time service is necessary for DCE is in order to keep track of time-outs within the distributed security service. Since the misuse of such things as encryption keys and access permissions can be a problem for security, they are often granted for a limited period of time (breaking codes is even harder if you don't have much time to do it in). On the other hand, they are exchanged between systems which have their own clocks, so keeping track of these time-outs requires synchronized clocks.

In addition to this, DTS provides a number of useful services which can be used directly by the application:

- retrieve time
- convert to local time
- obtain time zone information
- compare time values

DTS is implemented as a client/server application on the basis of RPC. Time servers on all systems exchange messages with each other in order to keep the clocks together.

External time sources, such as receivers for radio signals from the various national government agencies which operate atomic clocks, can be integrated into DTS. They use the TPI (Time Provider Interface) in order to pass UTC (Universal Coordinated Time) to DTS.

DCE DTS is based on DEC dts (Distributed Time Synchronization).

Directory

The DCE directory service helps you find things in the system, i.e., in all of the network covered by DCE. When given a name, the directory returns the unique network address of the resource. This is why this type of service is often called a naming service. In addition, the directory can store other information called the object attributes, which can contain very general information about the object in question.

As useful as this service is, it is not necessarily needed directly by the application: If the application uses RPC to communicate, the RPC service will make the necessary calls to the directory service.

In fact, the directory service is used by most other DCE services, including DTS, Security, RPC, and DFS. This makes it a very important component of DCE, even if you don't use it directly.

Each DCE cell has its own directory, called the CDS (Cell Directory Service). Requests to the directory service are normally serviced by the CDS, but if the name is not within the cell, a global directory agent will pass the request to a global name server, which is part of the GDS (Global Directory Services). The DCE GDS is an implementation of XDS (X/Open Directory Services, an X.500 API). As an alternative, the DCE GDS also provides support for the Internet DNS (Domain Name System).

The CDS data is stored in a distributed way in the form of replicas and references (pointers and links) within components called "clearinghouses". The actual lookup is carried out by special agents called clerks, which also cache the data in order to improve performance. The data in the CDS is controlled by the following access permissions:

- **read:** for viewing data

- **test:** for checking specific attributes
- **write:** for creating entries
- **delete:** for deleting entries
- **control:** for defining ACLs (access control lists, described under security)
- **administer:** for managing replication

The DCE CDS is based on DEC's dns (Distributed Name Service), and the DCE GDS is based on the Siemens Nixdorf DIR-X implementation of X.500.

Security

DCE contains a security service based on the Kerberos system [RFC 1510]. This is important, since security is more difficult to control in distributed systems than in centralized ones. The DCE Security service is used by DCE Directory, RPC, and DFS.

This section contains a brief description of DCE Security, and "Chapter 25. Security" contains a more thorough discussion of security in distributed systems.

The security service is a part of DCE, but the users (and administrators) decide how much control should be present in their particular system. This is referred to as DAC (Discretionary Access Control) and can be used to build a system that meets the C2-level security provisions of the Orange Book (see "The Orange Book" on page 306). After auditing is added to DCE Security, it should provide a full basis for C2.

Before accessing the system, every principal (i.e., user, computer, or server) must be identified and authenticated. This is done by checking a user ID and password.

Later, when a principal accesses some particular object, such as a file or printer, the authority to do so is checked against an ACL (Access Control List), which is generally defined by the owner of the object or by a system administrator. These access rights can be defined on the basis of the name of the principal, group, or organization, similar to the user, group, and other categories of UNIX.

In a client/server application using RPC, the server will normally check to see if the client is authentic and is authorized to use the service. This can also be used the other way around: The client can check to see if the server is authentic, i.e., is not an impostor which has sneaked into the network.

DCE Security also includes provisions for (optionally) encrypting data in order to ensure its authenticity, privacy, and integrity. Because encryption requires a lot of computing power, performance will dictate that it be used only when necessary. For example, the security system itself always encrypts passwords before exchanging them between systems.

A number of security services are offered to applications in the form of the following APIs:

- **Authenticated RPC:** checks for authentication on a call or message basis.

- **ID Map API:** to resolve principal names to UUIDs (Universal Unique Identifiers), which are globally unique, due to the way they are constructed based on addresses and time stamps.
- **Registry API:** for managing the registry database.
- **Login API:** defines and controls a principal's login context.
- **Key Management API:** retrieves and manages keys (passwords).
- **ACL API:** used to browse, edit, and test ACLs, or even to write an ACL manager, in order to provide access control for objects not supported by the vendor's DCE system.

DCE Security is based on MIT's Kerberos with enhancements from HP (ACLs).

Threads

A discussion of threads, and a comparison of threads to processes, can be found in "Chapter 6. Operating Systems".

Since threads incur less overhead than processes, they are important for writing servers, where a number of client requests need to be handled in parallel. In particular, the RPC model often leads to the definition of relatively small actions which are performed on each request. This is why threads are a necessary part of DCE. They are used by many of the DCE services and are the normal method for programming RPC servers.

Of course, the DCE thread services can be used to program clients whenever the application structure makes that beneficial.

When an operating system has native threads, these will normally be used by the vendor's implementation of DCE. For example, Solaris 2.3 (a UNIX variant) has threads which are implemented in the kernel. When it doesn't, the DCE code may be used to implement threads on top of the operating system's process services.

Since the different threads of a single process may access the same memory, there needs to be a mechanism for synchronizing this. DCE provides a simple method for this, in the form of the POSIX mutex (mutual-exclusion lock).

In addition to this, threads need to be written in a reentrant fashion, which means that the code is not changed during execution, a prerequisite for simultaneous use by multiple instances of a program. Since this may not be the case for subroutines provided by the runtime library of a compiler, DCE threads include jacket routines for some UNIX system calls, including input, output, fork(), and sigaction(). These jacket routines use a global lock to prevent simultaneous access to system resources.

Another service of DCE threads is the ability to define priorities and scheduling policies (first-in–first-out or round robin) for the threads of the same priority. Preemptive scheduling applies only to threads of different priorities.

DCE threads are based on DEC CMA (Concert Multithread Architecture), an implementation of POSIX threads.

DCE RPC (Remote Procedure Call)

RPC is the communication method supplied by DCE for use by all applications. Since communication is the basis for distributed processing, this makes RPC the most important, central service of DCE.

A discussion of RPC is also contained in "Part 4. Middleware", where it is compared to other forms of communication used in distributed processing.

RPC not only is intended for all applications written on the DCE platform, but also is used internally by other DCE services, including DTS, Directory, Security, and DFS.

The basic service of RPC is a communication method which is modeled after the (local) procedure call of programming languages such as C. Not only is this relatively easy to use, but it is also sufficiently powerful for solving a large number of problems.

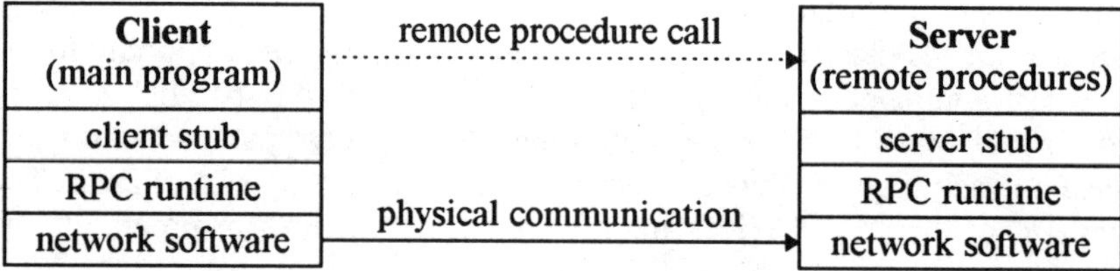

Figure 16. RPC Processing

Figure 16 illustrates the processing involved when a client calls a server via RPC. It provides a good example of the layering concept used in communications (see "Chapter 10. Structure of Networks" on page 111): The "logical communication" is a normal procedure call, but this is passed through some lower layers before the "physical communication" takes place. The steps involved are:

- The client program issues the call.
- The client stub code processes the call. With the help of the RPC library, it
  - marshals the data, i.e., converts it to a form suitable for transmission (and understood by all DCE implementations).
  - sends the request to the server.
- When the server stub code receives the request, it
  - unmarshals the data.
  - calls the server program.
- The server program processes the request.
- The response is handled analogously and eventually reaches the client program.

Hidden within this process are some other very important services of DCE RPC: data conversion, naming, and security.

The process of marshaling and unmarshaling data provides a way of converting the data between the formats used by different machines. The extent to which this is possible is part of the IDL (Interface Definition Language) discussed below.

The client program issues its request on the basis of the name used in the call. The DCE RPC service uses this name to access the DCE Directory service, which tells it the unique network address. This makes DCE RPC location-transparent: The client does not "see" or need to know the location of the server. This also makes it possible to change and install servers without changing the clients.

Based on the configuration and the runtime parameters used, DCE RPC uses security services to authenticate the client or server on a call or message basis, and to encrypt parts or all of the data transferred.

Since the communication is hidden in the RPC service, this is also transparent to the application. The original OSF implementation of RPC uses TCP/IP as its underlying communications protocol, but other protocols can be expected to be supported in the future.

The support provided by DCE for the development of client/server applications using RPC is illustrated in Figure 17.

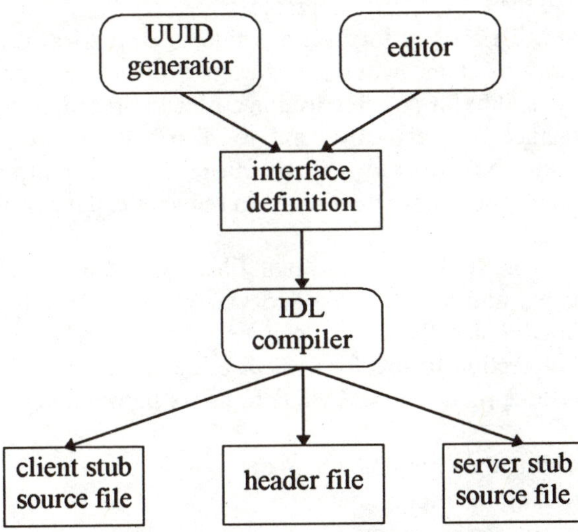

Figure 17. RPC Interface Definition

The UUID generator is used to generate a UUID (Universal Unique Identifier), which is necessary for identifying the client (in fact, a particular version of it) uniquely within all of the network covered by DCE. This ID is transferred by the RPC software during a procedure call in order to identify the remote procedure and ensure that it has the correct version.

The syntax of the call is defined using IDL (Interface Definition Language) and put into an interface definition file, which is read by the IDL compiler in order to create a header file and source code for the client stub and the server stub. These stubs contain all the code necessary for the RPC mechanism.

The client and server sources have an include statement for the header file. After compilation, they are linked with the stub objects and the RPC library to form the executable client and server programs.

DCE RPC is based on Apollo NCS (Network Computing Architecture) version 2.0.

DFS (Distributed File System)

The basic service offered by DFS is to make files on different machines available to the user (person or program) as if they were all on the local machine.

A discussion of distributed files and databases is also contained in "Part 4. Middleware", where they are compared to other forms of communication used in distributed processing.

DCE DFS uses DCE RPC and, by doing so, takes advantage of the DCE Directory service and the DCE Security service.

The use of the DCE Directory service makes DFS files location-transparent: They can be accessed by name without knowledge of where they are stored. This improves scalability, making it possible to move files to other machines as needed for reasons of performance and capacity, and to distribute the load among various machines. In addition, the Directory service can be used to improve fault tolerance, since files can be configured in such a way as to reduce the danger of loss and avoid a single point of failure.

The use of DCE Security means that files can be protected via the normal authentication method, and access controlled via ACLs (Access Control Lists). This support is built into DFS, and the user (file owner or system administrator) can decide how much access protection to use for each file. As an extension of the UNIX file system, which uses three permissions, DFS defines six permissions:

- **read:** for reading data (without change)
- **write:** for writing (changing) data
- **execute:** for running programs
- **control:** for controlling files
- **insert:** for inserting new records between old ones
- **delete:** for deleting, or removing, files

DFS also implements methods for file replication and caching, in order to improve performance and fault tolerance. DFS backup servers provide a method for backing up files.

When a vendor integrates DCE into an operating system, there needs to be a way of integrating DFS with the native file system of the operating system. DFS provides two ways of doing this:

The DCE LFS (Local File System) exists only locally, as opposed to the distributed DFS, but supports all of the functions of DFS, including replication, backup, authorization, and logging.

Alternatively, DFS can be integrated with UFS (UNIX File System), but without the extra features.

DCE DFS is based on Transarc's implementation of Carnegie Mellon University's AFS (Andrew File System).

DCE Diskless Support Service

This service makes it possible to run DCE systems on diskless workstations. It uses DFS to access files on other machines.

Among other things, Diskless Support Service makes it possible to define swapping files via DFS, so that they can be located on other machines.

DCE Diskless Support is based on technology supplied by HP and Transarc.

Standards

DCE is based on the following standards:

- File System Semantics: (POSIX 1003.1) [ISO/IEC 9945-1]
- Threads: (POSIX 1003.4a) [ISO/IEC 9945-1]
- Directory (X.500): [ISO/IEC 9594]
- Directory (DNS): [RFC 1034, RFC 1035, RFC 1101, RFC 1183, and RFC 1348]
- Kerberos [RFC 1510]
- DES [FIPS 46]

Trends and Products

In many respects, DCE has become a standard by which other systems are measured. It has shown that it is possible to integrate remote procedures, security, and directory services in a multiplatform environment. However, broad-scale usage depends on a number of other factors, including a typical chicken-and-egg problem: An infrastructure is not very useful until many applications support it, and applications developers often do not invest in such a technology until it is widely accepted.

Communications

Standard DCE RPC (version 1.0) runs on top of TCP/IP. However, a number of vendors are working on implementing it on top of other protocols, including SNA LU6.2, DECNET, IPX/SPX, Appletalk, Banyan Vines, and Novell NetWare.

This raises the question of whether these versions of RPC will guarantee interoperability between vendors. It is not yet clear whether the OSF Interoperability Labs will consider this to be their job.

Even though it seems natural for OSF to add other communications models, such as queuing or TxRPC, to their list, that has not happened yet. However, Oracle is reported to be working on SQL*Net over RPC and IBM on DRDA (Distributed Relational Database Architecture) over RPC.

Security

Standard DCE ACLs apply to such things as files and directories, but a clear need for many users is to have access control for databases. For example, support for DCE Security (and Directory) services in a number of RDBMSs is provided by products such as the following:

- Open Horizon's Connect provides for DCE single sign-on to:
    - IBM (DB2) (also supported via IBM DCE-RACF integration)
    - Informix (also supported via Informix DCE/Net)
    - Microsoft SQL Server
    - Oracle (also supported via Oracle 7 Advance Network Option)
    - Sybase

Products

DCE has been implemented on the following platforms:

- Apple Mac OS
- AT&T SVR4
- Bull BOSX
- DEC OpenVMS, OSF/1, ULTRIX
- IBM AIX, MVS, OS/2, OS/400
- HP HP-UX, MPE/iX
- Microsoft Windows 3.1 (by Gradient), Windows NT
- SCO Open Desktop
- SNI Sinix, BS2000
- Stratus System/88
- Sun Solaris

Summary of Part 2

By looking at the basic services offered by hardware and software systems, we can learn how and when to use them without going into their internal workings. However, we cannot always ignore the internal workings and just look at the upper surface of things, and still make good use of the systems. For example, when programs are written to the operating system services without regard for the performance of the hardware or the network, the result can sometimes ruin an otherwise good application.

Recent developments in hardware have made it possible to create new applications which were not feasible a few years ago. This covers both local processing and communication capabilities. In addition, new processors are giving us a new chance of attaining hardware-independent operating systems. These developments are also changing the way hardware and software will be bought in the next few years.

Operating systems traditionally provide the basis for all application development. They enhance the hardware with services that include files and databases, multiprocessing, memory management, interprocess communication and user interfaces.

Distributed processing can be achieved by putting communication services on top of operating systems, creating a network of individual operating systems, or by putting communication inside of the operating system, thus making one system extend over a network of individual computers. In any case, higher layers of software, whether they are called middleware, network operating systems, or something else, are rapidly becoming the new basis for the development of distributed applications.

Along with the operating system services, the other part of this basis is the communication services, which are covered in the next part of this book.

Part 3. Communications

Introduction to Part 3

In any distributed system, the service that ties the individual parts together is to be found in the communications system. In some cases, it is possible to forget about this service, and just deal with the distributed system as a whole. For example, this is how applications often see the services of distributed or network operating systems, as discussed in "Part 2. Systems".

In other cases, it is necessary to choose a communications service based on the basic processing model of the application, as discussed in "Part 1. Introduction". In this context, we will see that communications services based on different processing models do in fact behave very differently. Finally, there are some very basic properties of most computing systems, including communications, which often play an important role. These include such things as speed and error-handling capabilities.

"Chapter 9. Services" defines the services offered by communications systems in general and can be used either as an introduction to communications, as a reference, or as a checklist for use when choosing a product.

"Chapter 10. Structure of Networks" shows how the basic communications services are generally implemented in various layers or subsystems. This also shows which of these components are closest to the application and how they can be mixed with the other components.

"Chapter 11. Lower Layers" presents some of the most common low-level protocols used in LANs (Local Area Networks) and WANs (Wide Area Networks). It includes a discussion of the low-level services most likely to be relevant to applications, and an explanation of some important trends, such as switching and ATM (Asynchronous Transfer Mode).

"Chapter 12. The TCP/IP Family" begins the discussion of protocols by presenting the protocols and services used in the Internet. These technologies have been put into very widespread use in private and corporate networks as well, due at least in part to their open and economical availability, as with the UNIX systems on which they were originally implemented.

Within APE, the provision of communications services has been primarily a task of various birds. First and foremost among these have been the carrier pigeons, due to their long tradition in the market and a proven ability to quickly adapt and employ new technology, even when it required subcontracting to other species. For example, the deployment of a flock of solid-fuel-rocket–propelled carrier pigeons made big headlines even though it was never an important economic factor. A much greater success is to be found in the use of sophisticated modulation technologies which have enabled many songbirds to share bandwidth on the same spectrum and provide both sustained and burst-mode traffic with remarkably low interference levels.

Another recent success has been the exploitation of otherwise unused bandwidth, called the honking gap, in the magnetic guidance system of migratory geese.

Chapter 9. Services

Clearly, communications services are there to get data from one place to another. But what other services does your application require from the communications subsystem? For example, does it need high-speed transfer, or high reliability, or perhaps proof that the message was received by the partner, or maybe some way of finding out who is on the other end, or even very slow communications, but at a very steady rate without any delays?

This chapter provides a general definition of some of the most important services offered by communications systems. In the following chapters, individual communications protocols will be discussed, and described in terms of these services. Most of these services, along with the most important concepts involved, are defined in the OSI Basic Reference Model [ISO/IEC 7498-1].

Operational Services

Connections

Connections are something like the telephone call we need to establish before talking with someone at a distance. What is the meaning of this as far as the application is concerned? Is it just a necessary evil, a way of patching wires together before talking? In fact, it's more than that, and the difference between connectionless and connection-oriented communications protocols is very important for the application using the communications services. It affects not only the basic API to be used, but also the behavior of the application itself. In particular, it determines the way the application needs to handle errors.

This difference can be understood by looking at the example of mail versus telephones. A letter can be sent via mail without waiting to see if the recipient is available; when it arrives, it is left in the mailbox until the recipient takes it out. This is a connectionless protocol. On the other hand, in order to start a telephone conversation, the recipient has to take the phone off the hook before the conversation can start. Since a connection must be made between two telephones, this is a connection-oriented protocol.

If you send two letters to someone, it is possible for the second letter sent to arrive before the first one. This is an example of a sequence error. The same thing can happen in data networks where there is more than one path, or line, connecting the two partners. Correcting sequence errors is normally the task of a connection-oriented protocol. In general, connection-oriented protocols offer a higher level of service than connectionless protocols. For example, resequencing messages and segmenting and reassembling them are often tasks of a connection-oriented protocol.

Connection-oriented protocols often require less overhead, since they need to find the desired partner and allocate resources only once, namely, when the connection is established. They also often offer superior quality, since the connection provides a context for maintaining sequence and providing for flow control. And at the beginning of the connection, it is possible to negotiate the values of parameters and options governing the transmission of data that will hold during the connection. On the other hand, connectionless protocols sometimes often support services, such as broadcast, which are not offered by connection-oriented protocols.

When an application uses a connection-oriented protocol such as SNA (Systems Network Architecture), it can assume that either the messages sent will be received, or it will receive a "session outage notification" saying that the connection has been lost. This makes it unnecessary for the application to request responses for all messages, or to manage time-out mechanisms. In fact, an SNA network running on an SDLC (Synchronous Data Link Control) line requires timers only in the SDLC components (layer 2): If the last line available for a session fails, the information will bubble up through the layers and the session will be terminated. On the other hand, if the session is lost, the application may require knowledge of how many messages were received before the failure; this requires extensive error-handling methods, such as checkpoints or commit protocols.

In OSI terminology, an "association" is any cooperative relationship between peer entities, and applies to all layers except the physical layer. A "connection" is an association requested by an entity of the next higher layer for the purpose of data transfer, and applies to all layers except the physical and the application layers. Also, the OSI terminology uses the terms "connection-mode transfer" and "connectionless-mode transfer" where we use the more common terms "connection-oriented" and "connectionless".

In this book, we will use the term "connection" in a general sense, including different protocols at different layers. Here are some of the names used in specific protocols:

- **connection:** all OSI layers except application and physical, TCP
- **association:** all OSI layers except physical, but used most often in the application layer
- **session:** OSI session layer, SNA session-control services
- **conversation:** APPC (SNA advanced program-to-program communication)
- **dialogue:** OSI Transaction Processing

Here are the most important advantages of these two types of protocol:

- **connectionless:** the sender and receiver can operate independently of each other
- **connection-oriented:** relatively fast responses (since resources are allocated before data transfer), more services (sequence preservation, segmenting, etc.)

Connection-oriented protocols are not restricted to communications over LANs or WANs. For example, calling OPEN, READ/WRITE, and CLOSE to access a file is a kind of connection-oriented file handling. This interface shares a number of the properties of connection-oriented communications protocols, such as allocation of resources (e.g., I/O buffers) only once, and finding the partner (the file) only at the beginning of the connection.

A real network may be made up of a number of different protocols implemented in layers, where they may all be connection-oriented, or all connectionless, or mixed. If fact, it is quite possible to implement a connection-oriented protocol on top of a connectionless protocol or vice versa, something known in OSI as "mode conversion functions". For example, if you want to receive telephone calls when you are not home, you can install an answering device, which is a case of implementing a connectionless protocol on top of a connection-oriented one. An example of implementing a connection-oriented protocol on top of a connectionless one is TCP on top of IP.

Simplex and Duplex Transmission

Following parliamentary procedure during a debate involves applying definite rules about who can speak first, how contention situations are resolved, and how and when to interrupt one speaker or move on to the next one. Communications protocols have similar rules, and these also affect the interface to the application.

There are three ways in which the direction of transmission within any specific layer can be configured:

- **simplex:** data transmission in one preassigned direction
- **half duplex:** data transmission in either direction, one direction at a time
- **duplex (full duplex):** data transmission in both directions at the same time

Naming, Addressing, Routing

Before E.T. can phone home, he has to know his phone number, and then, depending on where his home is located, he may need to know an area code or a country code. After that, he may need to know that some area codes in the U.S. require a "1" before them, or that when you dial a European area code after the country code, you have to leave out the first "0" of the area code.

All this means that he has to know not only the "name" (e.g., Mrs. E.T.), and perhaps some further identification (to be sure he is referring to the right Mrs. E.T.), but also the "address" (phone number) and some information about the structure of the addressing scheme used by the telephone companies involved. And this is still easy compared to what the phone system may need to do in order to "route" the request through various nodes or switches in the intergalactic network between E.T. and his home.

- **name:** an identifier for a partner entity. There should be some way of specifying global names, which are unique in a global context, and local names, which are much shorter, but need be unique only within a particular system.

- **address:** an unambiguous name used by the system to identify an entity. In theory, this is the same as a name, but in practice, addresses are often complex technical structures used internally, whereas names are used externally. Also, addresses often identify the location or the device of an entity.
- **location transparency:** a property of a system which makes it possible to refer uniquely to a partner entity without specifying its location.
- **directory:** a service which translates names into addresses. It may also provide a means of storage for other information (attributes) about the named entities.
- **name server:** another name for "directory", normally applied to a server which offers its directory services to multiple clients.
- **broadcast:** transmission to all nodes of a certain scope, such as a single LAN.
- **multicast:** transmission to a number of destination addresses. This generally applies only to connectionless protocols.
- **unicast:** transmission to a single destination address (the normal case), used in contrast to broadcast and multicast.
- **distribution lists:** a method for specifying the recipients for a broadcast transmission. The term is often used in mailing systems.
- **routing:** a function which translates the address of an entity to a path (or route) by which the entity can be reached.
  - **static routing:** routing tables are preconfigured.
  - **dynamic routing:** routing tables are created and updated dynamically.
  - **alternate routing:** the system can select a new route without losing the connection when the old route fails.

For example, in a UNIX system communicating over TCP/IP, entities are referred to by their "host" and "service" names. A simple directory service, consisting of the files "/etc/hosts" and "/etc/services", converts these into addresses, or numbers called "IP address" and "port number". In order to keep things consistent, these files have to be maintained on all systems involved. A more convenient method is the directory service NIS (Network Information System) [see "NIS (Network Information System)" on page 148], which is a part of the NFS protocol suite (which runs on TCP/IP) and provides a centralized (client/server) directory.

Broadcast messages are often used within a LAN to notify all users of certain events, and are often quite common internally, such as when a node informs all others of its address or requests certain information from all others. This is the type which can cause performance problems when used extensively. Distribution lists are typical for electronic mail. Also, broadcast methods do not scale well, which means that they cause problems when the LAN grows above a certain limit.

Routing services are a part of many systems, and can be very complex. Static routing requires definition of routing tables for all possible communication paths, and provides a high degree of control. Dynamic routing determines the path at the time the communication takes place, which may require searching over multiple nodes and automatic maintenance of internal tables. It is much more convenient to use, but may cause unexpected performance problems. For example, when you buy an airline ticket, you might want to choose the lowest fare available, and accept any connection necessary to achieve it. Just as this service is now offered by some reservations systems, the telecommunications are beginning to offer "automatic least-cost route calculation".

Multiple Connections

In order to use a communications line efficiently, it is common to transmit messages for multiple connections on the same line. This technique, known as "multiplexing", involves somehow identifying the messages which belong to different entities and forwarding them to the correct recipient. Similarly, it is sometimes useful to allocate multiple lines to a single connection, in order to achieve a high capacity or improve fault tolerance. The individual services defined for this purpose are:

- **multiplexing:** the use of one connection to support multiple connections in the next higher layer.
- **demultiplexing:** the reverse of multiplexing.
- **splitting:** the use of multiple connections to support one connection in the next higher layer. Also known as "reverse multiplexing" and "bundling".
- **recombining:** the reverse of splitting.

In the higher layers, these functions are generally implemented in software, using message headers to carry protocol information that identifies the owners of the individual messages. In the physical layer, there are hardware methods, such as TDM (Time-Division Multiplexing) and FDM (Frequency-Division Multiplexing).

Segmenting and Blocking

Very often, protocols at the link or network level support only limited message sizes. Also, there is a tuning issue here:

- If the messages are too small, the overhead involved in packaging each message is inefficient.
- If the messages are too large, the probability of corruption and the resulting retransmission overhead makes operation inefficient, e.g., by using too much of the transmission capacity or too much of the storage available for buffers.

Therefore, transport protocols often have the capability to cut messages into smaller pieces (segmenting) and reassemble them when they arrive at the other end, and the capability to pack multiple messages into one piece (blocking) and take them apart again at the other end.

This service can also be relevant in other layers, including those near the application layer. The OSI terminology includes the following definitions:

- **segmenting:** a function which splits data units into multiple pieces before giving them to the next lower layer for transmission.
- **reassembling:** the reverse of segmenting.
- **blocking:** a function which combines multiple data units into one piece before giving them to the next lower layer for transmission.
- **deblocking:** the reverse of blocking.

To be precise, the OSI definitions differentiate between "segmenting and reassembling" and "concatenation and separation". The difference involves the question of which parts of the data (protocol information or net data) are involved. Here, we will use the terms "segmenting" and "reassembling" in a broader sense covering both meanings.

Control Functions

Not all devices are created equal. For example, a printer may not be able to handle data as fast as the computer can send it, so it needs a way to slow things down, or to control the flow of the data. In other situations, such as IP, the designers agreed to permit overloaded systems to discard data, making the end nodes responsible for repeating the transmission and keeping track of what has been transferred successfully and what hasn't. Here are a few basic definitions that cover this topic and some related things, such as keeping the messages in the right order.

- **flow control:** a function which controls the flow of data within a layer (peer flow control) or between adjacent layers (service boundary flow control).
- **sequencing:** a function performed by a layer in order to preserve the order of the data units submitted to it.
- **acknowledgment:** a function which allows a receiving entity to inform a sending entity of the receipt of a data unit.
- **reset:** a function which sets the corresponding entities to a predefined state with a possible loss or duplication of data.
- **expedited transfer:** expedited data units are transferred with priority over normal data units, and are used, for example, for control messages such as "cancel" or "reset". This has a meaning only in connection-oriented transmission.

For example, in SNA, flow control is called "pacing" and is used in both the data link and session layers.

The reset function is an error-correction mechanism which is normally applied after a loss of synchronization, i.e., when the two partner entities no longer agree on the state of the transmission. An example of this is resetting all sequence numbers, which may lead to loss or repetition of data units.

Synchronization and Transaction Control

Sometimes, it is necessary to synchronize multiple activities and ensure that either all of them complete successfully or all of them are aborted. For example, in a public telephone network, it may be necessary for a number of switches to be upgraded to a new software version simultaneously. In such cases, the basic unit of work is referred to as a "transaction", and the mechanism for implementing it is a "commit protocol" (see "Distributed Transaction Processing" on page 29). When such a commit protocol is used in a distributed environment, i.e., to implement "distributed transactions", it needs to be supported by a communications protocol, making synchronization and transaction control into a high-level communications service.

Synchronous/Asynchronous API

When you have a piece of work done for you, is it better for you to wait until it has been completed before doing something else? Or should you leave this up to your business partners, and check up on things later? Your decision will probably depend on your own schedule, on your experience with your partners, and on the consequences of the possible problems.

When an application uses a "synchronous (blocking) API", its processing is suspended until the requested action is completed. This way, it has immediate information about the success or failure of the operation, but it may have to wait some time at each call, thus preventing it from running at full speed.

When the application uses an "asynchronous (nonblocking) API", it does not have to wait for the operation to complete. However, if the application needs to be aware of which messages have been processed by the partner and when, additional code may be necessary. For example, it may be necessary to implement methods for saving or buffering messages until they are acknowledged, for checking which operations have completed, for correlating requests and responses, and even call-back or exit routines which are activated asynchronously when the operation completes. Ideally, if such methods are necessary, they should not be part of the application, but part of a subsystem, i.e., middleware, which provides a higher-level interface, such as a commit protocol.

Error Recovery

Did you ever play a game called "gossip"? If not, you may have played the same game, but called it "telephone". Or maybe you played a different game by the same name. This party game, which has always been a favorite among APE's communicating birds, goes like this: A small flock of birds sits in a row on a telephone wire and the first chirps a sentence into the ear of the second, who passes it along to the third, and so forth until it reaches the end of the row. Then, the original sentence is compared out loud with the final one, often resulting in a din of laughter and amusement. As a test, we could think up a sentence containing the word "gossip", and see if what comes out the other end contains the word "telephone". If you remember playing a game like this one, then you know how large the potential for communication errors is. Add technical problems caused by noise and the complexity of a telephone network, and it will be clear that detecting, correcting, and reporting errors is a very important part of data communications technology.

Link-layer communications protocols normally correct for data corruption and length corruption by using checksums and similar methods. Communications services for use at the application level should always provide this service. But even when the link layer provides these services, it is possible for messages to be lost, to be duplicated, or to arrive out of sequence. For example, messages can be lost when an intermediate node is overloaded and discards them. They can be duplicated when a response is lost and the message is re-sent. And they can arrive out of sequence when there is more than one route available, allowing messages to pass each other in transit.

In most cases, a connection-oriented transport protocol will provide reliable transport by implementing checks on sequence numbers, buffering messages, and retransmitting during the course of the connection on an end-to-end basis. Also, security mechanisms may be needed to ensure that messages are not modified by a malicious intruder in the network. This is often accomplished by encrypted end-to-end checksums.

Guaranteed Delivery

The term "guaranteed delivery" normally applies to connectionless protocols, since connection-oriented protocols prevent loss of messages within the connection. In order to provide this service when there is no connection, it is necessary to store the messages in safe storage until a subsystem at the partner's site has acknowledged receipt. In other words, the messages must be moved to disk storage and kept there until an acknowledgment is received from the partner.

Priority

There are a number of cases where some messages should have a higher priority than others. For example, when you hit the break key, this should be handled before other messages, so that it can in fact interrupt or cancel what has already been started. In real-time systems, priorities are sometimes assigned according to the time requirements of the devices being controlled.

Priority of certain messages over others means an intentional disruption of the sequence of messages. In application-level communications, it is sometimes implemented by using an extra connection or an extra queue for high-priority messages. In SNA, "expedited data" is transmitted with a higher priority than "normal data". In TCP, "priority transfer" is transferred with the same priority as normal data, but the recipient is notified of the higher-priority data, so that the application can handle it differently.

Data Conversion (Presentation)

It appears that E.T. had no trouble speaking English, and didn't have to use the AT&T translation service when he phoned home. But we earthlings don't do so well, and computers can be very insensitive about language subtleties. One of the major problems involved in truly heterogeneous systems is the representation of data. Each system has its own way of representing numbers, characters, and so forth.

For example, the IBM 370 architecture and the Motorola 68000 processors represent large integers as 32 bits, with the high-order bytes to the left (i.e., with the lower address), a method called "big-endian". In contrast, DEC VAX machines and Intel microprocessors keep the high-order byte to the right (i.e., higher address), a method called "little-endian". Most machines represent characters in 8-bit bytes, i.e., as one character per octet, but this is not always true; for example, the Honeywell format called "field data" defines 6-bit characters, and Unisys used 36-bit words which contained 4 bytes of 9 bits each. In fact, the Teletype character set is a 5-bit code, the original ASCII is a 7-bit code, and EBCDIC is an 8-bit code. Floating-point numbers are also represented differently, and are the subject of standardization by ANSI and IEEE [IEEE 754].

In addition to these differences, there are many more which can be even trickier. For example, some compilers add extra unused bytes (padding) to some data structures in order to make sure that integers, represented by 4-byte words, are aligned to a word boundary (an address divisible by 4). And anyone who has ported C programs between mainframes, UNIX machines, and PCs has learned to be careful about various conventions that define a character string to end with a binary zero, or begin with a length field, or occupy a fixed-length field that is left-justified and filled with blanks.

In order to provide a standardized solution to this problem, the OSI framework begins by defining three concepts:

- **abstract syntax:** the specification of data by using notation rules which are independent of the encoding technique used to represent them
- **concrete syntax:** those aspects of the rules used in the formal specification of data which embody a specific representation of that data
- **transfer syntax:** the concrete syntax used in the transfer of data between open systems

Security

In a distributed system, security can be a very important part of ensuring that the system works properly when it is needed, and the communications links are often the weakest point in this respect. Therefore, we have devoted a complete chapter to the topic of security (see "Chapter 25. Security" on page 293). In individual communications systems, there are a number of services which are relevant to security. These include:

- **integrity:** Can you be sure the data is correct?
- **confidentiality:** Can you be sure no one is eavesdropping?
- **authentication:** Can you be sure your communications partner is not an impostor?
- **nonrepudiation:** Can you prove that the other party received the message?

Network Support

When evaluating a specific application-level communication service, you need to know whether it will run on your network. For example, can you use a particular RPC on your particular LAN? In more general terms, the question is one of which lower layers can be used by the upper-layer protocol in question.

Robustness

The ability to detect and correct transmission errors is an important service of communications protocols, and has been discussed under the name of error recovery. This means that the machines you use are able to handle things like noise or short interruptions of the communications lines. But what happens when the system itself crashes—for example, due to a disk failure? Are all those things such as guaranteed delivery or correct sequence still valid?

When this kind of robustness is required, it is often achieved by special facilities in the hardware and the operating system or other software services, such as redundant disks and journaled file system (see "File Systems" on page 59). In order to be applicable to a communications component, this component needs to take these things into account and make use of the available facilities.

Accounting

The usage of communications facilities can sometimes be an important part of the total cost of a system. When the service is provided to a number of users, it may be necessary to charge each user for his fair share of the cost. This is the concern of accounting (see "Accounting Management" on page 227).

Quality of Service

A number of general characteristics, such as speed, performance, reliability, and availability, are almost always important to the application. Sometimes they are crucial; and sometimes you can afford to wait and do without until the service is back up.

Many subsystems, including communications protocols, or even operating systems, databases, and so forth, don't deal with these services directly, but pass the responsibility down to the next lower layer: If you have a problem, then you should buy a faster machine, buy a bigger disk, or lease a faster communications line. But even when this is the case, we often need a way to specify our requirements. Just as you might require a certain number of MIPS (Million Instructions Per Second) or SPECints (Standard Performance Evaluation Corporation integer) from a CPU (Central Processing Unit), or MB (Megabytes) from a disk, you will require similar capacity measures from a communications system. Also, the telecommunications providers are working on ways to make it possible to negotiate these parameters dynamically, i.e., when needed, and have put this into a package referred to as IN (Intelligent Networks).

The OSI terminology defines a number of QOS (Quality of Service) parameters associated with data transfer within any particular layer. Some possible parameters which may apply to either connection-oriented or connectionless transmission are:

- expected transmission delay, acceptable delay of individual messages
- probability of corruption
- probability of loss or duplication, acceptable loss of individual messages
- probability of wrong delivery
- cost of transmission
- protection from unauthorized access
- priority scheduling
- expected throughput
- probability of out-of-sequence delivery

There are also a number of QOS parameters which apply only to connection-oriented transfer. These include:

- connection establishment delay
- connection establishment failure probability
- connection release delay
- connection release failure probability
- connection resilience

Some QOS parameters which typically apply to the data-link layer are:

- error rate
- service availability
- transmission rate
- transit delay

Capacity

The capacity of a communications link is often one of the most important measures of its usefulness, and generally determines how much it costs. The capacity to transfer a certain amount of data in a particular amount of time is also often called "speed".

Today, this capacity is generally specified in bit/s or bps (bits per second). The older term "baud" is sometimes used synonymously, but there is an important difference: Baud actually means the number of pulses per second on the line (also known as the clock rate). If the line has more than one signal channel, or if the modem compresses the data, the capacity (in bit/s) will be higher than the baud rate. In any case, it is important to realize that this is only the capacity of the line, and that overhead due to the protocols used will reduce the capacity for transferring application data, sometimes significantly.

Another term often used for capacity is "bandwidth", which literally means the difference between the upper and lower frequencies in a band of electromagnetic radiation. When the characteristics of electromagnetic transmission are analyzed, the concept of bandwidth is important, but its meaning is not obvious to most users of data communications. As a result, it has become quite common to speak of bandwidth in very general terms without specifying frequencies, but then to refer to the capacity of the line in terms of bit/s.

Response Time

It is common to think of a communications line with a high capacity as being a fast, or high-speed, line. In many cases, this is adequate, since more data is transferred per second, making the line "fast". However, there are a few other measures that may conflict with this assumption.

One of these is "response time", which is the time required to receive a response to a request sent to a remote system. Since this time may depend on a number of other factors, such as the processing time and disk access required on the system(s) involved, it may be important to keep in mind that a "fast" line and a "fast" response can be two completely different things.

The response time also depends on the propagation delay of the transmission medium itself. For example, a modem connection over a telephone line may have a small capacity (slow) and a small delay (fast), whereas a satellite link may have a high capacity (fast) and a large delay (slow).

An example of high bandwidth but long response time can be seen in the interplanetary links used for beaming up animals over the APE's ADANet. These links need a very high bandwidth in order to carry the digitized image of even a very small animal. At the same time, there is a large propagation delay due to the long distances between planets. This makes these links similar to terrestrial satellite links, but even more extreme. Another important aspect of these links is the poor quality, due to meteorites, interstellar dust, and background radiation. At the same time, beaming up any species requires an extremely high transmission quality in order to keep the mutation rate down to a socially acceptable residual risk. This required a special design of the link layer: Even selective retransmission of corrupted blocks after one request-response cycle required such large buffering capabilities that a new anticipative heuristic error detection and correction algorithm had to be developed. Occasional glitches of this mechanism have resulted in some very interesting new creatures, referred to as "beaming mutations".

Latency

When you make a transatlantic telephone call, you may have noticed that the connection seems to disappear when both people try to speak at once. What happens here is that the connection is only half duplex, i.e., it supports communication in only one direction at a time. Whenever both people speak at the same time, the switching from one direction to another may make it impossible for you to hear the other person.

Similar, but more subtle, problems often occur with other telephone connections, where the effects of a switching device or a private branch exchange may cause small interruptions in the connection. In most cases, the people using the telephone will still understand each other well, and any telecommunications devices using the line will be able to detect and correct the small errors that occur.

The problem of latency, or delays, can have a number of causes. For example, data may be stored in an intermediate node and then forwarded to the next, causing a delay that depends on the load on that node. Also, transmission errors may be corrected by protocols which make checks on the data and repeat transmission of faulty messages. And finally, the propagation delay of the transport medium itself may be significant in certain cases.

Many data-processing applications need a certain average throughput, but don't suffer if there are a few delays here and there. Applications which require "low, deterministic latency" are sometimes referred to as "isochronous applications", and include imaging, multimedia, and videoconferencing. The data transferred by isochronous applications is also called "delay-sensitive traffic".

This requirement is one reason for the recent tendency to move error handling from the lower layers of communications protocols to the higher ones, making it into an optional end-to-end service instead of a part of the link-layer devices (see "ATM" on page 127). This way, it should become possible to use one single connection for voice, video, and data communications at the same time.

Chapter 10. Structure of Networks

Today, communications systems often consist of a lot of parts. These include the actual wiring and all the logic required to make this work in a reliable manner. On top of this is the software, which is responsible for formatting and handling the data in a way that is most useful to the applications that use it. The purpose of this chapter is to show how these components are organized. This information is useful for understanding the services offered by the different components, and for understanding how the different parts can be combined.

For application design, it is most important to know the services of the components used directly by the application programs. The hardware, wires, and protocols are hidden from the application, and needn't be considered in detail. However, even here, it may be important to know some specific services, such as capacity (bandwidth) or the maximum delay that can occur.

OSI Basic Reference Model

A general framework for communications protocols was defined in the OSI Basic Reference Model [ISO/IEC 7498-1]. This terminology has since gained widespread acceptance, even in protocols not defined within the OSI context. The basic concept involved here is one of layering, where the highest layer is closest to the application and the lowest is closest to the hardware. Two partners (peer entities) within the same layer communicate with each other in a logical sense via a layer protocol, and in a physical sense via the next lower layer. Each layer uses the services of the next lower layer and provides services to the next higher layer.

If necessary, a layer can be further split into sublayers. This has been done, for example, in the link layer, which has been split into LLC (Logical Link Control) and MAC (Media Access Control). Real implementations are not permitted to skip layers, but they may skip sublayers.

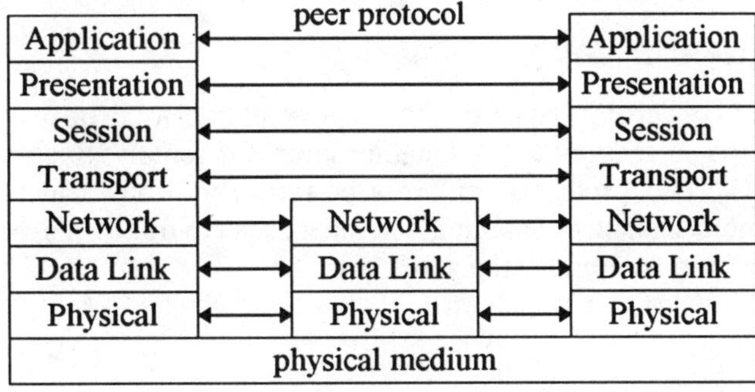

Figure 18. Communications Layers

In Figure 18, it can be seen that the lower layers are present in all nodes. In particular, the data link layer is used for point-to-point communication between two nodes, and the network layer is used for routing, or relaying messages from one node to another. The transport layer and all layers above it operate in an end-to-end fashion, without direct involvement of the intermediate nodes.

The Application Layer

In true OSI implementations, the application layer is the sole interface to the application. At first glance, it may look as if this layer were unimportant, since all basic communications services are covered by the other six layers. However, the services defined in the OSI application layer are very rich and have become the most important part of OSI.

Services

- naming and addressing
- determination of QOS (Quality of Service)
- synchronization (only for connection-oriented protocols)
- dialogue mode (only for connection-oriented protocols)
- error recovery
- security (authentication, access control, data integrity)
- identification of abstract syntaxes (for data conversion)

Examples

- ISO FTAM (File Transfer, Access, and Management)
- Internet ftp (file transfer protocol)
- ISO MOTIS (Message-Oriented Text Interchange System)/MHS (Message Handling System), i.e., X.400
- ISO Directory, i.e., X.500
- ISO DTP (Distributed Transaction Processing)
- ISO CMIP (Common Management Information Protocol)

The Presentation Layer

The problem of converting data from the representation used in one system to that used in another is solved by the presentation layer. Optionally, this may also include compression. The OSI protocols contain a powerful and universal method for this, making them more capable of handling heterogeneous environments, but at the cost of using more CPU and communications capacity.

Services

- data conversion, in particular
    - identification and negotiation of transfer syntaxes

- transformation of data between a local concrete syntax and a transfer syntax
- data compression

Examples

- ISO ASN.1 (Abstract Syntax Notation One)
- NFS XDR (Sun Network File System External Data Representation)
- OSF DCE RPC Data Marshaling (Open Software Foundation Distributed Computing Environment Remote Procedure Call)

The Session Layer

The session layer provides a means of organizing and synchronizing the data exchange between two partners.

Services

- session connections
- duplex and half-duplex transmission
- normal and expedited data transfer
- token management as a means of controlling the use of resources
- exception reporting
- multiple activities (logical pieces of work) within a dialogue
- synchronization
- flow control

Examples

- ISO Session Layer
- IBM SNA Session Control (not a layer)

The Transport Layer

The purpose of the transport layer is to provide transparent, reliable and cost-effective transfer of data in an end-to-end manner. In other words, this is the layer which hides all mechanisms used for routing data via multiple nodes, and makes sure it is packaged in an efficient way and arrives without error.

Services

- connection-oriented and connectionless transfer
- normal and expedited data transfer
- multiplexing and splitting
- segmenting, blocking, and concatenation
- error recovery, including sequencing
- flow control

Examples

- ISO Transport Class 0–4
- Internet TCP (Transmission Control Protocol)
- IBM SNA Transmission Control layer

The Network Layer

The network layer is primarily concerned with routing and relaying, i.e., with getting the data from one point to another across multiple intermediate nodes and different subnetworks (both in tandem and in parallel). It is the highest layer involved in these activities; all higher layers, including the transport layer, are concerned with end-to-end functionality.

Services

- connection-oriented and connectionless transfer
- addressing and routing
- provision of selected QOS (Quality of Service)
- multiplexing
- segmenting and blocking
- error recovery, including sequencing
- flow control
- normal and expedited data transfer

Examples

- ISO X.25 packet layer
- IBM SNA Path Control layer
- Internet IP (Internet Protocol)

The Data Link Layer

The data link layer provides point-to-point services for transferring data reliably from one node to the next in traditional networks. It is generally the most important component in error recovery when problems due to errors in the physical transport media are involved.

Services

- connection-oriented and connectionless transfer
- routing and relaying (however, generally used only within certain types of LAN)
- multiplexing and splitting
- error recovery, including sequencing
- flow control
- synchronization

Examples

- ISO/ITU-TS HDLC (High-Level Data Link Control)
- ISO/ITU-TS LAPB (Link Access Procedure Balanced), a variant of HDLC used in X.25
- IBM SDLC (Synchronous Data Link Control), a variant of HDLC used in SNA
- ISO/IEEE LLC and MAC (Logical Link Control and Media Access Control), used in LANs

The Physical Layer

The mechanical and electrical properties of transmission media are defined in the physical layer, as well as the procedural means for activating, deactivating, and maintaining them.

Services

- physical connections
  - point-to-point
  - multipoint
- transparent transmission of bit streams
- multiplexing
- notification of fault conditions
- QOS parameters

Examples

- ISO/ITU-TS V.24
- IEEE RS-232C

IBM's Blueprint

The preceding discussion of the OSI structure may seem a bit theoretical at times. Although it does provide a good representation of OSI protocols and a reasonable way of talking about others, it doesn't really cover all of those other protocols that populate our communications world. This is done at least partially in IBM's Blueprint for open communications.

This material was originally published (as a statement of direction) under the name "Networking Blueprint", and then extended into the applications layers under the name "Open Blueprint" [IBM GC31-7057-00]. The specifications for the transport-level structures were published under the name MPTN (Multiprotocol Transport Networking [IBM GC31-7073-00]. The MPTN architecture has been submitted to X/Open, and accepted as a standard [X/Open G506, X/Open C520, X/Open C521, and X/Open C522]. The IBM products that implement MPTN have been given the name "AnyNet", and now cover TCP/IP, IPX, and NetBEUI over SNA, and SNA over TCP/IP.

Thus, we can see that the IBM Blueprint covers a large number of real-world protocols, both proprietary and standard, and that its basic structure is either standardized or in the process of being standardized.

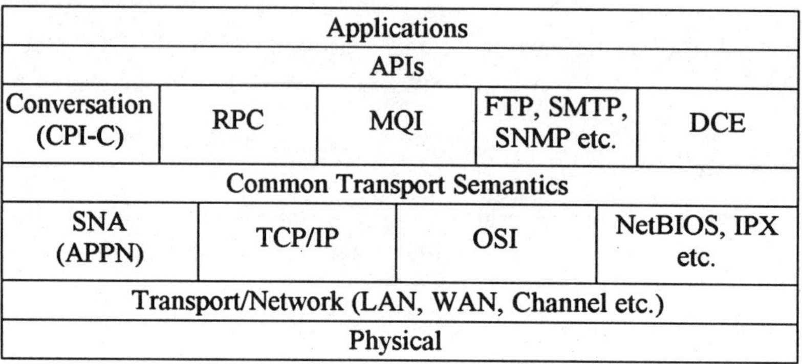

Figure 19. The IBM Networking Blueprint

Except for the lower layers (physical and subnetwork), the Blueprint can be divided into three major parts:

- transport services
- distribution services
- application services

Transport Services

The transport protocols covered by the Blueprint are:

- SNA APPN (Advanced Peer-to-Peer Networking): The SNA version with dynamic routing.
- TCP/IP: The Internet protocols.
- OSI: OSI TC4 (Transport Protocol Class 4).
- NETBIOS and IPX: Commonly used protocols in PC networks, providing less than full transport services.

An important aspect here is the definition of a new transport-level API, the CTS (Common Transport Semantics). CTS is part of MPTN, is an extension of the XTI API, and has been submitted to X/Open. CTS also includes the Berkeley Sockets interface. As the picture shows, this interface can be used over any of the transport protocols. For example, it is possible to use the Sockets interface over SNA.

Distribution Services

The term "distribution services" is used here to cover a number of protocols and services in the upper layers, including:

- communication services
    - CPI-C (Common Programming Interface for Communication): This is the IBM SAA (Systems Application Architecture) API for APPC, which has also been published by X/Open and can be used over OSI Transaction Processing. It is also referred to as "conversational" (see "APPC and CPI-C" on page 159).
    - RPC (Remote Procedure Call): Compliant with the OSF DCE RPC [see "DCE RPC (Remote Procedure Call)" on page 90].
    - MQI (Messaging and Queuing): An asynchronous, message-passing interface (see "Message Queuing" on page 191).
- DSOM (Distributed System Object Model): The IBM implementation of the CORBA standard for object management (see "CORBA" on page 175).
- DCE services (see "Chapter 8. DCE" on page 86)
    - Directory
    - Security
    - Time
    - Transaction Manager, including the X/Open protocols TX and XA

Application Services

Some of the application services included in the Blueprint are the following:

- **printing service:** Based on the Palladium implementation, which conforms to ISO/IEC 10175.
- **mail:** Includes the Internet standard SMTP and the OSI standard X.400.
- **file access:** Includes the DCE DFS as well as the IBM DDM (Distributed Data Management).
- **database access:** IBM DRDA (Distributed Relational Database Architecture) (see "Chapter 15. Remote SQL" on page 164).

Transport-Layer APIs

Today, many application programs use a transport-layer interface for all of their communications needs. In fact, the transport layer has proven to be one of the most natural places to split up the communications subsystem and to apply the concept of "mixing and matching", i.e., to choose the lower layers from one source and the upper layers from another.

The transport layer has the advantage of providing reliable end-to-end data transfer. Reliable means that such things as guaranteed delivery and correction of errors, e.g., corruption or loss of sequence, are taken care of. End-to-end refers to the fact that addressing and routing over intermediate nodes is taken care of (in the network layer), and such things as acknowledgments are done between the end points of the connection. There is also generally a choice between connection-oriented and connectionless transfer at the transport layer.

On the other hand, the transport-layer interface does not provide the services of the higher layers. In particular, there is no presentation service or data conversion. This means that either the applications must run in a homogeneous environment, where they all use the same data formats, or they must do their own conversion. Some other services which are provided only by the higher layers are the parameter formatting of RPC, the synchronization and transaction control of commit protocols, and the storage and distribution of mailing systems.

The way application programs use communications services is a good example of this (see "The Rising Level of Abstraction" on page 8). In the past (before the advent of SNA and VTAM), applications running on IBM mainframes handled such things as the start/stop line protocol and terminal control themselves. Today, a large proportion of applications use either a transport interface or a proprietary extension, such as Oracle SQL*Net. The next higher layer of services, including APPC, RPC, e-mail interfaces, and message queuing, are mature enough and sufficiently standardized to be the proper choice for most applications. This leaves only a few applications which should use a transport-level interface because of performance requirements or because the other services simply aren't necessary.

Berkeley Sockets

One of the most widely used APIs at the transport layer is the socket interface, which was introduced as part of Berkeley UNIX. It provides a stream-oriented interface which fits in very well with the UNIX file structure, and can be used either for local interprocess communication (in a UNIX domain, i.e., the UNIX file system) or for remote communication (traditionally via TCP/IP). The great importance of Berkeley Sockets stems from the fact that a very large number of standard UNIX applications, including TELNET, ftp, NFS, NCS, and X-Windows, use it for communication. The basic services of the Berkeley Socket API are:

- transport-layer API
- synchronous API
- connection-oriented and connectionless transfer
- stream-oriented data transfer
- support for numerous lower-level protocols:
    - local IPC (Interprocess Communication)
    - TCP/IP (Transmission Control Protocol / Internet Protocol)

- UDP/IP (User Datagram Protocol / Internet Protocol)
- XNS (Xerox Network Services)
- OSI TP4 (ISO Transport Protocol Class 4)
- SNA (as part of IBM's Networking Blueprint, also called "Snackets")

TLI and XTI

Since Berkeley Sockets is not standardized, and is adapted specifically to the UNIX stream interface, there was a need to invent a more general, protocol-independent transport-level API. This was done with TLI (Transport Level Interface), which was introduced as part of System V, and later improved and standardized by X/Open under the name XTI (X/Open Transport Interface) [Santifaller, page 250 and X/Open C438]. The basic services of the XTI API are:

- transport-layer API
- synchronous and asynchronous API (TLI both, XTI only synchronous)
- connection-oriented and connectionless transfer
- stream-oriented data transfer
- support for numerous lower-level protocols

The interface between TLI/XTI and the specific transport protocol has also been standardized, and is called the TPI (Transport Provider Interface).

Driver APIs

From a practical point of view, it is also very useful to have a standard interface to the device driver, i.e., the software component of the operating system which deals directly with the communication hardware, i.e., the network adapter or NIC (Network Interface Card). This way, various hardware devices and LAN technologies can be used by the same application or communications subsystem, and various applications can use the same hardware. Some examples of driver-level APIs are:

NDIS (Network Device Interface Specification)
ODI (Open Data-Link Interface)

Chapter 11. Lower Layers

In the previous part of this book, "Part 2. Systems", we saw that the lowest layer of computer systems, the hardware, cannot be completely hidden from the application. In particular, the speed of the processor is often visible to the user and also determines whether or not a particular application is feasible. In communication systems, the situation is similar, and the speed of transmission is one of the most obvious properties which show through up to the top, or application, layer. In addition, some other properties, such as the ability to support a constant transmission speed with little delay, are of immediate importance to some applications. In this chapter, these basic services will be discussed for some of the most important examples of communication technology. This brief discussion of lower-layer communication mechanisms also provides a basis for presenting some recent developments and current trends.

LANs

In order to connect a number of machines, such as PCs, within a limited area, LAN (Local Area Network) technology has become very popular. Typically, LANs support a relatively high capacity, such as 10 to 100 Mbit/s (megabits per second). On the other hand, due to the properties of the transmission medium, they can span only relatively short distances, such as less than 1 km, and support only a limited number of nodes. In order to increase the range, multiple LAN segments can be connected in a number of ways: "Repeaters" operate at the physical layer (layer 1) and extend the distance, "bridges" operate at the link layer (layer 2) and connect two LAN segments which use the same protocol, and "routers" operate at the network layer (layer 3) and can pass data from one type of LAN to another based on their addressing information.

Most LANs in use today use protocols which have been standardized by the IEEE and ISO and divide the link layer into two sublayers. The lower sublayer, MAC (Media Access Control), controls access to, or use of, the transmission medium, i.e., the wire. The upper sublayer, LLC (Logical Link Control), provides a link layer which is common to all of these LAN protocols, thus making it much easier to adapt the upper layers to different LAN technologies.

Ethernet

The most common LAN technology today is Ethernet, which has a very simple operating principle: When a station needs to send data, it first listens to see if another station is already transmitting. If not, it transmits and continues to listen. If it does not hear the same thing that it is sending, it assumes that a collision has occurred, and that the data is corrupted, stops transmitting, waits awhile, and tries again. This mechanism is also known as CSMA/CD (Carrier-Sense Multiple Access/Collision Detection).

The Ethernet protocol was originally developed as part of a research project, the Aloha net, which connected a number of campuses of the University of Hawaii, and used radio waves (i.e., the "ether") as a transmission medium. Subsequently, it was used for LANs by Xerox and named "Ethernet", then adopted by IEEE and named CSMA/CD, and then adopted by ISO.

Most often, Ethernet is used on a cable that has a capacity of 10 Mbit/s, but it can use only about 50 to 70% of this capacity efficiently. This is because a higher load leads to frequent collisions, which in turn increase the load due to retries. In order to keep this performance degradation from being worse than necessary, each station uses a random number generator to determine how long to wait before retrying a transmission, and increases this time interval when collisions are more frequent.

Token Ring

One possible solution for the problems caused by collisions in an Ethernet is the Token Ring protocol. Here, a special small frame, or block of data, called a "token" is constantly passed from one station to another in a ring. When a station needs to send data, it waits until a token passes by and replaces the token by a data frame. This way, there are never any collisions, and consequently much less transmission capacity is wasted under high load. However, this simple basic scheme would break down if the token were lost due to a transmission error. In order to prevent this, one station, the "master", monitors the ring in order to detect a loss of the token. The other stations then monitor the master, so that one of them can assume the role of the master if it fails. In addition, the cabling of the ring is double, so that a break in a segment can be repaired by (automatically) joining the two cables at the stations immediately before and after the break.

With all of these mechanisms in place, a Token Ring is very robust and is capable of utilizing more than 90% of the capacity of the cable without unacceptable performance degradation. On the other hand, due to this complexity, Token Ring devices are more expensive than Ethernet devices. Token Ring is widely used at speeds of 4 Mbit/s and 16 Mbit/s.

FDDI

One way of increasing the capacity of LANs is to move from copper wires to optical cables. The protocol generally used for optical LANs is FDDI (Fiber Distributed Data Interface). In comparison with copper wire, optical fiber (glass) has the advantages of having a higher capacity (since light waves have a higher frequency than radio waves) and being insensitive to electrical noise. On the other hand, the devices which convert the signals from electrical to optical and vice versa increase the cost of the network.

FDDI supports speeds of 100 Mbit/s and network lengths of up to 200 km. It uses a technology very similar to Token Ring, and has a variable-length frame.

Summary

All LAN technologies discussed here use a "shared medium" or "broadcast medium". This means that all data from all stations on the LAN is transmitted on the same cable, and thus broadcast to all other stations. As a result, the available capacity has to be shared by all stations. In addition, eavesdropping within the LAN is very easy. The distance spanned by a single segment is limited by such things as propagation delay, and the number of stations per segment is also limited.

In general, LANs are very useful and economical within these limits, but much more difficult to operate when extended past them. Until recently, the primary method of extending the capacity and distance covered by LANs has been the use of devices such as bridges and routers. Now, switching techniques, which are discussed below, are rapidly becoming more popular. Due to the nature of shared media, LANs are also well adapted for bursty data traffic, but provide poor support for isochronous, or delay-sensitive, traffic.

WANs

At the other end of the spectrum, both geographically and technically, we come to WANs (Wide-Area Networks). Today, the services available span a very wide range in terms of capacity, quality, and cost.

Circuit Switching

The starting point for WAN technology is the traditional telephone system, also known as the POTS (Plain Old Telephone System). The basic concept used here is "circuit switching", which means that a physical connection is established between two end points by switching together a number of individual lines. In the time since the telephone network was originally established, the technology used has evolved greatly, and so the connection which is established no longer consists of individual wires, but involves such things as virtual channels created by multiplexing over high-speed lines or satellite links. Nevertheless, the service offered here is one of an end-to-end or point-to-point connection with a minimum guaranteed capacity and quality. This, in turn, is subdivided into "leased lines", which are permanent connections for the duration of the subscription, and "switched lines" or "dial-up lines", which mean that the connection exists from the time it is established (i.e., dialed up) until it is broken down (i.e., hung up). The public telephone network based on this principle is also known as a PSTN (Public Switched Telephone Network).

Since the circuits set up by the POTS were originally intended for voice transmission only, the technology was optimized to support a certain relatively low frequency range, and not digital data. As a result, when the system is used for data transmission, the digital signals a computer uses are first converted to analog signals by a modem (modulator/demodulator), then transmitted across the line, then converted back to digital form by another modem. Today, typical modems for use on analog telephone lines cover a range of speeds from 2400 bit/s to 28,800 bit/s. Circuit-switched lines available as leased lines include the following:

- T1: 1.5 Mbit/s (in North America)

- T3: 45 Mbit/s (in North America)
- E1: 2 Mbit/s (in Europe)
- E3: 34 Mbit/s (in Europe)

In summary, the analog circuit-switched connections provided by the POTS are clearly well suited for voice and other isochronous traffic, since they are a medium dedicated completely to one user at a time. Also, high-speed leased lines are generally very expensive when compared with LANs. When used for data traffic, which is often bursty, or sporadic, in nature, circuit switching makes very inefficient use of the capacity of the line, unless it is shared by a large number of users. This requires some kind of multiplexing technique, such as packet switching (see below).

ISDN

One of the advances which have occurred since the analog telephone network was established is the introduction of digital transmission technology within the telephone network itself. This has made it possible to establish the ISDN (Integrated Services Digital Network), which gives the user digital transmission for the whole route from one end point to the other. When used for data transmission, ISDN does not require any modems, since the service is already digital. When used for voice, the signal is first digitized, in much the same way as music is digitized before being put on a CD (compact disk) or a DAT (digital audio tape). The result is a much better quality of transmission.

Two basic ISDN services are available. BRI (Basic-Rate ISDN) comprises two so-called B channels of 64 Kbit/s and one 16-Kbit/s D channel. In Europe, PRI (Primary-Rate ISDN) consists of one D channel and 30 B channels (for a total of 2 Mbit/s, i.e., an E3 line); the U.S. variant consists of 23 B channels (for a total of 1.5 Mbit/s, i.e., a T3 line). The B channels are used for data, voice, fax, etc., and can be used individually or combined. The D channel is used for control purposes, such as call establishment, but some PTTs also provide support for a 9,600-bit/s X.25 connection on it. When used this way, the D channel is always available for transmitting X.25 packets, since it is not part of the calling mechanism of the B channels. This way, X.25 fees are calculated in the normal way, i.e., per packet.

In addition to improving the quality and speed of transmission, ISDN has also made more services possible. For example, the user of a BRI can use the two D channels separately—both for voice, both for data, or for voice and data combined. Or, they can be combined to form one 128-Kbit/s connection. Another very useful service is CLIP (Calling-Line Identification Parameters), which gives the receiver information such as the telephone number of the caller before the call is established. By using this, the receiver has the ability to determine which calls will be accepted before they are accepted, i.e., before a fee for a call is incurred. This can be very useful in order to improve security, in much the same way as a call-back mechanism is used, or it can be used to reject "junk fax", i.e., unwanted fax messages.

In Europe, the protocol used by the D channel has been standardized by ETSI, and is called DSS1. This standard has been supported by the CEC (Commission of the European Communities) and, as a result, is now the normal case throughout Europe.

In summary, ISDN improves the speed, quality, and flexibility of the telephone system for both voice and data. However, it is still a circuit-switched service, meaning that without additional mechanisms, it does not provide efficient transmission of bursty data traffic. ISDN has taken a long time to move from its original conception to widespread usage, but it is now available from most PTTs around the world [Heywood].

Packet Switching

In order to make efficient use of dedicated lines for bursty data traffic, another method, called "packet switching", was invented. With this mechanism, data to be transmitted is first put into individual blocks called "packets", which are then transmitted to the next station, or node, in the network. Each node stores incoming packets in a queue, reads their addressing information, and forwards them to the next node on the way to their final destination. Since the packets are first stored in the node and then forwarded, this technique is also known as "store and forward".

One widespread packet-switching protocol is IP (Internet Protocol), the network layer (layer 3) of the Internet. If used alone, the service provided by IP would be a connectionless, unreliable transfer of packets, also called datagrams, which are all transmitted independently. Normally, IP is not used alone, but as part of TCP/IP or UDP/IP (see "The Traditional TCP/IP Services" on page 135).

Another common packet-switching service is X.25, which was defined by ITU-TS and adopted by ISO. Because of its origin in the public telephone network, X.25 was designed as a connection-oriented service. There are two types of connections: PVCs (Permanent Virtual Circuits) are established by administrative means, i.e. by subscription, and are analogous to leased lines. SVCs (Switched Virtual Circuits) are established dynamically, by a call procedure, and are analogous to switched lines. Since X.25 is connection-oriented, only the first packet (the call packet) of a connection requires full addressing information; all others just carry a circuit identification. In addition, the connection-oriented service includes prevention of loss, duplication, and out-of-sequence delivery.

In a typical packet-switched network, the connection between two adjacent nodes is operated by a protocol at the link layer (layer 2), which includes error detection and recovery by means of retransmission. Each (store-and-forward) node operates at the network layer (layer 3), which is primarily a question of routing. In order to ensure a reliable end-to-end connection, a connection-oriented transport protocol (layer 4), such as TCP, is operated on top of the packet layer. This protocol needs to do end-to-end error correction, since, even though each link may be reliable, a node can still fail.

In this example, we can see that error detection and correction is done twice, in the link layer and in the transport layer. Wouldn't it be more efficient to do it only once, in the (end-to-end) transport layer? To answer this question, consider the situation where a connection consists of a large chain of individual links (i.e., "hops"), each of which is running on a slow, unreliable line. If the probability of error on each single link is high enough, then very few messages will make it all the way from one end to the other without error. The resulting retransmissions will put an unnecessary load on all links, and performance will deteriorate unacceptably. From this example, we can see that error detection and correction on each individual link is a matter not of basic principle but of tuning, and it is a good design choice for low-quality lines. The case of high-quality lines is treated in the next section.

In summary, packet-switching networks are optimized for efficient transmission of bursty data traffic over slow, unreliable lines. They provide very poor support for isochronous traffic, such as voice or videoconferencing. Public X.25 services are available in most countries and are typically operated at speeds of 9,600 bit/s.

Frame Relay

Since packet switching was invented, the transmission technology used in public networks has greatly improved, so that higher speeds and better quality are now often available. What effect does this have on packet-switching networks? To begin with, the employment of error-correcting protocols on each link is now an unnecessary burden, since errors occur so seldom that they can be corrected more efficiently on an end-to-end basis. But that's not all there is to it: When a transmission line is run at a high speed, the switching node no longer has enough time to calculate checksums such as the CRC (Cyclic Redundancy Check) for each packet. This means that error detection and correction on each link not only is a bad choice, but is often impossible.

The frame relay service takes care of this by relaying frames (i.e., packets) from one node (or switch) to the next without error handling. It is connection-oriented (preserving the sequence of messages), and supports both PVCs and SVCs, as does X.25. Frame relay also detects transmission errors, but does not correct them; this is left up to a higher-level end-to-end protocol, i.e., a transport protocol. Finally, frame relay is designed for use on line speeds of up to 34 Mbit/s. The QOS (Quality of Service) parameters which are negotiated when a call is set up include:

- CIR (Committed Information Rate), i.e., throughput
- committed burst size
- excess burst size

Since frame relay relies on a store-and-forward technique, it does not guarantee good support for isochronous data, but is generally much better than packet switching, since there is less overhead in the individual nodes.

SMDS

Along with the connection-oriented frame relay service, a connectionless service has also emerged, the SMDS (Switched Multimegabit Data Service). SMDS was defined by Bellcore (Bell Communications Research), and has been followed by SIG (SMDS Interest Group) and ESIG (European SMDS Interest Group). A similar specification intended for European networks is CBDS (Connectionless Broadband Data Service), defined by ETSI. In order to make SMDS available as fast as possible, Bellcore designed the SIP (SMDS Interface Protocol) on the basis of an existing IEEE standard, DQDB (Distributed Queue Dual Bus), which was designed for use in MANs (Metropolitan Area Networks). Now, other interface protocols are also available, including interfaces based on frame relay and ATM.

In order to stress the fact that SMDS is a service and not a technology, it has been suggested that, in principle, it would be possible to employ SSCP (Supersonic Carrier Pigeons) as the underlying technology for SMDS [Klessig and Tesink, page 32]. In fact, APE's communication division has implemented a pilot program based on this concept. The project was late in getting off the ground due to disagreement on the proper way of converting the data from its electronic form to the native pigeon format. But after this was solved and the pigeons lived up to their highest expectations in supersonic travel, the project was very successful in meeting its secondary goal, which was to reduce the unemployment rate among young carrier pigeons. However, the major goal of achieving an information superflyway was not met, due to problems of congestion in the air space surrounding the end nodes, which ended in complete chaos within the PTC (Pigeon-Traffic Control).

SMDS is a connectionless packet data service which supports variable-length packets of up to 9188 bytes. It also provides a special service typical for connectionless protocols called group addressing (i.e., both unicast and multicast). In addition, "address screens" can be defined, in order to restrict access (incoming or outgoing) to specific addresses. This way, SMDS can be used to operate a VPN (Virtual Private Network) over a public network. The QOS parameters used for SMDS include the SIR (Sustained Information Rate) and the maximum burst size. Error detection and correction do not prevent loss, duplication, or out-of-sequence delivery, but these, along with corruption, are guaranteed to occur so seldom that they can be handled efficiently by a transport protocol (layer 4).

SMDS is intended for operation in high-speed networks, and its primary usage, like that of Frame Relay, is expected to be for connecting remote LANs. The following access classes have been defined based on the QOS parameter SIR:

class	SIR	intended use
1	4 Mbit/s	4-Mbit/s Token Ring
2	10 Mbit/s	Ethernet
3	16 Mbit/s	16-Mbit/s Token Ring
4	25 Mbit/s	?
5	34 Mbit/s	?

Table 7. SMDS Access Classes

In summary, frame relay (connection-oriented) and SMDS (connectionless) both support efficient transmission of variable-length packets over high-speed, high-quality lines (up to 34 Mbit/s). Both are intended for connecting LANs via a WAN in order to construct a "wide-area virtual LAN". However, neither one fully addresses the task of supporting isochronous data; this is treated in the next section.

ATM

As the speed and quality of the transmission lines continues to improve, the switching method used needs to be changed more and more. Today, many public networks are installing optical transmission lines that use technology based on the Sonet (Synchronous Optical Network) standard, which was developed by Bellcore and adopted by ANSI, or the European SDH (Synchronous Digital Hierarchy), which was defined by ITU-TS. These lines support speeds of up to 622 Mbit/s, which means that any small delay will result in huge amounts of capacity going to waste. (In fact, the standards for this technology include speeds of 52 Mbit/s, 155 Mbit/s, 622 Mbit/s, 2.5 Gbit/s, and 10 Gbit/s) [Gareiss and Heywood]. One of the primary objectives of ATM (Asynchronous Transfer Mode) is to support efficient use of these lines.

The cell-switching technique of ATM is basically similar to packet switching or frame switching as defined above. However, the packets are all very small, fixed-length "cells". In fact, ATM cells are 53 bytes long and have an information field of only 48 bytes. This way, delays due to queuing or packetization are kept very small, typically in the range of a few milliseconds or less. Since all cells have the same length and are forwarded without error correction, it is possible to reserve the necessary transmission capacity in advance, when a connection, or call, is established. This makes it possible to use ATM to provide good support for isochronous data. On the other hand, the fixed-length cells can also be used to multiplex sporadic data from multiple sources, i.e., to provide efficient transmission of bursty data.

The QOS parameters used in ATM subscriptions include the SIR, similar to the SIR in SMDS or the CIR in frame relay. The following service classes have been defined:

- **Class A, CBR (Constant Bit Rate):** connection-oriented, low latency, for traffic which requires low and stable delay, i.e., isochronous traffic, such as voice and video.
- **Class B, VBR (Variable Bit Rate):** connection-oriented, low latency, for packetized voice or video.
- **Class C, VBR:** connection-oriented, undefined latency, for typically bursty or sporadic data traffic, such as frame relay.
- **Class D, VBR:** connectionless, undefined latency, for typically bursty or sporadic data traffic, such as SMDS.
- **Class Y or ABR (Available Bit Rate):** for applications which can request the necessary capacity per transmission, i.e., "bandwidth on demand".
- **Class X or UBR (Unspecified Bit Rate):** with no guarantees on throughput or delay, as a least-cost alternative.

In addition, frame relay and SMDS can be implemented very well over ATM, so these two services should be included in the above list [Atkins and Norris].

Finally, ATM has been given a lot of attention in the data processing literature recently, and all major vendors and PTTs have either demonstrated or pledged support for it. As such, it appears to be one of those topics that has generated a lot of enthusiasm (see "Truth and Beauty" on page 10). This is due to the following properties of ATM:

- **high speed:** ATM can make efficient use of high-speed, high-quality transmission technology.
- **voice and data:** ATM can efficiently support both constant-bit-rate, low latency data, such as voice and multimedia, and data-processing traffic, which is typically sporadic and bursty in nature.
- **LANs and WANs:** The same ATM technology can be used well for both LANs and WANs.

In other words, ATM seems to be a grand unified communication technology which can be used at (almost) any speed, can support both voice and data (and multimedia) on the same network, and can seamlessly connect LANs and WANs over any distance. The ATM Forum has defined standards for 155 Mbit/s and 622 Mbit/s. The IBM proposal of 25 Mbit/s is based on the fact that it would make it possible to use existing Token Ring hardware to bring ATM technology directly to the desktop, but hasn't gained full support of the Forum.

Standards

The following list shows some of the most important standards for the lower layers:

- Ethernet [ISO/IEC 8802-3]

- Fast Ethernet [ISO/IEC 8802-3]
- 100VG-AnyLAN [IEEE 802.12]
- Isochronous Ethernet Integrated Services [IEEE 802.9a]
- Token Ring [ISO/IEC 8802-5]
- FDDI [ISO/IEC 9314]
- ISDN [ITU-TS I.120]
- X.25 [ISO/IEC 8208]
- FR [ITU-TS X.36 and ITU-TS X.76]
- SMDS [Bellcore TR-TSV-000772]
- ATM [ITU-TS I.361]

Trends and Products

As we have seen in the previous sections, networking technology has taken us from circuit-switched telephone networks to packet-switched data networks in WANs, and has been dominated by shared-medium techniques in LANs. Recently, cell switching or ATM has been given a lot of attention and is believed by many to be the primary method that will be used in the mid-term future, both for voice and data, and in both WANs and LANs.

However, ATM is not yet fully mature. A number of important standards are not complete, the devices are still relatively expensive, and the services are not yet available on a widespread basis from the public and private telecommunications carriers. At the same time, a number of alternative technologies are emerging.

Fast Ethernet is a faster version of Ethernet, which provides 100 Mbit/s instead of the usual 10 Mbit/s [Melatti]. 100VG-AnyLAN is another technology which gives us 100-Mbit/s Ethernet, but it also supports Token Ring and makes much more efficient use of Ethernet bandwidth because it reduces the number of collisions by using a priority-based access scheme. The same prioritization scheme provides a limited amount of support for isochronous applications [Rauch and Lawrence].

Iso-Ethernet, short for Isochronous Ethernet, provides a combination of normal Ethernet and ISDN. It consists of a total of 16.144 Mbit/s, divided into one 10-Mbit/s Ethernet channel, 96 64-Kbit/s ISDN B channels for isochronous multimedia traffic, and one 64-Kbit/s ISDN D channel for signaling.

Perhaps a more important advance is the development of switched LANs. For example, with an Ethernet switch, the full 10-Mbit/s Ethernet capacity is available to each device connected to the switch; only the switch has to run at a higher speed. Similarly, Fast Ethernet and FDDI can be switched, supplying 100 Mbit/s to each station. As an alternative, a switch (instead of a bridge or router) can be used to join two segments, meaning that the medium must be shared only by the devices on each segment, and not by all of them. One great advantage of switched LANs is that they make it possible to increase the capacity of the LAN without changing the LAN interface cards of any of the computers, as would be necessary when moving to a higher-speed shared-medium LAN.

In summary, we can see that the existing technologies, such as Ethernet, are being offered at higher speeds, that there are a number of partial solutions to achieving isochronous behavior, and that switching techniques are becoming more and more popular. In particular, LAN switching is beginning to replace routing. Many vendors have provided support for both ATM and other forms of switching technology. For example, IBM has announced a program called SVN (Switched Virtual Networking) along with products of the Nways family (refer to http://www.raleigh.ibm.com for more information), and Cisco has published an architecture called CiscoFusion (refer to http://www.cisco.com).

Chapter 12. The TCP/IP Family

TCP/IP is the protocol of the Internet, one of the world's largest computer networks. As a result, the two terms are often interchanged, or used to cover a whole range of protocols and services. To be a bit more precise, we also refer to these as the "Internet protocol suite" and reserve the term "Internet" for the network itself.

The protocols of the Internet have also become quite widespread outside the Internet itself. This is due to a number of reasons, including:

- TCP/IP is a proven technology.
- TCP/IP is widely used, thus affording a high degree of connectivity.
- The source code is available free (as part of Berkeley UNIX) and is a part of most commercial UNIX products.

History

The beginnings of the Internet go back to 1968, when the ARPA (Advanced Research Projects Agency) of the U.S. Defense Department started a research project which led to the creation of the ARPANet (Advanced Research Projects Agency Network), a forerunner of the Internet [Santifaller, page 12]. The contract to set up the first installation at four U.S. universities went to BBN (Bolt, Beranek and Newman), a company which subsequently had a large influence on the architecture of TCP/IP.

The protocol used at that time was called NCP (Network Control Program) and can be considered a forerunner of TCP/IP, the definition of which began in 1974 with an article by V. Cerf and R. Kahn. It may be worth noting that this is the same year that IBM released the first version of its SNA protocol, and is also about the time that work on the OSI architecture began. The goals of TCP/IP stated then were:

- independence from the network technology and the architecture of the hosts
- universal connectivity in the whole network
- end-to-end acknowledgments
- standardized application protocols

It wasn't until 1982 that the whole ARPANet was converted from NCP to TCP/IP. This is also approximately the time at which the Department of Defense defined TCP/IP as part of MIL standards and required it for contracts, and the time of the first TCP/IP implementation in the UNIX operating system.

An important contribution to the Internet suite, NFS (Network File System), came in 1984 from Sun Microsystems. The first version consisted of a file service, VFS (Virtual File System), and a directory service, YP (Yellow Pages), which is now known as NIS (Network Information System). During the next five years, NFS was extended to include such things as file locking, remote execution, and named pipes, and was ported to a large number of systems.

The specifications for the NFS protocols have all been published, partly as Internet standards, or RFCs (requests for comment), and are part of the SVID (System V Interface Definition). The source code is available for a small license fee, and NFS is available on most UNIX platforms, as well as on others such as DEC VMS, IBM MVS, and PC operating systems. In fact, it is the basis for a large number of LAN file servers for PCs.

Structure

Figure 20 shows the basic components of the Internet protocol suite, along with the corresponding OSI layers [Santifaller, pages 14 and 18].

OSI layer	TCP/IP component
Application	TELNET, FTP, SMTP, TFTP
Presentation	
Session	
Transport	TCP & UDP
Network	IP
Data Link	Subnetwork
Physical	

Figure 20. TCP/IP Components

The basic components of the Internet suite are:

- lower layers, such as:
    - ARPANet
    - Ethernet
    - X.25
    - Token Ring
- network layer:
    - IP (Internet Protocol)
    - ICMP (Internet Control Message Protocol)
- transport layer:
    - TCP (Transmission Control Protocol)
    - UDP (User Datagram Protocol)
- application services, such as:

- TELNET (Teletype Network)
- FTP (File Transfer Protocol)
- SMTP (Simple Mail Transfer Protocol)

The lower layers of the Internet suite are generally referred to as "subnetworks" and correspond to the two lower layers (physical and link) of the OSI model. Ethernet, a LAN protocol, has traditionally been the most commonly used subnetwork with TCP/IP, but many others are possible.

The use of X.25, normally in WANs, shows an interesting aspect of what happens when protocols are mixed: There are two implementations of the network layer (layer 3). This is because X.25 covers all three lower layers and IP is a layer 3 protocol. This means that there are two implementations, IP and X.25, which are concerned with addressing and routing packets through the network (see "Naming, Addressing, Routing" on page 100).

Even though it would be technically more efficient to remove this redundancy, it is very practical to keep it. All three layers of X.25 are available as a complete service in both public and private networks, so it would be difficult to remove one layer. The IP layer is common to all Internet implementations, so it can't be changed without changing all partners, which would also include all those not using X.25.

In fact, IP is the great common denominator in all parts of the Internet; every node in the network is known by its IP address. The other component, ICMP (Internet Control Message Protocol), is used only for control messages, and not for transporting data.

The transport layer includes two alternatives, TCP (Transmission Control Protocol), a connection-oriented protocol, and UDP (User Datagram Protocol), a connectionless protocol, as well as other, less frequently used protocols.

This structure also shows another aspect of protocol layering: TCP/IP consists of a connection-oriented protocol (TCP) on top of a connectionless one (IP). From the point of view of the internal workings of the network, the connectionless aspects are dominant: IP addresses packets individually and is free to discard them in congestion situations. From the point of view of the applications, the connection-oriented aspects are dominant: TCP requires addressing information only for connection establishment, and guarantees delivery of uncorrupted data in its correct sequence.

The traditional Internet application services are TELNET, for terminal access to remote hosts, FTP (File Transfer Protocol), and SMTP (Simple Mail Transfer Protocol). These have been extended greatly in the meantime, as mentioned below.

Figure 21 shows the basic components of NFS (Network File System) along with the corresponding OSI layers [Santifaller, page 140].

OSI layer	NFS component
Application	NFS, MOUNT, NIS, YPBIND, NLM, REX
Presentation	XDR
Session	RPC
Transport	TCP & UDP
Network	IP
Data Link	Ethernet
Physical	

Figure 21. NFS Components

The basic components of NFS are:

- RPC (Remote Procedure Call)
- XDR (External Data Representation)
- application services:
    - NFS (Network File System)
    - MOUNT
    - NIS (Network Information System)
    - YPBIND
    - NLM (Network Lock Manager)
    - REX (Remote Execution Service)

The Sun RPC is one of the most important contributions to progress in distributed computing. It raises the level of APIs for remote access above the transport layer in a manner which is well adapted to certain programming techniques. The concepts involved have been described in the context of processing models (see "Client/Server Computing" on page 27) and DCE [see "DCE RPC (Remote Procedure Call)" on page 90].

Another fundamental contribution of the Sun NFS group of services is the XDR, which is concerned with converting data between different formats used on different machines. In other words, it is an implementation of the presentation layer (OSI layer 6).

The major additions to the application services are NFS, which provides transparent remote access to files, and NIS, a directory service previously known as YP (Yellow Pages).

The Traditional TCP/IP Services

IP (Internet Protocol)

IP is the only protocol used in the network layer (layer 3) of the Internet. As such, it should have little direct relevance to the application program, and will be treated very briefly here. Our primary purpose is to give a brief description of IP addresses, in order to explain some of the debate going on at the moment.

IP is a connectionless protocol, meaning that each message, or packet, contains full addressing information. The IP implementation segments packets as necessary in order to provide the correct sizes for the link layer, but it does not take care of end-to-end error correction or flow control. In fact, messages are transmitted on a "best effort" basis, meaning that they may be discarded due to congestion problems. In the Internet protocol, these things are taken care of in the next higher layer, the transport layer. Internet addressing consists of the following parts:

- subnetwork address (used only in the link layer)
- IP or Internet address (discussed here)
- transport protocol address (specifies whether TCP, UDP, or some other transport protocol is to be used)
- port number (specifies a service within a host, or node)

IP addresses have a fixed length of 32 bits. This stems from the original ARPANet, where 7 bits (a maximum of 128 numbers) were reserved for a network ID and 24 bits (a maximum of about 16 million numbers) for a host ID. At that time, no one imagined that they would ever need more. But now we do need more, illustrating a very common problem in the computer industry (see "Records Are There to Be Broken" on page 8).

Since that original definition, much more has been done with IP addresses. There are class A, B, C, and D addresses, depending on how the available bits are divided up between network and host ID. In addition, the addresses now consist of three parts, network, subnetwork, and host ID, according to a subnetwork routing scheme defined in 1985 [RFC 950]. This means that the address contains routing information as well as a unique identification of the host referred to.

Since the IP address is 32 bits long, it can be thought of as consisting of 4 individual bytes. The normal convention for specifying IP addresses is to write the decimal equivalent of each byte, separated by periods, without leading zeros (dot notation). For example a class C address might be:

192.9.150.202 (dot notation) = C0 09 96 CA (hexadecimal)

In a traditional UNIX implementation of TCP/IP, each IP address corresponds to a "host name", which is a symbolic name used by applications in place of the IP address. The mapping between host names and IP addresses is stored in a file called "/etc/hosts". In large networks, this method is difficult to manage, because it requires updating files on a large number of computers. In many cases, this situation has already been improved by the use of directory services.

One other service that has been defined for IP, but rarely implemented outside of the military community, is security, as specified in [RFC 1108].

IPv6

The newest version of IP is particularly important because it breaks the 32-bit limit on IP addresses. This version was known as IPng (IP next-generation) on the basis of a proposal, but now has been standardized under the name of IPv6 (IP Version 6). The major enhancements contained in it are [Stallings 8/96]:

- **expanded address space:** 128 bits instead of IPv4's 32 bits
- **improved options:** options (for the transport layer) are put in separate headers, making the work easier for routers
- **address autoconfiguration:** provides support for dynamic assignment of addresses
- **resource allocation:** for specialized traffic, such as real-time data
- **security:** authentication and privacy (see "Secure IP" on page 358)

ICMP (Internet Control Message Protocol)

This network protocol (layer 3) is used for sending error messages and testing the network. It has very little direct relevance to applications, except for network management.

One message type worth mentioning here is the "echo" message, which may contain an arbitrary amount of data and is simply sent back to the originator. This is the basis for the very simple but very useful test utility "PING" (Packet Internet Groper), which periodically sends echo messages and reports the results.

Addressing and Routing

Before we leave the lower levels of the Internet, we should take a look at some of the services available for handling addresses and routes.

The SLIP (Serial Line Interface Protocol) is a very simple protocol used for transporting IP information over a serial line (i.e., ITU-TS V.24 or IEEE RS232C). PPP (Point-to-Point Protocol) is a newer and more powerful protocol for serial lines. In contrast with SLIP, PPP also has the ability to define and initiate network-level protocols, thus making it possible to use protocols other than IP. PPP consists of the following parts:

- LCP (Link Control Protocol): This is the link-layer protocol of PPP.

- NCP (Network Control Protocol): This is a way of establishing and configuring a network-layer protocol. A whole family of NCPs has been defined, such as IPCP (IP Control Protocol) for establishing IP communications.

It is generally expected that PPP will gradually replace SLIP. PPP also includes an optional authentication phase and methods for measuring link-level quality of service.

The EGP (External Gateway Protocol) is used for routing IP information over non-IP networks. The RIP (Routing Information Protocol) is used extensively within the Internet for routing between IP nodes.

BOOTP (Bootstrap Protocol) can be used as part of a procedure for initial load (bootstrapping) of a diskless workstation. Actually, BOOTP is used only to request the IP address and other configuration information from a server, based on the Ethernet or LAN address of the station. After this, if the system is also to be loaded from a server, this is generally done via TFTP (Trivial File Transfer Protocol).

The DHCP (Dynamic Host Configuration Protocol) is a new standard which makes it easier to dynamically configure IP nets. The DHCP server manages a pool of IP addresses and assigns them to hosts on request (a "lease" with a set expiration date). DHCP was developed with the help of Microsoft, and the first implementation of it is in Windows. One important shortcoming of today's DHCP is the lack of a method for synchronizing multiple DHCP servers.

TCP (Transmission Control Protocol)

This transport (layer 4) protocol is certainly the most important one within the Internet, and is being used more and more in other networks. Since it is almost invariably used in conjunction with IP, the two of them are referred to together, in the form TCP/IP.

The basic services of TCP can be summarized as follows:

- connection-oriented transfer
- full-duplex transmission
- error recovery, from
    - corruption
    - sequence error
    - loss
    - duplication
- flow control
- priority transfer (urgent data)
- addressing and multiplexing (port numbers)
- stream-oriented API

Most of these services apply to most transport-layer protocols, including the OSI TP4 (transport class 4), which shows the high degree of de facto standardization at this level.

One special characteristic of TCP is the stream-oriented transfer, which means that the user data is treated as a continuous stream of bytes, and not as individual blocks. Thus, the receiver has no way of knowing where the sender finished one block (or segment) and started the next. This structure is basically the same as the file structure used in UNIX systems (as well as MS-DOS, Windows and OS/2), and is also used in pipes (see "Pipes" on page 39).

The priority mechanism of TCP is also a bit different from others. Expedited transfer, as used in OSI or SNA, generally means that the data is to be transferred with higher priority than normal data. The TCP "urgent data" is transported with the same priority (i.e., without changing the sequence of data), but then the receiver is notified of the presence of urgent data and given a pointer to where it starts, so that the preceding normal data can be skipped or discarded.

The addresses of TCP users are called "port numbers" and are 16 bits long (for a maximum of 65,536 different numbers). Each host can define its own set of port numbers, but there are some conventions. In particular, some numbers are reserved for standard services. A few examples of these "well-known port numbers" are:

- FTP   21
- TELNET   23
- SMTP   25
- rlogin   513

In a traditional UNIX implementation of TCP/IP, each port number corresponds to a "service name", which is a symbolic name used by applications in place of the port number. The mapping between host names and IP addresses is stored in a file called "/etc/services". In large networks, this method is difficult to manage, because it requires updating files on a large number of computers. In many cases, this situation has already been improved by the use of directory services.

In order to address a service in a TCP/IP network, it is necessary to specify both the host and service names, or, equivalently, the IP address and the port number. In total, considering the parts, the IP address consists of:

- network number
- (optionally) subnetwork number
- host ID
- port number

All together, this address is called a "socket address". Similarly, the TCP/IP API (Application Programming Interface) defined within the Berkeley version of UNIX is called the sockets interface, or "Berkeley Sockets".

UDP (User Datagram Protocol)

Along with the connection-oriented TCP, the traditional Internet protocol suite has a connectionless transport protocol, called UDP (User Datagram Protocol). "Datagram" is a name typically used for packets transferred within a connectionless protocol. Each datagram is addressed and transferred independently of all others.

UDP is much simpler than TCP and less well known, but still widely used. For example, it is the basis for the very popular SNMP (Simple Network Management Protocol) and for Sun RPC. The basic services of UDP can be summarized as follows:

- connectionless transfer
- limited error detection (corruption, but not loss, duplication, or sequence error)
- addressing (port numbers)

Clearly, UDP is as limited as it is simple, since it does not prevent loss or duplication of messages, nor out-of-sequence delivery.

The port numbers used for addressing in UDP have the same format as TCP port numbers, but are separate. For example, the port number 514 refers to the "rsh" service in TCP, and to the "rwho" service in UDP.

RTP (Real-Time Transport Protocol)

As discussed in "Chapter 11. Lower Layers", packet-switching techniques, such as TCP/IP, are optimized for data traffic, and circuit-switching techniques, such as the telephone network, provide good support for real-time applications. In order to combine the best of both worlds, work is being done in a number of areas, such as ATM and iso-Ethernet. Within the Internet protocol suite, an important development is RTP (Real-Time Transport Protocol) [Estrin and Casner]. RTP is defined in RFC 1889, and RFC 1890 is a profile for carrying audio and video over RTP.

The RTP headers contain information which can be used to synchronize time between multiple applications and ensure correct sequence of messages. Another part of RTP, the RTCP (Real-Time Control Protocol), gives feedback on the quality of service of real-time traffic. In addition, an emerging standard RSVP (Resource Reservation Protocol) will make it possible to reserve resources in routers and other devices, in order to ensure more than just "best effort" data delivery.

Another important basis for multimedia applications is multicasting, which makes it possible to send a data stream simultaneously to multiple recipients. This feature is important for audio and videoconferencing as well as broadcast transmission. IP multicasting was defined in RFC 1112, and is controlled by the IGMP (Internet Group Management Protocol), which allows users to sign up to dynamically allocated group addresses (class D addresses).

RTP operates on top of IP and can be used along with other protocols, such as TCP and UDP, putting it into the transport layer. On the other hand, it is intended for use directly by the application, meaning that session and presentation layers will not be put on top of it. In summary, the services of RTP are:

- real-time stream transmission
- time synchronization
- sequence control
- multicasting

TELNET (Teletype Network)

As soon as a number of computers are connected within a network, a natural wish is to be able to work on a remote computer as if it were the one next to you, thus making your terminal into a kind of window to all other machines. This is what TELNET offers, a service similar to "rlogin" (see "The Berkeley r-Utilities" on page 142).

TELNET is a simple protocol which implements a remote login. In order to use it, you type the command "telnet", enter the name of the remote host, and then go through a normal login procedure. Then your terminal session runs on the remote computer. Its services can be summarized as:

- remote login
- character data (no graphics)
- (limited) data conversion

The services of TELNET make it much like a presentation-layer protocol. The data formats and conversions available are specified in terms of the NVT (Network Virtual Terminal), which is the generalized or generic form of the terminal's capabilities.

FTP (File Transfer Protocol)

Another way to access a remote computer is to transfer data to or from it in the form of files. This is the primary service of FTP, which runs as part of a normal terminal session (i.e., in foreground) and transfers files directly without using a spooling system. FTP is run similarly to TELNET, including the specification of login parameters. The most important services of FTP are as follows:

- file actions
    - send
    - receive
    - delete
    - rename
- directory actions
    - change current directory
    - create

- delete
- file format
  - text: only text characters and newline are allowed, but they are converted as necessary
  - binary: transparent data transfer, without conversion

FTP is implemented on top of TCP, so that it doesn't need additional mechanisms for ensuring data integrity. It uses TELNET NVT as a basis for text-mode transfer. One service which FTP lacks is a checkpoint/restart facility, i.e., the ability to restart the transmission of a long file from somewhere other than the beginning.

A close relative of FTP is TFTP (Trivial File Transfer Protocol). It is based on UDP instead of TCP, so it has its own methods for ensuring data integrity. Like FTP, TFTP also supports text and binary data transfer, but is otherwise more limited. Since it requires less protocol support, it is sometimes used in situations where resources are very limited, such as very small machines or for remote loading of the software which is needed to support full TCP/IP.

SMTP (Simple Mail Transfer Protocol)

The last two services described above operate in a synchronous manner, meaning that the user has to wait until things are finished before going on to the next step. In contrast, it is often useful to be able to send a message and have it stored until the recipient picks it up. This is the essential idea of electronic mail, supported by a protocol such as SMTP, which is certainly one of the most widely used TCP/IP applications.

The implementation of SMTP is similar to that of FTP, but supports only text mode transfer. Addressing is based on DNS (Domain Name Service). Its basic services are:

- sending messages
- text format: only text characters and newline are allowed, but they are converted as necessary

The complete message consists of an envelope, or header, and the contents. The header is normally created by the SMTP application, so the user doesn't have to worry about it. However, it is interesting to take a look at it, since it shows us what SMTP can do with its messages. The header consists of lines of the form:

    keyword: value

The possible keywords are:

    to   primary recipients
    cc   secondary recipients

<pre>
from   sender
reply-to   destination for responses, added by originator
return-path   address and route back to originator, added by destination system
subject   summary, provided by originating user.
</pre>

The addresses used in the header have the form "local-part@domain-name", and the SMTP application uses DNS to determine the correct IP address. For example, my mail address at Microsoft is:

tligon@microsoft.com

Here, "tligon" is my ID within the local mail system, and "microsoft.com" is the name of the mail domain in the Internet.

Some other things needed by an electronic mail system are not part of the SMTP protocol, but part of other programs which use it. These services include:

- queuing outbound messages
- retrying the transfer if the receiving system was not immediately available
- storing inbound messages
- providing for configuration of names and aliases
- providing a user interface for sending and reading mail

Originally, SMTP-based e-mail systems were implemented on UNIX machines, and all users accessed the system directly via a locally attached terminal. Since then, the standard has been implemented on a large variety of machines, and there are many ways of accessing the system where the mail is stored (referred to as the post office). One way of accessing the post office from another machine, such as a PC, is via the POP (Post Office Protocol), also known as POP3 (POP Version 3).

The Berkeley r-Utilities

The original integration of TCP/IP into UNIX was done at the University of California at Berkeley, and many of the results of that work are still in use today. This also had the effect of making TCP/IP more readily available, and played an important role in making it successful. In addition to putting the existing TCP/IP services into UNIX, the Berkeley team added some new ones, all of them "remote" versions of standard UNIX commands. Their names are the same as those of the local commands, but prefixed with an "r".

One of the annoying aspects of the older commands, such as TELNET and FTP, is that it is necessary to type in the login parameters "user-id" and "password" each time they are used. This also means keeping track of this information for each remote machine which is to be accessed by these commands. The solution to this problem is sometimes referred to as "single sign-on", and has since been implemented with varying degrees of security on a number of systems (see "Chapter 25. Security" on page 293).

The Berkeley implementation is based on a few tables which are stored (and managed) on each machine which is used as a server for the r-utilities. Requests from clients are considered trustworthy if they have a port number between 1 and 1023. They include the originator's user-id, which is checked against the tables, which in turn supply the information necessary for the login on the server. The common r-utilities, all of which support this "single sign-on" mechanism, are:

- **rlogin (remote login):** implements a terminal session on a remote machine, similar to telnet.
- **rcp (remote copy):** copies files between any participating machines. In contrast to ftp, rcp supports parameters such as "-r", which copies subdirectories as well.
- **rsh (remote shell):** makes it possible to execute individual commands on a remote machine.
- **rexec:** is similar to rsh, but with better security, since it transfers an encrypted password instead of relying on the server's tables.
- **ruptime:** displays a list of all active nodes.
- **rwho:** displays a list of all active users.

DNS (Domain Name Service)

As mentioned under "IP (Internet Protocol)" on page 135, administration of tables for matching names and IP addresses (i.e., "/etc/hosts" files) on a large number of nodes can be a tedious and error-prone task. The way to improve this is to install a directory service. The DNS (Domain Name Service) is a directory service created by the University of California at Berkeley for administration of names for IP addresses, port numbers, mailboxes, and so forth. Each name consists of a string of "domain" names, which are ordered in a simple naming tree. The top level, or TLD (Top-Level Domain), is limited to a certain set of values, including the following:

- **ARPA:** for Internet internal usage
- **COM:** for commercial organizations
- **EDU:** for schools and universities in the U.S.
- **GOV:** for government organizations
- **MIL:** for the U.S. Military (originator of ARPANet and Internet)
- **ORG:** for general organizations
- **"country code":** for countries outside the U.S.

For example, you might reach me at ThomasSLigon@compuserve.com or at tligon@microsoft.com ("tligon" is my user-id at Microsoft, which is registered as a commercial organization within the Internet in the U.S.).

When an application program knows the name of its partner, but not the address, it can get the address by making a query to the directory service. The API for interrogating the DNS is generally the same as the one used with the older built-in files, so conversion is easy. In order to improve efficiency, the application does not access the directory service directly, but via an intermediary called a "resolver" (because it resolves the name, yielding an address, a process also referred to as "name resolution").

The DNS implementation from Berkeley is called BIND (Berkeley Internet Name Domain Server). It includes a resolver which is capable of caching information in order to avoid unnecessary requests, and of performing recursive queries, in which the information returned by an unsuccessful query is used to perform further searches.

Today's DNS is an example of "static configuration": The correlation between names and IP addresses is contained in static, predefined tables. This is in conflict with the dynamic allocation of IP addresses used in DHCP. However, the IETF is working on a newer version of DNS that will support "dynamic configuration".

The NFS Services

The first version of NFS was released by Sun Microsystems in 1984, and included VFS (Virtual File System) and YP (Yellow Pages), which was later to become known as NIS (Network Information System). Later versions included file locking, support for diskless workstations, named pipes, and encryption. As such, it provides many of the functions expected of a NOS (Network Operating System).

Most NFS specifications have been published as RFCs, making them public-domain knowledge. This policy of openness has contributed greatly to the success of NFS, and has helped sales of Sun hardware, by making the functions open and interoperable. By 1989, NFS had been ported to a large number of operating systems and had been licensed by 260 vendors. Other vendors have implemented NFS on the basis of the specifications, and sell it without license to Sun. It is also available as an integral part of many UNIX systems, and as an add-on to many others.

In addition to the remote file access provided by NFS, the product includes a communications API [RPC (Remote Procedure Call)] at a higher level than the transport-layer TCP, and a method for converting data formats [XDR (External Data Representation)].

Sun RPC (Remote Procedure Call)

The basic concept of RPC and a programming interface was already defined in the section on DCE RPC [see "DCE RPC (Remote Procedure Call)" on page 90]. One of the earlier RPC implementations which became successful was contributed by Sun

Microsystems. In order to distinguish it from other RPC implementations, it is often referred to as "Sun RPC", but it is available on many other systems as well.

Sun RPC runs on top of either TCP or UDP, with the same basic services, but a few differences. In the UDP implementation, the length of parameters is limited to the length of a UDP datagram, which is often 2K to 8K. Also, since UDP does not guarantee delivery, some additional work is done by RPC, but the effectiveness of this may depend on the implementation of the server. The TCP implementation also allows a method called "batching", in which the client sends a number of requests before waiting for a reply from the server. The basic services provided by Sun RPC are:

- synchronous API
- addressing: each call uses 3 numbers (program, procedure, and version number) to identify the recipient
- directory: port mapper service
- security: the RPC protocol contains fields that can be used for authentication. The following two variants are in use:
  - NFS uses these fields for access control based on UNIX user-IDs.
  - Secure NFS uses an authentication mechanism which is encrypted by the DES algorithm.

The addressing of numerous services (remote procedures) via their numbers can be a tedious job. Worse yet, it could use up all the available port numbers. In order to solve these problems, a service called the "port mapper" has been defined. It works much like any other directory service: The application program gives it a name and gets back the necessary numbers, which it then uses for the subsequent RPC calls.

Unfortunately, the port mapper works only within an individual system, i.e., only after the machine the service is installed on is known. NIS would theoretically be a better solution, but it is used only for NFS, not for RPC.

Much like DCE RPC, Sun RPC contains its own language for specifying remote calls, and a compiler, called "rpcgen", which converts this into the C language.

XDR (External Data Representation)

The purpose of XDR is to enable communication between machines which have different data representations, but without the need for the application to be aware of the partner's data format. As such, it is an example of the OSI presentation layer (see "The Presentation Layer" on page 112).

Much like ASN.1, XDR has its own language for defining data structures (similar to C), and there are compilers for converting this to the internal data representation of the machine. In contrast with OSI ASN.1, which uses an "explicit format" for transferring data, in which each field is preceded by an indication of its type, XDR uses an "implicit format". This is simply a definition of the format of all possible data types to be transferred. Each system that communicates via XDR is then responsible for converting the data between XDR and its own internal format.

As a result of this definition, XDR does not require any protocol information. This makes it very efficient on machines whose internal representation is close to XDR, and less efficient when both partners use a non-XDR format. The service of XDR is:

- data conversion (presentation)

NFS (Network File System)

As the name says, NFS is a network, or remote, file system. The users, or clients, can access files stored on a remote file server. Using the term "distributed file system" for this would be exaggerated, since we are dealing only with distributed access, not with individual files distributed over multiple machines.

The files supported by NFS are basically the UNIX type of file, i.e., byte streams with an exact length. Such things as ISAM (Index Sequential Access Method) are not included. This makes NFS suitable for UNIX, MS-DOS, and related systems, so when it is implemented on a system such as MVS, this generally involves a new file system as well as a remote access method.

NFS does not assume that the underlying protocol is reliable. In fact, its design takes care to avoid problems of inconsistency caused by system crashes and subsequent restarts. This is done on the basis of RPC, which generally runs on top of UDP, and which in itself is not reliable.

The NFS solution to this is a "connectionless" or "stateless" file-access protocol, in which the server does not keep any information about the state of the client: There are no "open" or "close" calls. As a result, there is no connection which can keep a state, such as the current position within the file, and so "read" and "write" operations must specify the current position, instead of assuming it to be known. This information is stored in the NFS client.

Even though it is not considered a connection-oriented protocol, NFS does aim at being reliable. So, like any other system that tries to implement a reliable service on top of an unreliable (connectionless) one, it needs to take care of retries and time-outs; and in order to be efficient, it needs to cache information, such as the current directory of the remote system, as well as messages awaiting acknowledgment. One effect of this is that it uses time-out values which are a typical area for tuning: Too short means unnecessary load, and too long means unnecessary delays. The basic services of NFS are:

- stateless (connectionless) remote file access
- file functions
  - create
  - remove (delete)

- - rename
  - read
  - write
- file attribute functions
  - get
  - set
- directory functions
  - make
  - remove
  - read
- link functions
  - create link
  - create symbolic link
- security
  - NFS: comparable to standard UNIX
  - secure NFS: enhanced by DES encryption

In addition to access to normal UNIX files, NFS provides some support for two special file types, devices and named pipes. However, these files are available only on the local machine. This is not a severe restriction, since the function of named pipes is very similar to that of the socket interface to TCP, i.e., a simple stream interface.

In order to make file access transparent in the sense that the application can access local and remote files in the same way, it is necessary to add another layer on top of both. In most UNIX systems this layer is called VFS (Virtual File System), and in AT&T System V it is called FSS (File System Switch). Both of these provide uniform access to the UFS (UNIX File System), NFS, and sometimes other file systems.

This uniform treatment of different file systems has its limitation, due especially to the fact that UFS file access is connection-oriented (with open and close), whereas NFS is connectionless (i.e., stateless, without open and close). Most differences occur when changes, including deletion, renaming, or attribute modification, are made to an open file. The time-controlled caching and the blocking functions of NFS can also cause inconsistencies.

MOUNT

In order to access the files on a remote system (file server), the client needs some way of naming them. This is not part of NFS, but an extra service called "mount". From the user's point of view, "mounting" a file system means adding a directory of a remote file server to the local file system.

When an NFS client "mounts" a file system, it requests the mount service for the information necessary for accessing the files in that file system. After that, it can access the files via NFS with no further help from the mount server, which may be implemented on a different machine. In addition to this, the mount server keeps track of which file systems have been mounted by which clients. This information can become inconsistent as a result of failure of the client, and is often cleaned up with the help of broadcast messages during system startup. The services offered by MOUNT are:

- mount a file system (in read-write or read-only mode)
- unmount a previously mounted file system
- unmount all previously mounted file systems
- dump: return a list of all previously mounted file systems
- export: return a list of all exported file systems

Note that, since the name of the file system and its position in the local system's directory are determined by the mount operation, these names may be different on each client. In other words, two different clients may have two different names for the same file. In contrast with this, the DCE DFS uses a globally unique name for all files, determined by its global directory service.

In addition, MOUNT cannot be used transitively. In other words, files which have been mounted in the server are not visible to the client when it mounts a file system from the server. This also prevents loops in the directory structure.

NIS (Network Information System)

The original NFS implementation contained a service called YP (Yellow Pages), which, just like its paper cousin, is a directory, but, unlike its cousin, is a distributed electronic directory service based on RPC. In the meantime, YP has been renamed NIS (Network Information System). As a result of this development, many of the commands and internal names used by NIS begin with the prefix "yp". The primary use of NIS is to provide a centralized method for storing information such as user's names, which is more easily managed and more likely to be consistent than if it were stored on each individual machine.

NIS is a distributed database system used for sharing information such as that normally contained in the UNIX configuration files "/etc/passwd", "/etc/group", and "/etc/hosts". The protocol used in accessing NIS is called YPBIND. NIS consists of the following components:

- **NIS master server:** contains databases (called "maps") of information such as host names and passwords.
- **NIS slave server:** can be used to reduce the load on the master server. Its contents are controlled by the master server.
- **NIS clients:** the users of the information.

Each slave server contains a replica of a part of the directory applicable to a particular area, called a "domain". The tables, or "maps", stored by NIS are fairly simple: Normally an NIS request contains a name, such as the name of an IP "host", and NIS returns a string, in this case identical to the corresponding line of the file "/etc/hosts", which contains that host's IP address. By virtue of this simple structure, NIS can be used in place of the corresponding local files.

As such, NIS is a step forward in comparison to managing this information locally on each machine. On the other hand, this simple extension of local files is not sufficient for implementing a global directory with good security which is also flexible enough to handle other types of data. The next step of improvement can be seen in the directory and security services of OSF DCE (see "Directory" on page 87) or in the OSI Directory (X.500) (see "Chapter 18. Directories" on page 204).

Another disadvantage to using a directory system is the dependence on the directory server: When it fails, so do most applications. This situation can be improved by increasing the operational security of the server, and by increasing the redundancy in the storage of information, i.e., the number of replicas.

Locking

In a situation where multiple clients can access the same resources, in this case files, there is a need to prevent simultaneous, conflicting operations, such as when one application tries to update a record which another has already deleted. This is generally done by some type of locking mechanism.

Locking is not part of the basic NFS service, but is an additional (and optional) service, since locking is considered to be a contradiction to the stateless protocol used in NFS. The components of this are called KLM (Kernel Lock Manager) and NLM (Network Lock Manager). The situation is made more complex by the fact that not all UNIX variants have the same native locking mechanism. For example, System V supports file and record locking, but Berkeley UNIX does not include record locking.

As a result, the NLM service is an "advisory" locking mechanism, meaning that it has an effect only on those processes which use it to check for the existence of locks. A "mandatory" locking mechanism exists only in implementations which have been embedded in the operating system.

REX (Remote Execution Service)

Much the same as the Berkeley utility "rsh", REX starts a process on a remote host. However, rsh uses the environment variables and files on the server (the remote host). In contrast, REX uses the environment and files of the client (the local host).

The REX service is started by using the command "on", followed by the name of the remote host and the command to be executed. The "on" program communicates with the remote REX service via RPC in order to transport the variables and file data used in the command.

NCS

NCS (Network Computing System) is an implementation of NCA (Network Computing Architecture), created by Apollo Domain, which is now a part of Hewlett-Packard. The basic idea of NCA is one of access to remote objects, which are replicated as necessary. So-called strongly consistent objects are copied often enough to keep them identical; weakly consistent objects may be accessed even when they are not identical.

The NCS services are implemented on top of the Internet protocol UDP/IP as well as the proprietary Domain protocols. All are based on an RPC (Remote Procedure Call) mechanism. The concepts of RPCs were discussed in detail in "DCE RPC (Remote Procedure Call)" on page 90.

The basic services of NCS can be summarized as:

- access to remote objects
- location-independent access
- data conversion

The major components of NCS are:

- RPC: NCS was used as a basis for OSF DCE RPC, so they are quite similar.
- NIDL (Network Interface Definition Language): Language for defining RPCs, similar to OSF DCE IDL.
- NIDL compiler: Available for C and Pascal.
- Location Broker: Used to find information about remote objects. Similar to OSF DCE Directory and CORBA. Consists of:
    - LLB (Local Location Broker)
    - GLB (Global Location Broker)
    - Location Broker Client Agent
- DRM (Data Replication Manager): Keeps track of replicas and propagates changes.

NCS is available and widely used on HP systems. The general trend is expected to be a migration towards OSF DCE and CORBA.

Standards

The basis for standardization of the Internet protocols is the RFC (Request For Comment), which is an article published in electronic form on the Internet. These publications include articles describing problems or methods of operations for the Internet as well as specifications of protocols and services.

Basically, the comments requested by these publications form a review process, which is administered by the IAB (Internet Activities Board), which also decides which RFCs have reached the status of "draft standard" or "standard".

- BOOTP [RFC 951, RFC 1533, and RFC 1542]
- DNS [RFC 1034, RFC 1035, RFC 1101, RFC 1183, and RFC 1348]
- DNS usage [RFC 1032]
- EGP [RFC 827, RFC 888, and RFC 904]
- FTP [RFC 959]
- ICMP [RFC 792 and RFC 950]
- IGMP, IP multicasting [RFC 1112]
- IP [RFC 791 and RFC 1349]
- IPv6 [RFC 1883, RFC 1884, RFC 1885, RFC 1886, and RFC 1887]
- NFS MOUNT [RFC 1094]
- POP3 [RFC 1939]
- PPP [RFC 1540]
- RIP [RFC 1058 and RFC 1388]
- RTP [RFC 1889 and RFC 1890]
- security [RFC 1108]
- SLIP [RFC 1055]
- SMTP [RFC 821]
- Sun RPC [RFC 1057]
- TCP [RFC 793]
- TELNET [RFC 854]
- TFTP [RFC 783 and RFC 1350]
- UDP [RFC 768]
- XDR [RFC 1014]

Trends and Products

In addition to their use in the Internet itself, many protocols from the Internet protocol suite have come into very widespread use within corporate networks. They have been implemented in so many products that it would serve no purpose to mention them here.

Further development of Internet mail, in addition to the move from plain-text SMTP to multimedia MIME, is standardization work on the manipulation of mail. The IMAP (Internet Message Access Protocol) defines commands for retrieving messages and manipulating mailboxes (creating, deleting, renaming, and checking the status). The IMAP draft covers the manipulation of MIME messages, and an auxiliary protocol, IMSP (Internet Mail Support Protocol), allows IMAP to manipulate multiple mailboxes simultaneously.

A new protocol built specially for paging networks is the SNPP (Simple Network Paging Protocol). It is intended for sending messages to conventional alphanumeric pagers, and includes a confirmation mechanism in order to determine whether the message actually arrives at its destination. SNPP covers transmission over wireless networks, and should replace the usage of SMTP for paging devices.

Summary of Part 3

The communications layers present themselves to applications in many different ways. However, the best way is for them not to present themselves at all—but just to be there. For example, the application may access data, call a procedure, or invoke a method of an object, any of which may be located somewhere else, and the communications layers do their work without being noticed.

On the other hand, when the communications layers are visible, they can be seen in the form of the services they offer, such as connections, which support error handling, including protection against loss, duplication, and out-of-sequence delivery. Or we may also see some way of naming or addressing the partner application, and of converting data to its preferred format. And, finally, the application might notice how fast the data is transferred, or how much it is delayed.

Communications systems are generally divided into layers, from the top (application layer) down to the wire (physical layer). One of the best places to split these layers is on top of the fourth, or transport, layer, which supplies reliable end-to-end transmission. The layers above this are application-related services, and those below take care of transport, routing, and error recovery.

The lower layers of LANs and WANs are often optimized to provide good use of a certain type of transmission technology, which, however, is evolving rapidly. In order to adapt to these changes, the lower-layer protocols have themselves evolved from circuit switching to packet switching to cell switching. With the emergence of ATM, they are now on the verge of providing good support for both voice and data over the same lines, both locally and over large distances.

The Internet protocol suite not only is the basis for the Internet itself, but is used in many corporate networks. In addition to TCP/IP, the transport protocol, a large number of services are available, including FTP (File Transfer Protocol), SMTP (Simple Mail Transfer Protocol), NFS (Network File System), DNS (Domain Name System), and NIS (Network Information System).

Part 4. Middleware

Introduction to Part 4

The most important communications services from the point of view of applications are often referred to as "middleware". They bridge the gap between lower and upper layers, between local and remote computers, and between products from different software vendors. Our discussion of middleware begins with those services which are oriented largely towards synchronous processing or the client/server model, and continues to cover the asynchronous model and some additional supporting services.

"Chapter 13. RPC" gives an overview of RPC (Remote Procedure Call) and lists where it has been discussed in other parts of the book. The topic was treated thoroughly in the second part of the book, as part of the discussion of DCE (Distributed Computing Environment). Even though DCE RPC isn't the only RPC in use, it is the most modern one and shows all relevant aspects of the technique.

"Chapter 14. Distributed Transaction Processing" covers those communication protocols which are capable of supporting distributed transactions. This includes "APPC and CPI-C", which treats the most common application-level protocol of IBM's SNA (Systems Network Architecture), and the API which has been defined both for APPC (Advanced Program-to-Program Communication) and for OSI TP (OSI Transaction Processing).

"Chapter 15. Remote SQL" covers the techniques generally used for remote access to relational databases. In particular, the sections on IBM's DRDA (Distributed Relational Database Architecture) and the OSI RDA (Remote Database Access) discuss some of the important protocols, and the section on Microsoft's ODBC (Open Database Connectivity) shows how the standard SQL CLI (Call-Level Interface) has been combined with existing protocols to make a complete database-connectivity solution.

"Chapter 16. Distributed Objects" can be thought of as the object-oriented extension of RPC. However, in addition to the basic infrastructure defined in the CORBA (Common Object Request Broker Architecture) specification, the OMG (Object Management Group) has continued to define additional services in the form of objects that now include techniques such as distributed transaction processing, so they may grow to encompass (or provide an interface to) all processing models. Similarly, Microsoft's ActiveX, formerly known as OLE (Object Linking and Embedding), which provides much of the same functionality as the OMG specifications, is covered in this chapter.

"Chapter 17. Messaging and File Transfer" gives an introduction to different kinds of messaging services and how they can be used as a basis for distributed applications. It discusses a few different protocols and products, including remote queuing and mail. "Message Queuing" presents IBM's Message Queuing protocol and some similar products used for the asynchronous processing model. This is followed by "Electronic Mail" and "X.400", which present the topics of electronic mail and one particularly important standard for it.

"Chapter 18. Directories" is an introduction to directory services based on the X.500 standard. Directories are not a communications service as such, but are extremely important for managing communications systems, and it is becoming increasingly necessary to look for standards and ways of making different products work together.

"Chapter 19. EDI" discusses the topic of electronic data interchange based on the UN EDIFACT and ANSI X12 standards. These standards can be thought of as primarily a matter of defining data formats, and can be used in conjunction with most of the communications protocols presented above.

Within APE, there has never been any real agreement concerning the ownership of middleware. In practice, some parts have grown out of communications services provided by birds, and other parts have emerged as reusable application components produced by monkeys. The problem has been made worse by the fact that the components in question are very much a moving target: Today's middleware may be part of tomorrow's operating system, or may disappear as fast as it has appeared.

Chapter 13. RPC

Since procedure calls are so widely used in programming languages, it seems like a natural and very useful thing just to extend the reach of this method so that it can be used over a network. This is the task of RPCs (Remote Procedure Calls), which are, in fact, in very widespread use. In previous parts of this book, we have already had a good introduction to RPC, and it will be mentioned a few times more before we are finished, so the purpose of this chapter is to give an overview of what it available, and to discuss when RPC is adequate and when it isn't.

The basic idea of a request-response method of remote access was introduced in the chapter on processing models (see "Client/Server Computing" on page 27). Later, the structure of a typical RPC solution was explained as part of the chapter on OSF DCE [see "DCE RPC (Remote Procedure Call)" on page 90]. As part of the Internet protocol suite, the original Sun RPC implementation, used in Sun NFS, was briefly discussed [see "Sun RPC (Remote Procedure Call)" on page 144].

Among the higher-level protocols which can run on top of RPC, we will have a look at CORBA and ActiveX (see "Chapter 16. Distributed Objects" on page 175). In addition to this, there is also an extension of RPC which includes transaction-synchronization controls (see "TxRPC" on page 162).

With all of these good examples of RPC being used either directly by the application or indirectly, as part of a higher-level protocol, does this mean we should just use RPC for everything? Perhaps the most important reason not to is the difference between synchronous and asynchronous processing, something which is one of the most basic differences between communications services, and which is discussed often in this book.

On the other hand, consider the case where a program does use a synchronous model, and has been structured well into subprograms or procedures. In this situation, there is a very attractive idea that we could make a distributed version of the program just by replacing some of the local procedure calls by remote ones. However, this isn't so easy either. One reason for this is simply the amount of data passed at a particular interface, as compared with the communications capacity available on the network. This will be discussed in more detail in a chapter that describes the different places where the communications part can be inserted into a program (see "Chapter 27. Distribution Models" on page 318).

A number of other examples of where RPC is not applicable are discussed in a textbook on distributed operating systems [Tanenbaum 1995, page 95]. Some of these are:

- **global variables:** are not passed by RPC
- **weakly typed languages:** do not supply enough information to RPC
- **passing a pointer:** has no meaning on another machine
- **pipelines:** do not have the necessary client/server relationship

As an example of weakly typed languages, consider the "printf" statement in C. The first parameter in this call is a "format string", which contains information about how the other parameters are to be handled, and in particular what data types they have. As a result, the types of the other parameters are unknown at compile time, it is impossible to define an IDL, and there is no way for the stub to know how much data to transfer for each parameter (without containing all of the logic of the "printf" statement itself). Even though "printf" was a very popular call in C programs, it is no longer state of the art, and C++ provides us with strongly typed ways of achieving the same goal.

As an example of a pipe, consider the MS-DOS command "dir | sort" or the UNIX command "ls -l | sort". In this case, which part should be the client and which the server? Will this work when three programs are chained together? And what happens when the same programs are used in a different constellation? The lesson to be learned here is that client/server relationships and pipes have a different logical structure, i.e., they are two different kinds of animals.

In summary, RPC is one of the most useful methods for making distributed systems, but it is not good for all situations.

Services

The primary services to be looked for in RPC products are listed below.

- synchronous API
- data marshaling
- data conversion
- addressing
    - location-dependent, or
    - location-independent
- directory (to support addressing and management)
- security
    - authentication of client
    - authentication of server
    - encryption (confidentiality)

Standards

The most widely used standards for RPC are:

- Sun RPC [RFC 1057]
- DCE RPC

Trends and Products

One of the most important developments in RPC is Sun RPC, which is used in Sun NFS (Network File System). OSF DCE RPC, which was developed later, improved on this significantly, and includes built-in directory and security services. As a result, it has become the standard by which RPCs are measured, even when they are not based on the OSF code.

A few of the products which contain RPC implementations are listed here.

- HP Apollo NCS (Network Computing Architecture)
- Microsoft RPC
- OSF DCE RPC
- SunSoft ONC (Open Network Computing) RPC

Chapter 14. Distributed Transaction Processing

In order to implement distributed transactions, it is necessary to have a communications protocol which supports a two-phase commit. Three such protocols are APPC, which is also a general-purpose communications protocol, OSI TP, which supplies the commit control to be used with other data transfer protocols, and TxRPC, which is RPC enhanced by TP.

APPC and CPI-C

When IBM's SNA was announced in 1974, a number of LU (logical unit) types were defined, mainly to accommodate the existing protocols for terminals and printers of type IBM 3270. These LU types thus defined the higher-level protocols of SNA, including the device-specific details of terminal traffic [IBM GC20-1868-02].

For program-to-program communication, LU type 0 was defined, which allowed programs to communicate using any of a variety of variants of SNA. Two particularly important variants are the protocols used by CICS and IMS to communicate with RJE (Remote Job Entry) stations: CICS/3790 Full Function Logical Unit [IBM SC33-0236-00] and the IMS SLU Type P [IBM SC26-4186-01]. One of the main disadvantages of LU 0 has been that each application can define its own variant: this means that it does not provide any general basis for interoperability between programs.

Since there was no clear standard for program-to-program communication in SNA, many applications used LU 2, or 3270 terminal protocol, for all communications, including on-line processing and file transfer. This has a number of disadvantages:

- It is necessary to include 3270 control sequences in the data stream.
- Only printable characters are allowed.
- All data is in clear text (no encryption).

Later, LU type 6 was defined for program-to-program communication, and LU type 6.1 was defined for communication between CICS transactions. LU 6.1 includes general communications methods as well as transaction control.

The next version, LU 6.2, was defined by IBM in 1982 and was intended as a universal program-to-program communications protocol for all applications. The protocol is defined in [IBM SC30-3269-03], and the "protocol boundary" (the API, or services) in [IBM GC30-3084-03].

APPC (or LU 6.2) is a connection-oriented protocol, and the connections are called "conversations". They are implemented on top of SNA sessions, and in fact define a way of pooling and reusing sessions in order to improve performance, a technique frequently used in TP monitors. Due to its origin in the TP world of CICS, APPC also includes a commit protocol, defined by the following levels of support (synclevel, or synchronization level): none, commit (one-phase commit), and syncpoint (two-phase commit).

The name APPC (Advanced Program-to-Program Communication) has been the source of considerable confusion: Some sources define it as a synonym for LU 6.2, others as the API for LU 6.2, and yet others as a marketing name for LU 6.2 products. For most purposes, you can choose whichever version you prefer.

In 1987, IBM defined a new version of the API for APPC, called CPI-C (Common Programming Interface for Communications), as part of SAA (Systems Application Architecture) [IBM SC26-4399-04]. The functionality of this API is basically the same as that of APPC, so in that sense it isn't a higher-level interface, but it does have some real advantages:

- CPI-C is independent of SNA (such things as LU names and Logmode names are hidden in profiles).
- CPI-C is more precisely defined than APPC (so that applications that use it are more easily ported).

As a result of this, in 1990, the X/Open group was able to accept CPI-C as a standard interface for use with both LU 6.2 and OSI Distributed Transaction Processing protocol [X/Open C419].

As part of its Networking Blueprint [IBM GC31-7057-00], IBM has announced plans to base the CPI-C interface, which it refers to as "conversation", on both APPC and OSI TP, and these on its CTS (Common Transport Semantics), making it available on SNA, TCP/IP, and OSI networks.

The LU 6.2 protocol has been used as the basis for other, higher-level protocols, including the following:

- DRDA (Distributed Relational Database Architecture)
- SNA/DS (SNA Distribution Services)
- SNA/FS (SNA File Services)
- SNA/MS (SNA Management Services)

In summary, APPC is a connection-oriented protocol which also includes a two-phase commit, making it adequate for remote transaction processing.

OSI TP

The de jure international standard for distributed transaction processing is OSI TP (OSI Transaction Processing) [ISO/IEC 10026].

The basic component of an OSI TP system is called a TPSU (Transaction Processing Service User). A distributed transaction can span multiple TPSUs (at multiple locations), and these can be nested. The result is a "transaction tree", with the initiator of the global transaction at the top, i.e., at the root of the tree.

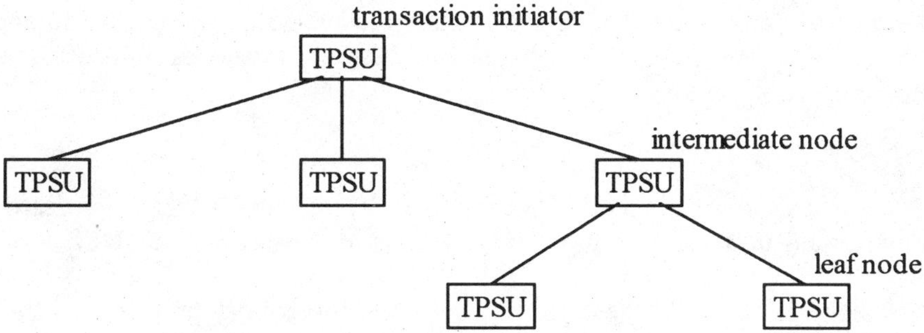

Figure 22. OSI TP Transaction Tree

OSI TP is a connection-oriented protocol, and the connections between TPSU instances are called "dialogues". Each dialogue can be established with a coordination level of either "none" or "commitment", and can span one or more transactions. Also, dialogues make use of the application-level connection, or association. Here, there is no predefined correlation; in other words, a dialogue can span an association boundary and vice versa. These dialogues can have either "shared control", in which both partners can transmit simultaneously, or "polarized control", in which they must alternate. This is basically the same concept as "duplex" and "half duplex", except that dialogues are concerned with only transmitting control elements, and not data. In addition, there are also two forms of synchronization: "handshake", which provides for a confirmation, and "commit", which provides for a full two-phase commit protocol.

All of this is very similar to LU 6.2, where "conversations" are established between "transaction programs" and are assigned a synchronization level of "none", "confirm" (one-phase commit), or "syncpoint" (two-phase commit). One difference, however, is that a conversation cannot exist longer than its underlying SNA session. Another difference is that OSI TP covers only distributed transaction control, whereas LU 6.2 is a general-purpose communication protocol which also includes data transmission. In the framework of OSI TP, this task is generally delegated to one of the following application-level OSI protocols:

- ROSE (Remote Operation Service)
- RDA (Remote Database Access).

In addition to the normal commit protocol, which is sufficient for covering cases in which failures of communication or database subsystems are visible to the TPSU, there are a number of refinements for other error situations, such as when a complete system crashes, or when a system hangs and doesn't respond. In general, error recovery is the task of the superior node in the transaction tree, and is carried out with the help of the "restart" instruction. However, if a subordinate node doesn't receive any notification from a superior for an extended period of time, the subordinate may need to apply a "heuristic" commitment or rollback, based on a best effort decision, in order to avoid locking resources indefinitely.

TxRPC

TxRPC (Transactional Remote Procedure Call) is an X/Open standard for communications in transaction-processing systems. It is based on OSF DCE RPC and OSI TP.

TxRPC is based on the RTI (Remote Task Invocation) protocol which DEC submitted to X/Open. RTI was developed by an industry consortium called MIA (Multivendor Integration Architecture), which consisted of NTT (Nippon Telegraph and Telephone), NTT Data, DEC, Fujitsu, Hitachi, IBM, and NEC and was set up to provide applications for NTT. RTI runs over OSI, TCP/IP, and LU 6.2.

Services

The primary services of remote TP can be summarized as follows.

- synchronous API
- remote transaction synchronization
    - ACID properties
    - one-phase commit
    - two-phase commit
- nested transactions
- heuristic commitment and rollback
- restart and recovery
- data-transmission features

One service missing in APPC is data conversion, or presentation. In fact, this is missing entirely in SNA, which really has no presentation layer. The only data conversion commonly available is a standard EBCDIC-ASCII translation.

The closest APPC comes to a presentation layer is the concept of "mapped conversations". When this option is used, each data record transmitted is delimited by a "length" and "type" field. The application system can then install routines which perform special processing, including conversion, for each record type. However, this remains within the responsibility of the user, and is not standardized.

Standards

The following list includes the three communications protocols which support remote TP with a two-phase commit protocol. In addition, the CPI-C API is also important.

- APPC [IBM SC30-3269-03 and IBM GC30-3084-03]
- CPI-C [IBM SC26-4399-04 and X/Open C419]
- OSI TP [ISO/IEC 10026]
- TxRPC [X/Open C505]

Trends and Products

APPC has been implemented on practically all IBM platforms, and many of them now support the two-phase commit protocol. It is also included in the offerings of many other vendors and third-party suppliers.

Within the IBM world, it is now possible to operate APPC over TCP/IP via the AnyNet products which implement MPTN. It is yet to be seen to what extent this variant will be supported by other vendors.

TxRPC has been implemented on:

- DEC ACMS TP monitor
- USL TUXEDO
- Transarc Encina

One recent addition to the family of TP monitors is:

- Microsoft Transaction Server

Developed under the code name of "Viper", this product includes DTC (Distributed Transaction Coordinator), which supports a two-phase commit and the XA protocol, and a method for pooling resources in order to achieve high performance. By providing these services from an ActiveX/COM interface, Microsoft intends this product to make many aspects of server programming easier by supporting such features as transaction support, multiple access, locking, and multithreading in a transparent way.

Chapter 15. Remote SQL

In many applications, storage and retrieval of data are very important, to the point where some of them do hardly anything else. Along with simple file systems, the most widely used method for this today is relational databases, and just as widespread is the use of SQL (Structured Query Language) to do it. Although the language has been standardized, there are many variants in use. In fact, SQL can also be used for nonrelational data, but with some limitations.

In order to extend this technique to a distributed environment, the most natural thing to do is to make some form of remote SQL, as most database vendors have done. From the user's point of view, the next step is to try to achieve more standardization, so that applications don't need to be rewritten and adapted every time they are used for a different database or a different communication protocol. And again, as always, there are two important aspects to consider: By standardizing the API (Application Programming Interface) used by the application, we can achieve more application portability, and by standardizing the protocol used, we can achieve more interoperability.

In this chapter, we will have a closer look at one of the more important remote SQL protocols, IBM's DRDA (Distributed Relational Database Architecture), and compare it to the OSI standard RDA (Remote Database Access). Then we will look at the accepted standard remote SQL API, ODBC (Open Database Connectivity), and see how it fits in with different protocols.

Background

Before looking into how SQL can be extended over a network, it will be worthwhile to take a brief look at the former situation, including the forms of SQL which exist and the proprietary solutions for making them network-enabled.

The more traditional form of SQL is referred to as "embedded SQL", meaning that the SQL statements are embedded in another programming language. Two languages are necessary, because SQL is highly specialized for the purpose of data storage and retrieval and does not have all the features needed of a programming language. In other words, it is not "computationally complete". In order to use embedded SQL, first, a SQL precompiler is used, which converts the SQL statements into function calls in the host language. Then the host language is compiled with its own compiler. The SQL-92 standard defines embeddings for seven languages (Ada, C, COBOL, FORTRAN, MUMPS, Pascal, and PL/I).

In one form of embedded SQL, known as "static SQL", all SQL statements are defined when the program is written, i.e., before it is compiled. In comparison, "dynamic SQL" allows SQL statements to be constructed at runtime. In both cases, the programmer may make use of a special data element known as a "cursor", which is a type of index or pointer to the current row of a table. However, since the cursor needs to be declared at compile time, it isn't truly dynamic. This has been corrected by the introduction of "extended dynamic cursors" in another variant of embedded SQL known as "extended dynamic SQL".

In comparison, static SQL is generally easier to program than dynamic SQL. In this respect, what is perhaps more important is that programs written this way are also easier for other people to read and maintain at a later time. In addition, assuming adequate support by the precompiler and DBMS, static SQL can be much more efficient than dynamic SQL. On the other hand, only dynamic SQL provides the flexibility to generate SQL statements on the fly. As a result, static SQL is often used for high-volume, but predefined OLTP (On-Line Transaction Processing), applied to "operational data", and dynamic SQL more for OLAP (On-Line Analytical Processing), applied to "informational data" (see "Distributed Data Storage" on page 40). In particular, some form of dynamic SQL is necessary in order to perform "ad hoc queries", i.e. queries which are not predefined in any way.

Another difference between using static and dynamic SQL involves the use of slow network links, such as the WAN links that often connect the branch offices of a bank to the central office. In an SQL query, an incorrectly formulated statement can easily lead to a flood of responses, for example, when the range of rows in a table is not restricted properly. If this is done on a slow link, it may easily use so much transmission capacity that the communication line is effectively blocked for all other tasks. This is another reason that organizations which have branch offices are often very careful about which type of SQL is used. Along with higher-speed lines, another solution to this problem may be the use of a multilayer application structure (see "Three-Tier Structure" on page 322).

A very popular solution to this problem is the use of "stored procedures", program routines which are automatically started by the DBMS when certain "trigger" conditions are met. This way, important parts of the application logic can be kept close to the data, thus reducing the load on the network. Stored procedures were introduced by Sybase in the 1980s as a vendor-specific enhancement to SQL. In the meantime, many variants have been produced, including some which can use any programming language. The ANSI and ISO SQL committees are also working on this topic, but under the name of PSM (Persistent Stored Module) [Geiger, page 97 and ISO/IEC 9075-4].

For applications which may use more than one database, even if these come from the same vendor, it is necessary to define the data source before accessing the data. This can be done with the CONNECT statement, which is also part of the SQL-92 standard. However, this is an example of an SQL statement which has been standardized, but not yet widely supported. In fact, experience shows that the farther we move away from pure data access and into database management, such as creating tables, the more nonstandard SQL statements are used.

The other major form of SQL is known as a CLI (Call-Level Interface). With this variant, no precompiler is needed; instead, whatever programming language is being used makes function calls to the database software. In fact, this is the same concept that is generally called API (Application Programming Interface). However, since the SQL standards documents also refer to SQL as an API, they use the term "call-level interface" instead.

To make things a bit confusing, there is another meaning for the abbreviation CLI, Command-Line Interface, meaning that the SQL statements can be issued from a command line, as for example under TSO or the UNIX or MS-DOS shell. This method is supported by most DBMS vendors and is very useful for ad hoc queries and for test purposes. Of course, command-line SQL statements can also be used within command procedures (i.e., CLISTS, shell scripts, batch files, etc.). In general, this form of SQL is somehow "just there" and doesn't need much discussion, so the abbreviation CLI almost always refers to the call-level interface.

Many of the native database APIs available today are call-level interfaces. Some examples are the OCI of Oracle and the DB-Library of the SQL Server from Sybase or Microsoft. Figure 23 shows a few examples of databases and the application interfaces available. In the case of IBM's DB2, the DDCS (Distributed Database Connection Services) client software has traditionally supported embedded SQL, but may be extended to support a call-level interface.

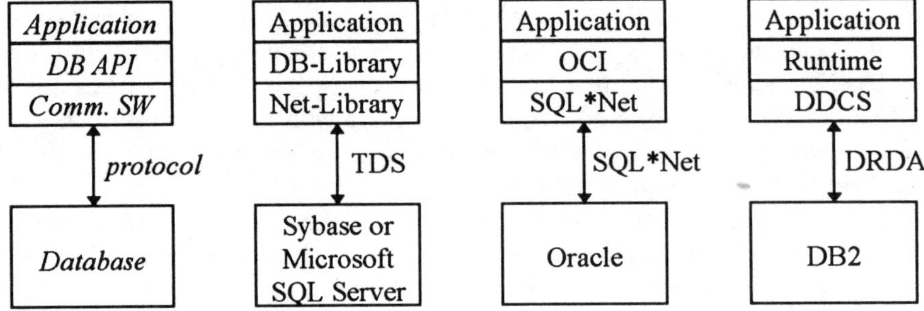

Figure 23. SQL APIs and Protocols

In Figure 23, the remote SQL protocols shown are the Sybase/Microsoft TDS (Tabular Data Stream), Oracle SQL*Net, and IBM DRDA (Distributed Relational Database Architecture).

DRDA

One of the most important vendor specifications, or de facto standards, for remote SQL is IBM's DRDA [Hackathorn]. The basic components of a DRDA configuration are shown in Figure 24:

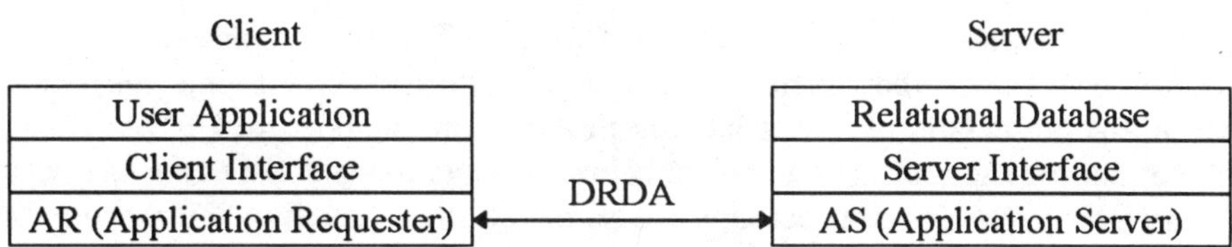

Figure 24. DRDA Components

As with any protocol, we will distinguish between the protocol itself, in this case DRDA, which defines the messages that are exchanged between the systems, and the service interface it presents to the application. With DRDA, the client application service interface, or API, is determined by the implementation of the AR (Application Requester), and is not specified by the protocol definition. It can theoretically be either embedded SQL or a CLI (Call-Level Interface). The IBM products which implement the AR are called DDCS (Distributed Database Connection Services) and generally implement embedded SQL.

As a next step, we will take a closer look at the protocol itself, which can be divided into a number of layers, as shown in Table 8.

CDRA	Character Data Representation Architecture
FD:OCA	Formatted Data: Object Content Architecture
DDM	Distributed Data Management
LU 6.2	Logical Unit Type 6.2

Table 8. DRDA Protocol Layers

The functions of these sublayers, and their corresponding parts in the ISO OSI model, are:

- **CDRA (Character Data Representation Architecture):** specifies single-byte and double-byte character sets, and belongs to OSI layer 6 (presentation).
- **FD:OCA (Formatted Data: Object Content Architecture):** specifies data types, such as floating point, and belongs to OSI layer 6 (presentation).
- **DDM (Distributed Data Management):** specifies commands and responses, such as establishing a connection to a database, executing SQL statements, and committing or rolling back transactions; it belongs to OSI layer 7 (application).
- **LU 6.2 (Logical Unit Type 6.2):** implements transport and synchronization (transaction control), i.e., OSI layers 4 (transport) and 7 (application).

Note that, in this case, the services of LU 6.2 (or APPC) which are used are more than transport level, since they include transaction control (commit and rollback). In addition, the presentation services lacking in APPC are included in DRDA. Also, the choice of putting the transaction control below presentation (in DRDA) or above it (in OSI) is really irrelevant, and perhaps a case of too much layering. Furthermore, the dependency on LU 6.2 is becoming less important, since the IBM MPTN architecture makes it possible to use APPC and CPI-C over other, non-SNA protocols, such as TCP/IP and OSI (see "IBM's Blueprint" on page 115). Security in DRDA is implemented on the basis of the LU 6.2 conversation-level security mechanism.

The amount of synchronization (or transaction control) offered by a remote SQL system can be categorized by the four levels defined by IBM:

- **RR (Remote Request):** *one* SQL statement to *one* database
- **RUOW (Remote Unit of Work):** *many* SQL statements to *one* database
- **DUOW (Distributed Unit of Work):** *many* SQL statements to *many* databases (but only *one* database per statement)
- **DR (Distributed Request):** *many* SQL statements to *many* databases (and each statement can refer to *many* databases)

The first DRDA specification, which appeared in 1990, went as far as RUOW (Remote Unit of Work), and has now become known as DRDA Level 1. The second specification, DRDA Level 2, appeared in 1993 and includes DUOW (Distributed Unit of Work) [IBM SC26-4651-01]. This requires the use of a two-phase commit protocol, which is implemented as a part of the AR on the basis of APPC. In future versions, this may be implemented in the AS, thus taking load off of the client and the network.

In summary, DRDA is a protocol for remote SQL which provides good support for both data conversion (presentation) and distributed transactions.

DRDA vs. RDA

RDA (Remote Database Access) is the ISO standard for remote SQL. All major vendors have contributed to it, including SQL Access Group, an industrial consortium with more than 45 members [ISO/IEC 9075 and ISO/IEC 9579].

From a technical point of view, there are a few important differences between DRDA and RDA. Perhaps one of the most noticeable is the fact that the first DRDA products from IBM support only static, embedded SQL, whereas the first version of RDA supports only dynamic SQL. From a programming point of view, this is a major difference, but various features of each protocol result in a situation that makes them very similar on the basis of performance.

Another important difference is the way they treat presentation. As an OSI protocol, RDA uses ASN.1 for this task, meaning that all data is transformed to a canonical form before being transmitted, and then transformed again by the receiver. In DRDA, in contrast, all data is sent in the native format of the sender, and transformed by the receiver only if necessary. In addition, the ASN.1 format tags all fields individually, making the overhead relatively large. As a result, the RDA presentation mechanism is universal, and each partner needs to take care of only its own native format and the transfer format; however, it requires high overhead and does unnecessary conversions when both systems use the same format. The DRDA presentation method, while being more efficient, has the disadvantage that the receiver needs to be able to interpret all native formats of all senders in the network, putting a big burden on future versions.

The SQL dialect supported is another significant difference. RDA is restrictive, in the sense that it supports only a specific subset of ISO SQL. DRDA is permissive, because the client will pass SQL through to the server without checking it. As a result, ISO RDA provides a good basis for ensuring interoperability between all implementations, but is impossible to extend without changes to the standard. DRDA makes it easier extend the SQL dialect of any implementation, but makes it necessary to investigate interoperability between any two products (or product versions) on a case-by-case basis.

Finally, there are some less technical issues involved. RDA is owned by an official standards body, and DRDA by a private company. Both organizations listen to their users and try to fill their needs, but neither guarantees satisfaction. From the standpoint of an individual user, the best choice will depend on how much each specification is accepted and used by the industry as a whole.

ODBC

The accepted standard for remote SQL based on a call-level interface is ODBC (Open Database Connectivity). It was created by an industry consortium under the leadership of Microsoft, and is based on the X/Open, ANSI, and ISO standards [Geiger]. ODBC can be used for accessing both relational and nonrelational data, both on the local machine and remote, and supports both multiple applications and multiple data sources.

Work on what was eventually to lead to ODBC was begun at Microsoft in 1988. At the same time, Lotus announced a plan called "Blueprint", which was aimed at achieving the same objectives. In 1989, the Microsoft API, then called "Open SQL", was reviewed by experts from a number of companies, and the feedback significantly influenced it. The next version, which was known as SQLC (SQL Connectivity), was then produced and the main contributors had become Microsoft, Sybase and Lotus, even though Lotus continued its work on Blueprint, now renamed "DataLens".

In late 1989, DEC called a meeting of almost all DBMS vendors; this was to be the beginning of the SAG (SQL Access Group). At that time, the plans were to create an interoperable version of SQL based on RDA. After this meeting, DEC joined the other three companies working on SQLC, and the SAG continued its work in parallel. In June 1990, version 1.12 of SQLC was presented to the SAG. Then several other proposals were submitted, from Oracle among others. SQLC was required to be limited to ANSI 1989 SQL, and was then accepted as the SAG CLI. At this time, the SAG CLI gained the attention of ANSI and ISO, and was able to benefit from their critiques.

In 1991, Microsoft hosted an SQLC design preview which was attended by more than 50 vendors. Then, in 1992, the product was named ODBC and a beta version shipped, including the basic SAG module and the Microsoft extensions. At about the same time, the SAG CLI was published by X/Open and accepted by ANSI and ISO as a base document for their work on a CLI. In 1993, the SAG CLI specification and ODBC Level 1 had converged.

The X/Open CLI was finalized in 1995, as were the ANSI and ISO standards. ODBC version 3.0 supports all of them [X/Open C451].

As mentioned earlier, portability and connectivity could be achieved by establishing a standard protocol for remote SQL, or database connectivity. The ODBC designers chose not to pursue this method, but to concentrate on the API instead. After all, at least one standard protocol already existed, and had not been adopted by the majority of DBMS vendors.

The ISO standard for database connectivity, RDA, achieves a very high degree of interoperability, but with a number of drawbacks. SQL compatibility is achieved by allowing only the 1989 ISO standard, thus restricting all partners to a subset of the available functions and disallowing such things as variable-length character data, BLOBs (Binary Large Objects), stored procedures, and so forth. Also, data conversion between machines with different architectures is universally and powerfully solved by the use of ASN.1, but at the cost of tagging and identifying every individual data element, with a resulting cost for performance. IBM's DRDA is in more widespread use, but hasn't become an accepted industry standard either. The ODBC solution doesn't require any specific protocol, but allows the use of all of them, including RDA, DRDA, TDS, and SQL*Net.

The other fundamental design decision was to base ODBC on a CLI instead of on embedded SQL. The main reason for this is to achieve "binary compatibility", the ability to move an application from one DBMS to another without recompiling it. When embedded SQL is used, it is necessary to take the source code, use the precompiler of the new DBMS, and then recompile the result. The ODBC solution makes it possible to use a standard application, such as Microsoft Excel, with different databases, such as Oracle or DB2, without recompiling it.

ODBC is based on the CLI standard of the SAG. The SAG was formed in 1989 as an industry consortium, and then merged with X/Open in 1994. In the meantime, the CLI specification has also been adopted by ANSI and ISO [X/Open C451]. As a result, ODBC supports dynamic SQL in a natural way, and can support static SQL by the use of stored procedures.

ODBC had the goal of providing the following services to applications, for any DBMS:

- a standard API

- all the functionality of the DBMS
- performance equivalent to the DBMS's native API

However, ODBC's goal does not stop at databases, but includes other types of data, including flat files and ISAM (Indexed Sequential Access Method) files. As a result, much of the ODBC literature refers not to a database, but to a "data source". Among other things, this makes it possible to use ODBC to access desktop databases which are not built on the relational model. On the other hand, the strict use of SQL in ODBC means that not all flat files or ISAM files can be accessed by it, since not all are amenable to the "row and column" paradigm of relational databases and SQL.

In order to achieve this, ODBC makes use of existing technology, forming a kind of standard "wrapper" for all data sources and their respective communications protocols. In Figure 25, the ODBC components are shown along with the application and the components of the data source, including communication software, which are used without the need to be changed in any way.

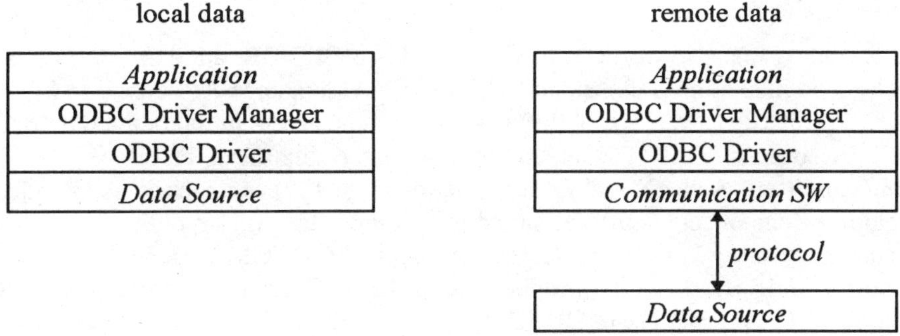

Figure 25. ODBC Architecture

As the figure shows, the two main components of ODBC are the Driver Manager and the Driver. The communication is handled by the software and protocol supplied by the DBMS vendor.

The "ODBC Driver Manager" is responsible for loading, unloading, and calling drivers as necessary. It provides the standard API to the application while managing the DBMS-specific drivers, and gives the application a way to choose and find the data source it needs to access. The Driver Manager also does a certain amount of error checking, making it unnecessary to put this in all drivers.

The "ODBC Driver" processes ODBC calls, submits SQL requests to the data source, and returns results to the application. Drivers are vendor-specific, since they need to access the vendor's API and, in a remote situation, the communications protocol.

The communications protocol used can come from any source, including the DBMS vendor or a third-party middleware vendor, as long as there is an ODBC driver for it. In addition, the number of layers can be extended, e.g., by including a "database gateway" in the middle and having it take over the job of managing the access to multiple databases, in order to move some load and complexity off of the clients.

One technique that ODBC uses to support all the functionality of existing DBMSs is the ability of an application to query ODBC to see if a specific driver supports any one of about 100 different options, such as, for example, "outer joins". This way, an application may provide different code for different situations, and choose on the basis of the available application. On the other hand, it can be coded on the assumption that a certain option is available and then use the standard ODBC API to check, instead of assuming that a certain DBMS is being used.

In summary, ODBC is based on call-level SQL and manages vendor-specific "drivers", which access the database API and manage any necessary communication. It provides a flexible but standard API, and allows the use of any communication protocol. This way, it achieves binary compatibility, making it possible for an application to be moved from one database to another without recompilation.

OLE DB

In this context it is also worth comparing ODBC to OLE DB, another interface which may be used in similar circumstances. ODBC is a C-language API based on SQL that is aimed primarily at interoperability with and remote access to relational databases.

In contrast, OLE DB is an object-oriented interface, based on the COM architecture (see "ActiveX and OLE/COM" on page 180). As such, it is intended for developing components, and it is suited for all data that can be defined in a tabular format, including relational databases. By using the DCOM system, OLE DB also provides remote access to data providers. In order to access relational databases, OLE DB tools will also make use of ODBC.

Since ODBC and OLE DB are both aimed at interoperability and standardized access to data providers, both are intended for use by software vendors and other component developers. For application programmers who want to take advantage of interfaces which are easier to program, Microsoft recommends using DAO (Data Access Objects). These are higher-level objects which are supplied with some data-access products.

Services

The basic service of a remote SQL protocol is to extend the Structured Query Language across a network. The variants involved differ mainly by the SQL programming method and the types of transaction control they support.

- synchronous API
- standardized API
- SQL method
  - embedded

- • static
- • dynamic
- CLI
- data sources
  - • relational
  - • nonrelational
- synchronization (transaction control)
  - • point-to-point
  - • distributed
- presentation (data conversion)
- security

Standards

The following list contains some of the most important standards for remote SQL. In addition to these, there are a number of proprietary protocols which have become quite successful.

- SQL [ISO/IEC 9075]
- SQL CLI [ISO/IEC 9075-3 and X/Open C451]
- RDA [ISO/IEC 9579 and X/Open C307]
- ISAM [X/Open D010]
- DRDA [IBM SC26-4651-01]
- ODBC available from http://www.microsoft.com/odbc
- OLE DB available from http://www.microsoft.com/oledb

Trends and Products

One method of achieving connectivity between diverse databases is the middleware approach, in which an independent third party develops software to bridge the gaps between these systems. Some examples of these products are:

- Gnosis
- IBI (Information Builders International) EDA/SQL (Enterprise Data Access)
- OpenLink Software

The following vendors have licensed DRDA (source: http://www.ibm.com):

- Attachmate
- File Tek
- GrandView DB/DC Systems

Part 4. Middleware

- Informix Software
- Object Technology International.
- Oracle
- Rocket Software
- StarQuest Software
- Sybase/MDI
- Wall Data
- XDB Systems

Nearly all DBMS vendors and major software vendors support ODBC, including the following:

- Borland: dBase dbf files, Interbase
- IBI (Information Builders International): EDA/SQL Link
- IBM: DB2
- Informix: Informix
- Lotus: Approach
- Microsoft: SQL Server and all major applications
- Novell: AppWare
- Oracle: Oracle Database and Oracle Transparent Gateway
- Powersoft: PowerBuilder
- Watcom

Some tools which make it easier to formulate ad hoc queries are:

- Andyne: GQL
- Brio: DataPrism
- Fairfield Software: Clear Access
- Intersolv: Q+E
- Microsoft: Query

Chapter 16. Distributed Objects

Now that object-oriented computing has become popular, and distributed computing is an important part of computing in general, what would be more natural than to develop a distributed version of objects? This was done in a number of small or experimental implementations, and then became the subject of standardization. This standard, known as CORBA (Common Object Request Broker Architecture), has been the object of much enthusiasm and is supported by a number of vendors. At the same time, Microsoft's ActiveX technology (previously OLE) has grown to cover much of the same content. As a result, these two specifications cover most of the work currently being done in the area of distributed objects.

CORBA

The generally accepted standard for distributed objects today is CORBA (Common Object Request Broker Architecture) from the OMG (Object Management Group) [Ben-Natan]. The OMG, founded in 1989, is a corporation which consists of over 400 members, including most of the major vendors and a large number of users. As such, CORBA is not an official standard, but a widely accepted, vendor-neutral specification.

The OMG produces architectures and specifications, but not products. However, all submissions to the OMG must include an implementation, which is intended to provide a proof of concept and to ensure commercial availability of the resulting specifications. This way, the OMG specifications are expected to provide the basis for portability and interoperability, while leaving the vendors sufficient room to produce their products in a way that differentiates them from the competition.

The basic architecture defined by the OMG, published in 1992, is the OMA (Object Management Architecture), which defines the role of the ORB (Object Request Broker). The actual CORBA specification (version 1.1), also published in 1992, was based on a submission by DEC, HP, Hyperdesk, NCR, Object Design and SunSoft. Another general specification is the OMG/OM (OMG Object Model), which defines the core object model and operations. It is extended by both the CORBA/OM (CORBA Object Model), covering remote messaging and distributed object graphs, and the ODMG/OM (ODMG Object Model), which covers database-related topics such as persistence and queries.

Structure

The ORB provides the basic object-object communication in a way which is location-, language-, and platform-independent. In other words, it makes it possible for one object to access another independent of its location, of which programming language was used to create it, and of the operating system and hardware it is running on.

In order to access a CORBA object, i.e., in order to invoke an operation of such an object, the application program executes code which accesses a local ORB. The

ORB looks up the necessary information, such as network address, in a directory and sends the request to the remote ORB responsible for the object in question. It also passes any response back to the originating application.

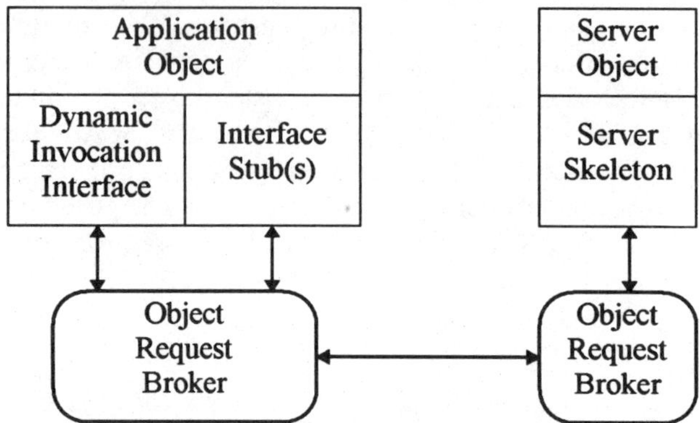

Figure 26. CORBA Configuration

As in RPC, the application code used to access an object is formulated in a special language, the IDL (Interface Definition Language). This is the same name as in RPC, but not the same language. Also, there is a special compiler, the IDL compiler, which converts this language into the relevant parts of the client and server programs.

In contrast with RPC, the object interface provided by CORBA includes attributes as well as operations. It also supports the object-oriented concept of "inheritance", which allows one object to reuse parts of another. In addition, CORBA includes a method for raising and handling "exceptions", which are special events that occur asynchronously to the normal operation of a program.

Another special feature of CORBA is the DII (Dynamic Invocation Interface), which makes it possible for an application to access an object of which it has no a priori information. In other words, instead of formulating the request in IDL at compile time, the application lets the DII create the request dynamically at runtime. The DII will generally retrieve the necessary information from a directory called the "interface repository".

In order to provide a means of accessing existing object services which may not comply completely with the CORBA standard, the ORB may contain a special layer known as the "object adapter". A few such adapters have been defined, including:

- **BOA (Basic Object Adapter):** includes the mandatory parts of CORBA, such as creation of object references, activation and deactivation of objects, invocation of methods, and authentication of the client.
- **LOA (Library Object Adapter):** allows objects to be implemented as library subroutines which can be activated without starting a new process or thread.

- **ODA (Object Database Adapter):** for accessing object-oriented databases which comply with the ODMG standard.
- **Other:** potentially anything necessary for providing a gateway to object systems which do not fully comply with CORBA. In particular, special object adapters may be used to achieve interoperation between different ORBs.

When a client accesses an object, the ORB must check the interface definition, including data types, and perform the marshaling of parameters. This is true for both statically defined calls (IDL) and dynamically defined ones (DII). In order to support this, the ORB makes use of a persistent storage of interface definitions in an "interface repository". This part is not yet fully specified.

Similarly, on the server side, the ORB needs information concerning which objects are available, which have been registered, and which authentication criteria are to be used. All of this, perhaps including the objects themselves, is contained in a persistent storage known as the "implementation repository" and used by the object adapter part of the ORB. The exact definition of the implementation repository is considered to be implementation-dependent and is not part of the CORBA specification.

The CORBA specification defines a very specific type of communication method between the client object and the server object. As with any program invocation or subroutine call, the communication is synchronous, meaning that the client requests a service and then waits until the service is rendered (or some other return code is supplied). In addition, there is a second model, the "deferred synchronous" model, in which the caller may issue a call, continue with something else, and later request the values returned by the service.

The first version of CORBA provided a complete definition of the API for accessing objects, but not of how ORBs should be implemented or how they should communicate with each other. In other words, it specified the services, but not the protocol. Therefore, it left the question of interoperability of ORBs produced by different vendors completely open.

This proved to be a significant problem, and was rectified in CORBA version 2, which also defines the ORB-ORB communication. In the meantime, a number of vendors created implementations of CORBA version 1 using their own methods of communication. Some of these, most notably those produced by DEC, supported multiple platforms, but there was no basis for interoperation between vendors.

In contrast with the ISO OSI standards, the OMG has not provided any facilities for testing conformance (do implementations conform with the standards?) or interoperability (can they work together?). As a result, the term "CORBA-compliant" has little meaning, and there is no established way of assessing whether one system will work with another.

Object Services

In addition to the CORBA specification, which can be thought of as basic infrastructure, the OMG has continued work on object technology by defining a number of object services. They are all defined in terms of IDL interfaces, and are thus to be made available in a platform-, language-, and environment-independent way. These specifications are part of various versions of the COSS (Common Object Services Specification) of the OMG.

Some of these services, such as naming, are fundamental to object technology. Others, such as transactions, are a necessary part of many, but not all, applications. At the time of writing, not all of the specifications listed below are complete, and, of those, not all are commercially available.

Naming

The Naming Service defines how names are associated with objects, and how an object can be found using its name. In order to make this totally platform-independent, and to provide a means for managing complex name spaces, names have not been defined as simple strings. Instead, they are structures, containing attributes for "identifier" and "kind".

In addition, names are contained within a "naming context", which may itself be contained within another naming context. The result is a "naming graph" which somewhat resembles the directory structure of many operating systems. In fact, the whole topic of naming is closely related to the problem of directories.

Event Notification

We recall that the basic CORBA communication is synchronous, meaning that both partners must be available at the same time. On the other hand, the Event Notification Service supports decoupled messaging, i.e., a reliable asynchronous messaging model, meaning that the two partners must not be active at the same time.

The Event Service distinguishes between "event suppliers" and "event consumers", i.e., senders and receivers. An "event channel" is responsible for transferring events from the supplier to the consumer and providing any other services supported, such as multicast or guaranteed once-only delivery. In the "push model", the sender takes the active role, and in the "pull model", the receiver does so. Events may be "typed", in which case they are defined via IDL, or "generic", in which case they are delivered transparently.

Note that the message-queuing nature of the Event Service does not change the basic synchronous nature of CORBA: The sending object accesses the event supplier synchronously via the ORB, and the receiving object accesses the event consumer the same way. The asynchronous communication is between the event supplier and event consumer objects via the event channel, not via the ORB. In order to use this facility, the behavior of the application must be designed around asynchronous message passing, as opposed to synchronous function calls or object invocations.

Life Cycle

Any object-oriented system needs a way to create and delete objects, and to copy or move them. These are often part of programming languages, but they need to be defined in a language-independent way that also covers such aspects as persistence and location. This is the topic of the Life Cycle Service, which was defined shortly after the CORBA version 1.1.

Object creation is done by a "factory object", which is any object which publishes an IDL interface that makes it capable of creating an object and returning a reference to it. Because of the properties of references and containment, objects can assume an arbitrarily complex structure, resulting in a complex "object graph". This makes it necessary for the copy service to include shallow, deep, and recursive copying.

Persistence

Many objects need to stay around after the program or process which created them terminates. This is the task of the Persistence Service and the PSM (Persistent Storage Manager) specification. In contrast to many such services offered previously, the specification is language- and platform-independent. In fact, the PSM uses a DDL (Data Definition Language) which is an attribute-only subset of the CORBA IDL. The Persistence Service also defines the concepts of "clusters" of data objects and "data stores", which consist of multiple clusters. Also, atomic transactions are defined and applied at the cluster level.

The Persistence Service is designed to be upwardly compatible with the ODMG standard for object-oriented databases (see "Databases" on page 59). Some of the services typically offered by an ODBMS, but not by the PSM, are concurrency, backup, recovery, and queries.

Relationship

Relationships between objects (also called associations) are a form of structuring systems consisting of multiple objects. The concepts are derived from two main sources: Programming languages contribute such concepts as references and containment, and relational databases contribute the entity-relationship model.

Externalization

Externalization and internalization provide a way to convert an object into a data stream and vice versa, and are therefore also known as "streaming services". When the data stream thus created is saved to disk, the externalization service provides a rudimentary form of object persistence. Note that this service is very similar to what is required of the presentation layer of the OSI reference model: some way of converting internal data structures to a stream of bytes that can be understood and reconstructed by another system.

Concurrency

The Concurrency Control Service is responsible for controlling concurrent access to objects, and is thus relevant to any multiuser environment, and in particular for a server which is accessed by multiple clients. Concurrency is also of particular importance to transaction processing.

Transaction

The Object Transaction Service is responsible for ensuring the ACID properties of transactions (see "Distributed Transaction Processing" on page 29). The current OMG work on this service is based on a joint proposal by a number of vendors, and discusses the relationship with existing standards such as the X/Open DTP Model, the X/Open TX and TA specifications, OSI TP and LU 6.2.

Time

The Object Time Services provide for clock synchronization between distributed systems, and also provide such functions as timers, alarms, and sequencing of events. The TTS (Trusted Time Service) is required by the Security Services.

Security

The Security Services are intended to supply such functions as identification and authentication, authorization (access control), secure communications, and auditing. In a distributed environment, security is difficult to achieve, and must be built into the system and based on standards. Adding it to the CORBA standard may require a significant amount of work.

Licensing

The Licensing Services are intended for controlling licenses to objects and for measuring usage.

Properties

The purpose of the Properties Service is to associate external attributes with objects, in addition to their internal attributes.

Query

The Query Service allows collections of objects, such as object-oriented databases, to be interrogated. The Query Service is expected to take account of the existing SQL standard and the OQL defined by the ODMG.

ActiveX and OLE/COM

ActiveX is the new name for Microsoft's object technology, previously known as OLE (Object Linking and Embedding) [Redcom 6/96]. With the introduction of DCOM

(Distributed Component Object Model), this technology also covers distributed objects.

OLE version 1, which was introduced in 1991, had the sole purpose of creating and managing compound documents [Brockschmidt]. This also explains the name of the technology, which provided a way of linking one document to another or embedding one into another. An important aspect of this step was the ability to manage documents consisting of parts that were created, edited, and displayed by different types of applications, including word processors, spreadsheets, and drawing tools.

The next major change in OLE, version 2, was introduced in 1993, and made OLE into an extensible, object-oriented architecture which could be used for much more than just compound documents. In fact, it was later to become the basis for an object-oriented operating system. Following that, many extensions to OLE were made, but without the need to change the basic architecture, so there was never a version 3. Finally, the Internet and the new language "Java" required some changes that would make it possible to create smaller components that could be downloaded on the fly and run in a platform-independent way. The result was ActiveX, which extended the scope of OLE and established a new name that was no longer tied to the idea of compound documents.

The architectural basis for OLE is COM (Component Object Model), which provides the way for binary objects to communicate with each other in a location- and language-independent way. This has now been extended to cover distributed environments and named DCOM (Distributed COM), a technology which had been known for some time as "Networked OLE".

In the past, OLE/COM has been known as a proprietary technology which was available only on Microsoft Windows operating systems. This should change due to two important developments. On the one hand, Microsoft is working with third parties (in particular DEC and Software AG) to port this technology to other platforms, including MVS and UNIX. And on the other hand, Microsoft has announced its intentions to put the control of the ActiveX specifications into the hands of an independent standards body (Microsoft press release of July 26, 1996).

Basic Concepts

Clients and Servers

Since ActiveX has its origins in compound documents, and has always been closely related to applications that support a GUI (Graphical User Interface), some of the terminology stems from these areas, even though the concepts are now much more general. For example, a "container" is a client object which maintains the persistent state of object instances (its "components"). For the purpose of comparison, here is a list of some related terms:

client	server
user	provider
container	component
main program	subroutine

In general, the left column designates the active, or controlling partner. However, this may break down in the case of container/component when the component is a "control", or element of a window, such as a pushbutton. In this case, the control may react to a user action by sending a message to the container. In fact, whenever a client object registers itself as a receiver of events from a server object, it reverses the client/server relationship, making the "server" call the "client" in order to send it an event.

COM

The architectural basis for ActiveX is COM and, more recently, DCOM. The COM specification defines a binary interface, making objects language-independent. In addition, DCOM makes them location-independent.

The COM specification provides direct support for encapsulation (hiding internal aspects behind a well-defined interface) and polymorphism (the ability to view different objects through the same interface). However, it doesn't provide any direct support for inheritance (the ability to use the characteristics of one object class to define a new one). The lack of inheritance in COM has been a point of criticism, since CORBA does support it. At the same time, it has been argued that inheritance is primarily important at the source level; binary objects can achieve the same level of reusability by means of containment and aggregation [Brockschmidt, pages 14 and 19].

The COM and DCOM specifications also handle the topic of addressing and routing. The Microsoft GUID (Globally Unique Identifier) is another name for the OSF DCE UUID (Universally Unique Identifier), and uses the same algorithm. Two special cases are the CLSID (Class Identifier) and IID (Interface Identifier). The COM locator service works with the registry and GUIDs to find objects.

A new addition in the ActiveX specification is the definition of "component categories". This should help make it possible to put components into groups with similar functions, and to find specific components. As a first step, three categories have been defined: "OLE Controls", "Internet Aware Controls", and "Windowless Controls".

Objects and Interfaces

ActiveX components are built of objects, the main structural unit defined in COM. Each object is in turn defined by its interfaces, each of which contains a number of member functions.

Interfaces are grouped into "standard" interfaces, which have a fixed meaning, and "custom" interfaces, which are user-defined. All objects must contain at least one basic interface, called "unknown". This contains three functions: "Query interface" is used to query all interfaces of an object, thus providing a type of dynamic invocation. The other two, "add reference" and "release", are used to control the life cycle of an object by influencing its instance counter.

The preferred method for designing an interface is via MIDL (Microsoft IDL), which is based on OSF DCE IDL. Objects are defined via the ODL (Object Definition Language), and information about them is stored in a "type library". This includes information about interfaces, member functions, and their arguments, attributes, and data types.

Interface definitions can be held in "header files" for use at compile time or queried at runtime. In practice, a client object will often query a server object for the interfaces that it (the client) supports. Any other interfaces of the server are ignored. This forms a kind of intermediate between fully static and fully dynamic invocation.

Object Services

The object services within ActiveX are defined as COM interfaces. In fact, even some of the fundamental technology just discussed, such as interface libraries, is provided in the form of standard interfaces which are part of the system.

Naming

Names of objects in distributed systems can become very complex. For example, names of NFS files depend on the "mount" instruction and are only locally unique. Names of files in DCE DFS are globally unique, but a global directory is necessary in order to manage them [see "DFS (Distributed File System)" on page 92]. On the other end of the scale, names may refer to other kinds of objects, such as a row or cell within a spreadsheet or an executable object, i.e., a piece of code. In addition, we may need persistent names for non-persistent objects.

In order to support this, OLE has defined persistent, intelligent names in the form of an interface called a "moniker". The interface supports simple and compound monikers, and includes a method for binding names to objects. It also provides methods for converting monikers to a display format and vice versa.

The "asynchronous moniker" is a relatively new COM interface defined in the ActiveX specification which makes it possible to download data asynchronously, and for the control to notify the container of the status of the transfer. This is especially important for Internet applications, because the application can continue working while the data for specific components is downloaded.

Structured Storage

Support for compound documents and compound objects requires a richer structure than that provided by the conventional file system. This is the task of structured storage, which thus supplies us with a kind of "file system within a file". In addition, this technique can be used for any kind of storage, including memory, files, and database records.

Structured storage consists of two interfaces: The "stream" interface provides for storage in a byte stream, as is customary in UNIX, Windows, and OS/2. The "storage" interface is similar to the directory of a file system. With these, structured storage objects can consist of an arbitrarily complex tree of storage objects, with storage objects or stream objects as leaves. The system also includes garbage collection and defragmentation features.

Providing a standard way for accessing structured storage has a number of advantages: for example, it makes it possible for a browser to navigate through a file directory and through the structure of a file without knowing the details of how the application stores its data. In addition, it should provide the basis for content indexing, a technique which makes searching entire networks feasible.

One concrete implementation of structured storage is Compound Files (previously known as "docfiles"). This system implements structured storage on disk files, with the addition of a locking mechanism for supporting multiple access.

Events

The basic services of an object (a server) used by other objects (clients) are defined in its interfaces. Since these interfaces are controlled or initiated from outside, they are referred to as "incoming" interfaces. But what if the server object needs to send unsolicited information to its client? This is handled by "outgoing" interfaces.

A (server) object which supports "outgoing" interfaces is called a "connectable" object. A client which connects to this object supplies a "connection point", which forms a sink, or receiver for asynchronous events. Then the server, or connectable object, can act as a source and call each connection point, sending it events. This kind of technique is commonly used for asynchronous events, and is also known as "callback routines". It keeps the system fully within the object-oriented framework, while allowing either object to assume the active role (thus breaking the strict client/server relationship).

Events are very important to systems which support a GUI because all keyboard and mouse actions appear as asynchronous events. But many other events, such as time-outs and notifications from communications subsystems, occur in a similar way. In OLE, there are a number of "standard event sets" or "standard notification interfaces" for defining standard events in header files.

Persistent Objects

Persistent objects are capable of saving some of their state information after the program or process terminates, and after the computer is turned off. When the object is loaded, or running, it is considered to be active, and while only its persistent state exists, it is thought of as being passive. Persistent objects are supported via the interfaces "persist file", "persist storage", and "persist stream". When an object supports one of these interfaces, a client or container object can tell it when to store its state and when to initialize itself from the stored state.

A new form of persistent data has been defined in ActiveX: The "data path" specifies a location, either in the client or somewhere else in the Internet, where data can be stored and retrieved.

Data Transfer

"Uniform Data Transfer" provides a means of transferring structured data from one object to another. Objects which transfer data do so via the "data object" interface. In addition, the "advise sink" interface makes it possible for the data source to inform the data sink when the data has changed, and thus needs to be transferred again. (This interface does not use the connection point interface, because it is older).

The "view object" interface includes functions such as "draw", which is used to display or draw an object on a device, such as a screen or printer. An object which supports this interface is referred to as a "viewable object".

The "data object" interface is also used to support the OLE Clipboard and OLE Drag and Drop. In order to participate in OLE Drag and Drop, an object must also support the "drop source" and "drop target" interfaces.

Automation

Since COM defines a language-independent binary interface, the objects written with it can be accessed by a programming language. However, this refers only to compiled languages. The purpose of "automation" is to make objects accessible to scripting or macro languages. This way, one scripting language, such as Visual Basic or Visual Basic for Applications, can be used to control multiple applications and to automate tasks that involve all of them together.

An object which can be automated this way is called an "automation object". This is achieved by using the "dispatch" interface, which makes all other interfaces accessible to the scripting language. The clients which can make use of these objects are referred to as "automation controllers" and include the scripting languages mentioned above.

In ActiveX the methods of OLE Automation are used to make ActiveX objects accessible from Visual Basic Script and Java Script, two scripting languages which have become important in Internet technology (see "Chapter 31. The Internet" on page 349).

Controls

Perhaps the simplest example of a control is a pushbutton. This is something that is activated from outside (pushed) and then has an effect on the computer software. In addition, as implemented in Windows, it has a number of other properties, such as a default color, keyboard mnemonics which make it possible to control it without the mouse, and so forth. Since most Windows objects, including pushbuttons, list boxes, scroll bars, etc., are controlled from outside by the mouse and keyboard, they all fall into this category.

"OLE controls", also called "OCXs", are objects which implement a number of interfaces, and thus support persistence, embedding, outgoing interfaces (events), in-place activation, automation, property pages, and keyboard mnemonics. Since OLE controls support automation, they can be used by Visual Basic. In fact, they were originally invented as the 32-bit replacement for the 16-bit "Visual Basic Controls", also called "VBXs".

OLE controls tend to be large objects, because they must support a large number of interfaces. This makes it easy for the client object to deal with them, but they are often too large to be downloaded efficiently over a slow link.

"ActiveX controls" are also COM objects, but are intended to be very small "applets" that can be downloaded efficiently. They must provide automation access for scripting languages, automatically register themselves when downloaded, and be able to find, store, and retrieve data either on the client or elsewhere in the Internet. Since ActiveX controls are not required to support such things as drawing themselves and menus, these functions are normally done by the ActiveX container. Technically, all OLE controls are also ActiveX controls, but the intended usage is clearly different.

Downloading

An ActiveX container, such as a web browser, may often need to download an individual component, such as a document, an image or an applet. In fact, HTML (Hypertext Markup Language) defines a special tag for this purpose, which contains a URL (Uniform Resource Locator) (see "URLs" on page 352). In ActiveX, this is done by the ICDS (Internet Component Download Service).

When the ICDS is invoked, its first step is to check the registry to see if a current version of the component is already on the local machine. Then, it locates the component by using registry entries known as the "Internet Search Path". These include not only security-related entries which may allow or restrict access to certain sites, but also local caches to be searched before using the URL and alternatives to be tried afterwards, in case the Internet location is not available. Next, the component is downloaded asynchronously, so that it doesn't interfere with other activities. Finally, the component, which may consist of a single file or multiple files and installation instructions, is installed on the local machine. This last step is done only after checking security criteria defined below.

During this process, the server should check the client's hardware platform and operating system, so that it can send the correct executable file. Servers which are capable of this are called "active HTTP servers". For other servers, it may be necessary for the downloaded package to contain code for multiple platforms, so that the client can choose and install the correct one. On the other hand, if the component is a Java applet, this is not necessary, since the executable is already in a platform-independent form.

Security

Since automatically downloading components is a potentially large security risk, ActiveX has added a security feature to this, known as the WTVS (Windows Trust Verification Service). Before the downloaded component is allowed to run, a number of checks are made to ensure that it is safe. First, the identity of the component's author is validated. Next, the component is checked to see if it has been altered. Both of these steps are carried out by using the mechanism of "digital signatures" (see "Digital Signatures" on page 301).

Finally, WTVS checks to see if the author can be trusted. This is done on the basis of three sources of information: the user's trust preferences, a list of previously trusted authors, and a direct user query. The first two may allow all sources, or may include categories, such as all commercial software vendors, or may be limited to specific vendors. They may also contain references to "certificate authorities", organizations which check the trustworthiness of software vendors and issue certificates used in digital signatures.

Licensing

A licensing service for ActiveX components has also been announced, but the specification, defined by a consortium of vendors, has not yet been published.

Java and ActiveX

Finally, ActiveX defines a way of supporting Java "applets" (see "Java" on page 355). When a Java applet, coded in a platform-independent form, is downloaded, it is wrapped in a COM interface, which makes it into an ActiveX control.

Business Objects

As we have mentioned before, the greatest benefit of object-oriented development is often experienced when objects are created at a high level in the application's hierarchy. This is because integration of many small objects is often cumbersome, whereas larger objects, or components, provide a more efficient basis for reuse of software. In particular, the concept of "business objects" is aimed at creating components which implement typical business logic [Foley, May 15, 1996].

Some of the work being done in this area is coming from Microsoft under the name of "LOBjects", which stands for LOB (Line of Business) objects. These objects will be based on DCOM and other ActiveX technologies, including:

- OLE transactions (code-named Viper)
- OLE DS (Directory Services)
- OLE MS (Management Services)

At the same time, IBM has defined plans for creating a layered framework of business objects, under the code name of "Project San Francisco". These layers, which are supposed to be offered on many different platforms, include:

- **general financials:** payroll, inventory control, accounts payable
- **CBOF (Commercial Business Object Frameworks):** customer master file, inventory, general ledger
- **GBOF (General Business Object Frameworks):** backup/recovery, save/restore, currency translation

In addition, the work of the OMG, as discussed above (see "CORBA" on page 175) is moving in the same direction. Of course, it will be based on the CORBA specification.

The following software vendors are also working on object-based versions of their products:

- Andersen Consulting
- Lawson Software
- PeopleSoft
- SAP
- Visteon

Services

The basic service of a distributed object implementation is location-dependent access to remote objects. As such, it is very similar to RPC, except that the fundamental concept is that of objects rather than procedures.

In summary, the following list shows the basic distributed object services:

- access to remote objects
    - operations
    - attributes
    - exceptions
    - statically defined in IDL (Interface Definition Language)
    - dynamically defined by the DII (Dynamic Invocation Interface)
- synchronous API
- location-independent access
- data conversion
- language neutrality: objects can be used by different programming languages
- upward binary compatibility: objects can be modified without recompiling all programs

Standards

The most important standards for distributed objects are listed here.

- CORBA [OMG/CORBA].
- ActiveX, available from http://www.microsoft.com/activex and the ActiveX Working Group at http://www.activex.org

Trends and Products

The CORBA specification has generated a lot of enthusiasm. For many, using distributed objects seems like the best way to create applications in today's environment. In addition, the large number of members in the OMG, including both vendors and users, is a good reason for optimism.

At the same time, there have been a number of disappointments. The first was the lack of interoperability in CORBA version 1.1, even though, according to the CEO of the OMG, interoperability is one of its primary goals [Ben-Natan, Foreword]. The second was the decision not to base CORBA communications on DCE RPC, meaning that the built-in security, directory services, and time synchronization had to be reinvented. (In discussing the goals of the OMG object services, Ben-Natan also mentions the desire to avoid "reinventing the flat tire" [Ben-Natan, page 14].

However, for many users, the lack of cooperation between the OMG (CORBA) and the OSF (DCE) has been less important than the lack of cooperation between the OMG and Microsoft (ActiveX and OLE). The growing number of organizations which had chosen to keep their mainframes and UNIX systems while using Microsoft Windows on the desktop were faced more than ever with the problem of how to make these systems work together. This may change due to an increased opening of the ActiveX specifications and increasing numbers of third-party interoperability products. Interestingly enough, Microsoft's Brockschmidt sees component software in general, and OLE in particular, as a way to "empower all users to solve problems themselves" and thus to free themselves from the "excessively competitive ways" of the software industry [Brockschmidt, page xxi].

There are also some other important differences between the various CORBA-compliant products, for example in regard to which programming languages they support.

The following products provide a CORBA-compliant interface (or will provide it in future versions):

- DEC: DEC ObjectBroker and ACA (Application Control Architecture)
- IBM: SOM (System Object Model), SOMobjects, DSOM (Distributed System Object Model)
- Iona: Orbix

Part 4. Middleware

- HP: HP Distributed Smalltalk, HP ORB Plus
- HP & SunSoft: DOMF (Distributed Object Management Facility)
- Hyperdesk: DOMS (Distributed Object Management System)
- SunSoft: DOE (Distributed Objects Everywhere)

A similar product is:

- PowerBroker (formerly Expersoft): XShell ORB.

Chapter 17. Messaging and File Transfer

In the past few chapters, we have discussed communications methods which have typically involved relatively short exchanges between a client and a server. Very often, when an application uses RPC, distributed objects, remote TP, or remote SQL, it requests a service from a supplier and waits for the response before continuing its current processing task.

In contrast with this, there are also a number of applications which either need to transfer large amounts of data and/or do not need to wait for responses before continuing. For example, an order-entry system may accept orders from a local source and send them to a central system for processing. To handle large numbers of orders, the application needs to send them as fast as possible, without waiting for responses from the central system. At the same time, it doesn't need a response to each order before submitting the next, so it should just pump them into the pipe as fast as possible. And if this application keeps local records of the orders submitted, then it will often have a completely separate return pipe, where the results of the orders are received and the local database updated.

The provision of a one-way pipe which does not wait for responses, and is thus often fast, is the task of "message queuing" systems. In contrast with this type of processing, we may need to distribute individual messages to many applications, often over a standardized mechanism to external partners, and so may choose a "message-handling system", or electronic mail. In contrast with this, transferring large pieces of data is often a task for "file transfer".

Message Queuing

As we discussed earlier, queues are a widespread and proven method for decoupling two applications, while still allowing them to communicate with each other. The applications may run at different speeds or behave differently, such as when one operates continuously and the other in bursts, or they may even run at different times, such as one during the day and the other during the night.

It is quite natural to extend this method to a distributed environment. The basic idea is simple enough: At least one queue is installed on each machine, and a special program, the queue manager, transmits the messages from one queue to the other. Figure 27 shows the structure of a subsystem which does this.

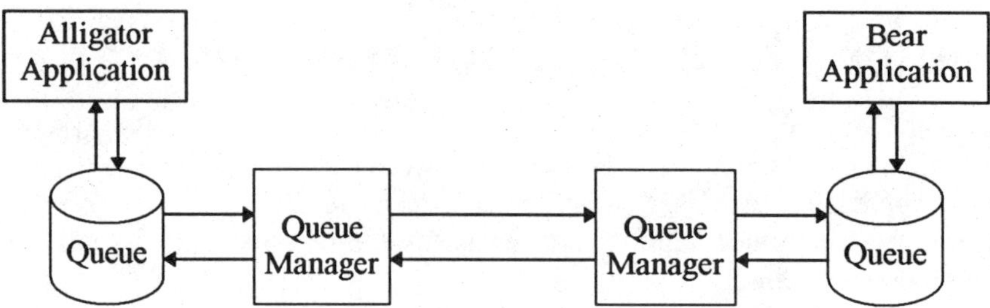

Figure 27. Remote Queuing

In fact, there is a little more to it than just transferring the messages from one queue to another. The protocol used has to make sure that no messages are lost or duplicated, and that their sequence is preserved. In addition, a highly robust system will include a commit protocol to ensure that each operation can be synchronized as necessary and will make provisions for recovery after failure of a system.

One particularly important remote queuing specification is IBM's Messaging and Queuing Architecture, which is called MQI (Message Queue Interface), and the products based on it, which are called the MQSeries [IBM GC33-0805-00 and IBM SC33-0850-01]. The specifications for MQI have been submitted to X/Open as a proposal for standardization. In accordance with IBM's Networking Blueprint, the lower layers under MQI can be either SNA (APPC) or TCP/IP.

The basic services offered by products of the MQSeries are remote queuing, i.e., an asynchronous, record-oriented API, guaranteed once delivery, and transaction synchronization. IBM refers to this as MDP (Message-Driven Processing).

A service missing in MQI is data conversion, or presentation. This is similar to the same deficit in APPC. In fact, MQI also offers a small consolation: Each record can be labeled with an 8-byte "format name", which makes it possible to define and handle individual record types in a user-specific way.

The MQI API

The MQI API consists of a number of calls:

- MQCONN: connect to a queue manager
- MQDISC: disconnect from a queue manager
- MQOPEN: open a queue
- MQCLOSE: close a queue
- MQGET: get a message from a queue
- MQPUT: put a message into a queue

At this point, a word about the term "asynchronous API" is in order. The asynchronous nature comes from the fact that the sending and receiving applications are completely decoupled from each other. In this sense, the queuing system implements a connectionless transmission between the applications.

On the other hand, the application is in fact connected to the queue manager (MQCONN) and to its queues (MQOPEN). In addition, writing to the queue is a synchronous call, i.e., the application waits until the message is put into the queue. This really makes remote queuing into a kind of mixed-mode transmission: connection-oriented to the queue, but connectionless to the remote partner.

The end result is an interface with an asynchronous nature, where the application can run independently of its partners, but where most of the advantages of connection-oriented transmission are kept.

Electronic Mail

Most people who use computers in large corporations today are familiar with e-mail, or electronic mail. On the surface, this technology is simply a way to send messages electronically, and thus faster than by traditional paper-based mail, which is sometimes called "snail mail". However, if you look a little deeper, most of today's e-mail systems offer many services, such as the ability to store outgoing messages until they are transmitted, to correctly address recipients all over the world, to request or send receipt confirmations, to convert content from one format to another, and to store incoming messages until they have been read.

As a result of this, e-mail has become a very powerful tool not only for direct use by end users, but also as a subsystem used by application programs. In other words, by adding an API, e-mail has been made into a special kind of middleware. The fundamental services offered are basically the same as those discussed in the context of messaging and queuing, but also include a number of features which were invented for the purpose of sending, manipulating, and managing person-to-person e-mail. In particular, e-mail is often used as the basis for groupware and workflow applications (see "Chapter 29. Groupware and Workflow" on page 334).

One example of the use of e-mail as a basis for an application is the DragNET, a network implemented by the FBI for exchanging DNA information between databases operated by the FBI and by local and regional police departments [Wayner 12/95]. The benefits of an e-mail solution here include its widespread availability, its ability to temporarily store messages, making it unnecessary to use expensive leased lines, and the ease of using it for application development, which involved adding a security mechanism and adapting its use to individual state laws. In this case, the relatively high overhead of e-mail, and its relatively slow response when compared with lower-level middleware, were not a problem to the application, because the messages are typically short (less than 1 KB) and transmission does not need to be faster than the typical laboratory work of a few days.

One of the most common standards for e-mail is the Internet standard SMTP (Simple Mail Transfer Protocol), and its extension MIME (Multipurpose Internet Mail Extensions), which were discussed above [see "SMTP (Simple Mail Transfer Protocol)" on page 141].

X.400

Another important standard is the ITU-TS X.400 standard, or its ISO equivalent, MOTIS (Message-Oriented Text Interchange System) or, more recently, MHS (Message Handling System) [ISO/IEC 10021]. An X.400 network consists of the following components:

- **UA (User Agent):** represents the user and serves as an end point in the network. The UA provides a user interface for message preparation and receipt, and services such as addressing and distribution information, reports, and time stamps.
- **AU (Access Unit):** a gateway to another service, such as fax or telex.
- **MTA (Message Transfer Agent):** forwards messages between UAs and other MTAs and serves as an intermediate network node. The MTA is analogous to a post office for paper mail, and many e-mail systems refer to the MTA as such.
- **MTS (Message Transfer System):** the collection of all MTAs in an MHS.
- **ADMD (Administrative Management Domain):** an administration entity which provides relaying and routing services (originally intended for use by public telecommunications carriers, or PTTs).
- **PRMD (Private Management Domain):** an administration entity without relaying and routing services (originally intended for use by private organizations).

Figure 28 shows the components of an X.400 message-handling service.

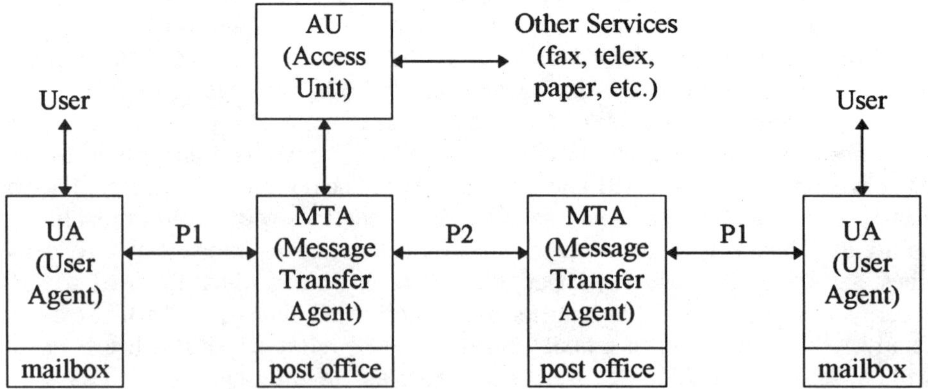

Figure 28. X.400 MOTIS/MHS Structure

The figure also shows the analogy to the traditional mail system: The UA (mailbox) is responsible for storing messages before and after transmission, and the MTA (post office) is in charge of routing and transferring messages from the originator to the recipient. In fact, these names are often used to designate the corresponding components of e-mail software.

An X.400 message consists of the following parts:

- envelope:
    - addressing information
    - identification of content type
- content:
    - header:
        - description of the body
        - service information, e.g. reply requested
    - body: in one of the following formats
        - ASCII (IA5 text)
        - telex
        - teletex
        - fax
        - SFD (Simple Formattable Document)
        - OSI ODIF (Office Document Interchange Format)
        - etc.

The content is defined to be one of the following:

- IPM (Interpersonal Message)
- EDIM (Electronic Data Interchange Message)
- service messages (e.g., delivery notification)

An X.400 address consists of the following:

- country
- ADMD
- PRMD
- organization
- organizational unit
- surname
- given name
- DDA (Domain-Described Attributes) for additional information, such as that used in gateways to other services

Naming

There are two common schemes for naming mailboxes. One is the Internet standard, and the other is defined by X.400 and X.500, and is also covered by an Internet standard, since it may be used for other purposes, such as names within a directory service which supports the LDAP protocol, even if it is not completely X.500-conformant. The relevant Internet standards are as follows:

- Names of the form "JamesSmith@myco.com" are defined in RFC 822.
- X.500-style names in the form "CN=JamesSmith,O=myco,C=US" are defined in RFC 1779.

Mail APIs

In addition to the standards for services and protocols, it is important to have a standardized API that applications can call in order to make use of electronic mail subsystems. One particularly important standard for this is the CMC (Common Messaging Calls) defined by the XAPIA (X.400 API Association). In addition, there is an X/Open API (adopted by IEEE). An industry specification defined by a consortium including Apple, IBM, Lotus, and Novell is VIM (Vendor Independent Mail).

Today, the most prevalent vendor-defined mail architecture is Microsoft's MAPI (Mail API), which is part of WOSA (Windows Open Service Architecture) (see "WOSA" on page 72) [Sheldon]. MAPI contains three APIs, the XAPIA CMC (Common Messaging Calls), Simple MAPI, and Extended MAPI. These cover services such as message store, address-book management, message transport, and configuration management. In other words, MAPI covers management and control of the e-mail system as well as transport of mail messages.

The XAPIA CMC API version 1 was defined on the basis of MAPI, and is now a subset of both MAPI and VIM. CMC version 2.0 includes more complex functions, such as enclosures and directory synchronization.

Access Protocols

The protocols defined by X.400 and by the Internet (SMTP) cover the communication between a mailbox and a post office, and between two post offices. This concept assumes that a mailbox (i.e., a user agent) is always available on the user's machine or LAN. However, with the emergence of the Internet, it has become increasingly important to access a remote mailbox provided by an organization such as an ISP (Internet Service Provider). For this purpose, there are two important Internet specifications [Kosiur]:

- **POP** (Post Office Protocol)
- **IMAP** (Internet Message Access Protocol)

POP is the older of the two, and is currently in version 3, and thus also known as POP3. It is also the easiest to implement, and is in widespread use. However, one important restriction involved with POP is its ability to retrieve either all messages completely or none at all. In comparison, IMAP has a number of additional features, including the following:

- selective retrieval of individual messages or parts of messages
- server-based searches
- shared mailboxes

Based on these additional functions, IMAP can be used as the basis for client/server e-mail systems which allow the user to download parts of the mailbox, process messages off-line, and then synchronize changes that have occurred on the client and the server. In addition, the server-based processing makes tasks such as searching more efficient and, together with shared mailboxes, can be used as the basis for workflow applications.

Secure Mail

Since electronic mail can be used both for exchange of interpersonal messages and as the basis for program-to-program communication, and is often used over wide-area networks, including the Internet, good security is an important aspect. In order to achieve this, there are two important standards. The X.400 standard includes security, and is based on certificates, as defined in X.509. An Internet standard, PEM (Privacy Enhanced Mail), also uses certificates and can be used with almost any e-mail software, including X.400 and SMTP systems.

Both of these standards provide the security services "confidentiality", "authentication of origin", "integrity of content", and "nonrepudiation of origin". In addition, the X.400 standard covers "nonrepudiation of receipt", a function that PEM provides only if receipt acknowledgments are created using PEM. The X.400 standard also includes "message security labeling" (access control) and, for communication between MHSs, "peer entity authentication", "security context" (access control), and "change credentials" (key management).

Thus, the services of both standards are very similar, and both are based on asymmetric keys and certificates. On the other hand, they differ significantly in their approach: The X.400 standard establishes a secure MHS, thus making "nonrepudiation of receipt" much easier. PEM, on the other hand, assumes a nonsecure message-handling system and establishes an end-to-end security that can be used on top of any mail software.

File Transfer

Instead of sending messages via an MHS or a queue, one fairly common way for applications to transfer bulk data is via file transfer. Some file transfer packages have an API for doing this, and practically all of them have a command-line interface which can be used by the application.

Perhaps the most common architecture for transferring files is ftp (File Transfer Protocol) from the Internet protocol suite [see "FTP (File Transfer Protocol)" on page 140]. FTP is now available on many systems, including UNIX, Microsoft Windows, and IBM mainframes.

In addition to this, one of the most important standards for file transfer is FTAM (File Transfer, Access and Management) [ISO/IEC 8571]. This standard defines a system which includes file transfer, and also remote access and management, including the following functions:

- read and write
- locate and erase data
- read and change attributes
- create and delete files

In order to achieve the high degree of heterogeneity and universality typical of OSI protocols, FTAM not only uses ASN.1 for data conversion, but defines the concept of a "virtual filestore". This is a conceptual definition of a structured file, including SAM (Sequential Access Method) and ISAM (Indexed Sequential Access Method). The physical filestore of the sending party is converted to the virtual filestore format before transfer, and then converted to the format of the receiving party afterwards. This way, each implementation must support only its own physical format and the virtual format, but there is a performance price to be paid, since there are always two conversions involved.

Comparison

Here are some of the most important differences between file transfer, mail (messaging), and queuing:

- File transfer is synchronous in nature, requiring both parties and the network to be available at the same time; queuing and mail are asynchronous.
- File transfer and queuing are point-to-point (unicast), whereas mail supports distribution lists (multicast).
- File transfer and queuing are often faster than mail.
- Some queuing systems include transaction control (commit protocol).
- File transfer and queuing initiators can generally send and retrieve data, whereas mail users can only send and wait to receive something sent by some other party.
- File transfer and queuing often require the establishment of special communication lines or connections, whereas mail is very widely available.

Perhaps it is worth noting as well that many older applications that use file transfer as a transport mechanism have dedicated "sender" and "receiver" processes, which together work very much like the queue manager of a queuing system, thus providing a means of decoupling the processing parts of the application. In other words, they really involve a private queuing mechanism and have an asynchronous nature, even though the basic file transfer mechanism is synchronous.

In summary, file transfer has long been a standard method for bulk data transfer between remote applications, but many of these may do better with a queuing system. On the other hand, for human users, file transfer packages will remain more convenient. In comparison, the main advantage of mail systems is their universal nature and widespread use, making them very easy and fast to employ, especially when different organizations are involved. A typical example of this is EDI, as we will see shortly.

Services

The services to be looked for in message queuing products are:

- asynchronous API
- record-oriented (i.e., message-oriented) API
- error handling, including sequence preservation
- guaranteed delivery (for example, the MQM on MVS/ESA also ensures message delivery after a system failure)
- robustness: support of commit protocol (for example, MQSeries supports syncpoint processing, including two-phase commit in CICS and IMS versions)
- triggers: the message queue manager can start an application based on the arrival of special messages
- security: depending on the implementation, it may include the use of APPC security or security checks at the API (e.g., MVS version)

The potential services of e-mail middleware, as discussed here, are partially covered by standards such as X.400 or by API standards. Other parts are specific to the software used for supporting the user in such tasks as managing mail stores.

- message archiving and retrieval (the message store in X.400)
- store-and-forward transmission to one or more recipients
- guaranteed-once delivery
- document conversion (e.g., X.408 character conversion, X.430 telex)
- priority control
- forwarding
- delivery confirmation
- receipt notification
- gateways to:
    - paper mail
    - other e-mail systems

- - fax
  - pagers (e.g., Eurocall)
  - telex
  - telephone
- security:
  - message origin authentication
  - proof of delivery
  - content integrity
  - content confidentiality
  - message sequence integrity
  - nonrepudiation of origin
  - nonrepudiation of delivery
  - message security labeling
- user interface (not part of X.400)
- API (asynchronous)
- message preparation and formatting, including enclosures and forms
- management of:
  - message routing
  - message stores
  - user definitions
  - address books
  - underlying transport systems
- directory synchronization

In file transfer software packages, typical services to be looked for include the following:

- synchronous API
- reliable data transfer
- bulk data transfer
- optimization methods, such as compression
- robustness, such as checkpoint/restart facilities
- security, such as encryption
- file management, such as create, delete, and rename
- job control, such as starting a job when transfer is complete

Standards

The standards for protocols, formats, services, and APIs of message queuing, electronic mail, and file transfer systems include the following:

- MQI [IBM GC33-0805-00 and IBM SC33-0850-01]
- SMTP [RFC 821]
- Names [RFC 822 and RFC 1779]
- POP3 [RFC 1939]
- IMAP [RFC 1731 and RFC 2060]
- PEM [RFC 1421, RFC 1422, RFC 1423, and RFC 1424]
- X.400/OSI MOTIS (Message-Oriented Text Interchange System)/MHS (Message-Handling System) [ISO/IEC 10021]
- XAPIA CMC (Common Messaging Calls) [CMC]
- OSI X.400 API [ISO/IEC 14392 and ISO/IEC 14394]
- X/Open X.400 API [X/Open C609]
- IEEE API [IEEE 1224.1 and IEEE 1327]
- VIM (Vendor Independent Mail), available from http://www.lotus.com
- Microsoft MAPI (Mail API), available from http://www.microsoft.com
- FTP [RFC 959]
- FTAM [ISO/IEC 8571]
- X/Open FTAM API [X/Open C415]

Trends and Products

The IBM products that implement MQI are referred to as the MQSeries (Messaging and Queuing Series), and many of them carry the name of MQM (Message Queue Manager). For a number of other platforms, the MQI protocol is supported by the ezBRIDGE Transact product line of SSI (Systems Strategies Inc.). Some of the platforms on which MQI is offered now or will be in the near future are:

- DEC VMS
- HP HP-UX
- IBM AIX/6000, Batch/TSO, CICS/400, CICS/6000, CICS/ESA, IMS/ESA, MVS/ESA, OS/2, OS/400, System/88, VSE/ESA
- Microsoft Windows
- Novell UnixWare
- SCO UNIX
- Stratus VOS
- SUN SunOS
- Tandem Guardian

Some other messaging products are [King]:

- Covia Technologies CI (Communications Integrator)
- DEC DECmessageQ

Part 4. Middleware

- Momentum Software MX (Message Exchange) and X-IPC (Extended Interprocess Communication)
- Peerlogic Pipes

A recent addition to this market is the announcement by Microsoft of

- Microsoft Message Queuing

This product (currently in beta test) was developed under the code name of "Falcon", and supports the functions of message-oriented middleware, including remote queuing and transaction synchronization. In fact, by embedding these in an ActiveX/COM interface, the services can be combined with Microsoft Transaction Server and accessed from languages such as Visual Basic. Microsoft is also working together with IBM and a third-party software vendor to provide interoperability with IBM's MQSeries products.

Very many e-mail systems are in use today, and a number are very widespread, especially the Internet SMTP format. As a result, there are also many gateway products, such as SoftSwitch Central, which convert from one format to another. In addition, a number of e-mail products support multiple formats.

Due to its good interoperability, its rich message format, including multimedia body parts, and its built-in functions, such as confirmation and delivery notification, the X.400 or MOTIS/MHS standard has gained wide support. As a result, it is often used for interorganizational connections and sometimes for e-mail backbones within large corporations. In addition, some newer products, such as Microsoft's Exchange Server, are based on the X.400 standard and have built-in support for X.400 transport format.

Some other mail-based messaging products and e-mail services available today are [King, Sheldon]:

- AT&T EasyLink
- Banyan Mail
- CompuServe Mail
- DEC All-In-1
- HP OpenMail
- IBM Profs, Ultimedia Mail/2 (MIME)
- Lotus cc:Mail, Lotus Communications Server
- MCI Mail
- Microsoft Enterprise Mail Server, Microsoft Exchange Server
- Novell NetWare Global MHS
- SoftSwitch EMX (Enterprise Message Exchange)

There are a number of file transfer products on the market which are based on proprietary protocols and are often optimized for specific purposes, such as high speed, robustness, or efficient network utilization. A more standard approach is supplied by many implementations of the Internet "ftp" standard, which originated in the UNIX community but is now offered on all major platforms. Products based on the "FTAM" standard also exist and are used mainly where high security is required or de jure standardization is important.

Chapter 18. Directories

Of all the technological advances available to us today, perhaps one of the most successful is the telephone. Although the telephone device itself is relatively simple, the infrastructure needed to support it, i.e., the telephone network, is very large and complex. Together, the telephones and the network make it possible to speak with people all over the world. But before we can speak to someone, we need to know that person's telephone number, which is a kind of unique network address that makes each telephone different from all others. And in order to find this number, we have come to rely on telephone directories, either printed or electronic lists of people and their respective numbers.

Similarly, distributed computing systems require some way of finding things. For example, the Berkeley DNS (Domain Name Service) discussed above [see "DNS (Domain Name Service)" on page 143] can be given a name (domain name) and return an IP address, which is used to identify a node in a TCP/IP network. Services like DNS are often referred to as "name services", but are also examples of the more general concept of "directory service". These systems can be used to manage many types of information, including:

- **general-purpose** information, such as names of people and organizations, their (street) addresses, and their telephone numbers
- information required by **e-mail** systems, such as e-mail addresses and distribution lists
- information required by distributed **applications**, such as names, interfaces, and capabilities of available services
- information required for **network and system management**, such as names and location of devices, their configuration parameters, and whom to contact when problems occur.

The use of a directory service for keeping this type of information has a number of advantages for the individual users and the organizations which administer the services, including the following:

- The information is available to all users (people and systems) in a consistent manner.
- Management of the information is much easier in the database of a directory service than in individual files installed on all machines.
- Security requirements are easier to implement.
- Entities, such as applications, can be moved more easily, because it is necessary to update only the directory, thus providing support for "location independence".

When a directory service is used for any of these purposes, it is often one of the central components of a distributed system, one that all others depend on. As a result, it can easily become a bottleneck, both in terms of performance and as a single point of failure. These problems then need to be solved by the use of replication techniques and distributed databases. In other words, the directory service, which is the basis for a distributed application, will itself be implemented as a distributed system.

One of the most important standards for general-purpose directory services is the OSI Directory Service, better known as X.500, the name used by the ITU-TS [ISO/IEC 9594]. The standard was originally conceived of by the ITU-TS as part of the X.400 MOTIS (Message-Oriented Text Interchange System)/MHS (Message Handling System), but it soon became apparent that it is very useful as a general-purpose directory service. In fact, X.500 is user-extensible, supports a distributed database and replication, and includes provisions for basic security mechanisms (authentication and access control).

The following list defines a number of the concepts and components that apply to X.500 directory services:

- **DUA (Directory User Agent):** provides the user access to the services of the directory.
- **DSA (Directory System Agent):** provides the storage and retrieval services for part or all of the database.
- **DIB (Directory Information Base):** is the conceptual database for all information stored in the directory.
- **DIT (Directory Information Tree):** refers to the hierarchical structure of the X.500 directory.
- **DAP (Directory Access Protocol):** is the protocol between DUA and DSA.
- **DSP (Directory System Protocol):** is the protocol between two DSAs.

One closely related, and important, standard makes it possible to access an X.500 directory via a simpler protocol defined within the Internet protocol suite.

- **LDAP (Lightweight Directory Access Protocol):** is an Internet version of DAP.

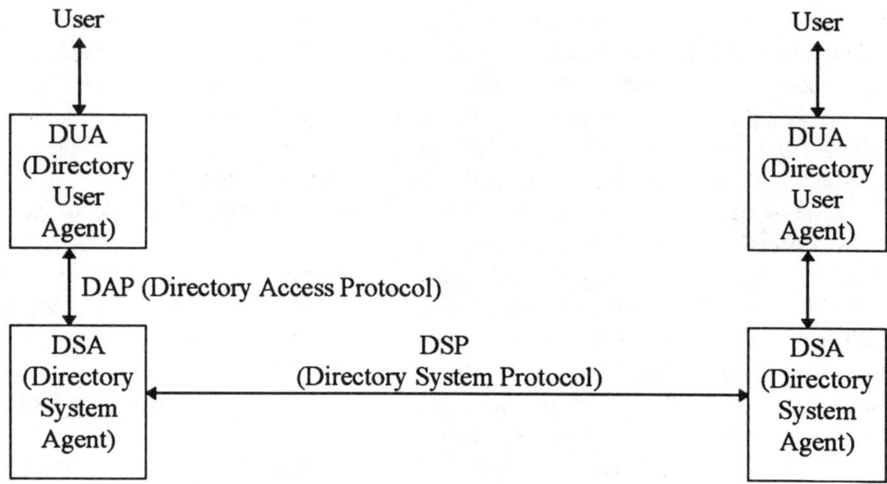

Figure 29. X.500 Directory Structure

When X.500 is used in conjunction with an X.400 e-mail system, the DUA may be not the end user but the MTA, or post office, of the message transfer service.

As with other OSI standards, the protocols are specified, but the user interface and the internal implementation are not. For the user, the importance of the protocols is one of interoperability: The DAP is used to access the information of the directory, and the DSP makes it possible for different directory products to participate in creating a distributed directory database. Providing support for the DSP allows products which are otherwise very different in structure and content to work together.

The directory operations are the elements of the DAP, and define what a user (person or machine) can do with the information stored in the directory database. They include the following:

- **bind and unbind:** used for establishing and breaking a connection to a DSA.
- **read:** used for extracting information from a specific entry when the name of that entry is known.
- **compare:** used to compare a specified value with the value of an attribute of an entry.
- **search:** used to search and retrieve information from a specified portion of the DIT (Directory Information Tree).
- **list:** used to retrieve information from all entries that are immediately subordinate to an explicitly identified entry.
- **abandon:** makes it possible to cancel operations such as read, compare, list, and search.
- **add, remove, modify entry:** used to add, remove, or modify the contents of an entry, i.e., of a leaf in the tree.

- **modify RDN:** used to rename an entry, i.e., to change the contents of the naming attribute(s) which determine the RDN (Relative Distinguished Name) of a leaf in the tree.

Other directory services include:

- Berkeley DNS (Domain Name Service)
- NIS (Network Information Service)
- Location Broker of NCS
- OSF/DCE directory service, which uses X.500 or DNS for global naming and its own CDS (Cell Directory Service) locally
- WINS (Windows-Internet Naming Service)

All of these directory services make it possible to implement a communications subsystem which provides location transparency: The application refers only to the name of the partner entity, and the subsystem retrieves the necessary addressing information from the directory server before sending a message or setting up a connection. This is how DCE RPC works.

Services

The services to look for in a directory system include the following:

- directory
    - distributed
    - structured (hierarchical, ...)
    - user-definable
- replication (X.525)
- security (X.509 = certificate management)
- API
- UI
- DB aspects
    - standard
    - logging
    - backup/restore
    - queries
- location-independent log-in
- single log-in
- central administration
- autodiscovery
- automatic synchronization
- integration with other directories

Standards

Some of the major standards relevant to directory services are:

- X.500 [ISO/IEC 9594]
- OSI Directory API [ISO/IEC 14392 and ISO/IEC 14394]
- XDS (X/Open Directory) API [X/Open C608]
- LDAP [RFC 1777 and RFC 1778]
- C API to LDAP [RFC 1823]

Trends and Products

With the growing size and complexity of distributed computing systems, directory services are becoming increasingly important. Services which support addressing at a lower layer, such as DNS, have been in use for some time. In addition, electronic mail systems almost always have some kind of address book, or directory. For example, the X.400 mail standard uses the X.500 directory standard.

Another area where directories have proven to be very useful is network management. For example, Novell NetWare has a directory known as NDS (NetWare Directory Service), and Banyan Vines has one called StreetTalk. These directories make it easier to keep track of various objects, such as network devices and user accounts, and help make applications location-transparent.

More recently, systems which use RPC or distributed objects need some kind of directory to manage the objects, their locations, their properties, etc. As a result, there is a need to build powerful, distributed directories to serve all aspects of distributed computing.

Finally, there is always the question of interoperability. In the case of directories, this is at least in part a matter of directory synchronization, which requires standard protocols and formats, and at least some common understanding of the semantics involved. In order to achieve this, some vendors either have supported X.500 or at least plan to support protocols such as DAP and LDAP. In fact, AT&T, Lotus, Microsoft, Netscape, and Novell have all announced plans to support LDAP as a protocol for accessing their directories and synchronizing them with others [Lewis].

Chapter 19. EDI

So far, most of this part has been concerned with how to transfer data and how the behavior of the transport mechanism affects the structure of the application program. The format of the data has been treated primarily as a method of bridging the gap between systems from different vendors, but none of this addresses the question of what the data means. Formatting and structuring data so that it has a meaning to the application is the main topic of this chapter. In other words, the chapter covers the semantic aspect of data exchange.

Today, many business transactions, such as purchase orders, invoices, and customs declarations, are done on paper. In order to increase the efficiency of these routine tasks, the data necessary for them can be transferred electronically, and this is the most general meaning of the term EDI (Electronic Data Interchange). However, since this data is exchanged between systems and not people, it is important to format it in such a way that applications from different vendors and different users can understand what it means without any special agreements. In other words, we need a standard format for transferring business data such as invoices. This brings us to the more specific definition of EDI, referring to the exchange of data structure according to standards.

The two most important standards for EDI are ANSI X12 and EDIFACT. Of these, ANSI X12 is the older and is in widespread use in the U.S. EDIFACT, which was defined by the UN and adopted by ISO, is based partially on X12, and has come into more widespread use in Europe. In addition, security services, such as digital signatures, are important for EDI [Wayner 10/94].

Interchange Agreements

Even though standards such as EDIFACT and ANSI X12 provide a good basis for formatting messages, there are still many aspects they do not cover. An "interchange agreement" is a way of defining these, generally in a bilateral agreement or contract between business partners. An interchange agreement may cover such aspects as:

- message standards (and versions)
- communications protocols
- security
- roles of third parties
- legal validity of EDI messages
- organizational constraints (e.g., service levels, time of availability)

A template which can be used for writing interchange agreements is contained in UNCID (United Nations Uniform Rules of Conduct for Interchange of Trade Data by Teletransmission).

ANSI X12

Like EDIFACT, which we describe in more detail below, the ANSI X12 standards consist of format and syntax, data element dictionaries, and data segment dictionaries. The two are very similar, so that application conversion and sometimes even interoperability should not be an insurmountable problem [Sokol, page 45].

EDIFACT

The other important standard for electronic messages is EDIFACT (Electronic Data Interchange for Administration, Commerce, and Transport) [ISO/IEC 9735], which was originally defined by the United Nations. In fact, the base standard is still complemented by message formats defined by the UN and many other organizations. Altogether, the EDIFACT standards cover four topics:

- syntax rules [ISO/IEC 9735]
- message-design guidelines
- directory of segments
- directory of data elements

EDIFACT defines a universal way of defining messages for business transactions, and can be used with almost any form of transport service. In fact, by choosing the correct character set, it can be used on anything from telex lines to floppy disks, file transfer, or X.400 e-mail. On the other hand, the standard is limited to this task, and does not cover issues such as data integrity, preservation of sequence, or security; these are left up to the underlying communication system or bilateral agreements between users.

To begin with, EDIFACT defines six different "character sets", including the telex character set and all ISO 8859 character sets necessary for European languages. Within these, "separator characters" are set out for marking the boundaries between the individual parts of the message. The default choice for the separators is a set of normal or printable characters. This makes it possible to use transport mechanisms such as telex for transferring EDIFACT messages without the need to convert the data beforehand and afterwards. These separators, along with their default representation, are:

'	apostrophe	segment terminator
+	plus sign	data element separator and segment tag
:	colon	composite data element separator
?	question mark	release character

These character sets and separator characters are then used to build "simple data elements", "composite data elements", "segments", "messages", and "interchanges". All of these pieces, along with their corresponding message headers and trailers, are shown in Figure 30:

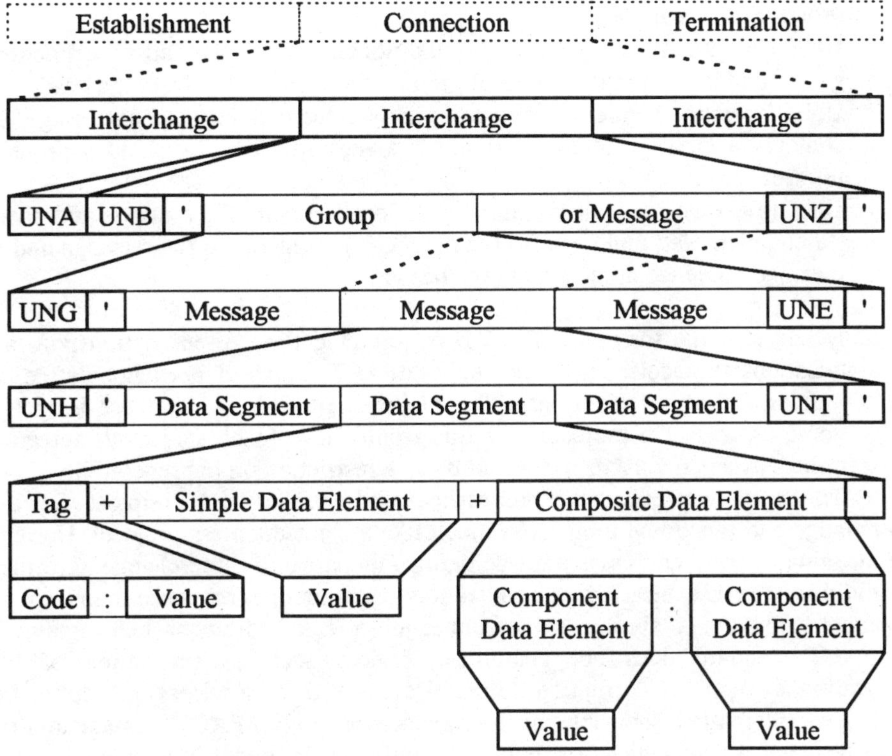

Figure 30. Structure of an EDIFACT Exchange

The message headers, which are defined as service segments, are used for specifying the structure within an interchange and for carrying control information. In the order in which they appear in the figure, they are:

- **UNA (service string advice):** conditional; defines the characters selected as delimiters and the character set to be used.
- **UNB (interchange header):** mandatory; identifies an interchange and the versions of the messages and directories used, identifies the sender and recipient (addressing), and contains an interchange reference number.
- **UNZ (interchange trailer):** mandatory; defines the end of an interchange and checks for completeness, and contains the number of messages or functional groups included and the interchange reference number from the header.

- **UNG (functional group header):** conditional; defines a functional group of messages, and contains sender and recipient, date and time, and a functional group reference number.
- **UNE (functional group trailer):** conditional; defines the end of a functional group, and contains the functional group reference number from the header.
- **UNH (message header):** mandatory; defines the beginning of a message, and contains a message reference number, a message identifier, and a sequence number.
- **UNT (message trailer):** mandatory; defines the end of a message and checks for completeness, and contains the number of segments in the message and the message reference number from the header.

In many respects, the formats defined here resemble those used in transport-layer communications protocols. However, the EDIFACT standard does not define any protocol rules, but only the formats. This makes it possible to use these formats to define some aspects of a protocol, but this would have to be subject to agreement between the partners involved, and would place a restriction on interoperability.

To be more precise, the addressing used (sender and recipient for each interchange and functional unit) looks much like a connectionless protocol. However, the meaning of these addresses must be defined as part of an interchange agreement. In addition, the use of headers and trailers with unique reference numbers and sequence numbers is similar to a connection-oriented protocol but, again, the EDIFACT standard does not guarantee services such as prevention of loss, duplication, or sequence corruption. In practice, all of these services are supplied by a lower layer, which is responsible for the transport of the EDIFACT message and may either be connection-oriented or simply contain the whole interchange in one piece.

Along with the business-oriented messages, EDIFACT also includes a number of service messages, which can be used for such things as acknowledgment of previously transmitted messages.

EDIFACT message formats cover text messages based on the character set used. Noncharacter data, i.e., graphics, can be included by making use of the features of the transport mechanism, such as the PEDI of X.400 MOTIS (Message-Oriented Text Interchange System)/MHS (Message Handling System). When a transport mechanism does not provide this type of support for embedded binary files, graphics can be transferred by means of mutual agreement, with the help of the messages CONDRA (drawing administration) and CONDRO (drawing organization).

EDIFACT also includes methods for implementing data compression (by suppressing insignificant characters) and repetitions of data segments and data elements.

Figure 31 shows an example of an EDIFACT exchange, as it may be used in a typical business situation involving a price quotation, an order, and an invoice.

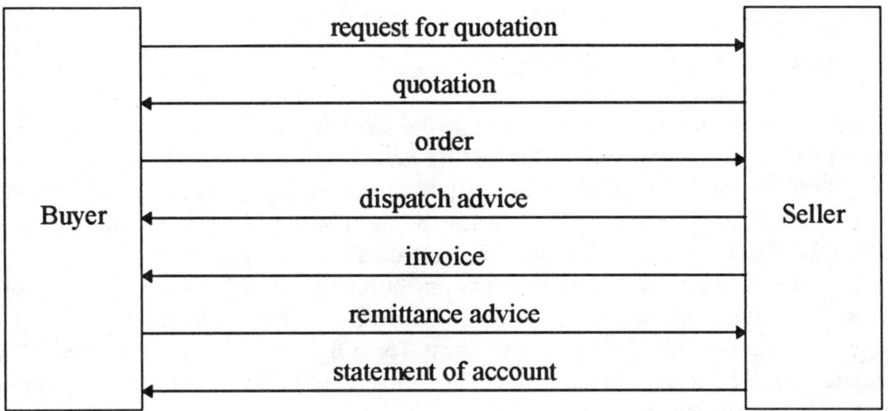

Figure 31. Example of an EDIFACT Exchange

In this figure, each step of the exchange is implemented by a different, standardized EDIFACT message.

One example of the use of EDIFACT messages is to be found in the SENANET (Senior Animals Network), which was implemented by APE. This is an international network which was set up to exchange social security information between different countries. Even though it is not a typical software vendor, APE was requested to do this project because of its good reputation in dealing with multiple species and in operating intergalactic networks. The exchange format chosen was EDIFACT messages transferred over X.400 electronic mail and secured by use of the Internet standard PEM (Privacy Enhance Mail). EDIFACT provided a common format which allowed each participant to make its own application software. X.400 was chosen as a common standard for e-mail, but since many of the participating agencies had non-X.400 mail systems or old versions, they were not able to implement X.400 security. PEM proved to be a convenient add-on that filled their security needs when exchanging confidential animal health insurance records.

Formatted Documents

Instead of using a standard for message formatting, such as EDIFACT or ANSI X12, it may be feasible to use a standard for document formatting. After all, the basic messages involved, such as orders and invoices, are normally created as documents, and it would be nice to have a format that could also be printed and used on paper when necessary.

The main international standard for document formatting is ODA/ODIF (Office Document Architecture and Interchange Format) [ISO/IEC 8613]. ODA defines three document formats:

- image form

- processable form
- formatted processable form

This way, documents can be stored in a logical structure, independent of their printed form, in a form which describes the printing layout, or in both. The processable form can be stored in SGML (Standard Generalized Markup Language) [ISO/IEC 8879], a tag language very similar to IBM's Script or BookMaster format. ODIF is actually part of ODA, and makes use of OSI ASN.1 for data conversion.

A similar, but older, proprietary specification is IBM's DCA (Document Content Architecture) and DIA (Document Interchange Architecture). Here, the storage formats are called FFT (Final Form Text) and RFT (Revisable Form Text). The latter should not be confused with RTF (Rich Text Format), which is a Microsoft specification for formatted text.

In addition to these formal standards for formatting office documents, development of systems for multimedia documents is still advancing rapidly, and includes specifications such as OLE and OpenDoc (see "Document Orientation" on page 71). In fact, OLE and CORBA now encompass methods (processing) as well as data, and form the basis for distributed object-oriented computing.

Are any of these standards suited for use by EDI applications? ODA/ODIF and DCA/DIA are really intended for office documents to be read by humans, whereas EDIFACT and X12 are for formatting business information in messages transferred directly from one application to another. In addition, EDIFACT messages can be transferred without loss on practically any medium. Distributed objects might well be usable for this task, but it will take time before the standards have become widespread enough, and even then, we might see distributed objects processing standardized EDIFACT messages.

In fact, the typical usage scenarios are very different: EDIFACT (standardized bilateral application-to-application communication) is most often used for relatively simple interorganizational applications which are just being converted from paper to electronic form, and distributed objects are most often used for complex processes within an organization.

PEDI

PEDI (i.e., X.435) is a protocol defined within X.400 MOTIS/MHS especially for use with EDI. It combines the general characteristics of e-mail systems with an interface designed for use by application programs.

Some of the advantages of using X.435 for the transport of EDIFACT messages are:

- asynchronous, guaranteed-once delivery
- worldwide connectivity
- acknowledgments

- concept of responsibility (e.g., for a message which has been acknowledged)
- multicast capability (distribution lists)
- security
    - message confidentiality
    - origin authentication
    - recipient authentication

Services

The services to be looked for in EDI standards and software systems include the following:

- message formatting (presentation)
- conversion (to other standards or paper)
- security services
    - message origin authentication
    - nonrepudiation of origin/receipt
    - integrity of content
    - message sequence preservation
    - confidentiality of content
- security mechanisms
    - digital signatures
    - digital cash
    - digital timestamps
- archiving
- API (synchronous or asynchronous, interactive or batch)

Since EDI addresses message exchanges between systems, an API is an important part of any EDI subsystem, so that the services can be made available to any application program that needs them.

Standards

The standardization efforts for EDI are a complex, ongoing process. The first, and easiest, step of this is the definition of basic syntax rules, as contained in ANSI X12 and EDIFACT syntax. The next step, still of a general nature, is the definition of base standards for general-purpose segments and messages. Finally, each branch of industry and government administration must set its own standards for messages, transport protocols, implementation agreements, and so on.

- ANSI X.12 [ANSI X12]
    - X12.1: Purchase Order Transaction Set

- X12.2: Invoice Transaction Set
- X12.3: Data Element Dictionary (includes revision service)
- X12.4: Payment Order/Remittance Advice Transaction Set
- X12.5: Interchange Control Structure
- X12.6: Application Control Structures
- X12.7: Request for Quotation Transaction Set
- X12.8: Response to Request for Quotation Transaction Set
- X12.9: Purchase Order Acknowledgment Transaction Set
- X12.10: Ship Notice/Manifest Transaction Set
- X12.11: Order Status Inquiry Transaction Set
- X12.12: Receiving Advice Transaction Set
- X12.13: Price/Sales Catalog Transaction Set
- X12.14: Planning Schedule with Release Capability Transaction Set
- X12.15: Purchase Order Change Transaction Set
- X12.16: Purchase Order Change Acknowledgment Transaction Set
- X12.20: Functional Acknowledgment Transaction Set
- X12.22: Segment Directory
- X12.23: Order Status Report Transaction Set
- X12.25: Customer Account Analysis Transaction Set
- X12.26: Product Transfer Account Adjustment Transaction Set
- X12.27: Price Authorization Acknowledgment/Status Transaction Set
- X12.28: Inventory Inquiry/Advice Transaction Set
- X12.33: Product Transfer and Resale Report Transaction Set
- X12.37: Shipping Schedule Transaction Set
- X12.38: Lockbox Transaction Set
- X12.41: Report of Test Results Transaction Set
- X12.43: Operating Expense Statement Transaction Set
- X12.50: Response to Product Transfer Account Adjustment Transaction Set

- EDIFACT (Electronic Data Interchange for Administration, Commerce, and Transport) [ISO/IEC 9735]
- UNECE/TDED [ISO/IEC 7372]
- ODA (Office Document Architecture) and ODIF (Office Document Interchange Format) [ISO/IEC 8613]
- X.435 PEDI [ISO/IEC 10021-8 and ISO/IEC 10021-9]
- UNTDED (United Nations Trade Data Element Dictionary)
- UNTDID (United Nations Trade Data Interchange Directory)
- UNECE (United Nations Trade Data Interchange Directory—EDIFACT Syntax Implementation Guidelines)
- UNEDED (United Nations EDIFACT Data Elements Directory)
- UNSM (United Nations Standard Message Types)

UNTDID defines messages, including Invoice, Arrival Notice, Passenger List, and Customs Declaration.

Trends and Products

Some organizations which support ANSI X12 and have developed industry guidelines and industry-specific message definitions are the following [Sokol, page 42]:

- **automotive:** AIAG (Automobile Industry Action Group)
- **chemical:** CIDX (Chemical Industry Data Exchange)
- **electronics:** EIDX (Electronics Industry Data Exchange)
- **electrical:** EDX (Electrical Industry Data Exchange)
- **metals:** Aluminum Association, AISI (American Iron and Steel Institute)
- **office products:** WSA (Wholesale Stationers Association)
- **paper:** API (American Paper Institute)
- **petroleum:** PIDX (Petroleum Industry Data Exchange)
- **retail:** NRMA (National Retail Merchants Association), VICS (Voluntary Interindustry Communication Standard)

EDIFACT messages have been defined for many different areas of applications (e.g., trade, customs, banking, automobile manufacturing, chemistry, etc.). One organization concerned with compiling this information is:

- EDIRA (EDI Registration Authorities), http://gate.dungeon.com/home/edira

Some of the organizations which have defined segments and messages specific to their fields are (source http://www2.echo.lu/oii/en/edi.html):

- AECMA (Association Européenne des Constructeurs de Matériel Aérospatial)
- CEFIC (European Chemical Industry Council), http://www.innet.net/cefic
- EDIFICE (Electronic Data Interchange Forum for Companies with Interests in Computing and Electronics), http://www-edt-fr/edifice
- IATA (International Air Transport Association)
- ODETTE (Organisation for Data Exchange Through Tele-transmission in Europe)
- SWIFT (Society for Worldwide Interbank Financial Telecommunications)
- UIC (Union Internationale de Chemins de Fer)

Since many commercial applications and databases already exist, there is a need to bridge the gap between their formats and those defined within the ANSI X12 or EDIFACT standards. This can be done at least in part by commercially available software products which are often referred to as "EDI converters" or "EDI translators".

Summary of Part 4

Middleware covers the upper-layer communication protocols and some other services used directly by applications. As such, it is the closest to the applications themselves, and must be chosen on the basis of the services and behavior required by the application.

In addition to the basic client/server protocol RPC (Remote Procedure Call), object-oriented APIs and protocols, CORBA (Common Object Request Broker Architecture), and ActiveX/DCOM (Distributed Component Object Model) are now available. IBM's APPC (Advanced Program-to-Program Communication) can be used for things such as client/server programming and DTP (Distributed Transaction Processing), while MQI (Message Queue Interface) is useful for asynchronous transfer of data. Remote SQL, in one of many forms, is used widely for remote access to relational databases, and three protocols (APPC, OSI-TP, and TxRPC) are available for distributed transaction processing. Electronic mail systems form another basis for asynchronous data transfer, and directories are an increasingly important part of communications systems. EDI (Electronic Data Interchange) provides a standardized way of formatting business-related information for exchange between independent organizations.

Table 9 shows which protocols are applicable for each of the basic processing models discussed in the first part of this book.

Middleware	Processing Model			
	C/S	DTP	Messaging	Remote Data
RPC	++	-	-	-
Objects	++	?	?	?
APPC	+	++	-	-
MQI	-	-	++	-
Remote SQL	-	-	-	++
DTP	-	++	-	-
Mail	-	-	++	-

Table 9. Middleware and Processing Models

Part 5. Systems Management

Introduction to Part 5

As more and more businesses base their activities on computers and networks, they become more and more dependent on the proper operation of these systems. The field of systems management is primarily concerned with keeping these systems and networks available.

For example, when the reservations system of an airline fails, flight reservations can, in principle, be made by manual methods. In practice, this is so much slower than the normal, electronic way that the number of reservations per hour falls drastically. The passengers fly with other airlines, or cancel their travel plans altogether. This can be converted to a well-defined financial loss, which Contingency Planning Research has estimated at $89,500 per hour of network downtime [McCarthy].

The losses in many other areas of business can be estimated in a similar way. For example, how much does an automobile manufacturer lose when the assembly line has to be stopped because of delayed deliveries? Other losses are more difficult or even impossible to estimate. For example, how much does a bank lose when its customers lose confidence in its ability to protect itself from bad investments or thefts?

At the same time that businesses depend so heavily on information technology, there are sufficient causes for failure (see "Murphy's Law" on page 7). A number of these were discussed by David Parnas in his recommendation not to implement the plans for an SDI (Strategic Defense Initiative) system [Parnas].

Perhaps the main cause of problems is complexity. This begins with the inherent complexity of digital technology and extends upward through a number of layers of software making up a distributed system consisting of hundreds or thousands of components from dozens of different manufacturers.

Another important cause of problems is the high rate of innovation: New releases may be issued as frequently as every 12 or 18 months. In practice, it is often necessary to install and adapt to these changes as fast as they are delivered, and, often, each one brings with it a whole new load of errors, incompatibilities, and other surprises.

Another source of requirements, if not problems, is the increasing autonomy of the users of the system. They demand applications faster than they can be written, require access to centrally stored data, often install their own components, and expect the system to run smoothly and be available 100% of the time.

The activities of systems management are analogous to those required for managing a company. The short-term operational tasks are centered on monitoring and control, and involve a lot of crisis management, in an attempt to keep everything running smoothly. The long-term jobs include the definition of goals, analysis of performance, and planning and installation of the next set of functions. In order to make this possible, the manager needs accurate and up-to-date information and the ability to influence the operation of the system. As a result of the complexity of the distributed system, the emphasis is on coordinating various parts, and as for the manager, "his chief daily task will be communication, not decision-making" [Brooks, page 111].

And, finally, systems management, like many other things, is a matter of cost. Once those PCs, LANs, WANs, and hosts are installed, how many people are needed to keep them running smoothly and up to date? One well-known estimate states that one person will be employed full-time for approximately every 30 users.

"Chapter 20. Elements of Systems Management" begins this part by describing what network and system management is all about. It describes the systems which need to be managed and the activities, or functions, that make up network and systems management. Then managed objects, a way of representing the managed resources, are introduced, followed by a brief description of the components involved, including managers and agents.

"Chapter 21. Management Protocols" introduces the communications protocols which are used for systems management. These protocols are the basis for understanding how the many components, both managed resources and management systems, can be combined. They also give a glimpse of the services that such a system can offer. Of these, the most widely used protocol arose within the Internet community, and is known as SNMP (Simple Network Management Protocol).

"Chapter 22. Desktop Management" is a relatively new, but very important aspect of systems management. It is very closely related to the development of "plug and play" PCs, but has not yet been integrated well into the rest of systems management. The most important standard in this area was defined by a consortium called the DMTF (Desktop Management Task Force), and includes specifications for an MIF (Management Information Format) and a DMI (Desktop Management Interface).

"Chapter 23. Components" describes the typical components of a management system. In other words, it presents management functions and services in the way that they are most often implemented in commercial products. A few of the many components typically used in systems management are network monitors, performance monitors, software distribution tools, and trouble-ticket systems.

"Chapter 24. Object-Oriented Management Frameworks" presents the concepts of object-oriented management tools on the basis of OSF DME and IBM/Tivoli TME. Since DME has not achieved the success of DCE, it should be considered not as a product but as a description of the current state of the art in systems management. TME (Tivoli Management Environment) provides a good example of the current state of distributed objects as a basis for network and systems management, showing where they are useful internally and externally.

"Chapter 25. Security", the last chapter of this part, is particularly important, due to the increased difficulty of achieving security in distributed systems. It begins by discussing which assets of resources, such as confidentiality of information or availability of systems, are to be protected, and against what types of threats, such as eavesdropping, viruses, or simple accidents by the users themselves. This is followed by a description of security services, such as authentication and access control, used to protect these assets. Finally, we go through the means of achieving the desired services, i.e., the security mechanisms, such as encryption and digital signatures.

Within APE, network and systems management has traditionally been the task of various dogs, the most famous of which are the bloodhounds and other sniffers employed in network monitoring. However, there is much more to network management than just sniffing a protocol, and the same holds true for APE's canines. For example, their social organization has helped them meet the challenge of integrating many different components while still keeping a unified team, or pack, and a number of watchdogs have provided good services in the area of security.

Chapter 20. Elements of Systems Management

Goals

The goal of systems management is to deliver a certain level of service to the user. This service includes functions designed to support the basic activities of the organization, such as computing and communications resources. The level of service can be defined in terms of the availability and performance of the installed systems. Some of the most important aspects are:

- **availability:** the percentage of the time that a particular service is available to the user. Some relevant measures are:
    - **percent availability:** the percentage of the time during which the system is available for use
    - **MTBF** (Mean Time Between Failures)
    - **MTTR** (Mean Time To Repair)
- **response time:** the time required for the system to respond to a user's request. This can be measured as an average or maximum value, and includes factors such as delays in processing, data access, and communication.
- **integrity:** protection against corruption of data or services.
- **fault tolerance:** ability to continue operations after failure of specific components.
- **flexibility:** ability to adapt to changes, such as new requirements or new technology.
- **security:** in the narrow sense, protection against misuse of data.
- **cost:** provision of the above services for a reasonable price.

The use of technology to support systems management has the purpose of reducing the costs for manual tasks, such as installing software (a routine job that can be automated) and fixing errors (a job that can be minimized by preventing some errors and handling others more efficiently).

The costs for effective systems management technology need to be weighed against the costs for the manual methods that would otherwise be necessary, and against the monetary benefit of the improved level of service they provide.

Methods

The management of distributed systems requires methods which function over a network and which encompass a large diversity of elements. These include techniques for the definition and standardization of the objects concerned, and for communication between the components of the managed and managing systems. These methods were developed within the framework of network management and have been standardized within the Internet and OSI protocols.

Even though the basic methods and terminology were developed within the narrower field of network management, they have been extended to many other topics. For example, the standardized definitions of managed objects began with such things as communications lines and protocol machines, and now include operating systems, applications, and even such things as contract relationships with suppliers and other business partners. (The latter are useful for managing such things as error reports sent to the vendor and the purchase-related aspects of devices for networked computing.)

In fact, the methods discussed here would also be well suited to such tasks as the telecontrol of a network of electric power lines or gas or oil pipelines. The available network-management applications, agents, and platforms, based on standard protocols and object-oriented definitions of managed entities, would be a good basis for such a system, and I am convinced that setting one up would be an interesting project.

Along with this development, the name of the field has evolved as well. Here, we have simply chosen the name "systems management" to indicate the whole field, in order to avoid such constructs as "integrated and automated network, systems, applications, and security management".

Managed Systems

In principle, the resources that need to be managed include all aspects of distributed systems. In fact, we fill databases with information about such things as the names of people responsible for specific tasks, and data about equipment suppliers. In practice, however, we are most often concerned with the technical components involved, which include:

- networks
- systems
- applications
- security

Each one of these areas requires a certain amount of monitoring and control, as well as definition of configuration. Many of the methods can be applied to all areas in a uniform way, but there are also a number of specialized tools for specific tasks.

Networks

The networking or communications parts of our distributed systems are a very important object of management activities. These devices and other resources are often scattered over widespread geographical areas, technically diverse, and prone to problems such as external interference and overloading. They require constant monitoring and careful planning and configuration, and often need to be adapted to new requirements or technical innovations. These resources include:

- lines
- modems
- bridges
- routers
- hubs
- LANs
- FEPs

As mentioned before, monitoring plays a particularly important role here, and this task is what many people think of first when they talk about network management. However, as a result of the increasing complexity and dynamic nature of the devices involved, other aspects, such as configuration management, are becoming increasingly important.

Systems

Traditional host-based systems, and, in fact, most or all large and medium-sized computers, have some kind of operator console. A look at the work done by the operator reveals how much has to be done in order to manage these systems. A lot of work has been done, and is still being done, on automating these activities and integrating them into the total management concept. The resources involved here include:

- operating systems
- subsystems
- middleware
- storage devices

In many cases, the software run on a typical host is stable enough that monitoring it for purposes of fault detection is hardly necessary. However, monitoring the load on the system is important. And then there are a large number of tasks, including scheduling and management of storage devices, which create a lot of work and are amenable to automation techniques.

Applications

All of the components mentioned so far are there to support the real work of computing, i.e., the jobs done by the application programs. These can be grouped into:

- standard applications
- user-specific applications

Management tasks involving applications include installation and configuration as well as starting, stopping, and monitoring them. In addition, there is a whole class of problems, including incorrect and inconsistent data, that can be detected only by the application. For these situations, the application needs a way of reporting problems directly to a central management entity.

Security

Protecting a networked environment from accidental and intentional disturbances is an important task which involves managing a number of resources, including:

- users
- access rights
- keys

The tasks involved here are concentrated on maintaining timely and consistent definitions which ensure the proper function of the security mechanisms. Also, the access to security systems needs to be restricted if the network is to be secure; for example, passwords cannot be exchanged without proper protection. As a result, the integration of multiple security systems is particularly difficult. This is an area where standardization activities are just beginning to have an effect on the products that are available.

Functions

Now that we have taken a look at the things that typically need to be managed, we should take a closer look at the tasks involved in managing them, so that we can judge the tools that are available and plan for their efficient use. We will begin with a general discussion that covers all areas of systems management.

The OSI network management framework [ISO/IEC 7498-4] defines the basic concepts of network management, including the functional areas and managed objects. This terminology provides a good basis for discussing all network and systems management, including non-OSI networks, and has been widely adopted within the industry.

The functional areas defined within the framework are:

- fault management
- accounting management
- configuration management
- performance management
- security management

As we will see, the products used for systems management often support activities which involve more than one of these areas or which cover only a small part of one area. As a result, we are constantly confronted with changing definitions, with reorganization and new configurations, just as with the managed systems themselves. In fact, this can even be seen in going from the OSI management framework [ISO/IEC 7498-4] to the OSI systems management functions [ISO/IEC 10164].

Fault Management

Fault management is concerned with the detection, isolation, and correction of faults in the system. Support for this function includes methods for:

- maintaining and examining error logs
- detecting errors
- sending and receiving notification of errors
- tracing messages and diagnosing problems
- correcting faults.

Faults can include a wide variety of malfunctions, ranging from small aberrations in performance to the total failure of a system. They may be temporary, meaning that they can be corrected by repeating the operation, such as when a communications line is occupied or when transmission is corrupted due to noise on the line. Or they may be permanent, such as when a piece of hardware fails or when an address is configured wrong.

Some faults can be detected by the component involved, as when a communications device or disk controller uses a CRC checksum to detect corruption of data. Similarly, an application program may perform plausibility checks on input data in order to prevent subsequent, undefined errors. This type of error can be reported or logged directly by the component which detects it.

Other faults may not be detectable by the components directly involved. For example, when a message is lost due to an outage of an intermediate node, or discarded by that node due to congestion problems, detection of the loss may require an end-to-end acknowledgment. Another example is that systems are rarely capable of providing notification of their own demise; other methods, such as a periodic "heartbeat" message, may be used to detect when a system has crashed.

After a fault has been detected, automatic recovery mechanisms may be activated. When this is possible, in such cases as retransmission of a message, it is generally the task of the subsystem, not of systems management. Even such recovery methods as using a different communications line are often implemented as part of the communications software, e.g., alternate routing. While some systems management products make it possible for the user to write automation scripts, this is rarely feasible for error handling.

Notifications of faults are generally written into an error log and reported to a systems management application. The task of reporting may involve the use of filters, which suppress duplicate events or forward the event only after a specific threshold has been reached. This way, the number of notifications sent over the network to the management application can be limited and controlled.

Once a fault has been reported to a management station, the task of diagnosing it can begin. In some cases, this is only a matter of localizing the component in which a malfunction has occurred. In other cases, diagnosis may be a very difficult job requiring significant amounts of time and expertise. For example, errors in the design or coding of software may affect the system in many different ways, some of which show no apparent relationship to their real cause. They may also depend on random situations such as the reuse of a specific memory address or the load on the system. And load-dependent errors may disappear when diagnostic routines such as message tracing are activated.

Fault diagnosis may include such methods as running predefined tests, analysis of error logs, analysis of protocol traces, use of code debuggers, and attempts to reproduce the error in a well-defined environment.

Correction of faults may include such activities as replacing defective hardware, installing software updates, correcting erroneous configuration parameters, preventing congestion, and deleting temporary files which cause a disk to overflow.

Accounting Management

Accounting management is concerned with establishing charges for the use of system resources and with identifying the costs for the use of those resources. Support for this function includes methods for:

- informing users of costs incurred
- setting schedules for calculating costs
- setting accounting limits
- combining costs for the use of multiple components

Accounting, or billing, is sometimes an extremely important part of a company's operations. For example, it is a significant part of the operations of telecommunications carriers. In addition, the ways customers are charged for services is often a primary factor determining their loyalty to a particular supplier. This can be improved by bills that are:

- **transparent:** showing exactly where the charges were incurred
- **machine-readable:** for example, in EDIFACT or spreadsheet format, making them efficient to process

On the other hand, good billing is often very useful to the supplier as well, because it provides valuable information about the customer's usage patterns. This turns it into a good tool for marketing and product planning.

The costs calculated by an accounting system, and reported or charged to the users, may be based on resources or on services. This distinction is an important characteristic of the accounting method, and demonstrates the wide range of possible accounting criteria.

Resources used for accounting include such things as CPU time, disk space, or usage metrics for some other device. For example, electronic mail systems often charge based on the size of messages stored on the system and how long they were stored.

Services used for accounting include such things as database access and business transactions. For example, airline reservations systems charge for each reservation made, banks often charge for each booking transaction, and public telecommunications providers charge for services based on time, distance, data volume, or a combination of these.

In addition, fees may also be calculated on the basis of other criteria intended to influence the pattern of usage. For example, a higher rate may be charged during peak hours, or rebates given for high volume or advance purchases, introductory offers made, etc.

In practice, accounting based on resource usage is often an unrealistic ideal; it may be the fairest method, but impossible to implement. This is especially true for systems with diverse usage patterns, where different users load the system in different areas, such as disk space, CPU, or communications. By comparison, accounting based on services is much easier for the user to accept, justify, plan for, and calculate as part of a total business budget.

However, even when service-based accounting is used for exterior purposes, some measurement of resource usage may be important for internal budget purposes and for planning further implementation steps.

From a technical point of view, the implementation of accounting management is very similar to that of fault management, since it involves the monitoring, logging, and reporting of information on specific activities. The difference is mainly a question of how this information is measured and used.

Finally, accounting also costs money, and a high degree of precision, i.e., a fine granularity of measurement, may be prohibitively expensive. As a result, in some cases it may be advisable to base accounting methods on simple flat-rate calculations.

In any case, the technology currently used for billing systems is often far behind the expectations for it. This is especially true for cases where the customers expect detailed use-based charging for a large range of services. In addition, these systems are often unable to cope with the development requests that result from market changes and new pricing plans. As a result, some new services have been delayed due to billing problems and some software suppliers have specialized in flexible systems for accounting management.

Configuration Management

Configuration management is concerned with controlling the operation of the system by means of defining, initializing, starting, and terminating services. Doing this requires providing and collecting data on the operations and exercising control over them. Support for this function includes methods for:

- setting parameters
- associating names and addresses with entities of the system
- initializing and closing, or starting and terminating services
- collecting information when required
- tracking changes required for and implemented in the system
- changing the configuration of the system

From this list of methods, it can be seen that configuration management applies to multiple phases of systems management, including:

- planning
- installation
- operation

Configuration management activities during the planning phase include defining the topology of a network and defining the hardware and software components to be installed and how they are interrelated. During installation, these activities include customizing products, setting parameters, and distributing configuration data and software. As a part of operation, configuration management involves activation and deactivation of services and components in order to adapt the configuration of the system to changing conditions or needs.

The configuration of a system, whether central or distributed, may be characterized as being either static or dynamic. Static configuration means that the characteristics of the system are defined before start-up and not changed during operation. For example, the system may be defined by the use of system generation statements or by writing a configuration file. This method has the advantages of being technically easier to implement and much easier to optimize in terms of performance.

Dynamic configuration means that the system can be changed without terminating its services. In this case, configuration data, stored in files, databases, or main memory, can be changed without disrupting normal operation. The advantages of this method include reduced work in defining the system and fewer losses in availability due to "planned downtime".

Even though static configuration of communications systems is quite common and sometimes the better choice, it has become fashionable to criticize this method, comparing it to the following situation: When someone wants to install a new telephone, the PTT broadcasts a message to all users, saying, "Please hang up within 5 minutes. The system will not be available for the next hour, so that new configuration tables can be loaded".

Since configuration management, in all phases of its applicability, is mostly involved with changes to the system, it is often referred to as "change management", or CCM (Change and Configuration Management). Another important aspect, referred to as "version control", is concerned with keeping track of various versions of components and providing support for ensuring consistency of systems made up of numerous components.

Configuration management of a complex system can be a very difficult task, involving a large amount of tedious work. Errors are often difficult to avoid and expensive to correct. As a result, it is important to have good tools which help do the following:

- keep accurate information
- ensure coherent and consistent definitions
- coordinate and synchronize changes
- automate repetitive tasks

Whereas the technical implementation of configuration-management methods for the planning and installation phases often leads to specialized products, the operational phase requires methods, such as monitoring and control, which are common to other areas.

Performance Management

Performance management is concerned with evaluating the behavior and effectiveness of the system. Support for this function includes methods for:

- gathering statistics
- maintaining and examining logs of system operation and history
- measuring performance under natural and artificial conditions
- altering modes of operation in order to influence the performance of the system

This list of methods is biased towards the operational aspects, but performance management applies to the planning phase of systems management as well:

- **planning:** performance modeling
- **operation:** performance measurement and optimization

Performance planning can be done in a very simple way, by monitoring the current system and planning upgrades wherever bottlenecks occur. This method has the advantage of being simple and fast to implement, and staying close to reality.

There are, however, cases that justify the use of specialized methods and tools to model the performance of a system, especially when the system or its operation is sufficiently expensive to warrant the cost or when it must be offered on a guarantee basis. These tools are most often based either on brute-force calculation of such things as instruction path lengths or on simulation techniques, such as queuing theory. Clearly, the effective use of such a tool for a complex distributed system is a difficult task, requiring thorough analysis in order to avoid false predictions.

The larger computer vendors generally have a fairly extensive set of tools for performance modeling, but only a small number of these tools are available for widespread use. This is due to a number of factors. For one, the tools are not used often enough to justify the step from an internal tool to a product with good documentation, guarantee, and so forth. Also, they often require very specialized knowledge in order to be used effectively. Next, in many cases, they are applicable only to specific products. And finally, the vendor wants to avoid publicizing results which would suggest changing the configuration in a way that would damage sales.

Another example of specialized tools consists of those for analyzing and designing network topology in order to optimize costs. This is a case where operational costs are often high enough to make going through this exercise worthwhile. Some of these methods have been published, while others are kept as trade secrets by the companies which own them and specialize in providing consultancy services in this area [Tanenbaum 1981, page 68].

Performance measurement is an area where methods and tools are much more readily available. Overall performance data can often be obtained with simple means and without expensive tools. More extensive data can be obtained from tools which either are standard components of the system or are sold as an optional component. Specialized systems management tools often contain performance-monitoring components. Of course, in a complex, heterogeneous distributed system, even these tools are not always sufficient for difficult analysis of problems involving multiple components.

Performance optimization or tuning during the operation phase is often a task done by specialists based on extensive knowledge of specific products. For smaller organizations which do not employ such specialists, it may be worthwhile to pay for consulting services for tuning purposes. On the other hand, falling hardware prices and rising costs for personnel often make extensive tuning work a bad investment.

Security Management

Security management is concerned with monitoring and enforcing the security policies established by an organization. Support for this function includes methods for:

- creation, deletion, and control of security services and mechanisms
- distribution of security-relevant information, such as encryption keys
- reporting and logging of security-relevant events, such as session initiation and access to protected resources

Ensuring security in distributed systems is a topic in its own right, to which an entire chapter of this book has been dedicated.

Many aspects of the technical implementation of security management are similar to other parts of systems management. In particular, control of security services and distribution of security information is similar to configuration management, and reporting and logging of security events is similar to the method used in fault management.

On the other hand, the special requirements for security make some aspects different. Since such things as passwords and encryption keys themselves must be protected, they cannot be stored or distributed as easily as other data such as software updates. As a result, integration and management of security subsystems are a bit more difficult. Also, standardized tools are just beginning to appear.

Systems-Management Functions

In addition to the abstract functional areas defined above, there are a number of concrete functions defined within the OSI management context [ISO/IEC 10164]. They are all defined in terms of managed objects, which are specified by their attributes and operations, and make use of inheritance. The operations are all CMIP (Common Management Information Protocol) operations, which means that new operations (other than Get, Set, etc.) are all CMIP actions.

These object definitions are defined formally and concisely, making them well suited as a basis for implementation. According to the OSI goal of providing state-of-the-art standards, they are all definitions of feasible functions and, in their content, if not in form, are often quite similar to existing products.

- **Object Management Function:** provides the basic object-manipulation services of CMIS.

- **State Management Function:** implements FSM (Finite State Machine) methods for managed objects.

- **Attributes for Representing Relationships:** defines attributes which are used to specify relationships between objects, and can help bridge the gap between managed objects and relational databases.

- **Alarm Reporting Function:** defines generic alarms (a special type of event).

- **Event Reporting Management Function:** gives the manager control over the events transmitted by a managed object.

- **Log Control Function:** provides logging facilities controlled by the manager.

- **Security Alarm Reporting Function:** provides event-forwarding discriminators for security alarms.

- **Security Audit Trail Function:** defines the event reports to be kept in a security log.

- **Objects and Attributes for Access Control:** specifies objects used for access control (security).
- **Usage Metering Function:** defines methods used for accounting.
- **Metric Objects and Attributes:** defines objects used for measurement, e.g. for performance monitoring or for accounting.
- **Test Management Function:** defines objects used for confidence and diagnostic tests.
- **Summarization Function:** defines objects used for gathering statistics and creating reports.
- **Confidence and Diagnostic Test Categories:** defines the categories of tests used for analyzing faults.
- **Scheduling Function:** used for scheduling the execution of tasks.
- **Management Knowledge Management Function:** defines a higher layer, or meta-layer, for management information, for the purpose of supporting dynamic definition of managed objects.
- **Changeover Function:** used for changing the state of a system.
- **Software Management Function:** defines the objects used for software distribution and installation.
- **Management Domain/Policy Management Function:** defines the objects used for controlling management domains and policies.
- **General Relationship Management Function:** used for managing relationships between objects.
- **Response Time Monitoring Function:** defines objects used for response time monitoring (performance management).
- **Time Management Function:** used for managing clocks.

Standards

For the purpose of defining general management functions, much of the literature has adopted the terminology of OSI management. On the other hand, the more specialized OSI systems-management functions are similar in content to existing products, but have not come into widespread use.

- OSI Basic Reference Model, Management Framework [ISO/IEC 7498-4]
- OSI Systems Management Overview [ISO/IEC 10040]
- OSI Systems Management [ISO/IEC 10164]

Managed Objects

The resources managed by the network- and systems-management application are referred to as managed objects and defined in an object-oriented fashion, in terms of their attributes, their operations, and the notifications they can send to the application.

Managed objects include such things as equipment (modems, lines, computers) and software components (communications packages, applications programs). Depending on the management protocol, there is normally a small set of standardized operations available, such as "get" and "set". Notifications are used to send asynchronous information (events, alerts) to the management application.

The set of all MOs (Managed Objects) within a system is referred to as its MIB (Management Information Base). To be precise, this is an abstract concept that includes all information that can be accessed by the management application, and does not imply anything about how the information is stored. In fact, the information can be stored at various locations in databases, flat files, or not stored at all, assuming that it can be generated when needed.

MIBs are thus the definition of the format (syntax and semantics) of a set of managed objects (resources). They are defined by a number of organizations, giving them varying degrees of standardization:

- **standards organizations:** e.g., ISO
- **consortia:** e.g., NMF
- **vendors:** e.g., IBM
- **users:** e.g., APE

Often, the term MIB is used to refer to the definition of these formats. These definitions are then often stored in a database or files of a network management platform, so that the management applications have access to the formats of the managed objects. When the user installs a new device, these format definitions are added to the database. This is often called "loading a new MIB". The ability to do this makes the management station flexible, i.e., it provides the user with an "extensible MIB".

Standards

The definition of management information in the form of objects began with OSI management, and was quickly adopted and implemented in a simpler form within the Internet management standardization. Soon after that, the Internet version became very popular, and the more powerful OSI version remained a standard for relatively few, specialized implementations.

- OSI SMI, GDMO [ISO/IEC 10165]
- Internet SMI [RFC 1155]
- Concise MIB Definitions [RFC 1212]
- MIB II [RFC 1213]
- RMON MIB [RFC 1513]
- ISO, NMF, OMNIPoint: various publications

Managers, Agents, and Frameworks

Very often, all or part of a network is managed by a central management station, which serves as a front end for the operators in charge of the network. The actual managed objects do not communicate directly with the management application; this is done by a component written specially for that purpose.

This situation illustrates the concepts of manager (or manager role) and agent (or agent role) defined in the OSI standards. The "manager" controls the managed objects by using operations such as "get" and "set" to interrogate or change the status of the objects. It also receives asynchronous notifications (i.e., events, alerts, or traps) from the managed objects. The "agent" serves as a bridge, or proxy, by communicating with the manager and interfacing directly with the managed objects via whatever special vendor-dependent techniques are necessary.

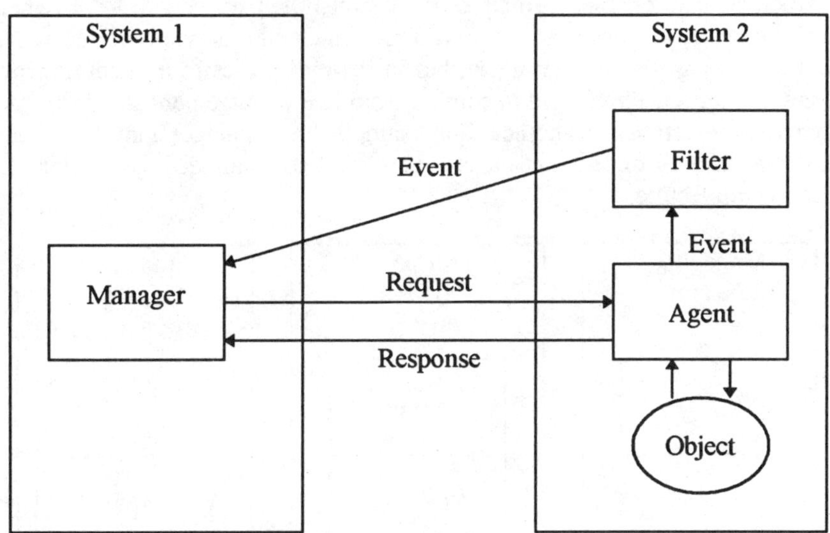

Figure 32. Management Components

Both the OSI and Internet standards use this concept; the major difference is one of complexity, both of the possible managed objects and of the operations they can support.

Two special managed objects in the OSI standards are logs and event discrimination filters. These are really part of the management system itself, since they provide services for management. However, since they are defined as managed objects, they can be controlled by the manager in a very natural way without any special methods.

"Logs" are simply log files where events created by individual agents are stored instead of being transmitted to the manager. The manager can read or delete them as necessary. "Event discrimination filters" are components that receive events from agents and apply rules, such as counting or comparing with a threshold. Depending on the outcome of this procedure, an event may be written to a log or forwarded to a manager. Since they are managed objects, these filters can be changed by the manager, for example in order to change the values of thresholds.

Just as in the client/server model, where a component can be both a client and a server, it is possible for a component of a management system to be both a manager and an agent. One use of this extension is the construction of a "manager of managers", which treats other managers as agents, thus defining a hierarchical structure to the management system. This can be useful for creating large systems which could not be managed by a single station, or for combining specialized managers, each of which covers only a part of the tasks, or for distributing management tasks over geographical regions or groups of people.

Another use of this principle is demonstrated in Figure 33, where an intermediate system is used as a proxy. From the point of view of the managing system, the proxy is just another agent, but in reality it accesses and controls another agent. Often, this concept is used to convert from one management standard (protocol and data representation) to another. For example, the manager may be based on a standard such as OSI or Internet management, and the managed system may have a proprietary architecture.

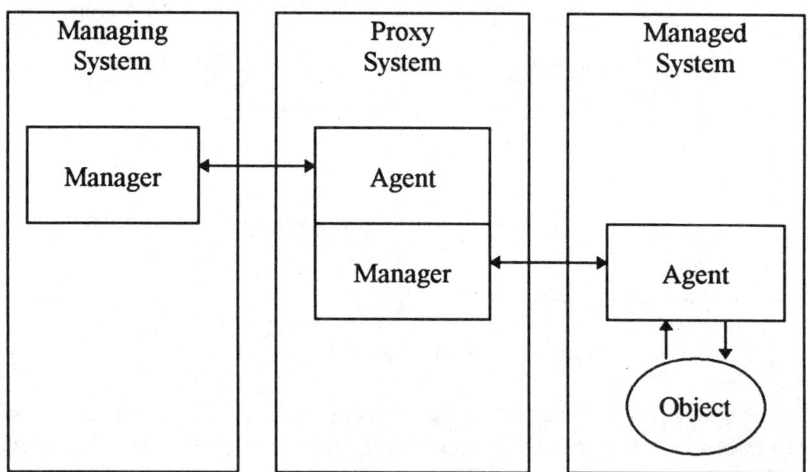

Figure 33. Proxy Agent

In any case, these concepts are asymmetrical, with one or more managers controlling a number of agents. This is also reflected in the types of operations and notifications involved. In fact, both OSI and Internet management use a predefined set of operations for all managed objects.

One further extension of these ideas results from allowing any possible objects and operations (or methods) defined for them, and any possible combination of components communicating with each other. The entities involved can communicate with each other in any way desired, whether symmetrical or asymmetrical. The set of objects defined for this purpose is then called a "management framework", and can be implemented on the basis of techniques such as CORBA (Common Object Request Broker Architecture), as was originally planned as part of OSF DME (Distributed Management Environment).

Standards

The concept of managers and agents is defined within the OSI standards and used in many situations, including Internet management. Object-oriented frameworks were defined within DME (see below) and have been implemented in proprietary products.

- OSI Systems Management Overview [ISO/IEC 10040]

Policies

An artist painting a picture is well advised to take two steps backward once in a while in order to see the whole piece in perspective. In a similar fashion, the network or systems manager needs to pause in day-to-day operations and look at the big picture in order to get a clear idea of the goals or purposes of all the individual activities of the work being done. This is where policies come in.

Goals are closely related to policies, but are not the same thing. For example, some typical goals of network management are:

- There should be a high level of network availability.
- There should be a high level of data integrity.

The policies are the next step toward achieving the goals. As such, some typical policies related to the above goals are:

- There should be no single point of failure in the network, i.e., the network should not fail due to the failure of a single component.
- The data on each file server should be backed up once per day, and three generations of daily backups and of weekly backups should be kept.

The first policy results in a characteristic of the network design, and thus has to be considered only when the network topology is changed. The second may result in a job description for certain employees or may be achieved via automated operations.

Another type of policy defines the security requirements of an organization, in order to direct the implementation of security services and mechanisms, such as access control. This is discussed in a separate chapter (see "Chapter 25. Security" on page 293).

In software development and maintenance, it is common practice to assign responsibility for a particular program or module to a specific individual. This improves efficiency, because the module "owner" knows (or gets to know) the module well. It also helps avoid conflicts, because only one person makes changes to each module, and helps avoid oversights, because each programmer has a clearly defined role. The same techniques are useful in other fields, including systems management, where it is very useful to define policies in terms of ownership and responsibility for management domains or for specific activities, such as backup.

As distributed systems grow in size and complexity, and more and more connections are made between systems belonging to different organizations, finding the cause of problems becomes more difficult. As a result, it is frequently necessary for one organization to have a way of looking into the status of another organization's network. This is particularly true when one of the organizations is providing a service, such as a transport network or a database service, to the other. In spite of this necessity, it is often difficult or even impossible to find an agreement that satisfies the two partners and provides both sufficient problem-resolving power and security. A crucial part of this is the definition of a suitable scope of visibility and of control for each organization's systems management. This is also an important part of systems management policy.

Policy definitions may come from within the systems management group, where they are made in order to give more clarity and structure to the work being done and to help guide employees in making decisions about priorities of individuals tasks. They may also come from a higher level of management, especially when they are the direct result of business goals or policies. In either case, the means for carrying out the policies often cost money, which means that they may need to be supported by higher management in terms of budgets. For example, 99% availability will generally cost more than 95%, and this cost must be justified by the benefit for the company's business.

Standards

The concept of policies is very general and, as such, in widespread use. A more concise definition can be found within the OSI standards.

- · OSI Systems Management [ISO/IEC 10164]

Domains

The management of a large, heterogeneous network which includes a number of different systems and communications products installed in dispersed locations is a big job which requires some kind of "divide and conquer" strategy in order to limit the complexity of individual tasks. This subdivision of management activities is the main goal of management domains.

In fact, there are two basic aspects of management that require this kind of division of labor:

- **human:** for defining the activities, responsibilities, and access privileges of individual human managers
- **technical:** for defining the technical scope of control of individual systems management applications or machines

In other words, the definition of management domains is a way of structuring the work done by both human and automated managers. It is something the network and systems operator does for the purely practical purpose of organizing the work in a way that makes it more efficient and easier to handle. There are no rules or standards for how to do this, but there are a number of aspects that should be considered:

- **size of job:** The work assigned to any individual human manager should be limited to what that manager can handle in order to avoid the necessity of ignoring important events.
- **expertise:** The work should be divided according to the expertise of the human managers. For example, different people might be assigned to the tasks of managing an SNA domain, a TCP/IP network, host applications, and UNIX system administration, which makes it easier to keep the proper specialist for each field. Alternatively, you may choose to break up this traditional division and assign someone to all lower-layer network components, to all higher layers, or to applications on all platforms, which makes it easier for them to keep track of the total network, or communications software, or distributed applications.
- **size of machine:** This is a question of scalability. There is only a limited number of events (traps, alerts), polling, requests, operator interfaces, and so forth that one machine can handle. How these can be spread over multiple machines is an important aspect of the product under consideration.
- **capability of tools:** Many of the tools involved are specialized for certain tasks, such as monitoring a specific LAN, monitoring the performance of an operating system, or distributing software to certain machines.
- **security:** It may be important to restrict the capabilities of an individual human or machine in order to prevent unauthorized access to the systems involved. For example, certain critical operations, such as updating routing tables or communications software, may be restricted to a small team of experienced network managers. Or limited read-only access to network resources may be granted to a large number of users or even to members of an external partner who shares a communications link with your company.

From a formal point of view, the definition of management domains is simply a question of compound objects, consisting of all managed objects in the domain. This makes it possible to define domains which are either disjoint or overlapping, the latter also being referred to as "shared control". And of course, operations on management domains can be defined just as easily as for managed objects.

From a technical point of view, the ability to define management domains depends on the products being used. Some important aspects of this are:

- **operator scope:** What methods are available for defining the visibility and privileges (profiles) of individual operators?
- **manager-agent configuration:** How can managers and agents be connected to each other? Is it possible to define a manager of managers?
- **interoperability:** Which components can interoperate with each other? (Which protocols do they use, which MIBs do they support?)
- **event routing:** How are events (traps, alerts) routed to management applications or event handlers?

Standards

The concept of domains can be found, in some form or another, in many systems, not only within management systems. A more formal definition can be found within the OSI standards.

- OSI Systems Management [ISO/IEC 10164]

Chapter 21. Management Protocols

How is network and systems management information transferred over the network? Which parts of this are standardized? These things are defined within the scope of the management protocol, which is used for communication between managers and agents.

As with any communications protocol, there are a number of aspects to be defined, including:

- **services** offered to the next higher layer (APIs)
- **protocol** used for communication with partners
- **format**, i.e., syntax and semantics of information

The information required for systems management can be transported in a number of places, including:

- within **normal messages** or their headers: For example, the X.25 Clear packet carries accounting information.
- in **special messages**: For example, the X.25 Reset packet is used for configuration of virtual circuits.
- in special **layer protocols**: For example, the network connection management subprotocol is used for managing the OSI network layer.
- in special **systems management protocols**: For example, OSI CMIP or Internet SNMP (see below) can be used to access MOs.

In the following, we will only deal with systems management protocols, since the others examples can be considered part of the inner workings of the network.

SNA/MS

One of the more widespread proprietary management protocols is SNA/MS (SNA Management Services), which is native to IBM's SNA (Systems Network Architecture). We will take a brief look at it here due to the importance of using it to establish gateway functions to SNA networks. This may involve adding a few management messages to individual devices connected to an SNA network, such as banking devices, or translating specific management messages at the boundary between an SNA network and a network using a different set of protocols.

The primary management message in traditional SNA is the NMVT (Network Management Vector Transport). This is a general-purpose SNA message which can be adapted to many situations. Some important special cases of the NMVT are the following:

- alert
- execute (RUNCMD)
- reply to execute (RUNCMD reply)

The alert is particularly important in heterogeneous networks, because it is the format which is generally supported by vendors of devices which need to send their status information to the network manager. The SNA alert contains a number of fields, called "code points", which describe the alert, probable causes, possible corrective measures, etc.

The RUNCMD is a primarily textual message which makes it possible for an SNA management station to execute a command on a remote machine and interrogate the results. For example, it can be used in such a way that a host NetView operator can issue an MS-DOS command on a PC and view the results.

In addition to the more traditional NMVT messages, SNA Management Services also contains genuine OSI management messages (see CMIP below), but transported over an SNA LU 6.2 conversation. This was added during the implementation of the "new" SNA, i.e., APPN (Advanced Peer-to-Peer Networking), which supports dynamic configuration.

CMIP

Within the OSI (Open Systems Interconnection) framework, the management services and their protocol are defined by the CMIS (Common Management Information Services) and CMIP (Common Management Information Protocol) documents. In this case, the services are so closely tied to the protocol elements that we can refer to them together without much danger of confusion.

Transaction Synchronization

When a number of components of a distributed system all work together, it is often important to keep them all in a consistent state. For example, all may need to run the same version of a communications protocol. Problems caused by different nodes operating with different software versions can be avoided in a number of ways, such as protocol implementations which assure backward compatibility or which negotiate the protocol version during connection establishment.

Even with these methods, it is sometimes desirable to make changes to a number of devices simultaneously, and to have either all changes take effect or none at all. This is particularly true for small devices which do not have sufficient resources to support multiple levels of protocols in a backward-compatible manner. It is also necessary when dramatic changes are to be made, such as switching to a completely new protocol, or even to a new physical interface on the existing media.

The requirements that result from this are exactly those of the ACID transaction, the basis for transaction-processing protocols: A number of operations are to be considered as a single action, the system stays in a consistent state at all times, no partial changes are visible until everything is finished, and these changes are then permanent (see "Distributed Transaction Processing" on page 29).

The CMIP protocol described above provides the mechanism for operating on individual attributes or on a whole group of attributes, but not for synchronizing these changes. This is made possible by the combination of CMIP with OSI Transaction Processing, as specified in a recent OSI standard [ISO/IEC 11587]. Since OSI TP covers only transaction control and not data transfer, it is natural to combine it with another protocol, such as Remote Operations (for data access) or CMIP (for management).

Services

The services of CMIP, i.e., of the OSI management protocol, can be seen easily by looking at the messages that can be transferred between management stations and managed resources. As in most protocols, these messages are called PDUs (Protocol Data Units). The actual service interface, or API, is closely tied to these messages.

These messages correspond to methods which act on managed objects. This puts us fully within the context of object-oriented programming, with the limitation that the methods are predefined, except for the "action", which provides a certain amount of flexibility. The "create" and "delete" messages control the life cycle of managed objects, "get" and "set" operate on their attributes, and "events" allow the managed object to send asynchronous (or unsolicited) messages to the management station.

The power of the CMIP messages is due in part to the full object orientation of the managed objects, including inheritance, and to the ability to define operations on large sets of objects ("scoping" and "filtering"). These services can be summarized as follows:

- **PDUs** (Protocol Data Units)
  - **Create:** sent by the manager to request the agent to create an instance of a managed object. Always confirmed.
  - **Delete:** sent by the manager to request the agent to delete an instance of a managed object. Always confirmed.
  - **Get:** sent by the manager to request the agent to get the values of attributes of managed objects. Always confirmed.
  - **Cancel-Get:** sent by the manager to request the agent to cancel a previous Get request. Always confirmed.
  - **Set:** sent by the manager to request the agent to set the values of attributes of managed objects. Optionally confirmed.
  - **Action:** sent by the manager to request the agent to perform specified actions of managed objects. Optionally confirmed.
  - **Event-Report:** sent by the agent to notify the manager of an asynchronous event. Optionally confirmed.

- **selection** of managed objects in the PDUs
  - **scoping:** specifies a part of the containment tree
  - **filtering:** specifies a Boolean expression for selecting objects
  - **synchronization:** specifies whether the operations of scoping and filtering are to be performed on an **atomic** or **best-effort** algorithm
- **transaction control** (ACID properties)

Variants

One important aspect of CMIP is that it requires all seven layers of OSI communications. In particular, it requires the ACS (Association-Control Service) and the ROS (Remote-Operation Service) within the application layer, and a full version of the presentation and session layers. This has been the subject of criticism for a number of reasons.

What happens when the communications path is not available? Then, no network management information about the remote entities is available. At first appearance, this sounds like a big problem. In fact, it has been the motivation for some users to define alternative, independent communications paths for management information. In practice, this is not a problem for most installations.

To begin with, during normal operations, most problems occur in things like lines and devices, not in the upper layers of communications software. Although getting the upper-layer components running for the first time might be a big job, they don't cause much trouble later, because they become stable after a period of extensive use and little change (this might not be true for some applications which continue to change). This means that the important problem, the loss of a connection to the remote site, is known to the management station and has first priority anyway.

Then, in most networks, when the path to a remote site is lost, all problems within the remote site either are unimportant compared to the lost connection or can be handled directly. For example, when a branch office of a bank loses its connection to the main office, this is a first-priority problem. Problems within the branch office, such as the failure of a printer or other peripheral device, can often be handled without the central management station.

The real reason for criticism of the seven-layer character of the CMIP protocol is the fact that it is too much of a burden for small devices, such as modems, bridges, routers, and hubs. This means that the only way to use CMIP for these devices is to implement CMIP on some intermediate node and use some other protocol between the node and the device.

A similar reason for alternative proposals is the desire to use the powerful and flexible CMIP formats within existing, non-OSI network protocols. This has led to the definition of a number of (nonstandard) variants:

- **CMOL:** CMIP Over LLC (Logical Link Layer), also referred to as CMIP Over LAN. This is intended for devices that are too small to support a full OSI implementation, and can be used for management of a LAN. However, since it has no network layer, there is no support for routing from one LAN to another.

- **CMOT:** CMIP Over TCP/IP. This is intended for use of CMIP functions within a TCP/IP net. It uses the TCP/IP protocol in place of the OSI network and transport layers and LPP (Lightweight Presentation Protocol) in place of the OSI session and presentation layers.
- **CMOS:** CMIP Over SNA. This was proposed by IBM, and uses SNA LU 6.2 (APPC) to transport CMIP messages. It, or something similar, is used by APPN internally for management purposes.

Although none of these proposed variants has become an official standard in its original form, all three have led to standards or specifications that are similar, and all of these have been implemented in real products.

SNMP

The Internet management protocol SNMP (Simple Network Management Protocol) was developed in about 1988 at a time when the CMIP standard was also under development, but not yet fully available. The original intention of its authors was to produce a useful management architecture that would be simple enough to be implemented rapidly, but at the same time would be as similar as possible to CMIP, in order to ensure a smooth migration path from SNMP to CMOT and finally to CMIP [Stallings 1993, pages 68, 272].

As time passed, this requirement was partially relaxed, resulting in MIB structures which are not completely compatible. But the big development was the momentum produced by the large number of vendors who implemented SNMP MIBs and agents, making SNMP into the major de facto standard in network management.

Services

As with CMIP, the services of SNMP can be seen by looking at the messages, or PDUs (Protocol Data Units), transferred by the protocol. Also, SNMP APIs generally correspond very closely to these messages.

- **PDUs** (Protocol Data Units)
    - **GetRequest:** sent by the manager to request the agent to send the values of a list of objects.
    - **GetNextRequest:** sent by the manager to request the agent to send the values of the next instances after those specified in a list of objects.
    - **SetRequest:** sent by the manager to request the agent to set a list of objects to the values specified.
    - **GetResponse:** sent by the agent as a response to any of the above requests.
    - **Trap:** sent by the agent to notify the manager of an asynchronous event.

All of the SNMP PDUs are coded in ASN.1, which was defined as part of the OSI presentation layer. This makes SNMP capable of doing the data conversions necessary for exchange between machines of differing architecture. All of the PDUs specify their objects in the form of a "variable binding", which is a list of pairs, each consisting of a reference to an object instance and its value (in a GetRequest, the values are NULL).

The GetNextRequest is a surprisingly powerful element: By requesting the name and value of the next instance (in the lexicographic ordering of object instances), it makes it possible to request everything from the agent without previous knowledge of it, i.e., to automatically discover the structure of the MIB.

The general method of usage for SNMP is for Traps to be sent only for serious errors, and for the status of all devices to be interrogated periodically by the manager (i.e., polled).

As mentioned above, SNMP was originally intended as an interim solution, so it is not surprising that it has a number of limitations in comparison with CMIP:

- SNMP is based on a connectionless protocol (UDP/IP), and so there is no guarantee that messages will be delivered. The application must either accept this lack of perfection or implement its own mechanisms. For example, polling should eventually retrieve the current state of all object instances, even when some Trap messages are lost.
- Polling can cause a significant load on the network. As a result, there is a limit to the number of nodes that can be supported by a single manager.
- The security mechanism of SNMP is minimal. This can add to the security deficiencies of TCP/IP networks in general.
- The complexity and flexibility of Managed Object definitions is very limited, and they do not support inheritance.
- SNMP does not support manager-to-manager communication.

SNMPv2

After SNMP established itself as the big de facto standard, and while CMIP implementations were still too scarce, it became apparent that the limitations of SNMP posed severe problems for some users, especially those with large networks. The important problems involved security and performance, and were addressed in two proposals, S-SNMP (Secure SNMP) and SMP (Simple Management Protocol). Both of these were then superseded by work on SNMPv2 (SNMP Version 2).

Another enhancement to be found in SNMPv2 is manager-to-manager communications, which can be important for integrating components of a large network when the load would be too much for a single management station. It can also be used for integrating specialized components of a heterogeneous environment or implementing a manager-of-managers strategy.

The main problem involved with SNMPv2 is its complexity, especially with relation to security. In fact, the 12 documents which define SNMPv2 cover a total of 416 pages [Stallings 1993, page 272]. As a result of this complexity and other issues, the security part of SNMPv2 is not finished yet [Stallings 8/96].

Services

The services of SNMPv2 can be seen by comparing the protocol's messages with those of SNMP.

- **PDUs** (Protocol Data Units)
    - **GetRequest:** sent by the manager to request the agent to send the values of a list of objects.
    - **GetNextRequest:** sent by the manager to request the agent to send the values of the next instances after those specified in a list of objects.
    - **GetBulkRequest:** sent by the manager to request the agent to send the values of multiple successive instances after those specified in a list of objects. Equivalent to multiple GetNextRequest PDUs.
    - **SetRequest:** sent by the manager to request the agent to set a list of objects to the values specified.
    - **Response:** sent by the agent as a response to any of the above requests.
    - **Trap:** sent by the agent to notify the manager of an asynchronous event.
    - **InformRequest:** sent by a manager to another manager. The semantics are defined in the M2M (Manager-to-Manager) MIB.
- **security**
    - **privacy:** prevents eavesdropping
    - **authentication:** ensures the validity of the source of a message, preventing, e.g., masquerade attacks
    - **authorization:** controls access to resources

Migration

Since SNMPv2 is intended as a replacement for SNMP, it is important to have an easy way of migrating from the old version to the new version. The basic method for doing this is to install a new SNMPv2 manager first, and then replace the agents as they become available. However, the protocols are not completely compatible, which is partly due to security requirements, so it is necessary to introduce some kind of adapter between them. There are basically two methods for doing this:

- **proxy agent:** This is an intermediary which acts as an SNMPv2 agent and an SNMP manager.
- **bilingual manager:** This is simply a manager that speaks both SNMPv2 and SNMP, removing the need for an intermediate step.

WBEM

Recently, a consortium consisting of BMC Software Inc., Cisco Systems Inc., Compaq Computer Corp., Intel Corp., and Microsoft Corp. has announced plans to create something called WBEM (Web-Based Enterprise Management). This will be based on existing standards, including HTML, HTTP, SNMP, and DMI, and will include the following additions:

- HMMP (HyperMedia Management Protocol)
- HMMS (HyperMedia Management Schema)
- HMOM (HyperMedia Object Manager)

Further details can be found at the Web site http://wbem.freerange.com.

Standards

The following list includes all relevant standards for management protocols. In addition to these, areas such as application management are often covered by vendor-specific specifications.

- CMIS [ISO/IEC 9595].
- CMIP [ISO/IEC 9596].
- CMIP with TP [ISO/IEC 11587].
- CMOT is not a formal standard, but the idea is supported by a standard for transporting upper-layer OSI messages over TCP/IP [RFC 1006].
- CMOL in its original form is not a formal standard, but has led to the standard known as LMMP (LAN/MAN Management Protocol).
- CMOS is not a formal standard, but the idea has been implemented in SNA/MS.
- LMMP [ISO/IEC 15802].
- SNMP [RFC 1157].
- SNMPv2 emerging Internet standard.

Trends and Products

After the original work on CMIP and SNMP was begun, SNMP quickly became the most widespread management protocol. This is due largely to its relatively simple nature, which made it possible for almost all vendors of network devices to provide support for it. On the other hand, CMIP has become established within many telecoms, or PTTs, and is used internally within IBM's APPN.

Due to this widespread use, SNMP has become the method of choice for managing networks, but it has not been established so well for managing operating systems and applications. This area has developed more slowly, and is often covered by proprietary methods or not at all. More recent developments suggest the possibility of using standards such as CORBA or HTML.

The use of management protocols is also closely tied to the definition of sets of managed objects, or MIBs (Management Information Bases). Within OSI management, MIB definitions cover little more than the OSI protocols themselves, but SNMP MIBs have been defined in a large number of RFCs and in at least as many device-specific vendor specifications.

Products which support management protocols can be divided into two categories, agents and managers. Agents for SNMP have been implemented by most vendors of network devices and operating systems, whereas agents for both CMIP and SNMPv2 are relatively small in number. Managers for all three protocols have been produced by many vendors of management software (see "Chapter 23. Components" on page 256). Since these software products are often general-purpose tools, it is possible to include support for all protocols. However, as long as the vendors of network devices do not provide support for the more complex CMIP and SNMPv2, these protocols will not come into widespread use.

Chapter 22. Desktop Management

When you install a new component in a PC, it is sometimes necessary to worry about conflicts involving interrupt request numbers of DMA addresses. Then you may need to choose among various device drivers and put them in a configuration file. Ideally, it should be possible to install and use the component without any further problems.

Similarly, in an organization that uses a lot of PCs, the people in charge of making the networks and distributed applications work may have difficulty doing it, because no one really knows how those machines are configured, not even the people who installed the devices. After all, keeping track of all those add-ons would probably cost more than the hardware itself.

This is the area addressed by the task of desktop management. Actually, there are two major concerns involved here:

- "plug and play": effortless, automatic installation of new components
- desktop management: systems management for all aspects of desktop systems

The basis for achieving these goals is a standardized but nonetheless flexible way of storing and accessing information about all components of desktop systems. This has been the subject of recent work done by the DMTF (Desktop Management Task Force), a vendor consortium that includes Microsoft, HP, and IBM. The result of the work is a specification of the DMI (Desktop Management Interface), which includes both information format and APIs [DMI].

In addition to the DMTF standard, there are a number of other issues involved in achieving the goals of plug and play [Halfhill 9/94]. In fact, they aren't so difficult when one vendor has control of the technology, as was shown by the Apple Macintosh and the IBM Microchannel Architecture.

Now there is a standard called "Plug and Play", abbreviated as "PnP", and written with capital Ps to distinguish it from the general concept "plug and play". PnP grew out of a standard first proposed by Microsoft and Intel, and is now controlled by the Plug and Play Association, which also includes Compaq. The standard is intended for PCs, and covers four areas:

- BIOS
- the operating system
- hardware devices
- applications software

In order to take full advantage of PnP, all of these components will need to support it. This way, dynamic configuration will include hardware and will be in effect during start-up, and the information will be available to applications. However, even without full support, upgrading individual parts of the system should improve the situation. As a result, PnP is expected to show some important results soon, but may take many years to have complete effect.

MIF (Management Information Format)

In the DMI specification, management information is defined in terms of ASCII files which bear a resemblance to Windows "ini" files, making them easy to create and to extend. Whereas "ini" files have a two-layer structure, consisting of "sections" and "entries", MIF files have three layers (component, group, attribute).

The groups can be repeated to form arrays ("tables"), which are addressed by "keys", so that addressing an attribute in a MIF file requires four parameters (component, group, key, attribute).

DMI (Desktop Management Interface)

Figure 34 shows the structure of the DMI components.

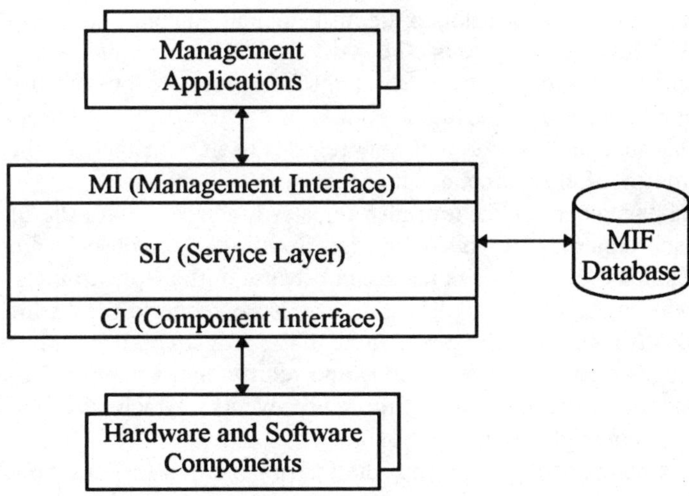

Figure 34. DMI (Desktop Management Interface)

The basic components of DMI are:

- **MI (Management Interface):** the API used by management applications
- **SL (Service Layer):** the intermediate layer, which provides the following functions:
    - synchronization
    - flow control
    - component name resolution

- **CI (Component Interface):** the interface to components, which is implemented by "component instrumentation" code
- **MIF (Management Information Format):** the language used for defining desktop management information

This structure may look familiar as well: It is very similar to the structure of WOSA (Windows Open Service Architecture) (see "WOSA" on page 72). The MI (Management Interface) contains the basic "get", "set", and "list" functions required for management tasks, much like SNMP and CMIP.

Local Access to DMI

DMI is a local interface, or API. It can, and often will, be used in an isolated fashion, i.e., on a stand-alone PC. When it is used, the following steps will take place:

- The SL (Service Layer) is a resident piece of code, which is most likely installed as part of the operating system.
- When a component is installed, its instrumentation code calls the SL to "install the MIF". The SL reads the ASCII MIF data and stores it in an implementation-defined way. Since the MIF contains attributes which define the instrumentation code, the SL now knows where to find it (path name, etc.).
- The instrumentation code will now register itself with the SL, specifying call-back routines for the functions it supports.
- The management applications also register themselves with the SL, specifying call-back routines to be used for receiving responses and indications (unsolicited events). This is necessary because of the asynchronous API.
- Now the management applications can issue requests for listing, getting or setting attributes. The SL passes these to the proper component instrumentation code (component name resolution) and returns the responses. In addition, the component instrumentation can send events, which are passed to the management applications.
- When a component is removed, the instrumentation code uses the "uninstall" request.

As a result of these activities, the following functions can be supported:

- Components can be installed automatically, add their MIF information to the repository, and read any other information they need.
- Applications can find any necessary configuration information in the MIF repository. In particular, the proper device drivers can be activated automatically, instead of being predefined by manual means.

- Management applications can monitor and control all devices which have been installed as DMI components. By using the "list" requests, they can read all of the MIF repository without any previous knowledge of its specific structure.

Remote Access to DMI

The DMI specification was defined as a local service, without specifying how it was to be accessed by remote management applications. This makes it independent of the management protocol used. However, thought was given to how it could be used, and there are a number of alternatives for this, as shown in Figure 35.

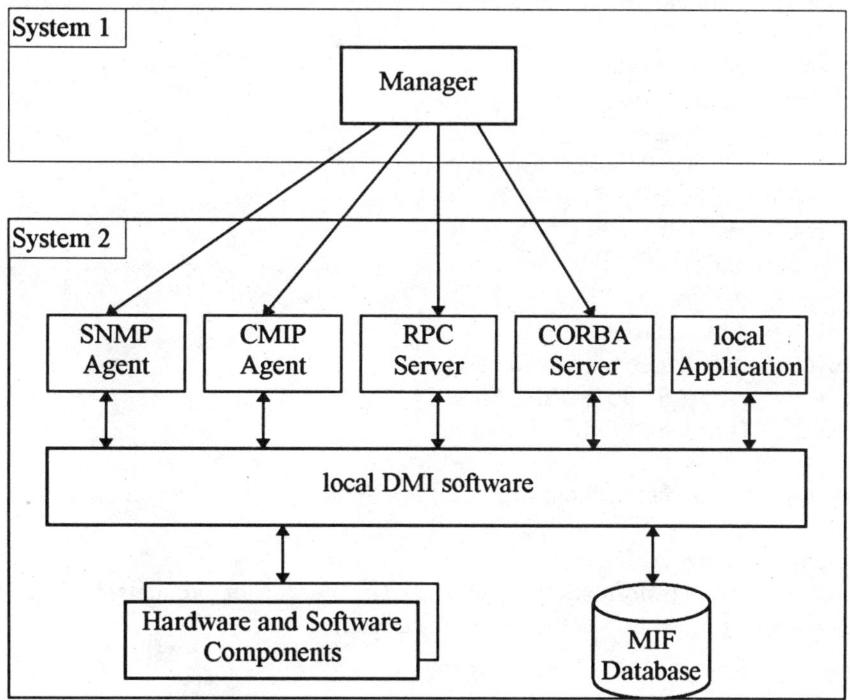

Figure 35. Alternatives for Accessing DMI

The possibilities for accessing DMI from a management application via a standard management protocol include the following:

- **SNMP:** The MIF structure can be modeled as SNMP objects. An SNMP agent can access DMI.

- **CMIP:** The MIF structure can be modeled using GDMO (Guidelines for the Definition of Managed Objects). A CMIP agent can access DMI.
- **RPC:** An RPC server can be defined which passes its requests to DMI.
- **CORBA:** An object can be defined which accesses DMI.

The DMI specification version 2.0 has some improvements for remote access. It provides a procedural interface, and defines the use of three RPC variants: DCE RPC, Sun ONC RPC, and TI RPC (used by Novell).

Services

The specification of the MIF format is formal, in terms of BNF (Backus Naur Form), but nonetheless simple to use. The MIF specification has the following characteristics:

- formal definition (BNF)
- Three-layered structure:
    - component
    - group and table of groups
    - attribute
- data types:
    - integers
    - strings
    - date and time
- internationalization: character set
    - 8-bit ASCII [ISO/IEC 8859-1]
    - Unicode [ISO/IEC 10646]

The DMI (Desktop Management Interface) has the following characteristics:

- asynchronous API
- only one call (information is passed in data blocks, not parameters)
- requests (issued by management application)
    - get
    - set
    - list
- responses (to requests)
- indication (events sent from component to management application)
- confirmation (of indications)

Standards

The primary standards relevant to this chapter are the MIF (Management Information Format) and DMI (Desktop Management Interface) defined by the DMTF (Desktop Management Task Force).

- DMI and MIF (DMTF) available from http://www.dmtf.org/tech/spects.html

Trends and Products

The following is a partial list of the vendors whose products have been certified to be DMI-compliant [Simpson, 11/96]

- Compaq: PCs and monitors
- Dell: PCs
- Digital Equipment: PCs and management software
- Hewlett-Packard: PCs, network adapters, and systems management software
- IBM: network adapters and systems management applications
- Intel: network adapters, systems management software, DMI browser
- NEC Technologies: PCs, DMI browser

Chapter 23. Components

The material in the past three chapters has been very general. It began with a discussion of general management functions, which led up to the formal standards for specialized functions. This was followed by a presentation of the most important management protocols, forming the basis for communication between managed resources and management applications. Although these protocols are not used for all tasks, they are still very general in nature. Finally, we had a look at an important standard for the management of desktop systems.

Now, in this chapter, we will examine the components of real management systems, or, in other words, the types of management products which are available. Very often, these products do not match up with the general categories of management functions. For example, management platforms usually cover both fault management (including monitoring and diagnosis) and configuration management (i.e., defining and controlling the structure and function of a system). On the other hand, software distribution, which is just a special case of configuration management, has become the topic of specialized tools, aimed at distributing large amounts of data in a reliable and efficient way and keeping track of the state of all components.

Management Platforms

After specialized management tools for a number of devices and networks came into widespread use, it became evident that there was a need to integrate these tools. In addition, there are a number of basic services, including communications support, naming, and user interfaces, that need to be treated in a more general manner than is possible with individual tools. This is the main objective of management platforms.

In practice, it is sometimes difficult to see the boundary between a platform and some of the applications that run on it, such as network monitors or other managers and agents.

The most fundamental part of a management platform is communications support in the form of an implementation of one or more management protocols such as SNMP and CMIP. In order to make this readily available for developers of specialized managers and agents, the platform also provides an API to this protocol, typically XMP, the X/Open management protocol. This makes it possible for applications to use the protocol without implementing all aspects of it in each application.

Since the managed resources are modeled in an object-oriented manner and named as objects, there needs to be some way of keeping track of which managed objects exist in the network, and where they are located. This means that it should be possible to add object classes (MIB definitions) to the system when they are required, and to add (i.e., register) object instances when new devices are installed. Then there must be some way of correlating these object instances with network addresses, so that the communications system can send requests to the right place. This is the task of registry or postmaster services.

At the user level, management platforms generally supply some way of integrating multiple applications into one management station. This involves the use of a standardized GUI (Graphical User Interface) as a method of making all applications visible and accessible from the same workstation.

Services

The services of management platforms can be found in the types of resources they can manage, including questions of connectivity, and the functions they perform. These include logging of events, active monitoring, control operations, and databases for storing such things as network topology and the state of individual components. The products should also be evaluated in terms of their ability to be adapted to tasks of various sizes and to be operated in a secure way.

- **management protocols:** e.g., SNMP and CMIP and variants such as CMOT and CMOL
    - **protocol API:** e.g., XMP
    - **conversion:** e.g., between NMVT alerts and SNMP traps
- **managed objects:** support for definition and administration of MOs
    - **registry:** of MOs
    - **naming:** of MOs
    - **addressing:** of MOs
- **management information base:** support for definition of MIBs
    - **standard MIBs:** certain standard MIBs will be built in
    - **extensible MIBs:** support for MIB extensions
    - **MIB loader:** addition of a new MIB definition
    - **MIB compiler:** a tool used for writing a formal MIB definition in a language such as GDMO and preparing it to be loaded into the platform
    - **MIB browser:** part of the end-user interface, a generic tool for looking at the status of all objects defined and registered
- **topology:** definition of network configuration
    - **manually,** via screens
    - **via API,** useful for automation and integration
    - **automatically,** i.e., auto-discover
- **databases:** used for such things as topology, registry, etc.
    - **standard SQL** interface allows implementation on database server
    - **open data model** supports integration and ad hoc queries
    - **APIs** support integration and automation
- **events:** support for receiving and handling events
    - **filters:** event discrimination filters, threshold checking
    - **API:** for defining filters

- **configuration:** definition of what happens with events
- **forwarding:** to other components, such as a trouble-ticket system (see "Trouble-Ticket System" on page 275)
- **actions:** triggered by events, e.g., automated error handling
- **logs:** support for management of log files
- **end-user interface:**
  - **GUI:** general support for windowing functions
  - **maps:** views of the network with icons that represent MOs and are correlated with their states
  - **API:** for extending UI
  - **domains:** definition of operator scope of visibility and control
- **scalability:** ability to adapt the management system to the size of the task, e.g., by configuring a cascaded array of management stations (manager of managers)
- **security:** ability to prevent misuse, e.g. via methods such as authentication and authorization. Optimally, this should be integrated into a total security system.

Standards

The standards which are applicable to management platforms include management protocols, APIs, and some consortium definitions of their functions.

- SNMP [RFC 1157]
- CMIP [ISO/IEC 9596]
- XMP [X/Open C306]
- XOM [X/Open C315]
- Carnegie-Mellon SNMP API
- NMF: various publications

Trends and Products

The following list includes the major management platforms. However, since the boundaries between platforms and other general-purpose management tools are not always clear, most of the other general-purpose tools have been included here as well.

- BMC: Patrol
- Boole & Babbage: Command/Post
- Candle: Candle Command Center
- Computer Associates: CA-Unicenter and CA-Unicenter/TNG (The Next Generation)
- DEC: Polycenter NetView
- HP: OpenView

- IBM: NetView (for AIX, ESA, OS/2, and Windows)
- New Dimension Software: Control-M
- Novadigm: various products
- Novell: NMS (NetWare Management System)
- Platinum: POEMS (Platinum Open Enterprise Management System)
- Tivoli: TME (Tivoli Management Environment)

Recently, as the popularity of the World Wide Web has grown, there has been interest in using the Web as a front end for management tools. For example, UB Networks has announced the use of Java in its management tools, in a product called Empower.

Network Monitor

As nice as general solutions are, there always seems to be a need for special tools for doing special jobs. The intelligence built into individual components, such as communications protocol machines or file servers, is a good basis for monitoring the state of the system at a high level. This can tell you which connections exist, how much data has been transmitted, and so forth. But what can we do when there are problems which just can't be detected by these components?

The solution to this difficulty often involves taking a deeper look into the insides of things, for example by sending test messages and analyzing the behavior of them in terms of signal quality and propagation time. The tools which do this are often called network sniffers or probes, because they peek under the covers of the system. They often monitor and analyze all traffic on the network, making them into a kind of wiretap or eavesdropping device.

Today, there are a number of these network monitors available. Many of them are specialized to specific networks, such as Ethernets or FDDI LANs, and many are stand-alone tools which run on a PC or on a dedicated test instrument which is connected to the network that needs to be analyzed. Increasingly, though, they can also be configured as agents that communicate with a central management tool, making them more interesting for use in large heterogeneous systems. When used as an agent, a decentralized tool such as a network monitor can significantly reduce the load on a WAN by performing polling of devices and event filtering locally.

The tasks of network monitors include testing the physical layer, analyzing protocols, especially in the link, network, and transport layers, but sometimes even in higher layers, and monitoring other aspects of network operations. There is often a considerable overlap with the next type of tool, the performance monitor, which often results in these two tasks being accomplished by a single tool.

One advantage of the protocol-testing capability of these tools is the fact that they can analyze the network even when individual components are malfunctioning or providing erroneous information about the operation of the network. In addition, they can provide information about the total situation, whereas individual components are often concerned with only a portion of the information.

The protocol analyzers in these tools can often be programmed to perform specific tests as needed. In fact, this makes it possible to use such a tool for conformance testing of protocol implementations.

Services

The services of these tools, called network monitors, LAN analyzers, sniffers, etc., include the following:

- testing of lower layers, especially physical
- capturing packets
- filtering to reduce volume
- protocol analysis, especially link, network, and transport
- editing data
- analysis of behavior
  - configuration
  - connections
- display of results
- replay of trace as a test tool
- usage
  - stand-alone
  - as an agent
- local operations (as an agent)
  - polling devices
  - event filtering
  - forwarding events

Standards

Before a network monitor can analyze a protocol, it needs to take account of the standard or specification of the protocol, so the user may prepare a list of relevant protocols as a checklist for buying such a device. Also, the RMON specification makes it possible for a remote RMON agent to collect information which can be used by a centrally installed network monitor.

- all relevant protocol standards
- RMON MIB [RFC 1513]

Trends and Products

Traditionally, protocol analyzers have been very expensive, special-purpose instruments. More recently, there are more and more software implementations which make use of standard equipment, such as a PC with an NIC (Network Interface Card).

In the latter case, the analyzer can see only the network traffic which the NIC presents to it. For many cards, this is only the traffic which contains the computer's own link-layer, or MAC (Media Access Control), address. A card which passes all network traffic to the computer is said to operate in "promiscuous" mode.

A few of the many network monitoring tools on the market are the following:

- HP OpenView Network Node Manager
- IBM LAN Network Manager
- Novell NMS (NetWare Management System), Novell LANalyzer

Performance Monitor

Prevention is better than cure. If you have some way of monitoring the disk usage on remote systems, you may be able to prevent the big problems that occur when applications are not able to write their data to the disk. For example, the application might crash, terminating important services; or it might leave important data inconsistent and unreadable, as happens when pointers or other references cannot be updated and stored completely.

The situation is similar for a number of areas, including the usage of disks, of processing power, and of communications lines. For example, an Ethernet LAN becomes very inefficient when the load is so high that a large number of collisions occur. The collisions disturb the normal transmission of messages, and the resulting retransmissions make the situation worse. If this cannot be prevented by simply providing enough bandwidth for all applications, there should be some way of monitoring the load and preventing situations where overload occurs.

This is where performance monitors come in. These are often stand-alone tools that monitor a specific LAN, but they can also be centralized systems that collect and analyze data provided by agents on the critical devices. These agents do the actual measuring task, which is often specialized to the system being monitored.

In addition, performance monitoring is important not only for networks, but for all kinds of systems, including large computers and their operating systems. Since the task of measuring performance often involves the lower levels of a system, there are a number of highly specialized monitors available, rather than a few generic tools.

In practice, performance monitoring often consists of monitoring or examining large amounts of data, and then presenting statistics to a management station. In order to do this efficiently over a network, it is necessary for a remote agent to monitor and filter the raw data, and then present the central management station with the results. Although this is often done using proprietary formats, it can be supported by the standard "Remote Monitoring" MIB.

Services

The services of performance-monitoring tools can be summed up as follows:

- monitoring of resource usage for
    - disk space
    - database utilization
    - CPU time
    - memory
    - transmission lines
    - behavior of applications
- alarms and notifications
    - when thresholds are surpassed
    - on other conditions, such as loss of connection
- collecting data
- analyzing data
    - locating problems
    - producing reports
- traffic generator for testing component performance

Standards

Very often, performance monitoring agents are special devices or software packages which are tied very closely to the resource to be monitored and are by nature proprietary. However, the RMON specification makes it possible for a remote RMON agent to collect information which can be used by a centrally installed performance monitor.

- any standards for the resources to be monitored
- RMON MIB [RFC 1513]

Trends and Products

The following list contains a few of the better-known performance monitors. There are many more, both general-purpose tools and those for monitoring the performance of special resources.

- HP: OpenView NetMetrix, OpenView Traffic Monitor, OpenView PerfView
- IBM: NetView Performance Monitor
- MAXM Systems: MAX/Enterprise
- OpenVision Technologies: AXXiON

Backup and Storage Management

In order for any system, whether it is distributed or not, to be reliable it is necessary to make backup copies of data, so that they can be restored when required. This is necessary not only when the primary disk fails, but when software errors or users' mistakes cause the data to be damaged or lost.

Very often, the service organization of a company is responsible for making backups of all data on mainframes and file servers, but anything stored on a local PC disk is the responsibility of the individual user. The backup policy and organizational procedures should be given thorough consideration in order to avoid problems such as overwriting backup storage too early, overwriting good data with bad, or simply making mistakes that corrupt large amounts of data.

On centralized mainframe systems, both the technology and organizational procedures for storage management have reached a high degree of maturity and sophistication. In distributed systems, such as PC LANs, some important tools have been developed, but there is still a need for much more.

One example of a method which is well established on mainframes, but is just beginning to appear on distributed systems, is HSM (Hierarchical Storage Management) [Reinhardt 6/94]. With backup methods, files are copied from primary to secondary storage (i.e., archived) without being deleted. This way, they are protected from loss, but the backup does not save any space on the primary storage, which tends to get more cluttered all the time.

In contrast, HSM moves (migrates) the files from primary to secondary storage when they aren't needed and moves them back (recalls them) when they are needed again. In general, the system supports multiple layers, i.e., a hierarchy, of storage devices, such as:

- magnetic disk
- optical disk
- magnetic tape

Optimally, an HSM system should operate completely automatically, migrating files to secondary storage on the basis of a policy such as the time since the last access, and recalling them when they are needed. In practice, it is not always easy to establish a really good policy for migration, or to recall files fast enough to satisfy users' needs. In addition, it can be difficult to combine the effects of HSM and of backup without problems.

One significant problem at the present state of development of storage management is compatibility between different systems. Whereas communications protocols and APIs have been standardized, the physical and logical formats used for storing backups are often different, so that a backup tape produced on one system cannot be read on another.

One well-known backup format is the TAR format (originally Tape Archive), which is widely used on UNIX systems. An example of a proprietary format is the MTF (Microsoft Tape Format) used by Microsoft.

An emerging standard is the SIDF (System-Independent Data Format), which is based on the Novell SMS (Storage Management System) data format. SIDF supports MS-DOS, UNIX, NetWare, OS/2, and FTAM file systems, and can be extended to support others. It is now under consideration as an ISO/IEC standard [Nadeau].

Services

The basic services provided by backup systems are:

- support of multiple storage media
- support of multiple networks
- standardized storage format
- automation

Some services provided by HSM are:

- a high degree of automation
- support of multiple layers of storage media
- independence from media type
- migration policies that take account of
  - storage capacity
  - time thresholds
  - exceptions by file type
  - forced migration
- fast recall (demigration)

Standards

Since backup and storage management is largely a matter of the operating system, the storage devices, and the network, any specifications for these components are relevant.

- standards for storage devices
- SIDF, which is under consideration by ISO/IEC

Trends and Products

A few products for storage management are:

- HP Omniback

- IBM ADSTAR Distributed Storage Manager

HSM is new to distributed environments. Vendors now supporting it are:

- Conner Storage Solutions
- Palindrome

In addition, Microsoft and Novell are expected to offer HSM solutions in the near future.

The recently defined SIDF format may become an important standard. The following vendors now have products which support the SIDF standard:

- Exabyte
- Palindrome
- Novell
- Mountain Network Solutions
- Cheyenne Software

Software Release Management

There are many situations in which it is necessary to manage multiple versions of software or something else. In this case, "managing" means keeping track of what versions exist, what changes were made, and so forth, and may extend to include specialized storage and retrieval, team support, or security.

For example, even when just one programmer develops software for a medium-sized system, there is always a need to save multiple versions of the same source code. This way, there is automatically a record of what changes have been made, and there is always a fallback version when the most recent changes prove to be a mistake. Instead of just making a new copy of the source code each time, it is very useful to save storage space by using a system which compares the two versions and saves only the differences.

Once a team of more than just two or three people is involved, the version management system needs a locking mechanism in order to prevent two people from inadvertently changing the same object at the same time and unknowingly corrupting each other's work. This is often referred to as "check-in" and "check-out". Of course, if parallel development activity is necessary, then it should be supported by a system which merges the changes made by two different people and helps to detect conflicts between the two.

When the version-control system is used for software development, it is also nice to have support for managing the rest of the process, such as defining compilation parameters, module structure, and dependencies between individual objects. These aspects fall under the category of "make", "build", or "configuration management".

Finally, any help the programmer can get in documenting the system will certainly be welcome, and some projects will profit by using general security mechanisms, such as access control and auditing.

On the other hand, source code is not the only thing that needs version management. The same requirements may apply to any kind of document, such as word-processor files, drawings, or spreadsheets. Also, for example, the people in charge of operating any large computer installation may need a way to keep track of multiple versions of binary executables, or object code.

On the product side, two of the most widespread and best-known tools arose in the UNIX community and are called SCCS (Source-Code Control System) and RCS (Release Control System). They support version management of source code (text format only), provide efficient storage (deltas), and include a locking mechanism. They are generally part of commercial UNIX systems. Some of the more recent commercial products go beyond this and support more demanding usage patterns.

Services

The services provided by software release management can be summarized as follows:

- version control
  - definition
  - storage
  - retrieval
- locking
- branching: support for parallel development of the same file
- merging: mixing the changes from two developers
- backtracking: undoing changes, finding their source
- status
- file types
  - text (for source code)
  - binary (for object code and other types of documents)
- efficient storage
  - file compression
  - deltas: storage of only the differences between versions, not complete new versions
  - database support
- configuration management
  - "make" or "build" utility
  - compatibility constraints
- documentation support
  - changes
  - problems
- reports

- security:
  - audit trail

Standards

The typical release-management products on the market don't follow any formal standards. However, many are modeled after SCCS and RCS, which provide a basic functionality that should always be present.

Trends and Products

Some of the more common products for managing multiple versions of software (and sometimes other documents) are:

- SCCS and RCS, supplied as part of many UNIX systems
- IBM CMVC (Configuration Management Version Control)
- Intersolv PVCS (Program Version and Control System)
- Legent Endevor
- Microsoft SourceSafe

Software Distribution

Ever since we left the age of pure terminal networks, the size and complexity of the software involved has grown tremendously. Today, many corporate networks contain thousands of PCs, each of which has software on it that comprises a few thousand files with a total of a few hundred megabytes. To this we have to add the numerous dependencies of the software on the hardware configuration, e.g., special device drivers for different printers, video adapters, network cards, etc. Since all of this software is being modified at an ever-increasing rate, the task of installing has become a big job indeed.

With this kind of a task, any automation that can be provided is very welcome, and, fortunately, there are a number of ways that this can be done, including mechanisms for distributing software packages efficiently across the network, automated installation procedures that first check the hardware and software prerequisites, a good inventory of what has been distributed, installed, or activated, and, finally, some way of removing or deinstalling software which is no longer needed. Many of these tasks have become the goal of specialized products which are frequently known as "software distribution".

From an abstract point of view, software distribution (and installation) belongs to the configuration management function of OSI management. However, it has developed into an independent area because the tools used have evolved specialized functions, such as automatic distribution to a large number of nodes, management of a database containing the status of these nodes, and support for extensive installation procedures.

In spite of this specialization, the tools used for software distribution can often be used for distribution of software in a very broad sense of the term, including programs, patches (program fixes), data files, and even tables of relational databases.

The OSI model describes software distribution in terms of managed objects, each of which is defined by its attributes and operations. The operations are the standard CMIP operations, whereby the actions are specific to their respective objects. The managed objects are:

- Software Distribution MO
- Software Unit MO
- Executable Software MO

The Software Distribution MO is much like a manager, and has only one action, namely "deliver", which is a request to transfer software from one location to another. The implementation of this action is not defined here, but it will presumably use the standard file transfer mechanism of the system involved or work via CD-ROM.

The Software Unit MO is much like an agent, and does the work related to installing software and tracking its status and history. It supports a large number of actions, including "install", "revert", "backup", and "restore". It keeps data in attributes such as "operational state", "file type", and "applied patches".

The Executable Software MO is a subclass of Software Unit, which means it inherits all attributes and operations of that class. In addition, it has one more operation, execute program, used for actually starting the program.

Services

In the following list of services, the OSI standard is reflected in the actions and the attributes of the inventory database. The other services are those typically supplied by the tools which are available on the market, but no one tool can be expected to provide all of them.

- platform: HW platforms and operating systems that can be used as
  - target machine
  - SW depot
  - control platform
- file transfer:
  - communications protocols
  - restart/recovery (resynchronization)
  - cascaded transfer (fanout), store and forward
  - compression, encryption, data conversion (EBCDIC/ASCII, etc.)
- control

- scheduling
- starting remote procedures
- push strategy: centrally initiated functions
- pull strategy: decentrally initiated functions
- support for other media, such as CD-ROM
- communication and coordination between multiple control machines or SW depots
- plausibility checks
  - for example, check disk space before transferring or installing
  - check for HW and SW prerequisites or other constraints, such as compatibility of component versions with each other
- actions (defined in OSI, via CMIP action request)
  - **back up:** make a backup copy
  - **create:** create a new software item
  - **deliver:** send file (push or pull strategy, depending on the source of the request)
  - **delete:** delete file
  - **execute program:** start program or initiate remote procedure (such as installation script)
  - **get:** retrieve attribute information (e.g., normal CMIP operation)
  - **install:** install a program package
  - **restore:** restore from a backup copy
  - **revert:** roll back to previous version (reverse effect of install)
  - **set administrative state:** set the administrative state attribute to values such as unlocked, locked, or shutting down; used for controlling the availability of the software item
  - **terminate validation:** terminate the validation operation
  - **validation:** check the integrity of the software item, such as by calculating the checksum attribute or testing for viruses
- other actions (not defined in OSI)
  - send/receive (or retrieve) file (push/pull strategy)
  - uninstall (deinstall) program package
  - activate/deactivate installed packages (implemented in OSI by setting state variables)
  - remote boot (IPL): Can the SW distribution package install a new version of itself, of the communications subsystem, of the operating system?
- configuration and installation methods
  - centrally or decentrally
  - Installp (UNIX)
  - MIF (DMTF), plug & play
- data formats

- ANDF (OSF Architecture Neutral Distribution Format)
- programs (object format)
- microcode
- flat files
- RDBMS tables
- format of transfer packets
- inventory database
  - tracking of all packages in depot and installed, including those pre-installed, i.e., installed without help of the SW distribution program
  - logging of distribution requests and results
  - printing of reports
  - in OSI model, data defined as object attributes, e.g.,
    - operationalState
    - administrativeState
    - fileType
    - fileLocation
    - fileSize
    - checkSum
    - appliedPatches
- integration
  - built-in integration with other systems management products, such as network monitor, HW inventory, and program version control
  - integration support via APIs, user exits, data interface, etc.
  - license control, e.g., via NetLS
- user interface: a standard UIF, such as X/Motif, Windows, or PM, can be a part of the integration of the software distribution package with other systems management applications.
- security
  - access control
  - security audit trail log
- automation

Standards

Software distribution (and installation) is closely tied to the operating systems used. As a result, there is a significant trade-off between special-purpose tools which are optimized for one platform and general-purpose tools which can support multiple platforms. Some relevant standards (that apply mostly to heterogeneous systems) are:

- OSI Software Management [ISO/IEC 10164-18]
- DMI and MIF (DMTF), available from http://www.dmtf.org/tech/spects.html

- ANDF (OSF Architecture Neutral Distribution Format) [X/Open G508 and X/Open P527]

Trends and Products

Since both software and networks are rapidly increasing in both size and complexity, efficient means for software distribution are becoming more and more important. At the same time, a number of products are being offered with specialties that range from close efficient support of relatively few platforms to a more universal coverage of very heterogeneous installations. A few of the products are:

- HP OpenView Software Distributor
- IBM NetView Distribution Manager (for AIX, MVS, NetWare, OS/2)
- Microsoft Systems Management Server
- Novell NetWare Navigator

License Management

Software is easy to copy. This causes problems for the vendors, who need some way of assuring that the software is being paid for. For programs which are sold and used individually, a large number of methods have been invented in order to protect the software from being illegally copied and used, but that is not the subject of this book. What we are interested in here is how to control the situation in a distributed environment.

When the computers where software is used and where it is stored are all connected via networks, the task of controlling the way the software is paid for is, at first, much more difficult, because it is so easy to copy or access the software over the network. On the other hand, this situation makes a much more effective means of control possible. This is a job for a license server or, at least, a license-monitoring tool.

When software usage is monitored and controlled by a license server, the user is allowed to copy it or to gain access to it over the network without any restrictions. But when the program is started, it does not run until it has received a usage key from the license server. This way, the server can manage the use of licenses in an efficient way, which is advantageous to both the vendor and the user. And this can be done in a very secure manner, similar to the operations of a security server.

Since the control over software usage is done at runtime, the user pays for only the number of copies used at any one time. In addition, there is a choice between any of a number of license-management policies, which determine how the licenses are made available to the users.

The use of a license server has a number of advantages for both the vendor and the user, including:

- simplified management
- improved control of usage
- reduced purchase overhead, simplifying accounting and making bulk rates possible

In order for this to work, each station that uses the programs under the control of the license server must have access to the server, and the programs to be controlled must be programmed so that they access the license service before becoming operational. In the case of NetLS, this is made possible by the ADK (Application Developers Kit), which is used by the vendor to program the applications, and the ARK (Administrator's Runtime Kit), which is used by system managers to define and control the licenses made available for the users.

When it is not possible to use a license server, for example because the applications in question don't support it, the next best solution is to use a tool that monitors the applications, thus checking on how many licenses are used. In some cases, these tools may also offer some way of preventing applications from being used improperly. Very often, they work by searching the network for certain files and checking for processes which are running.

Services

The services to be looked for in license servers are summarized below. License-monitoring tools also provide a number of these services.

- **software license management** at runtime
- **stand-alone** operation
- **network** operation
    - **networks:** network protocols supported
    - **platforms:** operating systems supported
- **user interface** for license administration
    - **GUI** for ease of use
    - **API** or command-line interface for automation
- **license management policies**
    - **use once:** application can be used only one time
    - **multiuse:** determines the number of subsequent usages allowed
    - **personal use:** restricts use to a specific user or user group
    - **concurrent use:** regulates the number of simultaneous users
    - **nodelock:** restricts use to a specific node (workstation)
    - **dynamic nodelock:** provides automatically generated nodelock licenses
    - **distributed:** accommodates multitiered software configuration
- **security**
    - **encryption:** of license keys

- **logging:** for security audits
- **reporting:** for analysis and planning
- **program interface:** for applications programs
  - **request** a license
  - **queue** a license request
  - **release** a license
  - **query** license status
  - **report** license usage history

Standards

There are a number of specifications for license management, but none have become accepted on a very widespread basis.

Trends and Products

Although standardized license management and the use of a license server would theoretically provide a very effective and flexible means of managing the use of software licenses, this method has not found widespread support. In other words, no standard has been accepted to the point that a really large number of applications support it. As a result, most tools available today belong to the category of license monitoring.

- NetLS (Network License System)

Help Desk

What is the first thing that happens after a network problem occurs? One of the better cases would be that an icon on a management screen changes color, so that the operator immediately sees the problem and takes action to solve it. An even better case would be for something like a performance monitor to warn the operator of a pending overload, and for the resulting action, maybe even automated, to prevent the problem from happening at all.

In many cases, the first person to notice the problem is the end user, and this is often someone without specialized training. The user then contacts a support group known as the help desk, where the problem is recorded and hopefully solved. The main job of the help desk is also referred to as first-level support, a kind of first aid for computer users. Second-level support is the next step, for problems that require specialists for particular tasks, which in some cases means the person who wrote the program that caused the problem.

Considering the complexity and frequency of change of today's systems, it is not surprising that many end-user problems are so-called user errors. This means that the help desk needs to spend a significant amount of time helping the users understand how to use the system, i.e., in a kind of tutorial activity.

In more ways than one, the help desk needs to speak the language of the user. So, in a multinational operation, there should be at least one help desk for each country, with another central level for those problems that cannot be solved locally.

So what kind of tools does the help desk need? There are really a large number, beginning with support for call handling, a database for recording and tracking open tasks and documenting past solutions, and good diagnostic tools. The first category is very much in line with what is referred to as a "call center", and applies to any business that provides telephone service to a large number of customers. The second, i.e., the database, is often referred to as a "trouble-ticket system" and is treated in the next section. Finally, diagnostic tools cover all aspects of network and systems management, including network monitoring and remote control of individual workstations.

Services

A few of the services which are specific to help-desk applications are:

- call-center support
- problem management (trouble-ticket system)
- diagnosis tools
- guidance in diagnosis
    - probable cause
    - corrective actions
    - contacts for first-level support

Standards

The specific tasks of help-desk applications have not been standardized. On the other hand, a number of standards may be relevant to the technology used in their implementation. This includes such things as CTI (Computer-Telephony Integration).

Trends and Products

Some of the suppliers of help-desk tools are the following [Hecht]:

- Applix
- Clarify
- McAfee/Vycor
- Peregrine Systems
- Platinum
- Remedy
- Scopus

- Software Artistry
- Vantive

One source for inexpensive help desk tools is [Dugger], along with the Web sites

- http://www.barry.edu/acchome/helpdesk.html
- http://www.helpdeskinst.com.

Trouble-Ticket System

Suppose an important piece of software in your installation keeps crashing in the same situation. Most likely, you will try to find a quick way of avoiding the problem, i.e. a circumvention. Then, you may go to the trouble of documenting it and reporting it to the vendor. What happens to it then?

The first thing that normally happens is that the report is registered, and you are told that your problem has been filed under number 10253 and will be handled as soon as possible. Some time later, you may be told that it was corrected as part of release 5.3 of the product. Or you may receive a temporary fix for your current release. And if you have to escalate the problem or even ask what the status is, hopefully you still know that number.

Everything that is happening at the vendor's site is going through the database where the problem was registered. This way, there is always an up-to-date record of what has been done, who is responsible, what the priority is, and so forth. And that big comments field of the error report has grown by the addition of those remarks saying that the problem was caused by someone else's code, or it couldn't be reproduced, or the developer needs more information, or the whole thing is really working as designed, so there is no problem at all.

This database has a lot of names, including trouble-ticket system and PTR system. PTR originally meant "Program Trouble Report", but it has generally been extended and redefined to mean "Problem Tracking and Reporting", and even misconstrued as "Problem Trouble Report".

In fact, all large software vendors and most small systems houses have one of these systems. It is an important tool in large organizations in order to keep the problems from getting lost in the bureaucracy, and it is important in small organizations in order to keep the problems from getting lost in the excitement and stress of trying to finish a test and meet a deadline.

Even though they don't say exactly how to do it, or whether to use a tool or not, the ISO 9000 Quality Assurance specifications do describe the area of problem management [ISO/IEC 9000-3].

A problem-tracking system is just as important for network operators as it is for software developers. With all the problems that can and do happen in a large system, it is absolutely necessary to have a way to document them, keep track of what has been done, report them to the suppliers or outsourcing companies, and analyze the behavior of individual devices.

Services

The services of trouble-ticket systems can be summarized as follows:

- **storage and retrieval:** all information kept in a database, including
  - description
  - responsible party
  - date opened
  - priority
  - status
- **additional information:** added to trouble ticket
  - device description
  - vendor information, such as telephone number, address, or contract status
  - automated inclusion of this information from other sources, such as inventory database
- **reports:** of selected information, such as
  - all open problems
  - all high-priority problems
  - all problems of a specific device or device type
  - statistics on behavior
  - MTBF (Mean Time Between Failures)
  - MTTR (Mean Time To Repair)
  - ad hoc queries
- **notification:** of support personnel
  - after events such as creation, closure, assignment, or escalation
  - via electronic mail
  - via voice mail
- **escalation:** automatic escalation of priority for problems which remain open for more than a predefined period of time
- **end-user interface:** for entering and retrieving information
  - GUI for easy access
  - API for integration and automation
  - other, such as electronic mail, for remote access

In addition, the trouble-ticket system can be very useful for coordinating the work of multiple network operators. It has also been proposed as a platform for automated actions. In fact, at least one APE employee has proposed implementing an expert system, or artificial intelligence system, on top of the trouble-ticket system.

Standards

One standard concerning trouble tickets is:

- NMF Forum 024

Trends and Products

A few of the commercially available products for problem management are:

- IBM AIX Trouble Ticket/6000
- Legent Paradigm/XP
- Remedy ARS (Action Request System)

Asset Management

One of the difficulties that arise in managing many of today's networks is that we don't always know what we are managing. Some companies don't even know how many PCs they have, and many don't know how these PCs are configured, i.e., how much memory they have, which video adapter or network interface card is installed, or even which operating system they use. This is really a very natural situation, due to the proliferation of PCs, their low cost, and the relative autonomy of many users, but it certainly doesn't make management any easier. The solution to this problem is often referred to as "asset management" [Black].

The primary component of any asset-management system is an "inventory database". This not only is useful for day-to-day management problems, but also supports activities such as planning, purchasing, and negotiating discounts. When the database is used this way, there is often a need for it to have bridges to the software in other departments, such as purchasing and accounting. In a similar fashion, it can be used to support license management.

Of course, there are many technical uses for an inventory database. With the help of a few programs or scripts, it can often be used to create system-generation input, such as the macros or tables used to define SNA or TCP/IP networks. This is a task that many large companies have automated by creating their own, user-specific database and related tools.

This raises the question of how the database is filled, and how it is kept up to date. Fortunately, for PCs, there are now tools that automate this process. They periodically interrogate all PCs on the network, collecting information about hardware and software, such as the CPU, RAM, add-on devices, BIOS version, operating system, and applications. This data is then available for such things as planning and controlling software distribution, troubleshooting, and license monitoring.

Standards

Many PC asset-management tools are based on the standards defined by the DMTF (Desktop Management Task Force).

- DMI and MIF (DMTF), available from http://www.dmtf.org/tech/spects.html

Trends and Products

Some of the products available for asset management are:

- Asset Software International: AssetPro
- DEC: Polycenter AssetWorks
- Horizons Technology: LANauditor
- Intel: LANDesk Manager
- Janus Technologies: Argis
- Microsoft: Systems Management Server with SQL Server
- Seagate: AssetManager (previously from NetLabs), LANAlert and Frye LAN Directory For Windows
- Symantic: Norton Administrator For Networks
- Tally: Cenergy

Print Services

In any distributed system, it is important to have some way of handling printing, including the definition of printing formats, queuing of information, and scheduling of print jobs. Whereas this service is normally considered a part of an NOS (Network Operating System), OSF has included it in its (now defunct) DME. This solution is interesting here, because it is an example of a printing service which is based largely on standards.

The DME PRS (Print Services) are based on Project Athena's Palladium, which, in turn is based on the OSI DPA (Document Printing Application) [ISO/IEC 10175]. In contrast with the OSI solution, however, PRS communicates not via OSI ROS (Remote Operations Service), but via DCE RPC. Based on the OSI DPA, the DME PRS consists of the following objects:

- **job:** one or more documents to be printed
- **printer**
  - **physical printer:** an entity that actually prints the document
  - **logical printer:** an entity used for defining characteristics of a print job
- **server**
  - **print spooler:** receives a job and queues it for printing

- **print supervisor:** receives the job from the spooler and submits it to the physical printer
- **scheduler:** a scheduling algorithm, such as FIFO
- **job-set:** a set of jobs to be printed
- **queue:** a job-set combined with a scheduler

This list of definitions shows how complex the total print service is. Used along with configuration files, called Print Object Databases, the system is capable of providing the following services.

Services

- send output to any printer
- address printers in a location-independent fashion (DCE directory)
- define proper output format
- control the operations of printers
- configure flexible mappings between logical printers, queues, and physical printers
- control schedules for printing

Standards

Some standards relevant to printing are:

- OSI DPA (Document Printing Application) [ISO/IEC 10175-1 and ISO/IEC 10175-2]

Trends and Products

Every distributed system, i.e., every NOS (Network Operating System), has some printing service. Most either are based on the UNIX LPD (Line Printer Daemon) or are largely proprietary.

Missing Links

Even though there are now many products and standards in the area of network and systems management, there are also a number of unsolved problems. Many of these are related to a lack of integration, with different tools for different activities, resources, etc. In other words, systems management shares many of the shortcomings of the heterogeneous, distributed systems that made management necessary in the first place.

Life-Cycle Management

The total management of systems covers all phases of the life cycle of the resources involved. This begins with planning, followed by purchasing, and leads up to day-to-day management activities, such as troubleshooting, problem management, configuration changes, software distribution, etc. After this, the problems in the system, such as bad performance or inaccessibility of individual components, often due to continuous growth and change, need to be analyzed and used for the next planning phase.

Very few products address the problem of complete life-cycle management, and none provides a full solution.

Integration

The previous section on life-cycle management makes it clear that the tools used for each phase of the cycle need to be integrated with one another. The data used for planning and purchasing should be available for operations; for example, device descriptions can be used for system configuration, for creating trouble tickets, and for routing these to the appropriate supplier. Data collected by automated asset-management and performance-monitoring tools should be available for the next planning phase.

However, even within one phase of the life cycle and within one activity, there is a need to integrate different components. For example, many network devices are managed via SNMP, many applications via log files or proprietary interfaces, and many PC components via proprietary interfaces or DMI. Diagnosing a problem in a distributed application may require information about all of these components, including PC client software, network devices, and host or server software. Even when all of the information is available, finding it may involve the use of different tools and may require a high level of expertise in each area.

The integration required of tools for network and systems management can be divided into the following categories:

- **user interface:** providing all necessary tools under one interface
- **process:** making it possible to coordinate all steps of the management process
- **data:** providing a common data repository for all management tools

A common, integrated user interface is achieved by management platforms where one vendor supplies the platform and specifies the interfaces to it, and many third-party developers supply tools which run within this framework. However, since the interfaces are not standardized, this works only when we stay with one platform vendor.

Process integration is achieved to a certain degree by tools from one vendor which access an interface supplied by another. For example, an event or alert forwarding and filtering system may be able to start automated actions, which can perform operations such as starting a monitoring tool or creating a trouble ticket. Similarly, software distribution may access the inventory database created by asset management, in order to choose which systems are update candidates.

Finally, data integration, in the form of an inventory database or repository, should play a central role in this scenario, since it has interfaces to many other components, including auto discovery, monitoring, problem management, performance analysis, planning, and purchasing. A number of industry consortia have been created for defining standards for this, but all have broken up without achieving their goals. At the same time, most major platform vendors have created their own specifications, but none of these has been accepted as a de facto standard, and in many cases the vendors haven't even adapted their own products to the specification.

Automation

One of the most frustrating things in network and systems management today is being hampered and burdened by otherwise modern and comfortable tools. In particular, graphical user interfaces often make it very easy to start working with a system, but they are sometimes poorly adapted to managing large systems. When making a simple change requires navigating through 5 or 10 screens, repeating the same procedure 1000 times is just too much. What we need is a way to automate these things, and apply them to whole sets of devices.

Automation is also an important factor in the cost of systems management. Most tasks can be accomplished by manual means, but require a much larger staff of highly trained personnel, something which is not easy to acquire.

This can be seen by looking at how the task changes with each power of 10. Managing 10 systems is often accomplished best without automation, because the cost of the automation tools in terms of installation and learning is too large in comparison with the benefit. Doing a good job with 100 systems requires some planning in advance, good bookkeeping, and a few automation aids such as shell scripts or command lists written specially for the task at hand. Taking care of 1,000 or 10,000 systems will be a nightmare with anything less that the best tools available today. Just keeping track of what is installed where, or which error reports have been corrected, calls for a database application with a good user interface.

There are a number of areas where the work of systems management can be partially or fully automated, including:

- installation
- configuration
- operation
- error correction

In practice, all of these areas except for the last one are well suited for automated systems management. In fact, there are a number of cases where error-correction techniques can be automated, such as retransmitting messages or selecting alternate routes. However, when this is done, it is normally a part of the communications subsystem and not the management application. The use of expert systems implemented on top of a management platform has been discussed often and tried a few times, but has not achieved the status of a normal product. In many cases, the basic management operations, such as polling devices or filtering avalanches of unneeded events, load the system to more than tolerable levels without the burden of a layer of artificial intelligence on top.

Along with the advantages of automation, there are some serious dangers which result from the fact that things are often done invisibly and without human intervention. This means that errors may be perpetrated before they are noticed. For example, automatic backup procedures may copy corrupted data onto a backup medium and overwrite the last available copy of the original, uncorrupted data.

Due to automation, the human operators might not be involved enough to be well informed and confident of their own ability. As a result, they are no longer able to react adequately to a real emergency when it does occur. This is what happened during the accident in the nuclear reactor at Three Mile Island.

Another interesting case occurred in the system responsible for early warning of intercontinental ballistic missile attacks. It was set up so that if the on-line machine failed, a standby would be automatically switched into service. Since the standby was otherwise not needed, it was used for test purposes, which is a common practice, since such a standby is a good copy of the real system. When the on-line machine failed, the standby had just read a tape containing data which simulated a massive attack, so this is exactly what it reported. Fortunately, the Pentagon judged that an attack was unlikely, since the Russian premier Khrushchev was just visiting New York, and so they decided not to launch a counterattack [Borning].

As a result, automated operations should be augmented by additional high-level monitoring, analysis, and logging mechanisms in order to make it possible to be sure that they are indeed running the way they should. Also, the operational staff should have additional practice sessions for those activities in which they are not routinely involved.

Total Management

As mentioned above, one of the primary problems involved in systems management today is the lack of complete and consistent management tools for a total system, including everything from a multitude of different network devices through operating systems up to and including applications. As a result, finding out why a problem has occurred and how to fix it often makes it necessary to use various tools and consult more than one expert.

On the other hand, the ability to manage the total system is a clear goal for many vendors of management products. When put in the light of managing everything necessary for a business, this concept has been given the name of "business process management" [Foley and Semich, and Foley, 4/15/96]. The basic contents of this program are basically the same as those described above: It is a matter of monitoring and controlling all of those resources in an integrated fashion. In addition to integration, one other major improvement that will be required involves applications management, because today this can rarely be integrated efficiently with the other management tools.

In the same vein, we noted earlier that the basic concepts and tools which have grown out of network management are general enough to be very useful for some completely different fields. Now, at least one vendor has published plans to use its network and system management tools for such things as managing factory production [Semich, 4/15/96].

The vendors are applying a number of strategies aimed at achieving an all-encompassing management solution. One of these, used by CA, HP, and IBM, is to publish a management API and try to get it established as an industry standard. Another is to work directly with the developers of the major applications in order to write application-specific modules and agents for the difficult task of managing some of these complex software systems. A similar way is to provide a generic, or extensible, agent that can be used by the application developers and end users to manage resources not covered by commercial products.

One method of achieving better systems and application management which Microsoft is using is to build more and more management functions into the operating system. For example, Windows NT has a built-in event manager and a built-in performance monitor with a graphical display. Any software developer can use the standard SDK (Software Development Kit) to write to the APIs that send events or publish counters and other data to be used by the performance monitor. Then, as soon as the application is installed and run, performance data can be analyzed, any Windows NT computer in the network can read event logs, and the events can be converted to SNMP traps and sent to a central console. Future additions to these capabilities include OLE MS (Management Services) and an improved directory service, partly described by OLE DS (Directory Services) and ODSI (Open Directory Services Interface).

Chapter 24. Object-Oriented Management Frameworks

With the general trend towards developing applications and operating systems on the basis of object-oriented methods, it is not surprising that network and systems management tools are also moving in this direction. However, in the case of management, the use of object-oriented technology has a special meaning when applied to the definition of managed resources and management protocols, because this is the basis for interoperability; in other words, it is the answer to the question "What resources can I manage with this tool?"

In fact, one of the oldest standardized management protocols is based on an object-oriented method for defining resources. OSI MIBs support full object orientation, including inheritance, but the protocol, CMIP, supports only a predefined set of functions. On the other hand, SNMP, created as a simplified version of CMIP, is not object-oriented, and the name "managed object" for the managed resources is really a misnomer. Similarly, the specifications of the DMTF, i.e., DMI and MIF, are not object-oriented.

The full use of distributed objects was not found until products, such as Tivoli's management framework, began to use CORBA or similar techniques. This was included in the DME OMF specification, which unfortunately was never finished. Today, there are a number of products which use distributed objects as the basis for their internal manager-agent communication.

As an introduction to these object-oriented frameworks, this chapter begins by a review of the DME specifications and then presents an overview of the Tivoli architecture.

OSF DME

It has become quite clear that distributed systems require a good set of distributed management tools. Also, the existing tools do not yet have the degree of integration or interoperability that is desired.

Once the OSF (Open Software Foundation) was well on the way to creating a vendor-independent platform for distributed applications, its DCE (Distributed Computing Environment), the logical next step seemed to be to follow this good example and create a vendor-independent management platform. This was the objective of the OSF DME (Distributed Management Environment). Like DCE, DME was to consist of existing technology selected through an RFT (Request for Technology) program [DME].

In spite of a number of similarities between the DCE and DME programs, there are a few important differences, which can be summarized by noting that DME was more prospective and less retrospective than DCE. Specifically, DME was based on some components which were not yet available and not proven to the same degree as the DCE components. As a result, some components had to be postponed or even abandoned, and others haven't been supported sufficiently by the vendors who should implement DME in their products.

The result of this is a design which does fulfill the major requirements for distributed systems management, and a number of components have been implemented and passed on to the vendors. The remaining components are in some respects exactly what many experts have requested or predicted as the future trend. Now we will have to wait and see how much of this will actually be supported by the vendors, i.e., how much ends up in the realm of real systems.

Services

The original DME plans covered three major areas:

- **NMO (Network Management Option):** a management platform that supports SNMP and CMIP
- **OMF (Object Management Framework):** an object-oriented management platform based on CORBA
- **distributed services:** a collection of individual services

The NMO is similar to existing management platforms, and the distributed services have been chosen from existing products. The OMF has been removed from the program because it depends on CORBA, which was not ready in time, and because the added value of DME on top of CORBA is relatively small.

NMO (Network Management Option)

The basic goal of the DME NMO is to provide a common management platform for both SNMP and CMIP. This was intended for use in a manager-agent configuration, as is common with SNMP and CMIP. Figure 36 shows the structure of a DME NMO.

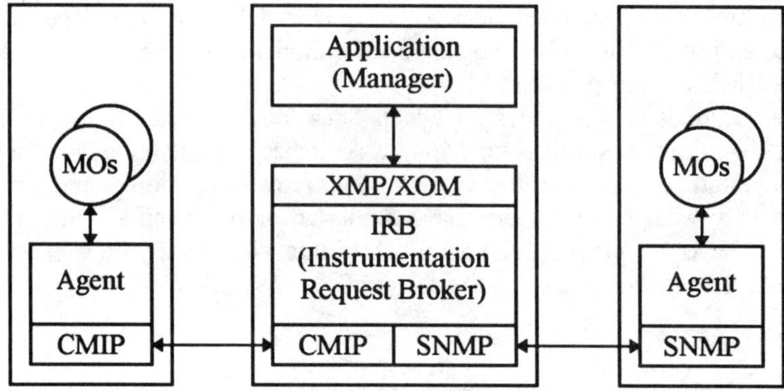

Figure 36. The DME NMO

The DME NMO platform consists of the following components:

- **XMP (X/Open Management Protocol):** A standard API for programming both SNMP and CMIP applications. This includes the XOM (X/Open OSI Management), a standard API for programming ASN.1, which is used to specify managed objects.
- **IRB (Instrumentation Request Broker):** An intermediate layer for the purpose of hiding the difference between SNMP and CMIP.
- **metadata:** An MIB repository for use by the applications.
- **PDK (Package Development Kit):** A development kit, including a compiler which converts GDMO MIBs into C structures.

The OSF DME NMO platform is based largely on technology from Hewlett-Packard, including the Postmaster, a distributed database for registry of MIB information.

OMF (Object Management Framework)

The basic goal of the DME OMF is to provide a fully object-oriented management platform. This was intended for use in a peer-to-peer configuration for management of complex systems. Figure 37 shows the structure of the DME OMF.

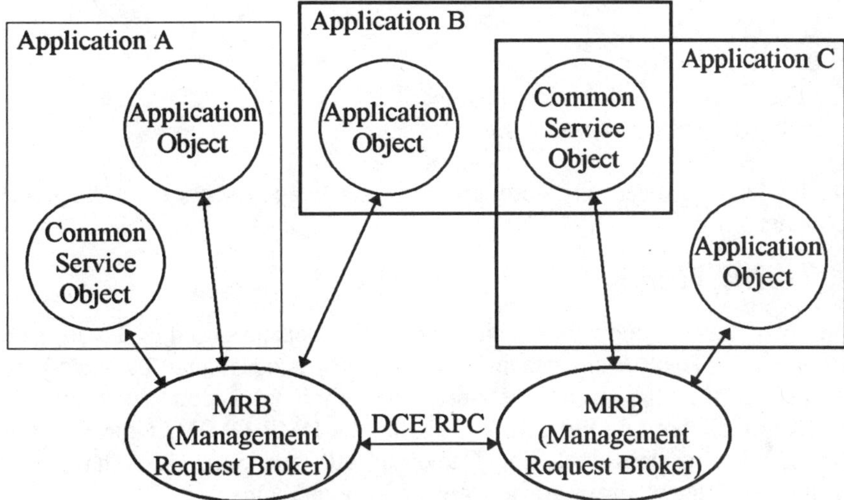

Figure 37. The DME OMF

The original intention of the OSF DME program was to produce an extended version of CORBA, called the MRB (Management Request Broker). Along with this, the CORBA IDL (Interface Definition Language) would be extended, under the name I4DL, since it covers four topics:

- interface
- inheritance
- implementation
- installation

The OMF plans also included an MUI (Management User Interface), an option which supports the development of GUI applications using the X Windows system.

The DME OMF MRB is based on technology from the WisDOM product of Tivoli. The MUI is based on technology from Hewlett-Packard and Tivoli. The OMF plans also included a sample application, the HMA (Host Management Application), based on the Tivoli product HUGS.

Distributed Services

As we have seen above, a lot of things are needed for a complete management solution, and they are not all covered by SNMP or CMIP alone (although the newer CMIP systems-management functions encompass most of them). These are the topic of the DME distributed services.

- EVS (Event Services)
- PRS (Print Services)
- SDS (Software Distribution Services)
- LMS (License Management Services)

The technology included in these services has been discussed in "Chapter 23. Components".

IBM/Tivoli TME

The family of network and system management products produced by Tivoli, generally known as TME (Tivoli Management Environment), is considered by some people to be a leader as far as the use of object-oriented technology is concerned, and Tivoli's WisDOM was chosen by OSF as the basis for the DME OMF. At the same time, a number of other vendors, including Cabletron, HP, and Sun, either have produced object-oriented frameworks or are actively working on them.

From this, we can conclude that some form of object technology will play an important role in future management systems. However, since the DME program was terminated, there is no clearly accepted general standard for this, and the objects and ORBs used by these systems do not yet provide a basis for general interoperability. Therefore, these aspects are best presented on the basis of a real system, and we have chosen the Tivoli system as an example. As with other product discussions in this book, this is not intended to be complete or to be a recommendation of one product over another.

Tivoli's Base Architecture

The Tivoli products use the basic manager/agent concept common to many management products. One of the main reasons for this concept is to make it possible to create remote agents which are intelligent enough to distribute much of the processing to the remote sites. This reduces the load on network capacity and on the central management station, making the solution more viable over slow WANs and more scaleable. In its extreme case, it also makes it possible to have multiple, distributed management consoles, which nevertheless share information with one another. In fact, most large management vendors support some kind of distributed management and intelligent agents.

Objects

For the communication between manager and agent or between managers, Tivoli made an early choice for object-oriented standards. The reasons for this are mostly the same as in any object-oriented system, and include:

- **modeling:** objects are well suited to modeling real-world systems

- **encapsulation:** objects are a good way of separating the internal implementation from the external interfaces
- **reuse:** objects are currently considered to be the best way to create reusable components
- **level of abstraction:** objects can be used to create a high level of abstraction

The current version of TME is based on the CORBA specification, version 1.2.

Security

As mentioned before, security is very important for distributed systems. In fact, due to the control they exert over other systems, such as applications, distributed management frameworks require an especially high degree of security. If it is not built into the management framework, users need to achieve security by keeping close control of who uses the management tools and how they are used. As an example, the use of a network monitor, or sniffer, may make it possible to read all data flowing over the network.

The TME products use a role-based management concept for achieving security of management applications. With this, each management operation is associated with a certain role, such as "user" or "administrator". Before the operation can be performed, the principal must be authenticated by the system, and must have sufficient privileges, which are checked by access control. This way, the security offered by TME is an improvement on the "all or nothing" security of some other management tools.

In the current version of TME, security is implemented in a proprietary way, but based on UNIX login or the Kerberos standard.

Distributed Coordination

In some cases, it may be important to coordinate multiple management operations, such as when various components need to be activated simultaneously. Other examples also mostly involve operations that belong to the category of configuration management, including remote control and software distribution. Whereas the OSI standard mentioned in "Transaction Synchronization" on page 242, was driven by the need of telecom operators to coordinate changes in telephone networks, the requirement for TME is based on the needs of distributed client/server applications.

One example of this requirement cited by Tivoli is the definition of a UNIX user, which requires changes to multiple files, including /etc/password, the user's home directory, and profiles. Another example, involving software distribution, is the need to ensure that the client and server parts of an application always use the same version of their protocol. In DCE RPC, this is enforced by the use of a version-checking mechanism, but it would be nice to prevent version clashes from happening in the first place.

TME supports distributed coordination by using a two-phase commit protocol, thus providing the basis for distributed, nested transactions.

Interoperability

Since TME is based on CORBA version 1.2, it does not automatically support interoperability with other management applications. In fact, CORBA 1.2 does not even address the issue of ORB-ORB communication. This is covered by CORBA 2.0, in the IIOP (Internet Interoperability Protocol), which is based on TCP/IP and not, as many people had hoped, on OSF DCE secure RPC. TME is an "extended implementation" of CORBA 1.2 which includes the use of the Tivoli security and transaction services. In order to keep these additional services, Tivoli has decided not to migrate immediately to CORBA 2.0.

On the other hand, Tivoli has publicly committed to using a later version of CORBA as soon as the OMG security and transaction services provide a sufficient basis for TME. In the meantime, they recommend the use of gateway or proxy objects in order to achieve interoperability with other management tools.

AMS (Application Management Specification)

An important specification produced by Tivoli is the AMS (Application Management Specification), which is based on the MIF (Management Information Format) specification produced by the DMTF (Desktop Management Task Force). The specification is supported by a number of application vendors, and AMS definitions form the basis for a number of management activities, including software distribution and installation, and monitoring. On the other hand, they do not require any changes to existing applications.

The basic component of AMS is an MIF definition called the ADF (Application Description File). In order to support complex applications consisting of multiple components, the ADF can be composed of a single GDF (Global Description File) and several CDFs (Component Description Files). The ADF defines the following aspects of distributed applications:

- **structure and topology:** including the platform (i.e., hardware architecture) and function (i.e., client or server), relationships between components (such as database servers), versions, and scripts for querying and changing relationships
- **distribution and installation:** defines distribution servers, components, targets, files, and the following operations:
    - **before/after:** programs run before or after installation
    - **before/after removal:** programs run before or after removal
    - **commit:** support for a two-phase commit for installation
    - **on error:** runs when errors occur during installation
- **dependencies:** define such things as required memory, disk space, existence of files, operating system version, configuration parameters (in Windows *.ini files or registry)
- **monitoring and events:** define how the application can be monitored, using methods such as log files, SNMP traps, or custom methods

- **operational control:** defines operations such as starting or stopping services or backing up and restoring data

Based on these definitions, the ADF for an application tells the management tools how to do the following:

- distribute the software
- install the application
- activate/deactivate services
- monitor the correctness of installation versions and parameters
- monitor events and performance

Otherwise, the AMS ADF is largely independent of how these aspects are achieved, and independent of both the management platform and the methods used by the application. Of course, there needs to be some common ground, e.g., both understand the same log file format, or both understand SNMP traps.

ADFs have some similarity to Microsoft PDFs (Package Definition Files), which are used by Microsoft System Management Server to define the aspects used for software distribution and installation, as well as inventory.

ARM (Application Response Management)

In order to measure application response time, usage, and availability, Tivoli and HP have jointly developed a specification called ARM (Application Response Management). In order to use it, the application developer adds "instrumentation calls" to the application at the beginning and end of each business transaction. These calls, supported by a developer's kit and a runtime library, make it possible for a management application, such as TME or HP OpenView, to remotely monitor and measure application performance.

Standards

DME is built (version 1) or at least designed (version 2) on the following standards.

- CMIP [ISO/IEC 9596]
- SNMP [RFC 1157]
- XMP [X/Open C306]
- XOM [X/Open C315]

Tivoli TME uses the following standards:

- CORBA [OMG/CORBA]
- DMI and MIF (DMTF), available from http://www.dmtf.org/tech/spects.html
- XSM (X/Open System Management) [X/Open G207]

- AMS, available from http://www.tivoli.com/AMS
- ARM, available from http://www.tivoli.com/ARM

Trends and Products

A number of products, including HP OpenView, conform to DME NMO, but without using the OSF DME code. DME OMF was never completed, but a number of vendors have already produced systems which work according to its object-oriented principles. The DME distributed services correspond very closely to existing products, but haven't been accepted by the industry as standards.

Distributed objects are now used as the basis for the manager-agent communication in a number of products, most notably Tivoli TME. However, none of these has reached the point of setting a de facto standard. In particular, the specifications for ORB-ORB communication have not yet become the basis for interoperability. These systems provide a powerful and flexible means for modeling complex managed objects. On the other hand, today's ORBs are much too complex to be used in simple network devices. As a result, we shouldn't expect ORBs to replace SNMP: They are likely to remain within the area of internal manager-agent communication and may be extended to the management of complex systems or applications.

In the future, a newer development, Web-Based Enterprise Management, including the specifications HMMS and HMMP, may provide a new standardized basis for management communication and data formats (see "WBEM" on page 248).

Chapter 25. Security

In 1984, a bank's branch manager manipulated a computer in order to embezzle $25 million. In 1988, a worm infected 2000 computers in the Internet, paralyzing them, though without destroying data. In 1990, a computer science student succeeded in entering and shutting down a computer belonging to NASA (National Aeronautics and Space Administration).

These incidents show how important computer security can be, but the spectacular break-ins that make the headlines are only a small part of the problem. In reality, something like 80% of the damage comes from inside the organization [Russell and Gangemi 1991, page 16]. And most of that comes not from malicious attacks, but from simple mistakes, due to laziness, poor training, or general ignorance of the problem.

In fact, the basic requirements for computer security are the same in distributed systems as in centralized ones. However, distribution and heterogeneity make it much more difficult to achieve the same level of security.

The examples also show how important the network is: Every communications link and remote system is a potential weak point, both for intruders and for routine errors. This applies not only to the more or less well organized enterprise network, but to the rapidly increasing number of external connections.

The importance of security has also been clearly recognized by the world's information technology managers. In the 1991 X/Open World Survey of opinion leaders in North America, Europe, and the Far East, it was noted that security had moved up the priority list from nowhere as a technology issue to second place [Tapscott and Caston, page 312]. And finally, security, like any other part of computing, is a matter of cost: The loss of confidential data, of critical information, and of computing or communications resources can all be quantified in terms of the loss caused to the basic business of the enterprise. The costs of security measures implemented to prevent this loss should be in a proper relation to the value of the resources protected by them.

The loss incurred may be a direct financial loss, such as when the reservation system of an airline is down: The potential customers may choose other airlines, choose other modes of transportation, or simply stay home. It has been estimated that any of the major airlines would be bankrupt after 72 hours of continuous downtime.

Another asset which may be lost is competitive edge. This can happen when competitors steal information about product development, enabling them to anticipate important developments.

A company may also lose public confidence. For example, information about losses in automatic teller machines may cause the public to lose confidence in the bank and to take their accounts elsewhere. Similarly, in order to keep public confidence, a company may choose to refrain from court action when an employee embezzles money.

The implementation of security is based on security services and security mechanisms, which are defined in the OSI Security Architecture [ISO/IEC 7498-2] and discussed in IBM's Security Architecture [IBM SC28-8135-00].

Overview

The basic goal of computer security is to protect valuable resources from loss. In the following sections, we will discuss what types of resources need to be protected, and what threatens them.

Resources and Assets

The resources to be protected by computer security include:

- **information:** business data, configuration data, etc.
- **services:** systems, applications
- **equipment:** computers, communications lines

In other words, we need to protect not only things like our company data, but the systems themselves. For each of these resources, it is necessary to protect the following assets:

- **confidentiality (secrecy):** preventing information from being disclosed to unauthorized persons
- **integrity (accuracy):** preventing information, equipment, and services from being corrupted, impaired, or modified
- **authenticity:** proof that a person or other agent has been identified correctly, or that a message is received as transmitted
- **availability:** assurance that information, services, and equipment are working and available for use

Threats

The threats to the above assets include:

- **accidental threats:** losses due to malfunction and error.
- **intentional threats (malicious attacks):** intentional damage or corruption of assets, sabotage.
- **passive threats:** those that do not change the state of the system. They may include loss of confidentiality, but not of integrity or availability.
- **active threats:** those that change the state of the system. This includes changes to data and to software.

Specific types of threat include the following:

- **masquerade:** The impersonation of one entity by another. For example, a program could display a logon screen in order to capture a user's password.
- **replay:** Repetition of a valid message in order to gain unauthorized access.
- **modification of messages:** For example, the name of an authorized user may be changed in order to gain illegal access, or the recipient of a banking funds transfer may be changed.
- **denial of service:** Loss of availability of a service. For example, a communications link may be intentionally disrupted or individual messages suppressed.
- **insider attacks:** Unauthorized or unintended actions of legitimate users of a system. This is the source of most known cases of computer crime.
- **outsider attacks:** Intentional violations of security by unauthorized principals. For example, wiretapping or access after guessing passwords.
- **trapdoor:** Alteration of a part of the system in order to produce unauthorized effects. For example, a programmer could implement an undocumented command in order to make access to the users' data possible.
- **trojan horse:** An authorized part of a system which also contains an unauthorized part, i.e., a form of masquerade. For example, a communications entity may also transfer specific data to an unauthorized user.
- **traffic analysis:** a form of eavesdropping or wiretapping, where analysis of traffic patterns may yield information which is not explicit.

Risk Analysis

Before implementing security measures, the following steps should be followed:

- Identify **resources** and **assets** to be protected.
- Analyze possible **threats**, and their likelihood and consequences.
- Estimate the **cost** of each loss.
- Analyze potential **countermeasures** and their costs and other disadvantages.
- Select appropriate **mechanisms** and include them in the security policy.

Security Policy

In general, each organization defines a security policy, which is a set of rules and practices that regulate how it maintains security.

This policy is based on the results of a risk analysis and cost considerations. It also takes any relevant national laws, industry agreements, and similar requirements into account. It includes such things as:

- definition of physical security measures, such as locks and safes

- definition of technical security measures, such as encryption and backups
- definition of security levels of software, e.g.. UNIX C2 security level (see "The Orange Book" on page 306)
- definition of organizational security measures, such as regulations concerning employees' behavior, how access rights to sensitive data are to be determined, when the two-person rule is to be applied, etc.
- definition of audit measures, such as what records to keep and for how long
- guidelines for actions to be taken when security requirements are violated

The value of defining a security policy can be seen by looking at an example of what can happen when no policy is in place. In the dark past, at a time when 8-bit PCs were just becoming popular, APE's LSD (Large Systems Division) won a contract to install an IBM-compatible mainframe at the Hamster University. This central computing installation was then connected to eleven remote sites by relatively high-speed links, and the sites were equipped with minicomputers and PCs which served as remote stations and terminals.

The acceptance test was set up according to rules which required 30 days of normal operation with a minimum of downtime; otherwise the contract would be void. Since the LSD crew was under pressure to fix outages as fast as possible, and didn't work according to a security policy, they didn't remember to use RACF to protect the MVS operating system files. As a result, the first student who logged on to TSO was able to rename all the files, and the LSD team spent a full night fixing up the mess. The lesson to be learned is that even the best security mechanisms are worthless if they are not used.

Security Services

Security services are the services provided by a system for implementing the security policy of an organization. They include the following:

- identification and authentication
- access control
- data confidentiality
- data integrity and recovery
- nonrepudiation (origin and delivery)

Identification and Authentication

All users of a system (e.g., people, programs, communications entities), referred to as "principals" in OSF DCE, must be uniquely identified. This is traditionally done with user IDs and other names. For a large, heterogeneous, distributed system, the task of keeping globally unique IDs for all principals is more difficult, and should be supported by a global directory or naming service.

The next task, authentication, is to ensure that the identification of the principal is correct. This is often accomplished by a login procedure with a password verification, but a number of methods are available:

- what you know
  - passwords
- what you have
  - locks and keys
  - cards (with magnetic stripes, microchips, or other devices)
- what you are (biometric methods)
  - fingerprints
  - retina patterns
  - voice patterns
  - writing patterns
  - keystroke patterns

Authentication most often applies to a user of the system, as a basis for later checking of access rights. However, it can also be applied the other way around: The user may require authentication of the system, in order to be sure that the system is not an impostor. Another variant is data origin authentication, in order to be sure that the data received by a process stems from the proper source.

When one system transfers authentication information (credentials) to another, the process is known as "certification". In any case, both distributed and local, passwords and credentials need to be protected, e.g., by encryption.

Another important concept in this context is "single sign-on". This means that the user can access multiple systems (or multiple parts of a distributed system) after a single identification and authorization process. The existence of a single sign-on is important both to the user and to the administrator, because it makes the task of managing IDs, passwords, and access rights in a large system feasible.

Support for single sign-on is generally based on the use of a (perhaps distributed) global authentication service, and requires that all security components use this standardized service.

As an example of the value of a single sign-on, consider the situation of the APE's MTS (Message Transfer System). This system was created by one of the APE's mandrills and has become established as a quasi standard and installed on a multitude of machines within the enterprise. For a number of reasons, such as the fact that the mandrill's team was never big enough to cope with this task, and the fact that the mandrill himself was too impatient to worry about the necessary details, the MTS has acquired a reputation for causing problems, and has become known as Mandrill's Trouble System.

The care and feeding of such a system on all of its hosts is a constant task which often involves restarting components, changing network configurations, fixing bugs, and creating new ones. When the animal in charge of such a machine needed the mandrill's help, the result was often a heated discussion about how to grant limited, temporary access to the mandrill's service team. But then it wasn't long until all UNIX machines in the enterprise had a user-id called "mts" and the same "well-known" password. For the mainframes, which forced passwords to be changed after 30 days, they just invented a combination of a few letters with the number of the month, so the password was well known here, too. As you might guess, the result of this disregard for security only added to the reputation of Mandrill's Trouble System.

If there had been an effective single sign-on, it would have been possible to change the mts password automatically for all of the machines. This would have restricted access to those who needed it. Of course, there would still have been plenty of other sources of trouble, things which need to be solved by quality assurance measures such as change management. As you might have guessed, the mandrill was never given a sufficient budget for any of these tasks, either. This also demonstrates another aspect of IT security: It often fails due to a lack of financing. As a result, the security team of any organization is well advised to start analyzing security breaches early, in order to be able to present a business case for security and be given a budget for it before it is all just swept under the carpet.

Access Control

Access control prevents unauthorized access to various resources (referred to as "objects" in OSF DCE) and is used to protect both the confidentiality and the integrity of data and other objects.

Access rights are generally defined within an ACL (Access Control List) and enforced by a program called an ACL manager. The services of the ACL manager are invoked by the resource manager, i.e., the file system or database management system.

In a system with DAC (Discretionary Access Control), the owner of each object can decide which, if any, access controls are to be applied.

In MAC (Mandatory Access Control), or policy-based access control, there is a set of access classes for objects and access privileges for principals. In order to access an object, the privilege of the principal must be greater than or equal to the class of the object. For example, a user with "top secret" privileges can read a document of class "secret", but cannot write into the document (this prevents "top secret" information from migrating into "secret" documents). Writing into the "secret" document would require the user to sign off and sign on again with a lower privilege level.

In a distributed system, uniform access control requires integration of the access control features of all components, such as communications and local storage.

Data Confidentiality

Data confidentiality services prevent unauthorized disclosure of data. This may be done to protect personal data, trade secrets, or military secrets.

On a single system, data confidentiality can sometimes be achieved by access control. For communications, it is generally implemented by encryption techniques.

Even on single systems, encryption is normally more secure than access control. For example, without encryption, a hardware technician who removes a damaged disk may be able to read parts of the original data, since the access control is no longer in effect.

Data Integrity and Recovery

Data integrity services prevent unauthorized modification of data. This includes protection from errors and from intentional modification.

Data integrity can be protected from malfunctions and accidental threats by the use of checksums, e.g., CRC (Cyclic Redundancy Check). Protection from intentional threats generally requires the use of encryption.

Nonrepudiation

Nonrepudiation with proof of origin protects against any attempts by the sender to falsely deny sending the data. This is analogous to the use of a seal by the sender of a letter. Nonrepudiation with proof of delivery protects against any subsequent attempt by the recipient to falsely deny receiving the data. This is analogous to registered mail.

These services are particularly important for EDI (Electronic Data Interchange), such as for electronic funds transfers, and are the object of further standardization work on message authentication. Both forms of nonrepudiation service are generally implemented on the basis of digital signatures.

Security Mechanisms

Security mechanisms are the means for implementing security services. In terms of the OSI layer concept, they can also be thought of as services of the next lower layer. Security mechanisms can be divided into the following categories:

- prevention
- detection
- recovery

Although it may be desirable to prevent security breaches as much as possible, it is generally not possible and certainly not economically feasible to do it all the time. Detection and recovery, defined under the heading of "pervasive security mechanisms" in the ISO Security Architecture, will be discussed here under Security Management. In fact, these security mechanisms generally involve long-term activities, and fit well into the concepts of network and systems management.

Commonly used security mechanisms include the following:

- physical security
- personnel security
- trusted computing base

- encryption
- digital signatures
- access control lists and security labels
- data integrity mechanisms
- authentication exchange
- traffic padding
- routing control
- notarization

Physical Security

One of the oldest types of security is physical security, i.e., "lock it up". For example, in order to prevent unauthorized access to your business correspondence, you might consider encrypting all files. On the other hand, it might be easier to just lock up the diskettes in a cabinet.

Even when good software-based security mechanisms are in place, there is always a need for physical security. For example, mission-critical servers need to be kept in a controlled environment, because even a secure operating system can be manipulated by means of software if the intruder can get access to the system's disks. Similarly, it may be necessary to prevent a PC from being booted from the diskette drive, since this offers a way of starting a malicious system that then has access to the PC's hard disk.

Personnel Security

Once we restrict access to a system to authorized people, we have to ask ourselves if these people can be trusted with operating or using the system. In other words, we need to apply security measures for the personnel of the organization. These may include the definition of security policies, means for enforcing them, and definition of the legal aspects of the policies.

Trusted Computing Base

In a similar vein, it is hard to imagine trusting the operations of a bank if we cannot trust the guards. Similarly, we should not trust an application if we cannot trust the operating system it runs on. The consequence of this train of thought is that a computing system contains certain basic components which need to be established as being a priori trustworthy. (These components are often used frequently and also need a high level of quality assurance.)

For example, we may decide to restrict access to all files which are part of the operating system, and thus protect them from accidental or malicious damage. But this makes sense only if we can trust the access-control mechanism, a part of the operating system, to do its job properly. In other words, this mechanism needs to be part of the TCB (Trusted Computing Base).

Encryption

Encryption, also known as "encipherment", is a method for transforming data from an intelligible (clear text) form to an unintelligible (encrypted or cipher text) form and back (decryption or decipherment). There are two forms of encryption algorithms:

- **symmetric (private key):** The keys for encryption and decryption must be known to both parties.
- **asymmetric (public key):** Knowledge of one key (public key) does not imply knowledge of the other key (private key). The public key may be either the encryption key or the decryption key, depending on the application.

Private key encryption, which is in wide use, requires keeping both keys secret. Public key encryption, in which one key is public, makes key management easier.

For example, using public key cryptography, the sender of a message can encrypt it with the recipient's public key. This way, it can be decrypted only by the recipient's private key, thus ensuring confidentiality. On the other hand, the sender can encrypt part or all of the message with the sender's private key. When the recipient is able to decrypt this with the sender's public key, this provides proof of the sender's authenticity.

Encryption of data needs to be reversible, but irreversible encryption of such things as passwords and checksums can also be useful. The keys for irreversible encryption can be either public or private.

Digital Signatures

Digital signatures provide the electronic analog of conventional signatures, and are used to implement nonrepudiation. The use of digital signatures consists of two steps:

- signing a data unit
- verifying the signed data unit

Digital signatures are generally implemented on the basis of encryption, by encrypting either the data itself or a special checksum. The signature process uses the private key and the verification process uses the public key.

One method for implementing digital signatures uses the services of a "certificate authority". The certificate issued by the authority includes a unique serial number, the holder's name and public key, an expiration date, the authority's name, and the location of the authority's revocation list. The digital signature for a document consists of a checksum encrypted by the author's private key and the author's certificate. The recipient of the document checks the certificate with the authority, decrypts the checksum using the author's public key, and compares this with the checksum calculated locally. If these agree, the document is considered genuine.

Another service which may be offered by the certificate authority is to check and monitor the trustworthiness of organizations before and after issuing them certificates. One such certificate authority is VeriSign (http://www.verisign.com).

Access Control Lists and Security Labels

These mechanisms define the rights of a principal to access a particular object. In general, they are applied at the destination, typically as part of the resource manager of the object (e.g., the file system or database management system). However, in some cases, such as connectionless transmission protocols, it is necessary to check the access rights at the origin.

ACLs (Access Control Lists) contain information about the rights of particular principals, groups or organizations to access (read, write, execute, delete, etc.) specific objects (files, directories, database tables, etc.). They are used for DAC (Discretionary Access Control). Security labels define the level of security of specific objects, and are used for MAC (Mandatory Access Control).

ACLs and security labels can be stored with the object itself, in a central database, or within a distributed security service. The method of storage has important consequences for the management of access rights, since it can be very cumbersome to manage ACLs which are spread over a large number of systems. For example, when some people leave the organization, how are the access rights assigned to them found and removed?

Access control may also be based on capabilities, which are tokens or tickets granted by a security service on the basis of defined access rights. The possession of the capability is evidence of the right to access an object.

Access rights may also be granted or restricted on the basis of additional criteria, such as:

- the time of access: e.g., only during working hours
- the route used to access the object: e.g., access restricted to specific terminals
- the duration of access

Data Integrity Mechanisms

Mechanisms used for the protection of data integrity include the following:

- checksums
- sequence numbers
- time stamps
- MDC (Modification Detection Code)

Checksums, such as CRC (Cyclic Redundancy Check), provide protection against accidental threats and errors. This technique is widely used in communications protocols and for storage media. The checksum is calculated on transmission (or writing) and again on receipt (or reading), when it is compared with the original value. If the two values don't agree, recovery mechanisms, such as retransmission, are invoked.

Sequence numbers are used to protect against loss of sequence (due to multiple parallel channels), loss of messages (due to congestion), and duplication of messages (due to retransmission) caused by accidental threats and errors. They can also provide limited protection against intentional attacks such as replay and modification.

Time stamps can be used for limited protection against replay of messages over connectionless transport media. They are also sometimes used for detecting messages which are delayed in temporarily segmented networks (due to inoperable links) and reappear after they have lost their validity.

MDCs (Modification Detection Codes) provide protection against intentional modification of messages. They are used in a way similar to CRCs, but computed using cryptography, and thus provide a higher level of protection.

Authentication Exchange

Authentication exchange is used to provide authentication of users, data origin, and peer entities (communications partners).

Authentication exchange may be implemented on the basis of cryptographic techniques, time stamping with synchronized clocks, handshake protocols, and digital signatures.

MACs (Message Authentication Codes), together with a corresponding acknowledgment, provide verification of the sender's authorization, protection of message content, and nonrepudiation with proof of origin and delivery. They are also calculated on the basis of cryptographic techniques.

Traffic Padding

Traffic padding, in which meaningless data is added to a message, can be used to protect against a loss of confidentiality due to intentional attacks involving traffic analysis.

For example, knowing the length of a password makes it easier to guess the password (or try all possible values). If a password can be anywhere between 6 and 14 characters long, knowing that it is a certain length, such as 8 characters, greatly reduces the number of possibilities. In order to make this invisible, some systems not only hide the characters of the password, but pad it in order to keep its length secret.

In order to ensure its effectiveness, traffic padding should itself be protected by cryptographic measures.

Routing Control

When a network consists of links with differing levels of security, routing control can be used to ensure that specific types of data, such as security labels, are transmitted only via secure links. After detection of an attack, it may be useful to change the routing pattern in order to avoid future damage.

Notarization

A notary, or trusted third party, can be used to provide a number of services to the other entities of a system. Notarization can provide proof of integrity, origin, destination, and time of transmission.

In some respects, the Kerberos security server used in OSF DCE can be thought of as a trusted third party, since the operating systems which use its services, such as user authentication, trust it to provide these properly.

Security Management

Security management is concerned with the definition of security policies, users and access rights, activation and deactivation of security services, and the monitoring of the proper operation of the system. The set of entities administered by a single authority is referred to as a "security domain".

The management of networks, systems, and security services often involves the exchange of information which is vulnerable to threats. For example, corruption of information for the configuration of networks and systems can cause serious losses in availability. Similarly, a violation of confidentiality of data such as passwords and encryption keys would open the door to practically any kind of attack.

As a result, the security of management services may be as important as the management of security services.

Security management includes the following functions:

- event detection
- recovery

Event detection involves normal events, such as successful logon or successful access to an object, as well as apparent violations of security policies. The events may be reported to a local or remote management station, written in an audit log, or used to initiate automatic recovery operations.

Recovery from security violations may be immediate, such as aborting an operation or disconnecting a user from the system. Temporary actions may involve disabling an entity, such as an information source. Long-term recovery operations include such things as changing keys or keeping a "blacklist" of nonprivileged users.

Security Objects

Security management is closely related to network and systems management. Just as network management defines MOs (Managed Objects) contained in an MIB (Management Information Base), security management defines objects in the SMIB

(Security MIB). In practice, the SMIB or parts of it may or may not be included in the MIB.

Security information objects include the following:

- users
- groups
- passwords
- access control lists
- privileges
- policies
- encryption keys
- event filters
- audit logs

Users, groups, and passwords are the basis for the identification and authentication service. Management of these objects can be very difficult in a heterogeneous, distributed system, because each system may have its own formats and rules for their use, and transferring them between systems requires some kind of protection mechanism, such as encryption.

In particular, synchronization of passwords is often very difficult. If any particular subsystem protects passwords properly, it may not be possible to propagate changes to these passwords to other subsystems. The result is a burden on the user, which leads to careless definition of passwords, reducing their effectiveness.

Access control lists, privileges, and security policies provide the basis for ensuring that the system is used only in an authorized manner.

Encryption keys must be changed periodically in order to prevent their misuse. In addition, private keys need to be distributed in a secure fashion. Effective key management services provide this function for the numerous entities requiring encryption.

Event filters determine how events are handled. For example, some events may be reported immediately (alerts), others may be forwarded after a certain threshold is reached, and some or all events may be written into a log. Management of event filters includes definition of changes in event routing and threshold levels.

Audit logs, or security audit trails, are a particularly important part of security services. In practical situations, it is often impossible, and almost always economically infeasible, to prevent all or even most security violations. As a result, mechanisms for later analysis are needed. Audit logs provide a record of all security-relevant activities, thus making it possible to determine the origin of a violation after it has happened.

In fact, in normal banking operations, national laws often require that audit logs be kept in permanent storage for as long as 10 years.

Management functions for audit logs may also include services for analyzing the logs or preparing reports.

The Orange Book

One particularly important standard for the discussion of computer security is the Orange Book, or TCSEC (Trusted Computer System Evaluation Criteria), of the U.S. Department of Defense [DoD 5200.28]. This standard, intended for the U.S. armed forces, defines basic requirements for security policy, accountability, assurance, and documentation.

The most important limitations of this standard lie in the fact that it primarily considers operating systems and confidentiality, but not communications, integrity or availability. In spite of this limitation, the Orange Book has played an important role in defining security criteria. In particular, it defines the following divisions of security protection (in order of increasing level of trust):

- D   minimal security
- C1   discretionary security protection
- C2   controlled access protection
- B1   labeled security protection
- B2   structured protection
- B3   security domains
- A1   verified design

The lowest level of security is D, which is really no security at all, and the highest is A1, which requires that the design of the system be verified.

The C1 and C2 levels use DAC (Discretionary Access Control), whereas B1 and B2 use MAC (Mandatory Access Control), as described above. This means that a C-level security system provides such things as access control, but does not enforce their usage, whereas a B-level security system requires different levels of access and prevents them from being mixed.

One security level which is quite valuable and also realistic (at least for isolated operating systems) is C2. In order for a system to comply with the C2 requirements, it must provide:

- secure login
- DAC
- auditing
- object and memory protection

Kerberos

One security mechanism which has recently won a lot of support is Kerberos, which stems from the Athena project at MIT. The current version, Kerberos version 5, is an Internet standard (RFC 1510). It was chosen by the OSF as the basis of DCE security (see "Security" on page 88), and is either supported or planned by a number of software vendors [Stallings 10/94].

Kerberos makes efficient use of network capacity by relying on a specialized security server (which consists of an authentication server and a ticket-granting server). In other words, it makes use of a "trusted third party", and this is why it was named after the three-headed dog that guards the gates of Hades in Greek mythology. Standard Kerberos implements authentication based on user names and passwords, but it can be adapted to use other techniques.

In order to ensure that all passwords and other security-relevant information are protected, Kerberos makes extensive use of encryption techniques. The original version used DES for this, but version 5 allows use of other encryption algorithms as well. After authentication is complete, the client receives a session key and a service-granting ticket, enabling it to access protected resources without further communication with the Kerberos server.

Kerberos version 5 also supports "authentication forwarding", which means that a client can access a server, giving it its credentials, and then this server can forward the credentials to another server in order to make use of additional services. For example, an application may request services from a print server, which in turn requires the services of a file server. Similarly, three-tiered client/server applications, such as those consisting of clients, application servers, and database servers, require similar features in order to access secure data.

Large networks can be made up of "realms", each served by its own Kerberos server. In order to enable access from clients in one realm to servers in another (interrealm authentication), "trust" relationships can be established between the realms. However, experience has shown that it is best to keep the number of trust relationships small by defining large realms, each supporting many thousands of clients.

Standards

Since security, in order to be effective, must pervade all parts of a distributed system, including communications, operating systems, and applications, there are just as many standards for it.

- Orange Book [DoD 5200.28]
- SILS (Standard for Interoperable LAN Security) [IEEE 802.10]
- Security Architecture [ISO/IEC 7498-2]
- Banking—Requirements for Message Authentication [ISO/IEC 8730]
- Banking—Key Management [ISO/IEC 8732]
- Security Alarm Reporting Function [ISO/IEC 10164-7]
- Security Audit Trail Function [ISO/IEC 10164-8]
- Security Frameworks in Open Systems [ISO/IEC 10181-1]
- GULS (Generic Upper Layers Security) [ISO/IEC 11586-1]

- DES [FIPS 46]
- Kerberos [RFC 1510]
- GSSAPI (Generic Security Services API) [RFC 1508 and RFC 1509]
- GSSAPI for Kerberos [RFC 1964]
- NIST DSS (Digital Signature Standard) [FIPS 186]
- TLS (Transport Layer Security): emerging Internet standard (RFC)
- SSL (Secure Socket Layer) (will be made obsolete by TLS), available from http://www.netscape.com, http://home.netscape.com/newsref/ssl/3-SPEC.html
- PCT (Private Communication Technology) (will be made obsolete by TLS), available from http://www.microsoft.com/intdev/security
- SET (Secure Electronic Transactions), available from http://www.visa.com/cgi-bin/vee/sf/standard.html, http://www.mastercard.com/set
- STT (Secure Transaction Technology), made obsolete by SET
- SEPP (Secure Electronic Payment Protocol), made obsolete by SET
- PEM (Privacy Enhanced Mail) [RFC 1421, RFC 1422, RFC 1423, and RFC 1424]

Security-related work is currently under way for the following standards [Langsford and Moffett]:

- OSI Directory: access control and directory authentication framework [ISO/IEC 9594]
- OSI CMIP: access control [ISO/IEC 9595 and ISO/IEC 9596]
- OSI FTAM: authentication and access control [ISO/IEC 8571]
- OSI EDI: message authentication [ISO/IEC 13208 and ISO/IEC 13209]
- OSI ROS: authentication [ISO/IEC 9072]
- Lower Layers Security Model [ISO/IEC 13594]

The following represents ongoing ISO work:

- Security Information Objects (SIO)—Part 1: Methods and Guidelines (ISO/IEC committee SC27 N604)
- Security Information Objects (SIO)—Part 2: Elements and Generic Class Specification (ISO/IEC committee SC27 N605)
- Guidelines for the Management of IT Security (GMITS)—Part 2: Managing and Planning IT Security (ISO/IEC committee SC27 N720)

De facto standards organizations, such as IETF, OSF, and NMF, are working on the definition of security objects (parts of the SMIB) [IBM SC28-8135-00, pages 6–16].

Trends and Products

Whereas a number of systems provide good security mechanisms, at least when used in an isolated configuration, real-life practice is very far from what is technically possible. This is due to many problems, including

- conflicting standards (heterogeneous systems)
- missing links (such as communications)
- cost of implementation and administration

On the product side, most security mechanisms must be built into normal products, such as hardware, operating systems, and communications services, in order to be effective. As a result, there are relatively few products which are specialized on security. Some of those which do exist often adopt a middleware style by filling gaps in other systems. They provide such services as single sign-on and password synchronization between diverse systems, or more efficient management and administration of the security aspects of other systems.

Some useful Internet sites for information on security are:

- http://www.yahoo.com/Computers_and_Internet/Security_and_Encryption
- http://www.alw.nih.gov/Security/security.html
- http://lcweb.loc.gov/global/internet/security.html

Summary of Part 5

Distributed systems are often very complex, involving diverse, or heterogeneous, operating systems, application programs, and communication networks. Many parts of the system are often installed in remote locations, such as branch offices, which do not employ personnel trained in the technical issues of data processing and communications. Keeping these systems running properly means ensuring their availability, performance, integrity, and security. In order to accomplish this, we need good methods and tools for network and systems management.

The systems, or resources, which need to be managed include communications networks, operating systems, application programs, and security systems. Management tasks cover detection and correction of faults, collection of accounting data, definition and control of the configuration, monitoring performance, and enforcing security. Managed resources are generally modeled as managed objects, which are implemented by an agent which communicates with a central manager.

The communications protocol used to connect the managed objects to the management station (the manager) is an important design issue. SNA/MS (Systems Network Architecture/Management Services) is used by IBM SNA networks. CMIP (Common Management Information Protocol) is the OSI protocol defined by the ISO and is used mainly by telecom operators. SNMP (Simple Network Management Protocol) is defined by the IETF (Internet Engineering Task Force) and has come into very widespread use, and is supported by most management platforms and a myriad of network devices.

Desktop management refers to the methods developed by the DMTF (Desktop Management Task Force). It is part of the basis for "plug and play" PCs, and also an important basis for remote management of PCs, including configuration management and asset management.

The commercial products offered for network management include general purpose, extensible management platforms, which provide a communication and presentation infrastructure. More specialized tools are network monitors, performance monitors, backup and storage management, software release management, software distribution, license management, and trouble-ticket systems.

The OSF DME (Distributed Management Environment) architecture and IBM/Tivoli TME (Tivoli Management Environment) demonstrate the current state of the art in object-oriented network and systems management platforms. Some other products also use these principles, but they do not yet provide a basis for interoperability with object-oriented components from other vendors.

Part 6. Applications

Introduction to Part 6

Just as computing in general is not an end in itself, distributed computing is a means of achieving some other goal, such as sharing information among members of a team, providing fast and reliable access to the operational data of a business, or enabling thorough and timely analysis of that same data. As such, the applications that can be built on top of distributed systems could be thought of as the goal of this book.

On the other hand, this book does not describe the goal itself (that might be your job); it describes the way to get to that goal. And in keeping with that, the following chapters provide examples of how the technology of distributed computing can be used to build applications.

"Chapter 26. Editing a File" begins this part by looking at one of the most common and fundamental activities in all of computing. It may come as a surprise that such an old and well-known application can run into really big problems when implemented in a distributed environment. In fact, some of these problems, and the solutions to them, provide us with a little review of some of the technology covered previously, along with some insights into how it works.

"Chapter 27. Distribution Models" then goes into depth about one of the most important design decisions for all distributed applications: How and where to split the application into pieces. All of the variants which are (theoretically) possible are examined in the light of what they mean in a real environment. The result is that, in most cases, there are not many good alternatives.

"Chapter 28. Migrating Monkey Instructions" tells the story of a project that had the job of implementing a distributed system, or at least the major distributed component of it. In this case, the basis for the project was the very pragmatic necessity of modernizing a large existing system (without disrupting business). By looking at the chosen alternative, and extrapolating to a few (theoretically) possible extremes, we see that something which looks unique on the surface really has parallels with many other techniques that are the basis for many new products.

"Chapter 29. Groupware and Workflow" discusses two related topics which address the problem of how distributed computing is used to share information among members of a team. "Groupware" is concerned with applications that share information such as documents, calendars, etc., and how the data is kept available and consistent for all users. "Workflow" goes a step farther by addressing the problem of automating and controlling the movement of data and tasks from one person to another.

"Chapter 30. Intelligent, Mobile Agents" is about how pieces of software can perform autonomous tasks in different parts of a network. Agents are generally entities which operate at some remote location and send back the results of their work in a concentrated form. For example, network management agents may filter events at a branch office and send only important alerts or summary information over the WAN to a central management station. Another type of agent actually has the ability to move around the network, for example in order to search for information and bring it back to the originator.

"Chapter 31. The Internet" is about today's biggest and most interesting network. Using the fundamentals presented earlier (see "Chapter 12. The TCP/IP Family" on page 131), this chapter covers some of the higher-level services, such as the World Wide Web, and the associated technology, such as HTML (Hypertext Markup Language) and Java.

Within APE, applications programming has traditionally been in the hands of the primates. Unfortunately, though, they have never enjoyed the good reputation they deserve. Many people think of a story where you give typewriters to 100 monkeys, let them type at random, and then see how long it takes before a Shakespearean sonnet emerges from one of the machines. In fact, the story was invented by humans as a purely hypothetical situation for illustrating probability calculations, and simply doesn't do justice to the highly qualified monkeys in APE's applications programming division.

Chapter 26. Editing a File

The most common activity among animals using computers is editing a file or processing a text document, and this is a piece of distributed computing as soon as the user process and the file are located on two different computers. The following example from one of APE's computing teams, ANSI (Animal Software Intergalactic), demonstrates many aspects of distributed computing, including some common problems which occur in a wide range of situations. Some of the activities which involve editing remote files include:

- **business:** processing documents shared by the animals of a workgroup
- **application programming:** modifying the source code of a program under test on a remote system
- **system programming:** defining configuration files on a remote system
- **network and system management:** examining error logs and security audit trails on a remote system

The members of the ANSI team normally work in their home office and develop software on a number of UNIX machines which are all connected by a LAN. In order to access these machines, a few of the animals use character-based terminals, some have X terminals (graphics terminals which support the X Windows protocol), but most use PCs with a number of applications which run locally.

After developing a number of successful applications, the team was requested to adapt some of these programs to the systems used by other divisions of the enterprise. Since not all UNIX systems are created equal, this task involved modifying and testing the programs on diverse machines. In order to avoid unnecessary travel and keep their team together, they chose to work as much as possible in the home office and access the remote machines via communications links.

The members of the ANSI programming team soon discovered that they could work very conveniently by using "rlogin" to access the remote machines (see "The Berkeley r-Utilities" on page 142). This gave them the ability to do anything on a remote machine that they could do on a local one, including entering commands (such as starting a compiler or a program under test), reading the results, and editing files.

The communication links were set up on the basis of a public packet-switched network because it offered a high degree of flexibility, left most network management tasks up to the service provider, and incurred costs only on the basis of usage. In addition, the X.25 protocol was a standard which was available on all systems in use by the programmers. Since the systems being used were UNIX, it was a natural choice to combine X.25 with the TCP/IP protocol (see "Chapter 12. The TCP/IP Family" on page 131). This provided an inexpensive path to all services on all the machines in use for development and testing. However, the animals soon ran into serious performance problems, and so they requested their networking specialist to look into the matter.

As we have seen earlier, both X.25 and IP are packet-switching protocols, so the ANSI team took a look at how the data transferred is "packetized", i.e., how the system determines how much data to put into each packet and when to send the packets off. This task can be done in a computer running a terminal emulation or in a special device, called a PAD (Packet Assembler/Disassembler), which is placed in between a terminal and the packet-switching network.

One common packetization mechanism is for the PAD to collect all characters from the keyboard until the return key is pressed, i.e., until it receives a CR (Carriage Return) character. In the other direction, the output from the computer to the screen is either sent in one packet or packetized at regular intervals, such as every 256 bytes. This method is quite useful for applications which run solely in a command-line interface, such as many of the early on-line bulletin boards.

On the other hand, there are a number of UNIX tools which do not work this way. For example, consider the editor "vi", which was used extensively by our programming animals. (Most either loved it or hated it, leaving little room for consensus, but ample material for debate.) When "vi" is working in command mode, it often interprets individual characters as commands, thus giving them a special meaning. For example, the character "n" tells "vi" to search for the next occurrence of a previously specified keyword, and to redisplay the entire screen with the part of the file surrounding the word it finds. Clearly, tools such as this no longer work when a PAD does not immediately transmit the character, but waits for a carriage return character.

Another example they looked at is forms processing, or entering data into screens formatted into fixed text and input fields. When a character is typed at the keyboard, the system must first determine whether the cursor is pointing to fixed text or within an input field, if the field accepts alphanumeric or only numeric data, and if insert mode is turned on. Depending on this, the character may be rejected, simply put into the field, or inserted, thus shifting the rest of the field's data to the right. Since the "system" which carries out this processing is the UNIX machine itself, it also needs to receive all characters immediately, and not some time later after the return key has been pressed.

This can be summed up by saying that traditional UNIX (i.e., pre–X Windows UNIX) normally operates with character-mode terminals. In addition to this, the input terminal cannot display the character from the keyboard directly on the screen, but must leave this up to the computer, which may need to display something completely different. In contrast, a terminal working in command-line mode can use "local echo", making it unnecessary for the computer to send the input characters back to the screen.

The next question that the ANSI team looked into is what effect this has on the communication. As you will recall, the team was using TCP/IP on top of X.25, and the communications software necessary to support this was developed as part of Berkeley UNIX (BSD), which has become a part of most commercial UNIX systems, so it is in very widespread use.

A quick review of some of the preceding chapters shows that this configuration is an implementation of the following layers of the ISO OSI model:

protocol	OSI layer	overhead
TCP	4 (transport)	24 bytes
IP	3 (network)	24 bytes
X.25	3 (network)	3 bytes
HDLC/LAPB	2 (link)	6 bytes
total	**2–4**	**57 bytes**

The rightmost column in the table (overhead) shows the number of bytes of control information required for each data packet (i.e., the length of the corresponding packet header and trailer).

Now when we add the one byte of data to this and consider the round trip, i.e., echoing the character back to the screen, we see that a total of 116 bytes are transmitted for each one character typed in. In other words, we have less than 1% payload. If we then assume that 5 animals are all typing at a speed of 2 characters per second (20 words per minute), then we see that there will be a total of 9280 (5*2*116*8) bits per second on the line, enough to fully saturate a 9,600-baud line. In practice, not all animals in the programming team will be typing constantly, but there will often be a full screen sent from the computer to the terminal, i.e., a block of about 200 to 2000 bytes. The end effect is that 5 programmers is about all that a line of this capacity can support without being overloaded and leading to long response times.

At this point, the ANSI team took a look at the protocols used to see if something could be improved there. One question that arose is why there are two implementations of the network protocol (layer 3). In other words, can we get rid of one of them? Asking the public network provider to give us something like X.25 without layer 3 certainly won't work. After all, this is how the provider routes the packets within its network, and the public packet network was chosen so that the programming team could let the carrier worry about these lower layers. Putting TCP directly on top of X.25 would be a better idea from the standpoint of protocols, but it is certainly not a choice we have, because the UNIX systems have TCP and IP built in and implemented together. In addition to that, many aspects of the networking depend on things like mapping host names to IP addresses, etc. If we change this on a few machines, they won't be able to communicate with all the others in the big Internet community.

The next thing they asked is why the TCP/IP headers are so much larger than the X.25 protocol overhead. This is mainly because both layers of X.25 are connection-oriented. This means that they need to use addresses only when establishing a connection, and layer 3 doesn't have to worry about layer 2 losing packets. TCP/IP requires much more overhead because layer 3 (IP) is connectionless, so it has to address each packet individually; and layer 4 (TCP), which is connection-oriented, has to keep enough information to fix all the problems that occur when IP loses packets, duplicates some, etc. This may sound a bit wasteful at first, but it was done on purpose and for some good reasons. It makes TCP/IP highly fault-tolerant, or robust, because even if not only individual packets but whole lines or even whole machines are lost, the rest of the network can recover and adapt, thus fulfilling one of the major design goals of TCP/IP.

Since the ANSI team didn't find any easy way to reduce the protocol overhead, they took a closer look at the way the data was being packetized, trying to see if it was really necessary to make a packet out of every single character. During a coffee break, they had a discussion with some colleagues from the mainframe programming group, and learned that host terminals, such as the IBM 3270, do this differently. Here, forms processing is done by the terminal, which then transmits a block of data, consisting of modified fields only, after the "enter" key is pressed. This results in efficient usage of communication capacity, which the ANSI team wanted to utilize in the UNIX environment as well.

What would be necessary in order to use 3270 terminals as a front end for UNIX machines? Could they just change some of the UNIX TELNET code and make it work? The deeper they looked, the more problems they found. Programs such as "vi" depend on character-mode transmission, and even forms processing would require changing the programs to separate the forms logic from the rest. Finally, they realized that, just as the tiger could not change his stripes, there would be no sense in stirring up the primordial soup of the UNIX character-based I/O. Even the mainframe colleagues were very understanding, since they were struggling with modifying a large number of application programs in which the terminal command codes and formats had been hard-coded in the application.

The next alternative they looked at was to stop using the "rlogin" technique and do all of the editing locally on a PC. After all, the PC had enough processing power to perform all of the editing and display functions without help from the UNIX host. The main question then was how and when to transfer the files between UNIX and the PC.

The first solution came from a programmer who was fond of using very simple PC editors, such as "notepad", which is part of the Microsoft Windows operating system. This was combined with NFS [see "NFS (Network File System)" on page 146], which made it possible to treat a file on the UNIX machine as if it were on the PC, and edit it with a PC editor. Unfortunately, the results were catastrophic! As it turned out, these simple editors work by loading the whole file into main storage (i.e., RAM) and then working with it there, without any further disk access. As a result, they can edit only files which are smaller than the available RAM, but then they work very fast. This technique, which was often well suited for working locally on a PC, meant that as much as a few megabytes were transferred as soon as the file was opened, thus completely blocking the slow communication line.

Fortunately, better solutions were not far away. For example, any editor capable of processing files larger than the available RAM, such as "write", which is also part of Microsoft Windows, is better, because it reads the file in individual blocks, as needed, instead of all at once. Also, some remote file access methods, such as DFS [see "DFS (Distributed File System)" on page 92] are capable of using caching and replication techniques to improve performance. And finally, I/O buffers and block sizes in the communications protocols can be adjusted in order to tune the system.

Once the ANSI team had solved the basic problem of remote file access, or editing files on a remote system, they turned their attention to the other problems involved in remote access in general. These included topics such as forms processing and user interfaces to various application programs. The solutions they found often involved performing display processing on a PC and keeping other parts of the application logic on a remote machine. However, the decision of where and how to split up the application was not always easy, so the next chapter has been written to discuss this in more detail.

By the end of the project, the APE programmers, who set out to modify a few application programs on a new machine, ended up learning a lot about communication. They looked at the protocol overhead of X.25 and TCP/IP, discussed some differences between connection-oriented and connectionless protocols, looked at character-mode vs. block-mode terminals, and tuned some caching and blocking mechanisms. As a result, they became involved in writing distributed applications.

Chapter 27. Distribution Models

In any distributed computing, such as a typical client/server application, some parts communicate with others via a network. Ideally, the network should be invisible to the application logic and should have no effect on the way the application behaves. In reality, however, the network often has a significant influence on application design and on the behavior, manageability, and security of both the application and the network.

Figure 38 shows the fundamental alternatives for distributing an application over a network. This figure, which is attributed to the Gartner Group, has been reproduced countless times in the literature; we have taken it from [Semich, 6/15/95] and modified it some. Why is this figure so popular? Perhaps because it presents a complete classification of the possibilities—a kind of Linnaean system for client/server computing. This way, the figure provides a good basis for comparing the alternatives and discussing their relative strengths and weaknesses, which is exactly the purpose of this chapter.

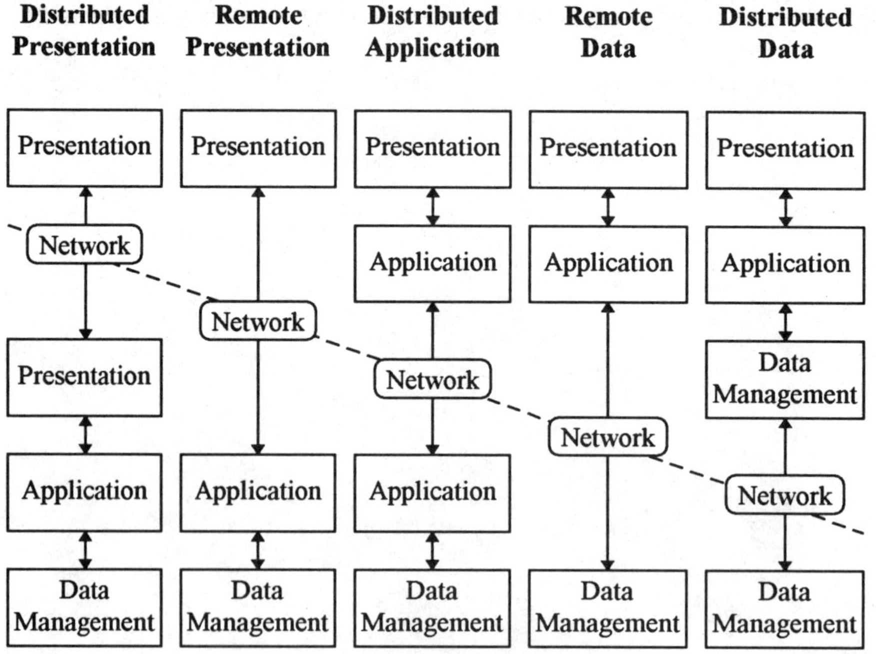

Figure 38. Distribution Models

Distributed Presentation

We would like to begin by discussing the left side of the figure, "distributed presentation". However, in order to do so, we need some background information, so we'll take a step back in time, to when nothing was distributed and all presentation, application, and data management logic was on one machine. This also puts us one step to the left of the picture, where the network disappears over the horizon of the presentation logic. In addition, the same effect can be achieved by stepping off the right side of the picture, which closes the circle, much like the point at infinity in projective geometry.

In this example, all processing is done on one single "host" machine, but the data is actually displayed on a terminal which has no "presentation logic", i.e., a terminal which cannot do anything except display the characters sent to it. The next step after this was terminals, such as the IBM 3270, which were capable of doing field formatting, insertion, and deletion locally, and transferring the data in blocks instead of single characters. This had the advantage of reducing the processing load on the host and the overhead on the network (see "User Interface" on page 64). At the time, these terminals were referred to as "intelligent", as compared to the "dumb" character-mode terminals. Today, they are considered "dumb terminals" in comparison to "intelligent" PCs and workstations. In both cases, part of the presentation logic, such as defining screen formats, is done on the host, and part, such as controlling the movement of the cursor within the input fields, by the terminal. In other words, this is a very real example of distributed presentation.

This character-oriented example of distributed presentation not only is very common today, but also works very well and produces a fairly small amount of overhead on the network. However, at the same time, it has a number of limitations: The terminals are not capable of complex graphical operations and cannot store sufficient data for things like context-sensitive on-line help. In addition, the host application is tied to the capabilities and formats of the terminal being used. Even though it is possible to separate application and presentation logic in the host, this is rarely achieved.

In many cases, the use of X terminals (see "User Interface" on page 64) is very similar, except that the terminal has all the intelligence necessary for a graphical user interface (instead of character mode). Again, the host supplies all the information necessary to set up the interface, such as screen definitions and fixed texts including help text. As a result, there is a high load on the network, due to the constant exchange of graphical data.

In summary, distributed presentation is a common method of presentation today, in the form of both character-mode terminals, such as the IBM 3270, and graphics terminals, such as the X terminal.

Remote Presentation

The next step in the evolution of presentation logic is to put all of it on a PC or workstation. Since the CPU, disk storage, and monitor of the PC or workstation are very closely coupled, it is possible to take full advantage of a modern graphical user interface, giving the user a large degree of control over screen formatting and multitasking, and providing support for such things as "cut and paste" and on-line help.

If we assume that all of the presentation is done on one machine (a client) and all of the application logic on another (a server), then this is an example of "remote presentation". But is this really possible? No, it isn't. To begin with, the very format of all those GUI windows, and the fixed-text parts of them, is certainly application-dependent. The same goes for the texts used for the on-line help. And, of course, any operations that produce new windows or controls, such as list boxes, require even more application logic. In other words, it is impossible to make use of a GUI without including some application logic in it. In fact, even character-oriented screens depend very much on application logic, which explains why host programmers rarely achieve complete separation of presentation and application logic.

In summary, remote presentation is virtually impossible. One published opinion on this is, "Forget about separating your functionality from your GUI. It doesn't work" [Sarna and Febish]. So, now that we have seen that at least part of the application logic will be on the client, let's try once more for a "clean" solution, separating things that are different to begin with. In other words, let's skip over the "distributed application" for the moment.

Remote Data

In its pure form, this alternative puts all the application logic on the client and all the data on the server. This has the advantage of making the data accessible to multiple clients, and it improves the manageability and security of data, since it applies only to the server. It may also improve cost efficiency by concentrating tasks such as high-volume storage or database management on a relatively small number of servers. "Remote data" (see "Distributed Data Storage" on page 40) is a very real and successful solution for the most common of all applications (see "Chapter 26. Editing a File" on page 313). In this case, the data is typically stored on a file server within a LAN, and many other applications make use of database servers within LANs. In most cases, there are common services which make the remote data appear to the application as if it were local [see "NFS (Network File System)" on page 146, "DFS (Distributed File System)" on page 92, and "Chapter 15. Remote SQL" on page 164].

On the other hand, there are cases in which remote data access produces more traffic than the available network can handle. For example, suppose that the user clicks a field of a GUI which causes a list box to appear, or the analogous situation on a character-oriented screen. The simplest solution is then to retrieve the whole list from the file or database server and give it to the GUI subsystem, which then takes care of all formatting, scrolling, etc. But this may be a problem if the list has thousands of lines. In addition, some protocols, such as remote SQL, often transmit a lot of overhead, such as bookkeeping information, in addition to the net data.

In summary, remote data is often a good solution, but it soon becomes impossible in cases where either the capacity of the network is low or the amount of data transferred is either large or difficult to control. The two possible solutions to this involve moving the network boundary either up, putting application logic in the server, or down, distributing the data.

Distributed Application

"Distributed application" means that some application logic is on the client and some on the server. The client part is generally necessary in order to implement an effective GUI. The server part may be necessary in order to solve problems that would arise from accessing large amounts of remote data. In addition, it may be desirable to implement some application logic, such as enterprise-wide "business rules", in a centralized server in order to improve manageability.

For example, consider a list box with thousands of lines. In order to control the network traffic, it may be necessary to implement functions that retrieve only a part of the list, such as the first/last 20 lines, the next/previous 20 lines, the 20 lines beginning with line "n", etc. The code for retrieving the data would be implemented on the server and the code for displaying it on the client.

As another example, consider the logic for calculating the fee for a service. This routine may require multiple data accesses but will generally return just one number. So putting it on the server will greatly reduce network traffic. In addition, it will also make it much easier for the business to change the way the fee is calculated, in order to make special offers and adapt to changing markets or competition.

In summary, distributed application logic may not seem to be a "clean" or "natural" solution at first, but it may well be necessary, in order to put presentation-intensive parts on the client and data-intensive parts or central business rules on the server. This is reflected, for example, in [Geschickter].

Distributed Data

Finally, another way of reducing unnecessary network traffic is to distribute the data itself across the network. This can involve the use of copies, or replicas, of files or database tables, and may make use of distributed file systems or distributed database managers (see "Distributed Data Storage" on page 40).

For example, if a banking application needs to display a list of all branch offices, or of account numbers, it would be possible to keep a copy of the list at the client's site. Instead of transferring the whole list every time it is accessed, it would only be necessary to transfer the changes. Since changes in branch offices and account numbers occur relatively seldom, but they are accessed often, this would be a significant improvement in efficiency.

Even though these five alternatives for distributing the application seem complete at first, there are some more alternatives, as shown in Figure 39.

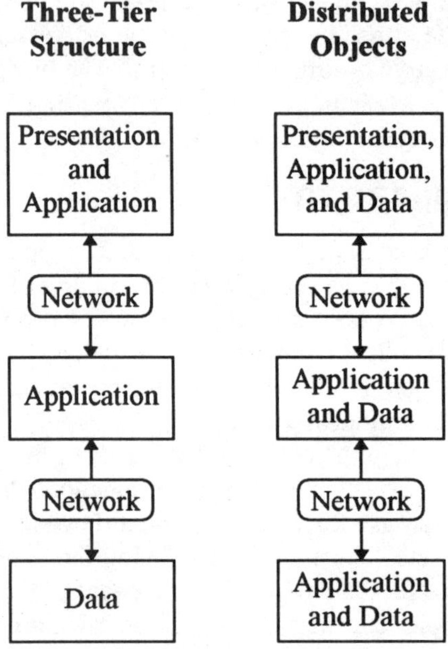

Figure 39. More Distribution Models

Three-Tier Structure

One further way to reduce performance problems that can arise from "remote data" is to add another layer. In this case, the client contains all presentation logic and enough application logic to support the presentation. The rest of the application logic, such as common business rules, is implemented on a dedicated application server, and the data on another server. Typically, the application server and the data server are both located on a central high-speed LAN, so that performance is not a problem. The application logic is split into a piece which supports the presentation and other activities closely related to the end user, and a piece which is best located close to the data and typically contains common functions for many applications. If necessary, the communication between the two can be structured in a way that minimizes network load.

Even though this solution requires an additional layer of software (and communication), it can be very efficient. All presentation-related logic is located on the client, where it can be very fast. The application server bundles multiple data accesses into a single "transaction" and returns only the result to the client. The data server is a specialized machine with a standard interface.

Distributed Objects

In all models discussed previously, the application logic has been shown separated from the data. This presumably arises from the traditional concept of application logic operating on a centralized database of "operational data" (see "Distributed Data Storage" on page 40). In some respects, this concept is not completely realistic, and in others it has become obsolete. For one thing, some application resources, such as screen definitions and help texts, need to be managed as data files, in order to support multiple natural languages (see "Internationalization" on page 18). Perhaps a more important example is the list box which displays a list of branch offices or account numbers. This is a case of operational data, but it changes slowly and needs to be stored at the site where presentation occurs. The result is a situation where both application logic and data are stored in both locations, and different data elements may be stored differently.

For example, the status of bank accounts might be stored centrally and accessed remotely, the list of branch offices might be stored centrally and replicated to the remote sites, and a list of user definitions might be stored and managed at each site (as for example in DCE DCS, see "Cells" on page 86). In each case, the application logic used for manipulating the data is tightly coupled to the data and there is a clear separation between internal aspects and externally visible behavior. This is called "distributed objects" here, because object-oriented techniques are the best way of describing the situation, no matter how it is implemented.

In summary, this solution offers the greatest degree of control, since each object can be tuned to its own special need. It also promises a high degree of flexibility, since the objects on the servers may be used by multiple applications on the clients. Internally, the objects may make use of techniques, such as distributed data, presented in the other alternatives.

Comparison and Implementation

Table 10 lists the distribution models discussed here, and gives a comparison of their network load, ease of development, potential benefits, and the middleware which may be used.

distribution model	network load	application development	potential benefits	possible middleware
distributed presentation	medium to high (GUI)	easy	low	3270, X terminal
remote presentation	?	unrealistic	—	—
distributed application	potentially low	difficult	high	all
remote data	high	easy	mixed	SQL, DFS, NFS, etc.
distributed data	mixed	easy	mixed	data mgmt. system
three-tier structure	mixed	difficult	high	all, plus remote data
distributed objects	mixed	difficult	high	all, pref. ORB

Table 10. Comparison of Distribution Models

Distributed presentation is easy to program, since the presentation service of the operating system transparently uses a terminal protocol to access the remote terminal. However, the benefit is small. One reason is its limitation to either character-oriented terminals or LAN environments (due to the high network load of graphics terminals). Another reason is simply the fact that it does not make use of the capacity of a PC or workstation to support many aspects of the application, especially those which are close to presentation and demand short response times. Remote presentation, even if it were realistic to implement, would not have significantly higher benefits.

The remote data model is also easy to program, since the application programmer can virtually ignore the existence of the network. The remote data access can be done via a standard API, such as SQL or standard file access. In fact, this standardization makes it possible to use the remote data model to create many applications without any programming. Application development tools, such as CASE tools, can automatically generate all the code required. As a result, the remote data model is very easy to program and often very useful. One limitation, though, is to be found in cases where the network is not capable of supporting protocols such as remote SQL. Another limitation is the lack of structure: Since all of the application is located on the client, it is difficult to create and manage reusable components.

The distributed data model is also very easy for the application programmer. Since data access is actually local to the application, this model has all the benefits of remote data. In addition, the distribution of data makes it possible to optimize the way data is transported over the network. This may involve putting different data elements at different sites, or replicating some elements, or using transaction processing to immediately synchronize other parts. In some cases, this can be a very difficult task, and a good strategy for data distribution will certainly require extensive knowledge of the application and its usage patterns. In other words, the burden of defining a good method of data distribution is shifted from the application designer to the database designer and manager. In summary, development is easy for the application programmer, but may be difficult for the database designer, and the two need to cooperate well. One case where this model has been very successful is groupware based on automatically replicated data (see "Chapter 29. Groupware and Workflow" on page 334).

This leaves us with only three models capable of producing a high benefit: distributed application, three-tier structure, and distributed objects. All three require splitting the application into at least two pieces, one on the client, close to the presentation, and one on the server, close to the operational data. Unfortunately, this is difficult! This is because this splitting can be done well only if the application usage patterns, data structure, GUI design, and network capabilities are all considered together. But application designers, database specialists, GUI specialists, and communications specialists all speak different languages! In fact, the task of coordinating PC GUI programmers (the client side) with host transaction programmers (the server side) is a very real example of a culture clash (see "The Culture Clash" on page 11). As a result, there is no way to automate the process, and no CASE tool which can generate the right splitting of the application.

At the same time, these models have the highest potential benefit, since the application can be split any way needed to support aspects such as performance (of the client, the server, and the network) and application structure (making common, reusable parts). In addition, they are also largely the same: The distributed application model is a bit overly simplified, since it ignores the need for data other than centralized operational data, so it can be thought of as a special case of the other two models. The three-tier structure model simply stresses the possibility of splitting the application more than once in order to achieve specific goals. The distributed object model is the most general, and stresses the use of object-oriented techniques, which keep application logic and data together, hide internal aspects, and provide support for more advanced concepts such as inheritance.

In summary, one model (remote data) is very easy to use and is very useful in many cases. Another (distributed data) is also very easy for the application programmer and sometimes very useful. However, the highest benefit can only be achieved by splitting the application (distributed application), perhaps more than once (three-tier structure) and preferably using object-oriented techniques (distributed objects).

Fat Clients and Fat Servers

Assuming that the application will be split into a client part and a server part, the question of how much to put on each platform arises. The term "fat client" refers to the situation where a large part of the application is on the client. One advantage of this is performance, since large parts of the code are local. Another important advantage is the ability to use complete components on the PC, and to take full advantage of GUI-oriented application-development tools. Finally, one disadvantage is the necessity to manage more code on the clients, something which can be a real burden if large pieces of software are changed often and thus need frequent distribution to all clients.

The other extreme, i.e., putting a large part of the application on the server, creates a so-called fat server. Here, the goal is to keep as many common parts of the application as possible on a central server, where they can be managed more efficiently. Another reason for doing this is network load, as discussed above in the move from the remote data model to the distributed application model.

One first step in creating fatter servers than pure file and database servers is the use of database "stored procedures". These are procedures which are written in a proprietary language supplied by the database vendor and stored on the database server. They are activated whenever certain conditions in the data are met, known as "triggers". One great advantage of stored procedures is their ability to reduce the network load, since they make it possible to bundle multiple data accesses into one transaction. They are also very useful for automatically enforcing data consistency constraints, such as proper normalization. In addition, they are also sometimes used for coding enterprise-specific business rules or application logic.

At present, stored procedures are very popular and have proven to be quite useful. However, they have a number of limitations. To begin with, they use proprietary techniques, such as the database language and triggers. In addition, these languages are not as powerful as normal procedural languages. One way to improve this is the use of transaction monitors (see "Transaction Monitors" on page 32). Another is to code the necessary logic in a higher-level language and make them available to the rest of the application not via SQL, but via the distributed object model.

Middleware

In a few limited cases, the choice of middleware is clear: The distributed presentation model uses a terminal protocol, and the remote data model uses some type of remote data access, such as remote SQL, DCE DFS (Distributed File System), or NFS (Network File System). In the distributed data model, the data management system, which may be a distributed file system or distributed database, is the middleware. In contrast, the really interesting models involving distributed application logic allow the use of all kinds of middleware. The correct choice here depends on the behavior of the application, and may be based on remote procedures, remote objects, messaging and queuing, or distributed transaction processing (see "Chapter 4. Processing Models" on page 27).

TP-Lite and TP-Heavy

In those cases where a high degree of synchronization is required, some kind of commit protocol will be necessary (see "Distributed Transaction Processing" on page 29). Here, there are a number of alternatives [Gray and Edwards]. The simplest method, referred to as "TP-Lite", involves nothing more than the transaction control of the DBMS, perhaps enhanced by stored procedures. In some cases, this is even possible with file systems that support transaction control, such as NTFS (the Windows NT File System). "TP-Lite" is capable of supporting transaction control (i.e., enforcing the ACID properties) between an application and a resource manager, such as a database, i.e., in a point-to-point configuration.

For more complex situations, it may be necessary to use a transaction monitor. The most fundamental difference here is the ability to coordinate transactions involving more than one resource manager, i.e., in a multipoint situation. As a result, transaction monitors can also handle heterogeneous resources, i.e., databases from different vendors. Very often, transaction monitors also support nested transactions, even when they involve multiple, heterogeneous resources.

In addition to these fundamental differences, the transaction monitor often provides other, more implementation-dependent features. For example, transaction monitors generally provide process management and can be programmed using standard procedural languages, making them more powerful than stored procedures. In practice, transaction monitors are sometimes used because of their compatibility with the traditional host environment, making it easier to migrate programs from the central host to a distributed environment.

"TP-Lite" is the easiest and most economical way of implementing transaction control in point-to-point configurations, which cover most applications. By contrast, "TP-Heavy" makes it possible to support more complex transactions, such as nested transactions, in a multipoint, heterogeneous environment, and often provides other related services.

Trends

Distributed application development is difficult today for a number of reasons. One is the fact that the automated tools available are good at creating GUIs (client) and SQL database access (server), but not at creating code for business rules. This is similar to the situation in compiler technology, where syntax analyses can be completely automated, but good code generation remains an art. For similar reasons, development of application logic should remain more difficult to automate than development of GUIs, but the situation is improving as the tools have begun to support object-oriented techniques better [Baum 3/1/95].

Part 6. Applications

Another reason lies in the different behavior of modern GUIs and database transactions. GUIs are user-controlled, meaning that the user can open windows and access data at will. Database transactions need to keep various parts of the data consistent, treating them all as part of an all-or-none transaction. This leads to a type of culture clash between GUI and DB behavior (see "The Culture Clash" on page 11). The resolution of this clash requires handwritten code which adapts the data to the GUI and vice versa, a type of logic known as "data choreography" [Chadda].

Finally, it is evident that object-oriented techniques in general, and distributed objects in particular, appear to be the best solution to a number of today's problems. However, they haven't reached that point yet. Before they can fulfill this dream, the following things need to happen:

- Developers need to learn more about object-oriented techniques.
- Tools, such as CASE tools, need to make better use of object-oriented techniques.
- Object-oriented middleware, such as ORBs (Object Request Brokers), need to improve with respect to performance, availability, and interoperability (see "The Rising Level of Abstraction" on page 8).
- Reuse of existing code needs to be improved by the development and establishment of more standardized high-level objects (see "Business Objects" on page 187).

Perhaps the most important of these is the question of reuse, one of the central themes of object orientation. Reusable object classes must be not only developed, but also standardized and accepted. Depending on the content of the classes, this may apply to the entire industry, to specific branches, or to individual organizations.

Another important question is what to do with existing applications. Some of the general possibilities include:

- **replacing:** replacing customer-specific applications by off-the-shelf software
- **reengineering:** completely renewing the business process and the applications involved
- **rearchitecting:** rewriting the application on a different platform while maintaining its logic
- **rehosting:** moving the application to another machine
- **refacing:** replacing existing character-oriented user interfaces by graphical interfaces

Some of the tools available for this include the following [Baum 1994; Semich 9/1/94; and Darling 1/15/95]:

- **code wrappers:** make existing programs behave externally like objects.
- **data recovery products:** used for reverse engineering legacy data.

- **CASE tools:** analyze, decompose, and regenerate legacy applications.
- **screen-scraping tools:** help add a GUI to a character-oriented user interface.

In the next chapter, we will cover a specific example which demonstrates some of the techniques possible for modernizing legacy applications.

Chapter 28. Migrating Monkey Instructions

Recently, one of APE's project teams was confronted with the task of migrating a large set of applications to a new environment. The situation is really quite common: An existing system had become obsolete, but there were many applications which depended on it. Designing a new system then proves to be the smaller, easier part of the task. The real problem is how to get all of those applications running on the new system. As one member of the team put it, "God created Heaven and Earth in six days, but He had no installed base to worry about."

After describing the staring point for this project, we will discuss the alternatives considered and then the solution which was successfully implemented.

Monkey Instructions

The starting point for this project was the MI, a proprietary system installed in the branch offices of APE's banking division. Why is it called MI? The real meaning has been obscured by history and historians. Most current technical documents simply refer to MI without ever bothering to use the long version of the name. And in everyday conversation, most animals refer to the system as Monkey Instructions, because it was developed by a well-known group of monkeys of the enterprise.

Some of the original specifications refer to MI as the "Mask Interpreter", and this provides a good clue to the function of the system. The main use of MI is to display masks (also called screens, panels, or forms) on the terminals and to accept input from the keyboard. Today, this would be called a "user interface" or "presentation layer". In order to do this, "monkey instructions" exist for defining the actions done as a result of input from the user. These instructions are then executed by the Mask Interpreter, much as BASIC instructions are executed by a PC.

Most MI programs work together with banking applications that run on central hosts, or mainframe computers. As a result, monkey instructions have also been developed for communication between the MI machines in the branch offices and the central hosts. This also demonstrates the most important advantage of the MI: It made it possible to move the task of display processing (i.e., presentation) off of the host and onto a dedicated machine in the branch office. This not only reduced the load on the processing power of the host, but also greatly reduced the amount of data transferred over the communication network. This is because all static information (e.g., fixed texts) could be stored on the MI instead of on the host.

As the use of the system grew, the monkey instruction set was enhanced so that it could also be used to encode business rules and other logic. Today, MI is a complete programming language which can be used for creating full banking applications that run on the MI machines in the branch offices. In other words, MI programs can be written for almost any task, but are still used mostly for display processing and host communication. To use the words of one member of the migration team, "There is more to monkey business than making faces."

At the beginning of the migration project, the MI installation could be characterized by the following facts:

- MI machines are installed in about 2000 branch offices.
- More than 5000 MI programs are in use.
- Most MI programs work closely with host programs.
- MI and host programs are constantly being revised.
- Replacement of the MI machines is expected to require 1–2 years. The peak phase of this plan foresees as many as 10 installations per day.

The Alternatives

Whenever it is necessary to replace an existing system by a new one, only a few basic alternatives are available; everything else is a matter of technical detail. We will discuss these general alternatives here in the context of the MI migration project.

Reengineering

The most radical solution is based on a very simple idea: "Throw everything away and start from scratch." Here, the advantage is the possibility of creating a completely new system based on the most modern techniques available. On the dark side, it provides no systematic way of finding the necessary application expertise, and no way of estimating how much knowledge is missing. This is particularly dangerous with a system which consists of a large number of programs written mostly by programmers who have since changed jobs or even changed employers. This alternative was favored vehemently by a few technicians of the MI team, but was never considered seriously by APE's management.

Another reengineering method is much more systematic and consists of two steps: (1) capture existing application knowledge, and (2) recode the application. This is done most efficiently with the help of CASE (Computer Aided Software Engineering) tools which provide support for analyzing the existing programs, representing the application knowledge in a system-independent from, and generating code for the new target system. Even though this reengineering approach is much more realistic than the first, it never gained support from APE's management and the MI project team, partly because no one involved had enough experience with the method to make a reliable estimate of the cost.

In fact, all reengineering suggestions were discarded because of the difficulty of finding all the application knowledge required for a new implementation. And even if this were possible, no one came up with a way of incorporating the changes which would be made during the long and difficult reengineering process.

Conversion

If the existing applications aren't to be reengineered, then it may still be possible to convert them from the old environment to the new one. This task of "conversion" is also referred to as "porting" or "migration without redesign", especially when the main task is to move the code from one machine to another. If the same programming language is available on both machines, this boils down to changing things like operating system calls and external interfaces, then recompiling and testing. If the same language is not available, it may still be possible to automatically convert one language to another. In any case, it is sometimes possible to automate part or all of the task, leaving the rest to be done manually. In most cases, this also leaves a large testing job in which there may be a number of surprises.

Since the conversion technique avoids the necessity for understanding all application logic, it is generally faster and more certain than redesign. However, it is less able to make use of new technology, since conversion methods are not feasible for all possible changes. In the case of MI, a special conversion tool was written and used very successfully.

Software Emulation

In the last of our three alternatives, the applications are neither redesigned nor converted, but left unchanged. Instead, an "emulator", or "virtual machine" is created in order to simulate the old environment on top of the new one. The big advantage of this technique is the fact that it has a very high chance of success and relatively small development cost. One disadvantage is to be found in the fact that it involves keeping old technology on a new system, and provides no migration path to the new system. Another potential disadvantage lies in the extra layer of software, which sometimes leads to performance problems. As we will see, even though the MI migration is generally described as a conversion solution, it also involves a significant piece of emulation.

The MI Solution

The migration solution implemented for MI can best be described as a combination of conversion and emulation. The first step is a fully automatic conversion from the old MI language to a new MI language. The second step is an environment which supports the new language. These steps are called "compilation" (conversion from one language to another) and "runtime" (runtime support for the new language) in the MI environment.

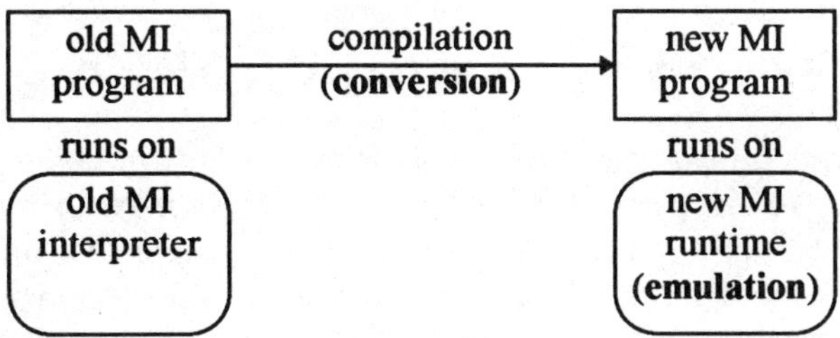

Figure 40. MI Conversion and Emulation

This example shows how the techniques of conversion and emulation can be combined in such a way that the full spectrum between both extremes is possible. If the new language is the native language of the new system, the runtime is trivial, and we have a case of 100% conversion. If the old and new languages are the same, the compilation is trivial and the runtime does all the work, resulting in 100% emulation.

In the case of MI, the new language was chosen somewhere between these two extremes. This was done in such a way that the following goals could be met:

- Compilation is 100% automatic and complete.
- The new language is an improvement of the old one, providing a migration path to the technology of the new system.

This resulted in the following success for the MI migration: All 5000 applications were always available on both old and new systems, even though they were constantly being modified during the entire transition period of 1–2 years. As a result, it was possible to protect the investment made in the existing applications, but still replace the obsolete MI machines. At the same time, the converted applications made partial, but not full, use of the new technology. This provides a good starting point for reengineering some of the applications to make full use of the new facilities as soon as the transition period is finished.

Chapter 29. Groupware and Workflow

When PCs came into widespread use, two applications, word processing and spreadsheets, soon proved to be particularly valuable. In fact, PCs, using local processing power for display and formatting, were much more effective for word processing than mainframes and minis, which soon made many PCs into modern replacements for typewriters. Spreadsheets, on the other hand, were a true revolution in computing, providing a completely new way of doing calculations without programming, and soon became the basis for large parts of day-to-day business operations at the personal and departmental level.

Given this, and the advent of inexpensive LANs (Local Area Networks), it was also time to enable teams, or workgroups, to share their work and collaborate on producing documents, whether they were texts, spreadsheets, or something else. One of the most important tools for doing this was (and still is) the LAN file server. This is basically a PC (or some larger machine) that provides file storage for all PCs on the LAN, and normally supports some basic locking and security mechanisms in order to ensure consistency when multiple users access the same files.

The other main tool for information sharing is e-mail (or electronic mail), which makes it possible to exchange messages (and sometimes other documents) by sending them over the network. Many earlier LAN e-mail products were fairly simple, used a proprietary protocol, and were based on shared files. Today, many of these systems have been replaced by more powerful e-mail products in order to meet higher demands in terms of volume, robustness, file types (including binary files), enterprise-wide networks, and external connections using standard protocols (see "Electronic Mail" on page 193).

Closely related to e-mail is the topic of discussion groups, news groups, or forums. Discussion groups are groups of users who send all mail regarding a certain topic to a distribution list, or alias, which contains the names of all the members of the group. This way, each member can post a question to the whole group, and anyone who knows the answer can reply to the whole group. Similarly, a BBS (Bulletin Board System) or forum is generally a collection of messages or files concerning a specific topic which are available to all users of the system. In any case, individual users may be assigned read-only access or read/write access, and there may or may not be someone in charge of moderating the discussion.

Groupware

These two tools, file servers and e-mail systems, already provide the most important basis for information sharing, and are often referred to as "groupware", i.e., products for supporting collaborative work by groups of people. However, there is no exact definition for the term "groupware", and it is used for a wide spectrum of products, beginning with file servers and e-mail and extending to such things as scheduling tools and complex distributed applications.

When a calendar is put on a file server, it can be shared, just like any other electronic document. This way, you can inform other people about when you are available and when you are out of the office. With the addition of basic security techniques, you can make parts visible to all people, such as when you have an appointment, and other parts visible to selected people, such as who is attending the meeting. Also, you can give certain people the ability to change your calendar and make appointments for you. Another step, known more as scheduling, makes it possible for you to schedule a meeting automatically by checking other people's calendars and then asking them if they will attend or not.

Whenever a number of people are organized into a team in order to work together on a specific project, it is useful to supply them all with a list of participants, including names, postal addresses, telephone numbers, and e-mail addresses. If the work involves external contacts, such as customers or suppliers, they should also be included in this address book. As a first step, this could simply be a shared text file on a server, but the next step is for it to be integrated into the e-mail system and divided into shared and personal address books. When security is involved, it is very convenient for the same names to be used for both addressing e-mail and defining access rights. Of course, we could take this a step further and extend it to the enterprise network and provide gateways to other organizations, or the public telephone directory, or many other things. In any case, it brings us to the topic of directory services in general, and how to integrate them and provide for directory synchronization (see "Chapter 18. Directories" on page 204).

Some other topics which are sometimes included in the category of groupware are fax, electronic forms, multimedia, and telephony integration. Fax gateways make it possible to send and receive fax messages from PCs, and sometimes integrate this with an e-mail system. Electronic forms provide a way of filling out forms electronically and submitting the information to other applications for storage, retrieval, and processing. Multimedia features make it possible to include pictures, sounds, video clips, etc., in electronic documents, such as texts and e-mail messages. Although CTI (Computer Telephony Integration) is often considered a field in itself, it is sometimes included in groupware in order to record telephone messages and embed them into shared documents [Trammell].

Finally, groupware can be construed to include any kind of shared or distributed application used by all members of a workgroup. This may include shared databases or any line-of-business application and leads us to the topic of how these applications can be developed, and what tools can be used to do it. In any case, no discussion of groupware would be complete without at least mentioning Lotus Notes. In fact, not only is it the leading product for creating groupware applications, its name has often been used almost synonymously with the term "groupware".

For the purpose of this discussion, the most important aspect of Lotus Notes is the method which it has introduced to the way groupware applications are developed. This consists primarily of an information storage system which is automatically replicated to all servers and accessed via client applications built with tools which are supplied with the system.

The basic data storage and retrieval mechanism of Lotus Notes, called the "Notes database", would more accurately be called a "document repository". It is not a relational database, but a document storage with a minimal amount of additional structure. This structure is just enough to make it possible to group, manage, sort, view, and distribute the information efficiently. At the same time, it is simple enough that it is easy to access. In addition, the Notes database has a built-in replication mechanism which is capable of synchronizing data across multiple Notes servers, a feature which is the main basis for its success [Baum 5/1/95]. Finally, Notes is supplied with a set of development tools for creating client applications with a graphical user interface.

Together, these features make it very easy to create distributed applications: You define a basic information structure, create some forms and other front-end applications, and install the system. Then, the forms can be used to input and modify data, and the results are kept synchronized at all locations. As a result, Lotus Notes now supports more than a million users and many applications, created both by the end users themselves and by numerous third-party software vendors.

In some ways, the method behind Lotus Notes can be compared with the revolution caused by the invention of spreadsheets: First, it is similar, because it has created a new type of application and a new market. Second, it is different, because it is not a conceptual breakthrough, but rather the application of existing techniques. Finally, it may be similar in that it has led to the success of the product which pioneered the concept, but the product will be followed by competing products which try to do the same thing better.

Data replication, which is the heart of Lotus Notes, has existed for some time within relational databases. As long as the application doesn't need immediate synchronization of all data, replication is a "good enough" solution, and much less demanding than distributed transactions (see "Distributed Data Storage" on page 40). Built-in and automatic replication of Lotus Notes is also very easy to use, and requires very little management as long as the load it produces is not too much for the network being used [Yavin]. However, if the number of users, the number of servers, or the amount of data exceeds a certain size, automatic replication is something that requires effective strategies and careful planning. For this purpose, Lotus Notes now includes more powerful ways of controlling replication, including definition of replication plans, network topology, server-server and client-server replication, selective replication (modifications only), granularity (field-level replication), and priority. Of course, a demanding and complex replication scenario extends the product out of the area where it is simple to use and raises the question of where is it more effective to invest development effort, in the application design or the replication strategy.

Among the competition, both Collabra Share and Microsoft Exchange now support replication. In contrast with Notes, the replication mechanism in Exchange is based not on a proprietary protocol, but on e-mail, so it does not require a constant network connection (e-mail is a store-and-forward technique, see "Electronic Mail" on page 193), and can by used over any of a number of protocols, including SMTP and X.400. Similarly, the "public folder" concept of Exchange is to a certain extent analogous to the "Notes database". Also, the application-development tools available for Exchange include all standard Windows tools, in contrast with the Notes-specific tools. On the other hand, at the time of this writing, Microsoft Exchange is still new enough that it does not have the same number of applications, number of third-party groupware developers, or size of market share as Lotus Notes.

Workflow

Under the concept of "groupware", we have now seen a number of ways to support the work of the individual members of a team, and make it easier for them to share information. In almost all cases, the sequence of tasks performed with the help of these applications is determined more or less ad hoc by each user. Better support for this aspect, i.e., for controlling the overall process, is the primary task of "workflow" tools. In other words, groupware tools help optimize the individual tasks of a team, and workflow tools help optimize the process, thus reducing time lost waiting for the results of some previous step.

For example, consider the steps involved in processing travel expenses. First, the person who has returned from a business trip will generally fill out a form and include receipts for the expenses. Second, the traveler's supervisor is required to check for correctness and proper allocation of the resources of the project's or department's budget. Next, someone else will process the request, and check for consistency with company policies and tax laws. Finally, the employee can be reimbursed for the expenses. The purpose of groupware tools is to ensure that data needs to be entered only once, and is passed from one step to another, and that each step can be done with a minimal amount of work. Workflow tools help the company define the steps according to company policy, provide a means for forwarding the request from one instance to the next, and help eliminate time wasted between steps. Optimally, they should take into consideration availability of resources, including vacation and sick leave, and provide adequate reports to both management and the individual involved.

Similarly, many other business processes can be subjected to workflow techniques, such as claims processing within an insurance company or order processing, inventory, and stock management. In some cases, these may be more complex than the example involving travel expenses, and may require such things as legally binding signatures on electronic documents.

In summary, workflow is responsible for tracking, automating, and management of business processes. As such, it may be used for automating existing processes, or as a planning and implementation tool as a part of BPR (Business Process Reengineering). In any case, the use of workflow tools always requires an analysis of the business process involved, and this task of analysis may be as difficult and enlightening as the use of the tool itself.

The scope of workflow automation methods generally begins with tools for analyzing and modeling business processes. This is followed by some kind of automation of the process, involving determining the proper recipient for the next step, transferring the data, and notifying the person involved. This automation may involve a "push" strategy, where tasks get pushed into a person's in-box, or a "pull" strategy, where the people select their next tasks from the system. The push method is more suited for routine tasks, whereas the pull method is more useful for highly variable tasks [Thé 8/15/95]. The method of routing the information from one task or instance to the next may involve an ad hoc strategy or be conditional, i.e., dependent on other factors or business rules, and may require the use of recursive loops or parallel paths.

In fact, many of these aspects have already been automated in one form or another, as part of existing, user-specific applications. In this respect, the task of workflow is to provide general-purpose tools for automating business processes. In any case, the tasks involved vary greatly in complexity, and the tools available on the market vary greatly in function, complexity, and price.

Perhaps one of the greatest problems in the area of workflow or business process automation is the question of flexibility [Thé 10/1/94]. How is it possible to automate a business process that is constantly changing (see "The Law of Change" on page 5)? Worse yet, how is it possible to automate a process which no one can even describe? In any case, the art of good workflow automation requires a feeling for the right degree of automation, something that makes work easier and more efficient without making it too rigid. The same thing goes for the tools to be used in workflow scenarios: They should help you analyze and automate the business processes, but without requiring too much time, and should be flexible enough to make it possible to adapt the process to all the changes that will inevitably be required.

When considering automation of business processes, we should take another look at our original example of travel expenses. Here, full electronic automation is hampered by the necessity for submitting receipts, such as airline tickets and hotel bills. As a result, the request is often handled in paper form, even when it is supported by something like a spreadsheet for calculating expenses. In order to eliminate this, the receipts can be scanned and converted to electronic form, then stored on some high-capacity medium. Then, there needs to be some way of viewing them, and it is useful to be able to annotate them, for example to store comments such as which telephone calls were on a business account and which were private. All of these steps are examples of the use of imaging techniques in workflow automation.

Imaging techniques, including scanning, storage, retrieval, viewing, and OCR (Optical Character Recognition), are therefore necessary as a part of full automation of workflow. As a result, they are often thought of as being part of workflow technology, even though they are useful in other areas as well. Interestingly enough, some products which do nothing other than imaging are often referred to as workflow products, even when they provide no methods for automating or managing the workflow or business process itself. In fact, the term "workflow" is defined just as loosely (if at all) as the related term "groupware".

Services

The services to be looked for in groupware and workflow products include the following:

- groupware
    - information sharing: file servers, file sharing
    - e-mail
        - transports: X.400, SMTP
        - APIs: CMC, MAPI, VIM
    - discussion groups and BBS (Bulletin Board System)
    - calendar/schedule
    - address book/directory
        - standards: X.500
    - fax
    - forms
    - document integration: text, graphics, multimedia
    - telephony integration
        - voice mail recording/embedding
- data storage and retrieval
    - support for standard databases
    - data replication and synchronization
        - selective (modifications only)
        - field-level
        - priority control
        - topology: star, mesh, etc.
- workflow
    - tracking, automation, and management of business processes
    - push vs. pull strategy
    - routing
        - ad hoc, conditional, parallel, recursive loops
        - definition via scripts or GUI tools
        - flexibility, ease of management
    - imaging
        - storage and retrieval
        - file formats: BMP, GIF, JPEG, PCD, PCX, TIFF
        - scanning, display, processing, annotation, OCR
- network support
    - standard protocols, such as TCP/IP and IPX/SPX

- platform support
  - hardware
  - operating system, client and server
- application development support
  - GUI tools
  - data import/export, access to databases
  - ODBC support
  - access to legacy code
  - forms, views, queries, charts, graphs
  - support for standard tools
  - workflow modeling tools
- security
  - encryption
  - digital signatures

Standards

In the area of groupware, there are no specific standards. However, the standards for the underlying technology, such as e-mail, may be very important for achieving interoperability and platform independence. For workflow, the underlying technology includes imaging document formats such as GIF and JPEG, and both groupware and workflow depend on network protocols and directory services. On the other hand, for workflow, some fundamental concepts have been defined by an industry consortium.

- networks: e.g., TCP/IP
- e-mail: e.g., SMTP, X.400, CMC, MAPI, VIM
- directory: e.g., X.500
- workflow: WFMC (Workflow Management Coalition)

Trends and Products

In the area of groupware, there are a number of products for specific tasks, such as e-mail, file sharing, scheduling, faxing, and telephony. As a groupware application development and support platform, Lotus Notes has set the current standards and is the leader. However, others, such as Microsoft Exchange, have entered the arena with the intention of doing the same thing better. Products in the area of workflow range in function from very simple to very complex and differ just as much in price.

- Action Technologies: ActionWorkFlow Manager
- Attachmate: OpenMind
- Collabra Software: Collabra Share

- DEC: LinkWorks
- FileNet: Visual Workflow, WorkFlo
- IBM: FlowMark, WorkGroup
- Keyfile: Keyfile, Keyflow
- Lotus: Lotus Forms, Lotus IPS (Image Processing Server), Lotus Notes, Lotus Organizer
- Mesa Group: Conference+
- Microsoft: Electronic Forms, Exchange, Schedule+
- NCR: ProcessIT
- Novell: CMS (Collaborative Message Server), GroupWise, MHS, SoftSolutions
- PaperClip: PaperClip Workflow
- Reach Software: WorkMAN
- Recognition International: Plexus FloWare
- Staffware: Staffware
- ViewStar: ViewStar System
- Wang: OPEN/Workflow
- Xsoft: InConcert

Chapter 30. Intelligent, Mobile Agents

We have seen that it can be very useful to split up an application into two parts, one close to the user and another close to the necessary resources. This is an important part of the client/server model, where the clients often handle the user interface and the servers often provide such things as data storage. A similar division is also common in network management, where there is usually one or more central managers and a number of remote agents. For most operations, the manager serves as a client and interrogates or controls the agent; for event handling, the agent takes the initiative and the manager plays the role of an event server.

One of the biggest problems with this approach is its rigidity: The agents, or servers, have to be designed, written, and installed on their respective systems before any client or other user can access them. Considering the difficulty sometimes encountered in finding a good design for the interface between client and server, this can be a slow process, not to mention the organizational difficulties that exist when the computers are owned and run by different people.

At the same time, we have heard a lot about viruses, worms, and other creatures that invade remote computers and play games with their resources. These programs are able to move around in a network, find things they want, wait when necessary, and then become active when conditions are right. While all this sounds like great fun for hackers, it is certainly a real problem for the users of the resources.

Why shouldn't we combine the best of both worlds? Optimally, the user should be able to create new agents, tell them what to do, and send them off to roam about cyberspace (i.e., the Internet), doing all the tedious work that should be done by computers. Later, when the results have been put together, the agent phones home and gives a report to its creator.

This is a vision of useful digital creatures that:

- are easy to create
- understand what we want
- go where necessary
- work while we are sleeping
- give us clear, useful answers
- make sparing use of resources (networks, terminals, etc.)

Actually, this idea is technically feasible now, and many aspects of it already exist. At the same time, so much of it is new, and rapidly changing, that it is not even clear what it should be called [Halfhill and Reinhardt; Wayner 5/94; Reinhardt 10/94].

Of course, there are still some problems to be solved. One is security, i.e., how to keep malicious agents from acting just like viruses or even worse. Along with this danger of malicious use, there is an increased danger of errors: The more removed a process is, the harder it is to keep track of it. For example, an error could cause a mobile agent to go into an endless loop and incur huge expenses. In fact, even static, stable agents can cause such things as mail-forwarding loops, sending messages around in a circle. The emerging technology has solutions to these problems, but many people are still very cautious about adapting it.

Foundations

Daemons

In UNIX, any process which runs in background mode, i.e., without a terminal, is referred to as a daemon. Most daemons are intended to run constantly, and to do such things as handle communication requests.

Scripts and Macros

One important way in which repetitive tasks can be automated is through the use of scripts, which are a way of specifying actions that would otherwise be done manually. For example, terminal emulation software may contain a way of specifying a script for the logon procedure, or for a database query.

A macro is generally defined as a construct which consists of multiple instructions of a given programming language. For example, in the MVS operating system, the assembly-language "open" macro generates a number of instructions, including a call to the operating system.

When used in connection with user interfaces, both terms generally refer to a way of saving and modifying actions which would otherwise be done with the keyboard or mouse. Thus, a macro (or script) is recorded when a series of keystrokes and mouse actions is carried out and saved for later use. The saved version can normally be modified, and generally consists of some sort of programming language.

These methods can be used to create a program, or "agent", which can be used to do a job that would otherwise be done manually. However, these programs always run locally, i.e., where they were created. In the case of a script for querying a remote database, the result is normally an automated version of a terminal session, with all the drawbacks of network load.

Intelligent Agents

In the case of network management, both the Internet protocol (SNMP) and the OSI protocol (CMIP) use the concept of agents. Especially in the case of SNMP for large networks, the amount of network traffic generated for management purposes can become prohibitively large.

For example, in order to determine when a specific variable, such as disk space used, reaches a certain value, such as 90%, the management station needs to poll the disk space variable periodically or to receive periodic events containing this value. One possible solution to these problems is to filter and otherwise analyze the management data at the source, before sending it to the central manager. The tool for doing this is called an "intelligent agent".

Smart Mailboxes

E-mail filtering and routing is a method of selecting specific messages from a stream of incoming mail, and forwarding them to their proper destination. One of the traditional tools for doing this is the UNIX mailfilter, and many electronic mail systems have similar functions. With these, the user can define automatic operations, such as having messages from a specific sender or containing a certain keyword be put in a special place or forwarded to someone else.

Many implementations of this method today work in connection with an on-line service, and are active only when the user is logged onto the service. These client-based solutions provide a good example of the way added intelligence in mail agents can be used. Some large institutions have implemented server-based solutions which work in the background and prepare the information for the user without intervention. The primary difficulty with these implementations is the cost of developing and installing proprietary programs.

Telescript and Magic Cap

Suppose we have a job, such as searching for a clearly defined piece of information, which involves a significant amount of processing, perhaps at multiple sites. Clearly, it would be very useful to have this done off-line, e.g., by an agent that we simply create and send out to those sites. But how can we instruct this new agent how to operate on some remote machine, and access its services, when we don't even know what kind of operating system that machine has? And how can we make sure it won't become a Frankenstein's monster that wreaks havoc when it gets there?

One possible solution to this problem is a programming language called "Telescript", which was developed by General Magic, a company which has partnerships with AT&T, Matsushita, Motorola, Philips, and Sony. A Telescript agent is simply a program written in the Telescript language, and is capable of moving to other destinations. In other words, it is an object that can move.

The Telescript language has the power of other languages, such as C, in addition to special features like the command "Go", which instructs the agent to move to another site, as well as ways to access the services of the hosts it runs on. In order for this to work, each computer in the network needs to have a Telescript interpreter, so that the language can run without being compiled for the specific machine involved.

The basic services of the Telescript language are:

- a common language for all hosts in the network
- access to services, such as files
- moving the agent to another host

- creating new agents
- communicating with other services
- accounting, with charge limits
- security, using authentication and digital signatures

Another creation of General Magic is an operating system called Magic Cap, which is intended for use on PDAs (Personal Digital Assistants) and perhaps other devices such as fax machines, telephones, or televisions. The name Cap comes from the acronym CAP (Communicating Application Platform), which stresses the importance of communications in this concept. Magic Cap has a new GUI, which is supposed to make it easier for people to use the devices it runs on. Also, it is the first system that runs Telescript, and it already runs on the Apple Macintosh.

One important use of PDAs and other portable devices is mobile computing, where the user works off-line much of the time, but periodically connects to a network from different locations. These connections may also be made over such things as cellular telephone networks or wireless WANs, meaning that only a low-speed, relatively unreliable link is available and bringing in the old WAN problem. This situation makes it particularly important to limit communications to a small volume over brief connections, which favors the use of a messaging model.

General Magic software is used in Apple's Newton PDA, and further handheld wireless devices are being developed by Sony, Motorola, and Matsushita.

AT&T's PersonaLink

PersonaLink is a new network run by AT&T and based on General Magic's Telescript. It is intended for use by the general public and will provide such services as e-mail, information retrieval and on-line shopping.

All devices which make up or use PersonaLink must support the Telescript language, which is then used for all communications and all access to resources within the network. This way, all network entities form the substrate for intelligent, mobile agents. The first devices used to access the network will be based on the Magic Cap operating system, which has Telescript built into it.

Perhaps the greatest difficulty to be expected with PersonaLink is the fact that it requires a new basis for every device that uses it. However, by making one powerful language the common ground for all activities, it ensures a high degree of interoperability and the ability to support the newest agent technology.

The services of the AT&T PersonaLink network can be summarized as:

- data types
    - voice
    - graphics
- on-line services
    - news

- shopping
- gateways to
  - AT&T Mail
  - X.400
  - fax
  - paging
- intelligent routing
- smart mailboxes
- security
  - authentication
  - encryption
- accounting
- billing limits for agents

IBM's Intelligent Communications

IBM's new Intelligent Communications network aims at many of the same goals as PersonaLink, except that its users are expected to be more from the professional community than casual or first-time users. Also, it is based on a different implementation strategy. In fact, it can best be described as a super hub for connecting many diverse, but existing services. As such, it does not require a new software architecture on all devices connected to it.

The IBM Intelligent Communications network can be thought of as an improved on-line service that provides many gateways between different communications methods, including transformations wherever possible. For example, it should provide a means for converting faxes to text or e-mail to voice. The basic mail service is also aimed at providing a single in-box, a single bill, and filtering and prioritization services for mail messages.

The communications within the Intelligent Communications network is message-based and runs on TCP/IP, and the internal directory service is based on the X.500 standard. In this network, all the services retain their full function. This means that, in general, each service has its own interface and retains any programmable intelligence it may already possess.

The messages passed around the network are in the form of "Intelligent Communications objects", which contain both data and dynamic scripts. Access to these objects is implemented by intelligent agents, called "proxies", which can be configured to support the preferences of the users or the characteristics of a particular device. Also, service proxies can be constructed to access existing host-based services.

The "Alter Ego" is a programmable rules engine that contains the logic for mail prioritization and routing. This makes one of the most important differences between the AT&T and IBM networks clear: The intelligent agents (proxies) in the IBM network are expected to be very powerful and to cover a lot of existing services, but they are not as easily created, modified, or moved as the Telescript agents in the AT&T network.

The services of the IBM Intelligent Communications network can be summarized as:

- conversion between internal formats
  - e-mail
  - fax
  - voice
- directory
- gateways to external service providers
  - Prodigy
  - Internet
  - other e-mail services
- external directory services
- security
  - authentication
  - encryption
- accounting

Internet Agents

Considering the experimental and innovative nature of the Internet, it shouldn't be surprising that many of the methods discussed above already exist somewhere in the Internet. At the same time, they may lack the consistency or reliability of a commercially backed system.

CommerceNet is a set of commercial services built on top of the Internet; its members include companies such as American Express, Citicorp, IBM, Intel, and Pacific Bell. One major activity of CommerceNet is to promote standards for security and billing, both considered as weaknesses of the Internet, even though a number of alternatives are available.

Among these standards is a new version of the HTTP (Hypertext Transport Protocol), which is the basis for WWW (World Wide Web). This new version, called Secure-HTTP, should make secure (i.e., authenticated and encrypted) communication among WWW clients and servers possible.

Another important standard is Secure-Tcl, which is used for creating intelligent agents. Just as Tcl (Task Control Language) can be used on UNIX, Secure-Tcl scripts can be embedded in MIME (Multipurpose Internet Mail Extension) messages, enabling them to travel to remote sites (referred to as "tunneling") and execute there. In fact, Safe-Tcl can be thought of as an "open Telescript", since it performs many of the same functions, but without being proprietary: Instead of requiring a new (Telescript) infrastructure, it builds on existing Internet services.

Within the Internet community, a number of mobile agents have been created; often they are called "spiders" or "robots". Many of them are programmed in Perl, but some in Tcl, C or C++.

Chapter 31. The Internet

Recently, there has been an enormous amount of public interest in the Internet and in the idea of an "information highway", and most computer companies either have taken part in creating this enthusiasm or have joined the movement after recognizing the business potential involved. And even though today's "information dirt road" has a long way to go before it comes close to the hopes and dreams being placed on it, it does give us a good glimpse of many of the possibilities involved. At the same time, the degree of public interest has already determined that the future information highway will evolve from today's Internet.

Why are so many people so excited about the Internet, and how will it affect our jobs and lives? One book devoted to this topic is *The Road Ahead* [Gates]. The chapter called "Friction-Free Capitalism" discusses how technology has already begun to open up many old and new business opportunities to small organizations and individual people, and the next chapter continues this theme in the context of education. All of this is summed up later in the observation, "we are all created equal in the virtual world". These remarks, along with the Gates/Microsoft dream of "information at your fingertips", make it clear that a big part of the lure of the Internet is a matter of empowerment (see "Power to the User" on page 4).

On the other hand, the Internet is used not only for business and education, but also for entertainment, games, hobbies, and other cultural activities. While these activities often have little to do with economic or political power, they do represent new opportunities for individuals to pursue their interests, and so they are also a type of empowerment to "do it my way". As such, the ability to tap vast resources in pursuit of special interests, and the enthusiasm that goes with this, demonstrate how it is possible to be creative through the use of an ostensibly "noncreative" technology (see "Truth and Beauty" on page 10).

Finally, not much of this is new to the people who have known and used the Internet during the past 20 years. In fact, the Internet is closely related to the UNIX phenomenon, which is driven much more by the open, free exchange of ideas among a talented community of followers than by the technical merits of a single operating system. The really new aspect here is the widespread, global public interest that has recently arisen. This, together with the technological advances available, will be the real basis for the coming "information highway".

The size of the Internet has been doubling each year since 1988, measured in terms of network traffic, connected networks, hosts, or users. It currently links tens of thousands of networks in over 50 countries, 20 million people use it each day, and it connects 300 million computers. Use of the Internet by commercial organizations is no longer prohibited, and the operation of the backbone has been put on a commercial basis [Johnson 4/94]. More than half of the computers now connected to the Internet belong to commercial enterprises. In addition, the Internet protocol suite, based on TCP/IP, is being used more and more within enterprise networks.

At the same time, there has been significant criticism of the Internet in terms of reliability and security. In the past, these have been serious limitations of the Internet, but the situation is now changing rapidly. The commercial interests involved, including the operation of the backbone and of commercial ISPs (Internet Service Providers), already provide enough reliability for many applications, and this should improve as time goes on. Security in the Internet has been the topic of IETF RFCs and a number of industry consortia, so that, today, the necessary technology has been defined and is available, even though it is not in widespread use.

Internet Services

In a previous chapter (see "Chapter 12. The TCP/IP Family" on page 131), we have discussed a number of technical topics such as communications protocols and application-layer services. These are all part of the "Internet protocol suite", and their importance is due partly to their technical merit and partly to their widespread availability. However, the main importance of the Internet is not its technology, but its content.

From its beginnings as a research network, the Internet grew to be a worldwide network of Universities and other academic institutions and nonprofit organizations. At that time, it was funded by public sources and commercial usage was prohibited. Since then, the operation of the Internet backbone has been put on a commercial basis, and the Internet itself is open for commercial usage.

As a result of this heritage, the Internet contains a huge amount of information, including university publications, archives of research organizations, and commercial databases, such as product information from the major computer vendors. This information is so vast and diverse that whole books have been written on how to find things in it. Here is a brief overview of the major services [Johnson 4/94].

- **Archie:** An Internet resource discovery protocol that locates information in publicly available files and directories. Archie is basically a distributed index to all files available for anonymous FTP, and is operated by McGill University in Montreal. Archie can be accessed via TELNET or e-mail.
- **Gopher:** An Internet resource discovery protocol which enables clients to access information from servers. Gopher was developed by the University of Minnesota at Minneapolis, and is operated on about 1,400 servers throughout the Internet. Gopher is accessed via a special protocol which is available in the form of shareware front ends or commercial products.
- **Gopherspace:** The collection of all information available to the Gopher service.
- **Veronica:** An Internet service which allows searching of titled Gopher items.
- **MIME:** Multipurpose Internet Mail Extensions. Allows for the transfer of non-textual documents, such as binary files and multimedia, by e-mail.

- **WWW:** World Wide Web. An Internet hypertext-based resource discovery protocol that allows users to create, edit, or read hypertext documents. WWW uses the HTML (Hypertext Markup Language), and is accessed via a "Web browser" (see below).
- **USENET:** A distributed conferencing system carried on most parts of the Internet.
- **WAIS:** Wide-Area Information Servers. An Internet information service that allows easy searching and retrieval of information in remote databases. WAIS was developed by Brewster Kahle, founder of WAIS Inc.

The World Wide Web

The recent public interest in the Internet has been concentrated on a service known as the WWW (World Wide Web). The Web is based on the concept of "hypertext", which is based on the idea of direct links between parts of a document or between different documents. The WWW extends this by supporting links that can refer to documents on any machine anywhere in the network, in this case anywhere in the worldwide Internet.

The original WWW was developed by CERN (Center for European Nuclear Research) in Geneva. Later, this activity was turned over to INRIA (the French National Institute of Research for Computer Science and Control). In the meantime, commercial and public interest has led the Web to become a common effort supported by almost all software vendors and used for many types of distributed application.

The technical basis for the Web is a language called HTML (Hypertext Markup Language) [RFC 1866] and a protocol called HTTP (Hypertext Transfer Protocol). HTML is an ASCII-based language in which rules for formatting are declared in the form of "tags", i.e., special character sequences, such as "<p>" for beginning a new paragraph or "<h1>" and "</h1>" for delimiting a header at level 1. The original version of HTML was a true subset of the OSI standard SGML (Standard Generalized Markup Language), which, in turn, is very similar to IBM's Script and BookMaster markup languages.

The major, and very important, extension made by HTML is the tag "<a href=...>", which can include any Internet address (see "URLs" below). This simple, but perhaps revolutionary, idea makes it possible to create hypertext documents which span the globe. To the user, this tag, also referred to as a "link", appears as a highlighted field (normally blue and underlined), which, when selected, opens a new document in a new place. This hypertext concept may also be familiar from such things as on-line help texts or multimedia encyclopedias.

Further extensions to HTML have made it possible to use these links to activate many other types of objects, including multimedia and interactive programs, such as links to databases and existing host transactions.

Web technology is also the topic of a consortium, called the W3C (World Wide Web Consortium), with over 40 members. For more details, refer to the Web site http://www.w3c.org.

Web Browsers

In order to use the technology of the World Wide Web, we need a piece of software that communicates with a server via HTTP, understands HTML, and is capable of rendering, or displaying, whatever is contained in the various tags or links within the HTML source. These tools have become known as "Web browsers", and are now available for all major PC and workstation operating systems.

The first Web browser was called Mosaic, and it was originally developed and distributed as a freeware program by the NCSA (National Center for Supercomputing Applications). Commercial versions of Mosaic are now available from Spyglass and Spry, and a number of software vendors, most notably Netscape and Microsoft, have developed their own Web browsers.

Web Servers

Along with the Web browsers, or clients for the WWW, we need Web servers for providing the services of the Web. Originally, this was just a matter of supporting TCP/IP and HTTP communications and publishing static HTML documents. In the meantime, it has been extended to include interactive interfaces, dynamic downloading of application components, and gateways to many other systems, such as external databases.

In order to be useful, a Web server needs to have typical server properties, such as robust multitasking, high-capacity communications including support for many parallel connections, applications programming support, and security.

Most Web servers support the CGI (Common Gateway Interface) standard, an API for making dynamic Web pages. CGI has a few limitations which prevent it from achieving high performance, the main one being the fact that it spawns a new process for each request. As an improvement over the CGI standard, Netscape has defined its own API, the NSAPI (Netscape Server API), and so has Microsoft, namely the ISAPI (Internet Information Server API). Both companies are trying to have their specifications accepted as the new standard.

URLs

When using the WWW and related services, it has become customary to use an extended form of addressing called the URL (Universal Resource Locator) [RFC 1808]. The format of a URL is

- protocol-name://domain-name/path-name

For example, a test document for testing Web pages can be found in

- http://www-dsed.llnl.gov/documents/WWWtest.html

Here, "http" is the protocol used for the Web, "www-dsed.llnl.gov" is the domain name of a computer operated by a government organization [see "DNS (Domain Name Service)" on page 143], "/documents" is the path name, and "WWWtest.html" is the file name of the test document.

Some of the protocols which appear in URLs are:

- file: any file (local or remote) accessible to the browser
- ftp: File Transfer Protocol
- gopher: Gopher service
- http: Hypertext Transmission Protocol
- ldap: Lightweight Directory Access Protocol
- nntp: Network News Transmission Protocol

Searching

In many cases, using the Web means starting with a well-known URL, or address, such as "http://www.microsoft.com". From there, you can navigate via hyperlinks, and this may take you to many other sites, i.e., other machines in other locations. But what do you do when you are looking for a specific piece of information, but you don't know where it might be? Fortunately, there are good ways of searching the Internet.

Suppose we want to search for the definition of "RJ 11". We may already know that this is a plug which is used for telephones and modems, but we would like to know how the wires are connected, because we need to connect it to a different plug from another country. What we can do here is visit one of the "search engines" on the Web and search for "RJ 11". However, since this is likely to give us too many answers, such as a large number of vendors who sell devices with this plug, we would like to restrict the search more. One good way to begin is to search for "RJ 11 and FAQ"; FAQ (Frequently Asked Questions) is a tradition on the Internet, and provides a good starting point for further inquiries.

The following list includes a number of WWW search engines, most of which are free of charge. Some of the most famous ones are Yahoo, Lycos, and WebCrawler.

ALIWEB Multiple Keyword Form Search	http://www.leo.org/www_index/aliweb.html
All-in-One Search Page	http://www.albany.net/allinone/
AltaVista Main Page, DEC	http://www.altavista.digital.com/
Document Center—Search Page	http://doccenter.com/doccenter/doc2.html
Infoseek	http://www.infoseek.com
Lycos search engine	
Welcome to Lycos	http://lycos.cs.cmu.edu
Search The Internet with The Internet Sleuth, has links to other search engines	http://www.isleuth.com/
WebCrawler Searching	http://www.webcrawler.com
WEBster—The Cyberspace Surfer	http://192.147.238.100/masterlist.html
Welcome To GO, CompuServe search engine	http://www.compuserve.com/search/index.htm
WWWW—World Wide Web Worm	http://wwww.cs.colorado.edu/wwww
Yahoo Search	http://www.yahoo.com/search.html

Table 11. World Wide Web Search Engines

At this point it may be worth asking how these programs are able to search such a huge network effectively and return an answer within such a short time. In fact, what they do is to periodically collect information, such as key words, from as many sites as possible. This is put into a database so that inquiries only have to search the database.

Documents on the Net

Once we find something on the Internet, we may discover that it is in a format that our machine doesn't understand. We may need to get a popular tool for uncompressing a compressed file, or we may need a program that reads this format or converts it to another. In both cases, the solution might be a commercial program, or it might be a program which we can download for free from the Internet. In any case, it is useful to know the meaning of the file-name extension, since there may be many different programs which can read the file, and we would like to choose which one to use. Some document types which are commonly found on the Internet are listed here:

- **.doc:** Microsoft Word for Windows document
- **.gz:** compressed by GNU-Zip, needs to be uncompressed by GNU-Unzip
- **.htm or html:** HTML (Hypertext Markup Language); can be read by any Web browser or Web authoring tool
- **.ps:** Postscript printer format; can be viewed with a Postscript viewer or sent directly to a Postscript printer
- **.rtf:** Rich Text Format document; can be read by many word processors, including Microsoft Word for Windows
- **.txt:** unformatted ASCII text, can be read by almost any editor or word processor
- **.wpd:** WordPerfect document
- **.Z:** compressed by UNIX compress, needs to be uncompressed by UNIX uncompress
- **.zip:** compressed by pkzip, needs to be uncompressed by pkunzip (or winzip)

Java

The programming language Java was invented at Sun Microsystems in 1990 for the purpose of programming consumer electronics. Since then, it has become very popular as a language for creating Internet applications. It is produced by Sun, but has been licensed by a number of other companies, including IBM and Microsoft [Semich and Fisco].

One very important aspect of Java is that it is compiled to an intermediate language, called "byte-code", which is then executed, or interpreted, by the JVM (Java Virtual Machine). This makes it possible to create small application programs, called "applets", in a language (byte-code) which is independent of the target platform (hardware and operating system). The main application, typically a Web browser, can then download these applets whenever they are needed, also making it unnecessary to install the applet software on the target machine.

The concepts of virtual machine and emulation, which have been discussed previously (see "Hardware Emulation" on page 53 and "Software Emulation" on page 332), are very important here. In most compilers, the lexical analysis of source language requires much more time than all the rest of the work, i.e., syntactic and semantic analysis and code generation. This means that a well-designed intermediate language can be interpreted much more efficiently than a human-readable source, such as BASIC. As a result, the JVM interpreting Java byte-code is not as fast as the CPU running compiled C, but much faster than a source-level interpreter running BASIC.

One further effect of the virtual machine is that it insulates the Java application from the local machine's operating system, file system, hardware, and so forth. This makes it easier to implement security features which are aimed at protecting the local machine from bad applets, both those containing bugs and those created with a malicious intent, such as viruses. Of course, this also makes it more difficult to extend programs using features that are not supported by the virtual machine.

The actual Java language is based on C++, and is very similar to it, but simpler [van Hoff, Shaio, and Starbuck]. For example, it does not have pointer arithmetic, structures, unions, multidimensional arrays, multiple inheritance, or templates. In addition, Java objects must have a static type, and instead of pointers, Java allows only the use of object references. This effectively removes the most common source of errors in C programs: bad pointers. Although C++ can be written in such a way that type casting and pointer arithmetic are avoided, there is nothing in the language that forces the programmer to adhere to good style. One other source of errors (during portation) is eliminated by making integers and long integers the same size on all machines, something which is unfortunately not true for C and C++.

All of this makes Java object-oriented. In addition, it supports abstract classes in the form of Java "interfaces", which are very similar to CORBA IDL, making it easy to combine the two.

Java also supports multithreading, something which is important for graphical user interfaces, even when the machine is used by only one person. The Java runtime is small enough that Java can run efficiently on PCs which have only 4 MB of RAM. The memory management of Java's runtime also includes a "garbage collection" service, meaning that memory blocks which are no longer used are automatically returned to the system, thus eliminating another typical error, called "memory leaks".

Since one of Java's important features is its ability to download executable code from the Internet directly to the PC, it is important to have built-in security features, in order to avoid downloading dangerous bugs or viruses. Java accomplishes this through four mechanisms [Lemay and Perkins]:

First, the language itself and the compiler were designed to avoid a lot of typical C/C++ errors, such as bad pointers, addressing outside an array, and memory leaks.

Second, the JVM screens, or verifies, byte-code programs before letting them run. The verifier checks things like address ranges, access restrictions, stack overflow/underflow, and data types (strong typing). This step also makes checks which are normally done by the compiler, in order to ensure that the code has not been altered or produced by a malevolent compiler. Since the verifier is an important part of Java security, Sun has announced plans to implement validation suites that will test the correct and safe operation of Java compilers and runtime software.

Third, the class loader checks for address and access restrictions when it loads a class into the system. In addition, it keeps track of the source of the class, which is categorized in realms, such as the local machine, the local network, and the global network (the Internet). Each realm is treated differently depending on the security preferences of the user. In addition, the class loader prevents a class from replacing another one that came from a realm that has higher protection. For example, the local machine's file-access class cannot be replaced by a file-access class that was downloaded from the Internet.

Fourth, the JVM insulates the local machine from the Java application. This means that the application has no direct access to the local machine, and in particular never has a pointer to an address outside of its own space.

Java byte-code is often downloaded to a client machine running a Web browser that implements the JVM. However, if a server also has a JVM, then the Java code can also be uploaded to it. With this technique, Java applets can be made and sent around the network to do many kinds of tasks, as envisaged by the agents in the Magic Cap of General Magic [Gosling] (see "Telescript and Magic Cap" on page 344).

One recent addition to Java is JDBC (Java Database Connectivity), which can be used to access databases from the Java language. JDBC is based on ODBC (see "ODBC" on page 169) and is very similar to it, with the exception that its interface was specially designed for the Java language. There is also an adapter that makes it possible to use existing ODBC drivers for databases which do not yet have JDBC drivers.

Scripting Languages

In order to create Web server applications, it is possible to use programming languages, such as C++ and Java. In addition to these, there are also a number of scripting languages which are available, including:

- Java Script (technically not related to Java)
- Perl
- Tcl (Task Control Language)
- VB Script (based on Microsoft's Visual Basic)

Internet Security

Security, on which the Internet has traditionally been weak, has been an important area for further development during the past few years, since the Internet was put on a commercial basis. Now there are good technical solutions for practically all security issues concerning the Internet, but many of the solutions are not yet in widespread use. The security mechanisms used with the Internet can be divided into three categories:

- **firewalls:** providing isolation between corporate networks and the Internet
- **secure channels:** providing secure communications paths
- **secure applications:** including specialized application-specific security

Firewalls

The concept of a firewall is quite old and is in very common use. Basically, a firewall is a network node which connects an internal, or corporate, network to an external network, such as the Internet, and restricts traffic to certain allowed types. For example, the firewall may allow only certain IP addresses to communicate with each other, or may filter traffic based on the application being used. In doing this, the firewall may also translate the IP addresses, making the internal addresses invisible to the outside world.

Starting with this basic concept, there is a wide range of functionality available in commercial firewall products, resulting in a similar range in cost, administration effort required, and resulting network performance. Often, firewalls are implemented on the basis of multiprotocol routers or application servers, which may then be known as proxy servers.

Secure IP

One important new Internet standard which will soon be introduced is a secure version of the IP protocol (layer 3) [Stallings 12/96]. Secure IP will be an optional part of the existing IP standard and a mandatory part of IPv6, and includes both authentication and encryption services. Since secure IP operates at the IP level, it takes effect for all transport-level protocols using IP, including TCP and UDP.

The implementation of secure IP includes both an authentication header and a privacy header, called the ESP (Encapsulation Security Payload) header, which can be applied in either order. When encryption (privacy) is applied first, it covers only the original message, and the IP header is handled in the usual way by the intermediate network nodes. When authentication is applied first, encryption covers the original message, the authentication header, and the original IP header. This way, authentication is included in the encryption process; the original IP address is hidden by virtue of its encryption, and a new IP header is added for use by the external network nodes.

One recently announced product which implements secure IP is S/WAN (Secure WAN), which was codeveloped by RSA Data Security and TimeStep.

TLS (Transport-Layer Security)

The name TLS (Transport-Layer Security) refers to a standardization which is in progress within the IETF. It is a security service, including authentication and encryption, which works as the transport layer, i.e., the Sockets or TCP layer. It is based on a combination and improvement of the following two security services:

- **SSL** (Secure Sockets Layer) Version 3.0 from Netscape
- **PCT** (Private Communications Transport) Version 2.0 from Microsoft

Since TLS is soon to be an Internet standard (RFC) and is based on two widely accepted specifications, it is likely to become the general standard for transport-layer security over the Internet.

WTS (Web Transaction Security)

The name WTS (Web Transaction Security) refers to a standardization which is in progress within the IETF. It covers security in HTML and HTTP, and is also known as "secure HTTP".

PEM (Privacy Enhanced Mail)

One of the better-established Internet standards for achieving security of mail systems is PEM (Privacy Enhanced Mail). It is discussed in more detail, along with X.400 mail security, in "Secure Mail" on page 197.

SET (Secure Electronic Transactions)

One important example of an application-layer security service is the industry standard SET (Secure Electronic Transactions), which is used for extending the credit-card system for payment over nonsecure networks, such as today's Internet. SET is based on the convergence of two previous specifications:

>**STT** (Secure Transaction Technology) from Microsoft and VISA
>**SEPP** (Secure Electronic Payment Protocol) from Mastercard

SET is supported by American Express, Mastercard, VISA, and a number of software vendors, including IBM, Microsoft, and Netscape. As such, it can be expected to become the standard security service for payment transactions over the Internet.

Internet PCs

Now that access to the Internet, in the form of the World Wide Web, requires only a Web browser, and not a full set of operating system services, application software, and so forth, why not make a simple PC that just accesses the Internet and does nothing else? After all, applications will be downloaded from the Web as applets whenever needed. This is the idea behind the "Internet PC" [Simpson 3/96].

Since the Internet PC doesn't need any application software, but only a Web browser with a Java Virtual Machine, there will be nothing to install. That will certainly make it much easier to use than ordinary PCs. And since it doesn't need all that software, it probably doesn't need disks and diskettes and so forth. That should also make it cheaper.

The result of all of this is a PC that will cost about $500, require no maintenance, and be very easy to use. Since that price doesn't include a monitor, it will be hooked to a television or the monitor of a regular computer. The companies which have advocated this idea the most are IBM, Oracle, and Sun.

Intranets

For some time, the term "intranet" has meant the internal network of an organization, as opposed to "an internet" (any combination of multiple networks) and "the Internet". The three types of networks may or may not use the same technology, such as TCP/IP, though they differ in their organizational structure. But after the World Wide Web became popular, it also became clear that the same technology, involving the use of things like Web browsers, HTML, etc., could be very useful within an organization, i.e., on its intranet.

Since the Internet has traditionally been week on security and reliability, the distinction between internal and external Web technology is particularly important for most organizations. As a result, the discussion of the uses of Web technology has very often distinguished between global and internal uses.

Very often, the Internet is used for things like e-mail, news groups, and research. In contrast, while intranets often support these types of activity, they also support things which are much more tightly coupled, such as when the members of a project team collectively work on the same documents, or when they use groupware and workflow applications. In addition, intranets are often used for disseminating information which needs to stay within the organization, or for supporting organization-specific applications. Now, Web technology on an intranet may be used to provide easy and widespread access to data and applications which reside on older, or "legacy", machines. When used this way, an intranet which uses Web technology is also referred to as a "dataweb" [Varney].

The articles published on this topic make it clear that most, if not all, major software vendors are working on or already offering software that supports the use of Web technology together with traditional platforms. For example, IBM has a gateway between HTML and DB2 and another between HTML and CICS. In fact, there are already so many products, often referred to as "gateways" or "connectors", that it would be silly to try to list them here.

The reasons for this rapid development are also clear: Due to the great popularity of the Web and to its ease of use, many users want to employ the same techniques internally. At the same time, the vendors see the need to protect their investment in existing products, so they are very eager to make them accessible to Web technology. The result is that most traditional products now have some kind of Internet- or Web-like interface.

In summary, if you want to use your favorite Web browser to access existing data and use existing products and applications, there is probably already a rudimentary way of doing it. And if you need a powerful, efficient, and secure way of doing it, there may some way available now or in the near future.

ISPs and On-line Services

Along with the technical aspects covered here, it is worth taking a quick look at how the Internet is operated. The backbone is run commercially, and each organization which attaches directly to the backbone pays a fixed monthly fee for all services. Private individuals who use the Internet generally establish a dial-up connection to an ISP (Internet Service Provider). The ISP operates a fixed connection to the backbone, a number or dial-up connections for users, and generally charges a small monthly fee and additional fees for the time the user is connected to the service. This way, a user can dial up a local ISP and access all Internet services worldwide without any extra charges.

Along with organizations that provide connections to the Internet, there are a multitude of organizations, sometimes referred to as "content providers", which supply the actual services. Among these are not only the traditional Internet participants, such as universities and research institutions, but also many commercial organizations which supply information either for free or for a usage fee. Among these are the "on-line services", many of which were established before the WWW became popular and are now in the process of converting their services to the HTML standard.

On-line services typically provide the user with such things as:

- electronic mail
- news groups
- discussion forums
- information databases
- software for downloading, including shareware and vendor-supplied software such as device drivers and test versions
- Internet access (ISP services)

A few of the better-known on-line services are:

- America Online
- CompuServe
- Delphi
- AT&T EasyLink
- MSN (Microsoft Network)
- Prodigy

Standards

Many of the standards relevant to the Internet were quoted earlier (see "Chapter 12. The TCP/IP Family" on page 131). Some of the standards specific to the World Wide Web are:

- HTML [RFC 1866]
- URL [RFC 1808]
- Java, available from http://www.sun.com/java

Trends and Products

Based on the first version of HTML, Web browsers offered a number of very useful aspects. They made it possible to access (static) Web pages and to navigate the World Wide Web from any desktop computer. In other words, they provided a universal graphical user interface to all servers. At the same time, this method was very much like using a terminal or terminal emulation software to access a host, instead of using client/server or distributed applications. As a result, it has been referred to as the "3270 of the 1990s", and was described as a movement back to host systems, accessed by remote terminals.

However, this situation did not last long. The next extensions to HTML made it possible to download active components or applets, and to combine Web browsers with practically every other type of software. Therefore, HTML and HTTP may become both the universal user interface and the universal communications middleware for distributed applications. This has the great advantage of setting a de facto standard which can be used as the basis for distributed applications on all platforms. At the same time, it does not solve many of the typical problems involved in creating such applications. In fact, when designing the application, it is still necessary to consider such things as communications capacity, synchronous versus asynchronous data transfer, distributed transactions, and where and how to split up the application.

A number of vendors now produce Web browsers, including:

- Microsoft: Internet Explorer
- Netscape: Navigator
- Spry: Mosaic
- Sun: HotJava

Web servers are also offered by a number of vendors, most notably:

- Microsoft: Internet Information Server
- Netscape: Communicator
- Oracle: WebServer
- O'Reilly: WebSite

Perhaps more important than the Web servers are the many interfaces, gateways, connectors, and so forth. Practically all software vendors are now offering or developing some way for their existing products to be used in Web applications or otherwise used with, in, or over the Internet.

Many vendors are developing Java implementations. IBM has even written a JVM for its mainframe operating system MVS. These vendors include the following:

- Adobe Systems
- Borland
- Gupta/Centura Technologies
- IBM
- Lawson Software
- Microsoft
- NAT Systems
- Oracle
- PeopleSoft
- SAP
- SAS
- Seer Technologies
- Symantic

The following companies are working on Internet PCs:

- Acorn (Acorn Computer Group)
- IBM: IPC (InterPersonal Computer)
- Oracle: NC (Network Computer)
- Sun
- Sunriver (Sunriver Data Systems)
- Transphone
- WebBook (The WebBook Company)

Summary of Part 6

Creating distributed applications can be anything from very easy to very difficult, depending on the requirements they must fulfill. In some cases, we can simply use an NOS (Network Operating System), a distributed file system, or some other type of middleware, and forget the network completely. In others, we need to choose an adequate processing model, decide where to split the application, and design the interfaces and data formats.

A look at what happens when we edit a file on a remote system gives us an example of some of the difficulties involved in using standard tools, including standard communications protocols, file systems, and editors. A deeper look at what happens here also shows where the process can be optimized, and this includes the choice of protocol and things like buffer management in the application.

In order to be more thorough in designing a distributed application, we can begin by examining all possibilities for splitting the code into different pieces on separate machines. The alternatives which are theoretically possible cover the simplest case of remote terminals, which does not offer much advantage, and the case of remote data, which often requires a high network capacity. Splitting the application in the middle has the highest potential benefit, but requires the largest amount of design work.

When classical host/terminal applications are modernized, so as to take advantage of the benefits of intelligent workstations, it is often necessary to migrate existing application logic. One example of this, involving presentation logic, shows that techniques of compilation and emulation can be used in a natural way to support existing, or "legacy", applications while providing good performance and use of the newer technology.

The other common area of distributed computing involves the activities of a team, or workgroup, sharing data and applications, most often on a local network. Groupware applications make it possible for all members of the team to share data, such as text files and spreadsheets. Communication and coordination enhances this by the use of tools such as electronic mail and shared electronic calendars. Workflow applications take this a step farther by controlling the overall work process. These applications are often combined with imaging technology in order to reduce the amount of paper used and speed the movement of work from one person to another.

Today, many distributed applications consist of a remote client which uses the services of a central server. In a number of other cases, such as management applications, it is advantageous for the central manager to delegate tasks to a remote agent, in order to reduce the load on both the central process and the network. The same concept can be used to make many other tasks more efficient, even those which do not involve a central system. This is further improved by adding intelligence to the agent and giving it the capability of moving around within the network.

The biggest network in use today, the Internet, not only is the technological basis for many applications, but is, in many respects, the application itself. This is simply because what we have come to know as the Internet is not only a network but a collection of systems which provide high-level services and content. Recently, one Internet service, the World Wide Web, has received a great amount of attention, both within the computing industry and from the general public. As a result, the technology used has been rapidly improved and applied to other areas, such as intranets, or corporate networks. In addition, the public interest has led to a great expansion of the content offered on the Web, and will certainly continue to have a positive effect on the price and availability of products and services.

Appendix

Glossary

ABA: American Bankers Association. The ABA has defined security standards for banking applications.

ABI: Applications Binary Interface. A standardized ABI makes it possible to move an application (in binary format, i.e., object code) to another platform without recompilation.

abstract syntax: The specification of data by using notation rules which are independent of the encoding technique used to represent them.

acknowledgment: A function which allows a receiving entity to inform a sending entity of the receipt of a data unit.

ACL: Access Control List. In DCE security, a list defining which principals have which type of access to a particular object.

ActiveX: Microsoft's object technology, previously known as OLE (Object Linking and Embedding).

address: An unambiguous name used by the system to identify an entity.

ADF: Application Description File. Part of AMS.

ADK: Application Developers Kit. A part of NetLS.

ADMD: Administrative Management Domain. An administration entity in an X.400 MHS (Message Handling System) which provides relaying and routing services.

AIX: Advanced Interactive Executive. A UNIX variant developed by IBM.

AMS: Application Management Specification (Tivoli).

ANDF: Architecture Neutral Distribution Format (OSF, DME SDS). A format for software for distribution to machines independent of their hardware architecture.

ANSI: American National Standards Institute. Standardization body in the United States.

AnyNet/MVS: A feature of IBM VTAM which allows mixing different protocols, previously called MPTF.

APE: Animal Proliferation Enterprises. The fictitious organization used for examples in this book.

API: Application Programming Interface. A standardized API makes it possible to move an application (source code) to another platform (requires recompilation).

APPC: Advanced Program-to-Program Communication. The universal program-to-program communication protocol in IBM's SNA, defined as LU Type 6.2.

applet: Any small application. In particular, a Java applet.

APPN: Advanced Peer-to-Peer Networking (IBM SNA). A method for routing and configuring SNA networks dynamically.

Archie: An Internet resource discovery protocol that locates information on publicly available files and directories.

ARK: Administrator's Runtime Kit. A part of NetLS.

ARM: Application Response Management (Tivoli and HP).

ARPA: Advanced Research Projects Agency (U.S. Department of Defense), initiator of the ARPANet.

ARPANet: Advanced Research Projects Agency Network, a forerunner of the Internet.

ASCII: American National Standard Code for Information Interchange. A character-interchange code developed by ANSI.

ASN.1: Abstract Syntax Notation One. OSI method for defining data in a machine-independent way.

association: In OSI terminology, any cooperative relationship between peer entities; applies to all layers except the physical layer.

AU: Access Unit. A gateway to another service, such as fax or telex, within an X.400 MHS (Message Handling System).

audit: Recording and examining of all security-relevant activities in a system.

authentication: In computer security, the process of proving that a user (person or system) is authentic, i.e., not an impostor.

authorization: In computer security, the right of a user to access resources.

backup: Data copied to a secondary medium so that it can be restored if the primary medium fails.

bandwidth: A term used to denote the capacity of communications lines.

baud: The number of pulses per second on a communications line. Closely related to the capacity, measured in bps (bits per second).

BBN: Bolt, Beranek and Newman, a company which made substantial contributions to the first versions of the Internet and TCP/IP.

BIND: Berkeley Internet Name Domain Server. The Berkeley implementation of the DNS (Domain Name Service).

BLOB: Binary Large Object. A data type used for storing arbitrary, large data elements, such as image files, in a relational database.

blocking: A function which combines multiple data units into one piece before giving them to the next lower layer for transmission.

BOA: Basic Object Adapter. Part of the CORBA specification.

bps: Bits per second. Used for measuring the capacity of communications lines.

broadcast: Transmission to a number of destination addresses.

byte-code: The name of the intermediate language used by the JVM (Java Virtual Machine).

CAE: Common Applications Environment (X/Open, EWOS).

CBOF: Commercial Business Object Frameworks. Part of IBM's plans for business objects.

CCITT: Comité Consultatif International Télégraphique et Téléphonique (International Consultative Committee for Telegraphy and Telephony). Previous name of the ITU-TS.

CCR: Concurrency Commitment and Recovery. An OSI application-level service.

CDRA: Character Data Representation Architecture. Part of the IBM DRDA remote SQL protocol.

CDS: Cell Directory Service. The local directory service of OSF DCE.

CEN: Comité Européen de Normalisation (European Committee for Standardisation).

CENELEC: Comité Européen de Normalisation Electrique (European Committee for Electrotechnical Standardisation).

CERT: Computer Emergency Response Team. Monitors and advises on Internet security issues.

checksum: A sum, or the result of some other calculation, used to check if data has been corrupted during transmission or storage.

CI: Component Interface. A part of DMI (Desktop Management Interface).

CICS: Customer Information and Control System (IBM). IBM's standard transaction monitor.

CIL: Component Integration Lab. Vendor consortium which defines OpenDoc.

CISC: Complex Instruction Set Computer. A computer hardware architecture with a large set of complex instructions. Cf. RISC.

CIX: Commercial Internet Exchange Association. A worldwide group of Internet service providers.

CLI: Call-Level Interface. An SQL API, as opposed to embedded SQL.

CLI: Command-Line Interface.

client: An entity, such as a program, which requests services from another entity, the server.

CMC: Common Mail Calls. A mail API defined by the XAPIA (X.400 API Association).

CMIP: Common Management Information Protocol. The OSI protocol for network management.

COM: Common Object Model. A specification written by DEC and Microsoft to ensure interoperability between their object brokers.

COM: Component Object Model. Microsoft's object broker and the basis for OLE.

concrete syntax: Those aspects of the rules used in the formal specification of data which embody a specific representation of that data.

connection: In OSI terminology, an association requested by an entity of the next higher layer for the purpose of data transfer; applies to all layers except the physical and application layers.

CORBA: Common Object Request Broker Architecture. A standard for distributed objects defined by the OMG (Object Management Group).

COS: Class of Service. In SNA, a specification of transmission characteristics, such as bandwidth, priority, and security, similar to QOS (Quality of Service).

COS: Corporation for Open Systems.

COSE: Common Open Software Environment. Founded in 1989 by IBM, HP, SCO, Sun, Univel, and USL to provide a common open software environment across their UNIX platforms.

COSS: Common Object Services Specification. A set of object specifications defined by the OMG and based on CORBA.

CPI-C: Common Programming Interface Communications. The API for APPC (LU 6.2) defined in IBM's SAA and accepted by the X/Open group.

CRC: Cyclic Redundancy Check. A method for detecting data corruption, e.g., during transmission or on disk storage.

CTS: Common Transport Semantics. A common interface to transport-level communications (OSI layer 4) defined in IBM's Networking Blueprint.

cyberpunk: Someone who disregards netiquette (network etiquette), the rules of conduct for use in networks.

cyberspace: Virtual Reality. Also, the Internet.

DAC: Discretionary Access Control. A means of (optionally) restricting access to resources based on the identity of the user.

DAP: Directory Access Protocol. The protocol between X.500 DUA and DSA.

DARPA: Defense Advanced Research Projects Agency. A part of the U.S. Department of Defense which developed the ARPANet, a forerunner of the Internet.

DBCS: Double-Byte Character Set. A character code defined by IBM.

DBMS: Database Management System. A software system that controls the storage of data in order to provide such services as availability, consistency, and integrity.

DCE: Distributed Computing Environment. A distributed computing platform, or NOS, produced by OSF and sold by its member companies.

DCOM: Distributed Component Object Model. The basis for Microsoft's ActiveX.

DDCS: Distributed Database Connection Services (IBM products which implement the SNA DRDA remote SQL specification).

DDE: Dynamic Data Exchange. An interprogram communications method defined within Microsoft Windows.

DDM: Distributed Data Management. A distributed data protocol defined by IBM.

deblocking: The reverse of blocking.

DEC: Digital Equipment Corporation.

demultiplexing: The reverse of multiplexing.

DES: Data Encryption Standard. A private-key encryption algorithm defined by FIPS.

DFR: Document Filing and Retrieval [ISO/IEC 10166].

DFS: Distributed File System. The file system of OSF DCE.

DHCP: Dynamic Host Configuration Protocol. A part of the Internet protocol suite.

DIB: Directory Information Base. The database of an X.500 directory.

digital signature: In computer security, an authentication tool that verifies the identity of a sender and the origin of a message.

DII: Dynamic Invocation Interface. Part of the CORBA specification.

directory: A service which translates names into addresses.

distribution lists: A method for specifying the recipients for a broadcast transmission.

DIT: Directory Information Tree. The hierarchical structure of an X.500 directory.

DME: Distributed Management Environment. A distributed management platform produced by OSF.

DMI: Desktop Management Interface. An API defined by DMTF.

DMTF: Desktop Management Task Force. A vendor consortium which has defined DMI.

DNS: Domain Name System. A part of the TCP/IP protocol suite that converts host names to IP addresses.

DOE: Distributed Objects Everywhere. An object broker created by SunSoft.

DOMF: Distributed Object Management Facility (OMG).

DPA: Document Printing Application [ISO/IEC 10175].

DRDA: Distributed Relational Database Architecture. An architecture developed by IBM for remote access to relational databases.

DRM: Data Replication Manager. A part of NCS.

DSA: Directory System Agent. Provides the storage and retrieval services for part or all of an X.500 directory.

DSMIT: Distributed Systems Management Interface Tool (IBM AIX).

DSOM: Distributed System Object Model. An object broker from IBM.

DSP: Digital Signal Processor. A specialized chip used for processing audio and video signals.

DSP: Directory System Protocol. The protocol between two X.500 DSAs.

DTP: Desktop Publishing.

DTP: Distributed Transaction Processing.

DTS: Distributed Time Service. The time-synchronization service of OSF DCE.

DUA: Directory User Agent. Provides the user access to the services of an X.500 directory.

DUOW: Distributed Unit of Work. Part of the IBM DRDA remote SQL specification.

duplex (full duplex) transmission: Data transmission in both directions at the same time.

dynamic routing: Routing in which tables are created and updated dynamically.

EBCDIC: Extended Binary-Coded Decimal Interchange Format. A character-interchange code.

EC: Event Controller. A part of DME EVS.

ECMA: European Computer Manufacturers Association.

EDI: Electronic Data Interchange.

EDIFACT: Electronic Data Interchange for Administration, Commerce, and Transport. An EDI standard defined by the United Nations.

EDL: Event Definition Language. Used in DME EVS.

EGP: External Gateway Protocol. A part of the Internet protocol suite.

EHLLAPI: Emulator High-Level Application Programming Interface. An API defined by IBM for use with 3270 terminal emulation.

e-mail: Electronic mail.

encipherment: Also encryption. A means for rendering information unintelligible in order to prevent unauthorized use.

encryption: Encipherment.

ERB: Event Request Broker. A part of DME EVS.

ESP: Encapsulation Security Payload. Part of secure IP.

EVS: Event Services. A part of OSF DME.

EWOS: European Working Group on Open Systems.

expedited transfer: Expedited data units are transferred with priority over normal data units. Has a meaning only in connection-oriented transmission.

FD:OCA: Formatted Data: Object Content Architecture. Part of the IBM DRDA remote SQL specification.

filter: Also event discriminator. In OSI network management, a program which receives notifications, applies rules such as threshold criteria, and optionally forwards notifications to another entity.

FIPS: Federal Information Processing Standard.

flow control: Function which controls the flow of data within a layer or between adjacent layers.

FSS: File System Switch. A part of the Internet suite contributed by AT&T.

FTAM: File Transfer, Access, and Management. The OSI file service.

FTP: File Transfer Protocol. A part of the TCP/IP protocol suite.

GBOF: General Business Object Frameworks. Part of IBM's plans for business objects.

GDA: Global Directory Agent. A part of OSF DCE.

GDMO: Guidelines for the Definition of Managed Objects. The method for specifying managed resources defined within OSI management.

GDS: Global Directory Services. A part of OSF DCE.

GLB: Global Location Broker. A part of the NCS Location Broker.

GMITS: Guidelines for the Management of IT Security. An OSI standard.

Gopher: An Internet resource discovery protocol which enables clients to access information from servers.

Gopherspace: The collection of all information available to the Gopher service.

GOSIP: Government Open Systems Interconnection Profile (NIST).

GSSAPI: Generic Security Services API [RFC 1508 and RFC 1509].

GUI: Graphical User Interface.

GUID: Globally Unique Identifier. The Microsoft version of the OSF DCE UUID (Universally Unique Identifier).

GULS: Generic Upper Layers Security. An OSI standard.

HAL: Hardware Abstraction Layer. A lower-layer part of some operating systems containing the hardware-dependent code.

half duplex transmission: Data transmission in either direction, one direction at a time

HDLC: High-Level Data Link Control. A general link protocol defined by ITU-TS and ISO.

heartbeat: A message which is sent periodically to another system in order to determine whether it is still alive (operational).

HLLAPI: High-Level Language Application Programming Interface (IBM 3270 emulation interface).

HMA: Host Management Application. A part of the original DME OMF.

HMMP: HyperMedia Management Protocol. Part of WBEM.

HMMS: HyperMedia Management Schema. Part of WBEM.

HMOM: HyperMedia Object Manager. Part of WBEM.

HP: Hewlett-Packard.

HSM: Hierarchical Storage Management.

HTML: Hypertext Markup Language. The basis for WWW (World Wide Web).

HTTP: Hypertext Transport Protocol. The protocol used by the World Wide Web.

HUGS: Host/User/Group/Subnet.

hypermedia: An extension of hypertext that includes multimedia elements such as photographs, audio, and video.

hypertext: Text which provides links between key elements, allowing the reader to move through information nonsequentially.

i18n: An abbreviation for "internationalization".

I4DL: Interface, Inheritance, Implementation, Installation Definition Language. Part of the original OSF DME OMF.

I&A: Identification and Authentication (security). The method by which the identity of a user is determined and verified.

IAB: Internet Activities Board, standardization body for Internet specifications (RFCs).

IBM: International Business Machines Corporation.

ICDS: Internet Component Download Service. A part of Microsoft's ActiveX.

ICMP: Internet Control Message Protocol. A control protocol in the network layer of the Internet.

IDL: Interface Definition Language (DCE, CORBA, UI-Atlas).

IEC: International Electrotechnical Commission.

IEEE: Institute of Electrical and Electronics Engineers.

IETF: Internet Engineering Task Force.

IGMP: Internet Group Management Protocol. An Internet standard for multicasting.

IMA: Interactive Multimedia Association. A vendor consortium concerned with multimedia.

IMAP: Internet Message Access Protocol. A proposed Internet standard for the manipulation of messages and mailboxes.

IMS: Information Management System (IBM).

IMSP: Internet Mail Support Protocol. A proposed Internet standard for using IMAP with multiple mailboxes.

IN: Intelligent Networks. Telephone or telecommunications networks which make it possible to specify such things as QOS (Quality of Service) on demand.

infobahn: A nickname for the "information highway".

information highway: A U.S. government program for modern high-speed telecommunications. See also NII.

internationalization: The process of creating software which is usable internationally.

internet: A network of networks joined by a common internet protocol.

Internet: The worldwide network previously operated as a research network, but increasingly used for commercial purposes. It predominantly uses the TCP/IP protocol and others which are overseen by the Internet Society and the IAB (Internet Architecture Board).

IP: Internet Protocol. The network-layer protocol in the Internet suite.

IPC: Interprocess Communication.

IPD: Installed Product Database. A part of DME SDS.

IPng: Internet Protocol next generation. The new IP addressing scheme required to overcome the limitations of the existing one.

IPX: Internet Packet Exchange (Novell).

IRB: Instrumentation Request Broker. A part of OSF DME.

IrDA: Infrared Data Association. An industry consortium which has defined a standard for infrared wireless communication.

ISAM: Index Sequential Access Method. A file system that provides record access either by index or sequentially.

ISO: International Organization for Standardization.

ITU-TS: International Telecommunication Union—Telecommunications Sector (formerly CCITT).

JTC: Joint Technical Committee—Information Technology (ISO/IEC).

JTM: Job Transfer and Manipulation.

KLM: Kernel Lock Manager. A part of the locking mechanism used with NFS (Network File System).

l10n: An abbreviation for "localization".

LAN: Local Area Network. A physical connection that allows communications between devices on the same premises.

LCP: Link Control Protocol. A part of PPP.

LFS: Local File System (DCE).

LLB: Local Location Broker. A part of the NCS Location Broker.

LLC: Logical Link Control. The upper sublayer of the IEEE LAN standards.

LMS: License Management Service. A part of OSF DME.

LOA: Library Object Adapter. Part of the CORBA specification.

localization: The process of adapting a piece of software to a particular locale.

location transparency: A property of a system which makes it possible to refer uniquely to a partner entity without specifying its location.

LSAPI: Licensing Services API. Defined by Brightwork, DEC, Gradient, Microsoft, and Novell, and planned for implementation in Windows.

LU: Logical Unit. A port through which end users access an SNA network.

LU 6.2: An LU of type 6.2, or the protocol used between these entities. The architectural basis for APPC.

MAC: Mandatory Access Control. In computer security, a method which restricts access to objects based on the authorization level of the user.

MAC: Media Access Control. The lower part of the link layer of IEEE communications protocols, defined especially for use with LANs.

MAC: Message Authentication Code. In computer security, an encrypted code attached to a message to ensure that the message is not altered during transmission.

MAN: Metropolitan Area Network. A network used for connecting nodes within the boundaries of a city.

MAPI: Messaging API. A mail API defined by Microsoft.

Matrix: All computer networks that exchange electronic mail.

MDC: Modification Detection Code (security).

MHS: Message Handling System. The OSI mail system, a store-and-forward system for delivering arbitrarily structured messages. The newer term for the ISO/IEC equivalent of ITU-TS X.400.

MI: Management Interface. A part of DMI (Desktop Management Interface).

MIA: Multivendor Integration Architecture (NTT, NTT Data, DEC, Fujitsu, Hitachi, IBM, and NEC).

MIB: Management Information Base. The collection of all MOs (Managed Objects) accessible to a management application.

MIDL: Microsoft Interface Definition Language. The Microsoft version of IDL, used for defining RPC interfaces.

MIF: Management Information Format. A data format defined by DMTF (Desktop Management Task Force) and used with DMI (Desktop Management Interface).

MIME: Multipurpose Internet Mail Extensions. Allows for the transfer of nontextual documents, such as binary files and multimedia, by e-mail.

modem: modulator/demodulator. A device used to convert signals from digital format to analog for transmission over telephone lines, and vice versa.

Mosaic: An Internet service, the most popular browsing software for WWW.

Motif: A window manager selected by the OSF and based on the X Windows protocol.

MOTIS: Message-Oriented Text Interchange System, the older term for the ISO equivalent of ITU-TS X.400.

MOUNT: An Internet service used with NFS (Network File System).

MPP: Massively Parallel Processing. Indicates that a large number of processors operate in parallel to make one computer.

MPTF: Multiprotocol Transport Feature (IBM VTAM, now AnyNet/MVS).

MPTN: Multiprotocol Transport Networking (IBM and X/Open).

MQI: Message Queue Interface. A remote queuing protocol defined by IBM.

MQM: Message Queue Manager. The name for some IBM products which implement MQI.

MRB: Management Request Broker. Part of the original OSF DME OMF.

MS: Microsoft.

MTA: Message Transfer Agent. An intermediate node in an X.400 MHS (Message Handling System).

MTBF: Mean Time Between Failures.

MTTR: Mean Time To Repair.

MUI: Management User Interface. A part of OSF DME.

multiplexing: The use of one connection to support multiple connections in the next higher layer.

MVS: Multiple Virtual Storage. An IBM mainframe operating system.

name: An identifier for a partner entity.

name server: A server which offers directory services to multiple clients.

NASA: National Aeronautics and Space Administration.

NBS: National Bureau of Standards (U.S., now NIST).

NCA: Network Computing Architecture. Used in Apollo/HP NCS.

NCP: NetWare Core Protocol. A protocol in part of Novell's products.

NCP: Network Control Program. A communications protocol which was a forerunner of TCP/IP.

NCP: Network Control Program. The name for the software that runs IBM's 37x5 family of communications controllers.

NCP: Network Control Protocol. A part of PPP.

NCS: Network Computing System. An implementation of NCA by Apollo (now a division of HP).

NCSA: National Center for Supercomputing Applications. Author of the original Mosaic program, an Internet WWW tool.

NDIS: Network Driver Interface Specification (Microsoft/3Com).

NDS: NetWare Directory Service (Novell). The directory service in Novell NetWare.

NEC: Nippon Electric Corporation.

netiquette: The etiquette of using the network.

NetLS: Network License System (Apollo/HP).

NFS: Network File System. A part of the Internet suite contributed by Sun Microsystems.

NIDL: Network Interface Definition Language. A part of NCS used for defining RPCs.

NII: National Information Infrastructure. U.S. legislation on telecommunications, also referred to as the "information highway".

NIS: Network Information System. A UNIX directory service from Sun, previously known as Yellow Pages.

NIST: National Institute of Standards and Technology (U.S., previously NBS).

NLM: Network Lock Manager. A part of the locking mechanism used with NFS (Network File System).

NMF: Network Management Forum. Consortium of users and suppliers.

NMO: Network Management Option. A part of OSF DME which uses SNMP and CMIP.

NOS: Network Operating System. A generic term used for an operating system which supports components distributed over a network.

NTP: Network Time Protocol (Internet).

NTT: Nippon Telephone and Telegraph.

NVT: Network Virtual Terminal. The terminal abstraction of TELNET, an Internet protocol.

ODA: Object Database Adapter. An addition to the CORBA specification, used for object-oriented databases.

ODBC: Open Database Connectivity. An SQL CLI (Call-Level Interface) defined by an industry consortium (Microsoft, Sybase, Lotus, and DEC).

ODIF: Open Document Interchange Format (OSI).

ODL: Object-Definition Language. A formal language, along with a compiler which converts ODL to C++ or Smalltalk (ODMG).

ODM: Object Data Model. A definition of object-oriented data modeling (ODMG).

ODMG: Object Database Management Group. Part of the OMG.

ODP: Open Distributed Processing.

ODTP: Open Distributed Transaction Processing.

OID: Object Identifier. A unique ID assigned to each object when it is created (ODMG).

OLE: Object Linking and Embedding. A standard for document-oriented and object-oriented computing, defined by Microsoft.

OLTP: On-Line Transaction Processing.

OMA: Object Management Architecture. The basic reference model of the OMG.

OMF: Object Management Facility (HP NewWave).

OMF: Object Management Framework (DME).

OMG: Object Management Group. Corporation of vendors and users that defined CORBA.

OMNIPoint: Open Management Interoperability Point (NMF).

OpenDoc: A standard for document-oriented computing, defined by CIL, which is expected to compete with Microsoft's OLE.

OQL: Object Query Language (ODMG).

ORB: Object Request Broker (DME OMF, DOMF, OMG).

ORPC: Object RPC. An object-oriented extension of DCE RPC created by DEC.

OSF: Open Software Foundation.

OSI: Open Systems Interconnection. A set of standards defined by the ISO to facilitate communications between computers of different manufacture and technology.

PAC: Privilege Attribute Certificates (security).

pacing: The sliding-window flow-control method used in SNA.

PCMCIA: PC Memory Card International Association. Refers to a standard for small PC expansion cards.

PCT: Private Communications Transport. Secure transport layer (Microsoft).

PDF: Package Definition File (Microsoft).

PDIF: Product Data Interchange Format.

PDK: Package Development Kit. A part of OSF DME.

peer: In OSI, an entity of the same layer.

PEM: Privacy Enhanced Mail. An Internet standard for secure e-mail.

PGO: Principal/Group/Organization (DCE Security).

PGP: Pretty Good Privacy. A public-domain implementation of the RSA encryption algorithm.

PIN: Personal Identification Number (security).

PING: Packet Internet Groper. An "echo" message used for testing IP networks.

PKA: Public Key Algorithm.

PnP: Plug and Play.

POSIX: Portable Operating System Interface. A set of standards defined by the IEEE.

PPP: Point-to-Point Protocol.

PRMD: Private Management Domain. An administration entity in an X.400 MHS (Message Handling System) which does not provide relaying and routing services.

protocol: In OSI, a set of rules and formats which determines the behavior of the entities during communication.

PRS: Print Services. A part of OSF DME.

PSF: Product Specification File. A part of DME SDS.

PSM: Persistent Storage Manager. Part of the OMG Persistence Service, one of the object services based on CORBA.

PSM: Persistent Stored Module. The ANSI/ISO equivalent of stored procedures, a method for storing and activating program logic within a database.

QOS: Quality of Service.

RACF: Resource Access Control Facility (IBM).

RAM: Random Access Memory. The main memory of a computer used for running programs. In contrast to disk storage, the contents of RAM are lost when the computer is turned off.

reassembling: The reverse of segmenting.

recombining: The reverse of splitting.

reset: A function which sets the corresponding entities to a predefined state with a possible loss or duplication of data.

REX: Remote Execution Service. An Internet service contributed by Sun.

RFC: Request for Comment. An Internet publication, also used for standards.

RFT: Request for Technology (OSF).

RFT: Revisable Form Text (IBM DCA).

RIP: Routing Information Protocol.

RISC: Reduced Instruction Set Computer. A hardware architecture with a small set of simple instructions. Cf. CISC.

RJE: Remote Job Entry (IBM).

RMON: Remote Monitor (SNMP).

ROS: Remote Operation Service. An OSI standard for request/reply communications.

routing: A function which translates the address of an entity to a path (or route) by which the entity can be reached.

RPC: Remote Procedure Call. A method of communication which provides procedure calls over a network.

RSA: Rivest Shamir, Adleman (public-key encryption algorithm).

RSVP: Resource Reservation Protocol. An emerging Internet standard.

RTCP: Real-Time Control Protocol. Part of RTP.

RTF: Rich Text Format (Microsoft).

RTP: Real-Time Transport Protocol. An Internet standard.

RUOW: Remote Unit of Work. Part of the IBM DRDA remote SQL specification.

SAA: Systems Application Architecture (IBM).

SDLC: Synchronous Data Link Control. The original link layer of IBM's SNA (Systems Network Architecture).

SDS: Software Distribution Services. A part of OSF DME.

security policy: A set of rules and practices that regulate how an organization maintains security, including physical, technical, and organizational security measures.

segmenting: A function which splits data units into multiple pieces before giving them to the next lower layer for transmission.

SEPP: Secure Electronic Payment Protocol. A specification from Mastercard, made obsolete by SET.

sequencing: A function performed by a layer in order to preserve the order of the data units submitted to it.

server: An entity, such as a program, which provides services for another entity, the client.

service: In OSI, a capability provided by one layer to the next higher layer.

SES: Security Exchange Service (OSI).

SET: Secure Electronic Transactions. An industry specification for secure electronic commerce.

SGML: Standard Generalized Markup Language [ISO/IEC 8879].

SIDF: System-Independent Data Format. A format used for backup storage, under consideration by ISO.

SILS: Standard for Interoperable LAN Security [IEEE 802.10].

simplex transmission: Data transmission in one pre-assigned direction.

SIO: Security Information Objects (OSI).

SKC: Secret Key Cryptography.

SL: Service Layer. A part of DMI (Desktop Management Interface).

SLIP: Serial Line Internet Protocol. A simple protocol for connection to Internet hosts via serial lines.

SMI: Structure of Management Information (CMIP, SNMP).

SMIT: Systems Management Interface Tool (IBM AIX).

SMP: Simple Management Protocol. A precursor of SNMPv2.

SMP: Symmetric Multiprocessing.

SMS: Storage Management System. A data format used by Novell for backup storage.

SMTP: Simple Mail Transfer Protocol. The traditional Internet e-mail protocol, which supports textual messages.

SNA: Systems Network Architecture. A network architecture (formats and protocols) defined by IBM.

Snackets: Another name for "SNA Sockets", the IBM implementation of the Berkeley Socket API over the SNA protocol.

SNMP: Simple Network Management Protocol (Internet).

SNMPv2: Simple Network Management Protocol Version 2 (Internet).

SNPP: Simple Network Paging Protocol. An Internet protocol for use with paging devices.

Sockets: The Berkeley API for programming the (transport layer) protocols TCP and UDP. More precisely, the term "socket" refers to a special file handle in this interface, and "socket address" to an address of a partner.

SOM: System Object Modeling (IBM).

SPAG: Standard Promotion and Application Group (Europe).

SPEC: Standard Performance Evaluation Corporation. Defines standards for measuring performance of hardware.

splitting: The use of multiple connections to support one connection in the next higher layer.

SPX: Sequenced Packet Exchange (Novell).

SQL: Structured Query Language. The data-access language used with relational databases.

SQL*Net: A remote SL protocol used by Oracle.

SSL: Secure Sockets Layer. Secure transport layer (Netscape).

S-SNMP: Secure SNMP. A precursor of SNMPv2.

static routing: Routing in which tables are preconfigured.

STT: Secure Transaction Technology. A specification from Microsoft and VISA, made obsolete by SET.

SVID: System V Interface Definition. (AT&T).

SVR4: UNIX System V Release 4.

TCB: Trusted Computing Base. In computer security, that part of a system which can be trusted a priori.

TCOS: Technical Committee on Operating Systems (IEEE).

TCP/IP: Transmission Control Protocol/Internet Protocol. The transport-layer (TCP) and network-layer (IP) protocols of the Internet.

TCSEC: Trusted Computer System Evaluation Criteria (DoD Orange Book).

TDS: Tabular Data Stream. A remote SL protocol used by Sybase and Microsoft.

TELNET: Teletype Network. An Internet virtual terminal service that allows a user on a local host to login to a remote host.

TFTP: Trivial File Transfer Protocol. A simple file transfer protocol in the Internet suite.

TLD: Top-Level Domain. The highest level of naming in the DNS (Domain Name Service).

TLI: Transport-Level Interface.

TLS: Transport-Layer Security. An emerging Internet standard.

TP: Transaction Processing.

TPI: Time Provider Interface (DCE DTS).

TPI: Transport Provider Interface. The interface between TLI/XTI and the transport protocol.

TR: Token Ring.

transfer syntax: That concrete syntax used in the transfer of data between open systems.

two-person rule: A security measure which states that certain actions may be taken only by two people together.

TxRPC: Transactional Remote Procedure Call (X/Open).

UA: User Agent. The endpoint in an X.400 MHS (Message Handling System).

UDP: User Datagram Protocol. A connectionless transport protocol used in the Internet.

UFS: UNIX File System.

UI: UNIX International.

URL: Universal Resource Locator. A standard way to refer to resources in the Internet that specifies the type of service as well as the exact location of the directory or file in question.

USENET: A distributed conferencing system carried on most parts of the Internet.

USL: UNIX System Laboratories.

UUCP: UNIX to UNIX Copy Program. A UNIX mail network packaged with most UNIX systems.

UUID: Universal Unique Identifier (DCE RPC).

VAN: Value-Added Network.

variable binding: In SNMP, a list of pairs, each consisting of a reference to an object instance and its value.

Veronica: An Internet service which allows searching of titled Gopher items.

VFS: Virtual File System, a part of the Internet suite contributed by Sun Microsystems.

VITAL: Virtually Integrated Technical Architecture Lifecycle. Apple strategy for integrated distributed systems.

VR: Virtual Reality. Cyberspace.

VTAM: Virtual Telecommunication Access Method (IBM).

WAIS: Wide-Area Information Servers. An Internet information service that allows easy searching and retrieval of information in remote databases.

WAN: Wide-Area Network. A network for connecting nodes over wide geographical areas.

WBEM: Web-Based Enterprise Management. An emerging industry standard, including HMMS and HMMP.

WFMC: Workflow Management Coalition. An industry consortium which defines standards for workflow.

WINS: Windows-Internet Naming Service. A proprietary Microsoft directory used for correlating names with IP addresses.

WOSA: Windows Open Service Architecture (Microsoft).

WOSA/XFS: WOSA Extensions for Financial Services.

WTS: Web Transaction Security. An emerging Internet standard covering secure HTTP.

WTVS: Windows Trust Verification Service. A part of Microsoft's ActiveX.

WWW: World Wide Web. An Internet hypertext-based resource discovery protocol that allows users to create, edit, or read hypertext documents.

X.400:. The ITU-TS mail system, a store-and-forward system for delivering arbitrarily structured messages. Equivalent to OSI MHS (Message Handling System).

X.500:. The ITU-TS directory service. Equivalent to OSI Directory.

XA: An X/Open API for use between transaction managers and resource managers.

XAPIA: X.400 API Association. A multivendor consortium which defined CMC (Common Mail Calls).

XDR: External Data Representation. A presentation-layer component of the Sun NFS (Network File System) services.

XDS: X/Open Directory Services (X/Open API).

XDS: X.500 Directory Services (ITU-TS).

XMP: X/Open Management Protocol. An API used for programming both SNMP and CMIP applications.

XNS: Xerox Network Services.

XOM: X/Open OSI Management. An API for programming ASN.1.

X/Open: Nonprofit corporation for defining standards, mainly in the UNIX area.

XPG: X/Open Portability Guide.

XTI: X/Open Transport Interface.

XTP: X/Open Transaction Processing.

YP: Yellow Pages, a directory service, part of the Internet suite contributed by Sun Microsystems, and now known as NIS (Network Information System).

YPBIND: The protocol used to access YP.

Bibliography

Allen, Dennis. "The Entertainment Factor", *BYTE,* Vol. 19, No. 5, page 10 (May 1994).

ANSI X12. *ANSI X12 Series: A collection of all ANSI-approved X12 standards.* American National Standards Institute (1992).

Atkins, John, and Norris, Mark. *Total Area Networking. ATM, Frame Relay and SMDS Explained.* John Wiley & Sons, Chichester, England (1995).

Balzer, Robert M. "Living in the Next-Generation Operating System", *IEEE Software,* pages 77–85 (November 1987), reprinted from H. J. Kugler, ed., *Information Processing 86,* North-Holland, Amsterdam (1986).

Baum, David. "Backing into Client/Server", *Datamation*, Vol. 40, No. 20, pages 71–77 (October 15, 1994).

Baum, David. "The Right Tools for Coding Business Rules", *Datamation*, Vol. 41, No. 4, pages 36–38 (March 1, 1995).

Baum, David. "Groupware: Is It Notes or Nothing?" *Datamation*, Vol. 41, No. 8, pages 45–48 (May 1, 1995).

Bellcore TR-TSV-000772. *Generic Systems Requirements in Support of Switched Multi-Megabit Data Service.* Issue 3, Bellcore (October 1989).

Ben-Natan, Ron. *CORBA: A Guide to Common Object Request Broker Architecture.* McGraw-Hill, New York (1995). ISBN 0-07-005427-4.

Berson, Alex. *Client/Server Architecture.* McGraw-Hill, New York (1992).

Black, George. "Save Money through Asset Management", *Datamation*, Vol. 42, No. 7, pages 62–64 (April 1, 1996).

Booch, Grady. *Object-Oriented Analysis and Design with Applications*, Second Edition. Benjamin/Cummings, Redwood City, Calif. (1994).

Borning, Alan. "Computer System Reliability and Nuclear War". *Commun. ACM,* Vol. 30, No. 2, pages 112–131 (February 1987).

Brand, Richard. "Iso-Ethernet: Bridging the Gap from WAN to LAN", *Data Communications International,* Vol. 24, No. 9, page 103 (July 1995).

Brockschmidt, Kraig. *Inside OLE,* Second Edition. Microsoft Press, Redmond, Wash. (1995). ISBN 1-55615-843-2.

Brooks, Frederick P. Jr., *The Mythical Man-Month. Essays on Software Engineering.* Addison-Wesley, Reading, Mass. (1972, 1982).

Capra, Fritjof. *The Tao of Physics*. Bantam Books, Toronto (1975).

Cattell, R. G. G., ed. *The Object Database Standard: ODMG93*. Morgan Kauffman (1994).

Chadda, Parmeet Singh. "Dancing with Data: Check Your Choreography", *Datamation*, Vol. 41, No. 14, pages 59–63 (August 1, 1994).

CMC. *Common Messaging Call API. Version 2.0*. X.400 API Association, Cupertino, Calif. (1995). Available from the Electronic Messaging Association, http://www.ema.org.

Conway, M. E., "How Do Committees Invent?" *Datamation*, Vol. 14, No. 4, pages 28–31 (April 1968).

Cox, Brad J. *Object-Oriented Programming: An Evolutionary Approach*. Addison-Wesley, Reading, Mass. (1986, 1987).

Cox, Brad J. "There Is a Silver Bullet", *BYTE*, Vol. 15, No. 10 (October 1990).

Custer, Helen. *Inside Windows NT*. Microsoft Press, Redmond, Wash. (1993). ISBN 1-55615-481-X.

Darling, Charles B. "Tap Into a Rich Legacy of Data", *Datamation*, Vol. 41, No. 1, pages 65–75 (January 15, 1995).

Darling, Charles B. "Is It Time to Change Your NOS?" *Datamation*, Vol. 41, No. 16, page 71 (September 1, 1995).

Date, Chris J. Article in InfoDB (1987), cited in Berson (1992).

DME. *Distributed Management Environment. DME Features and Functionality*, Open Software Foundation, Inc. (1989).

DMI. *Desktop Management Interface. Specification. Draft 4.5*, Desktop Management Task Force (April 1994).

DoD 5200.28. *Department of Defense Trusted Computer System Evaluation Criteria (TCSEC)*, U.S. Government Printing Office, Washington, DC, No. 008-000-00461-7 (December 1985).

Donne, John. "Meditation 17". Quoted in Witherspoon, Alexander M., *The College Survey of English Literature*, Harcourt, Brace & World, New York (1942).

Dugger, Randy. "Build a Help Desk on the Cheap", *Datamation*, Vol. 42, No. 14, pages 33–34 (August, 1996).

Estrin, Judy, and Casner, Stephen. "Multimedia over IP: Specs Show the Way", *Data Communications International*, Vol. 25, No. 10, page 93 (August 1996).

FIPS 46. *Data Encryption Standard.* National Bureau of Standards, Federal Information Processing Standard, Publication 46, U.S. Department of Commerce (January 1977). http://www.nist.gov/itl/csl/fips.

FIPS 186. *Digital Signature Standard.* National Institute of Standards and Technology, Federal Information Processing Standard, Publication 186, U.S. Department of Commerce (May 1994). http://www.nist.gov/itl/csl/fips.

Foley, Mary Jo. "Control Business Process with Platinum, BMC or Tivoli?" *Datamation*, Vol. 42, No. 8, pages 40–46 (April 15, 1996).

Foley, Mary Jo. "Objects for Business Apps are Coming! But Slowly", *Datamation*, Vol. 42, No. 10, pages 52–56 (May 15, 1996).

Foley, Mary Jo, and Semich, William J. "Run Your Business with Systems Management Tools", *Datamation*, Vol. 42, No. 8, pages 32–34 (April 15, 1996).

Gareiss, Robin, and Heywood, Peter. "Tomorrow's Networks Today", *Data Communications International,* Vol. 24, No. 1, page 55 (September 21, 1995).

Gates, William H. III. *The Road Ahead.* Viking Penguin, London (1995).

Geiger, Kyle. *Inside ODBC.* Microsoft Press, Redmond, Wash. (1995). ISBN 1-55615-815-7.

Geschickter, Chet. "Client-Server's New Cry: Break Up the Application". *Data Communications International,* Vol. 23, No. 5, page 25 (March 21, 1994).

Gilb, Tom. *Principles of Software Engineering.* Addison-Wesley, Reading, Mass. (1988).

Gosling, James. "Gosling on Java", *Datamation*, Vol. 42, No. 5, pages 30–37 (March 1, 1996).

Gray, Jim, and Edwards, Jeri. "Scale Up with TP Monitors", *BYTE,* Vol. 20, No. 4, page 123 (April 1995).

Hackathorn, Richard D. *Enterprise Database Connectivity: The Key to Deploying Enterprise Applications on the Desktop.* John Wiley & Sons, New York (1993).

Halfhill, Tom R. "Emulation: RISC's Secret Weapon", *BYTE,* Vol. 19, No. 4, page 119 (April 1994).

Halfhill, Tom R. "80x86 Wars", *BYTE,* Vol. 19, No. 6, page 74 (June 1994).

Halfhill, Tom R. "Transforming the PC: Plug and Play", *BYTE,* Vol. 19, No. 9, page 78 (September 1994).

Halfhill, Tom R. "The New PC", *BYTE,* Vol. 20, No. 10, page 52 (October 1995).

Halfhill, Tom R., and Reinhardt, Andy. "Just Like Magic?" *BYTE,* Vol. 19, No. 2, page 22 (February 1994).

Hansen, Wolf-Rüdiger (Ed.). *Client-Server-Architektur. Grundlagen und Herstellerkonzepte für Downsizing und Rightsizing.* Addison-Wesley, Bonn (1993).

Hayes, Frank. "Personality Plus", *BYTE,* Vol. 19, No. 1, page 155 (January 1994).

Hecht, Bradley. "The Help Desk Market: Disarray and Disrepair", *Datamation,* Vol. 42, No. 18, pages 57–64 (December 1996).

Heywood, Peter. "ISDN: A Long Time Coming ... But Still No Quick Fix", *Data Communications International,* Vol. 24, No. 15, page 48A (November 1995).

IBM GC20-1868-02. *Systems Network Architecture, Sessions between Logical Units.* International Business Machines Corporation (April 1981).

IBM GC26-4876-02. *Information Warehouse: An Introduction.* International Business Machines Corporation (April 1993).

IBM GC30-3084-03. *Systems Network Architecture, Transaction Programmer's Reference Manual for LU 6.2.* International Business Machines Corporation (September 1990).

IBM GC31-7057-00. *Networking Blueprint Brochure.* International Business Machines Corporation (November 1992).

IBM GC31-7073-00. *Multiprotocol Transport Networking. Technical Overview.* International Business Machines Corporation (May 1993).

IBM GC33-0805-00. *IBM Messaging and Queuing Series. An Introduction to Messaging and Queuing.* International Business Machines Corporation (March 1993).

IBM GH20-2157-00. *Transaction Processing Facility. ACP/TPF Concepts and Architecture.* International Business Machines Corporation (January 1979).

IBM GH20-7488-00. *Transaction Processing Facility. TPF Concepts and Structure Manual.* International Business Machines Corporation (June 1989).

IBM S82G-3743-00. *IBM C/C++ Tools: User Interface Class Library. User's Guide.* International Business Machines Corporation (November 1993).

IBM SC26-4186-01. *IMS/VS Programming Guide for Remote SNA Systems.* International Business Machines Corporation (July 1987).

IBM SC26-4399-04. *Systems Application Architecture, Common Programming Interface, Communications Reference.* International Business Machines Corporation (September 1991).

IBM SC26-4651-01. *Distributed Relational Database Architecture Reference.* International Business Machines Corporation (March 1993).

IBM SC28-8135-00. *IBM Security Architecture. A Model for Securing Information Systems.* International Business Machines Corporation (March 1993).

IBM SC30-3269-03. *Systems Network Architecture, Format and Protocol Reference Manual: Architectural Logic for LU 6.2.* International Business Machines Corporation (December 1985).

IBM SC33-0236-00. *CICS/OS/VS 3790/3730/8100 Guide.* International Business Machines Corporation (November 1985).

IBM SC33-0850-01. *MQSeries. Message Queue Interface. Technical Reference.* International Business Machines Corporation (April 1993).

IEEE 754. *IEEE Standard for Binary Floating-Point Arithmetic.* Institute of Electrical and Electronics Engineers (1990).

IEEE 802.9. *IEEE Standards for Local and Metropolitan Area Networks: Integrated Services (IS) LAN Interface at the Medium Access Control (MAC) and Physical Layers.* Institute of Electrical and Electronics Engineers (1995).

IEEE 802.10. *IEEE Standards for Local and Metropolitan Area Networks: Interoperable LAN/MAN Security (SILS).* Institute of Electrical and Electronics Engineers (1992).

IEEE 802.12. *IEEE Standards for Local and Metropolitan Area Networks: Demand Priority Access Method, Physical Layer and Repeater Specification for 100 Mb/s Operation.* Institute of Electrical and Electronics Engineers (1995).

IEEE 1224. *IEEE Standard for Information Technology—Open Systems Interconnection (OSI) Abstract Data Manipulation—Application Program Interface (API) [Language Independent].* Institute of Electrical and Electronics Engineers (1993).

IEEE 1327. *IEEE Standard for Information Technology—Open Systems Interconnection (OSI) Abstract Data Manipulation C Language Interfaces— Binding for Application Program Interface (API).* Institute of Electrical and Electronics Engineers (1993).

Inmon, William H. *Building the Data Warehouse.* John Wiley & Sons, New York (1993).

ISO/IEC 7372. *Trade Data Interchange—Trade Data Elements Directory (Endorsement of UNECE/TDED, volume 1).* International Organization for Standardization and International Electrotechnical Commission (1993).

ISO/IEC 7498-1 (=ITU-TS X.200). *Information Processing Systems—Open Systems Interconnection—Basic Reference Model.* International Organization for Standardization and International Electrotechnical Commission (1992).

ISO/IEC 7498-1 AD1. *Information Processing Systems—Open Systems Interconnection—Basic Reference Model Addendum 1: Connectionless Data Transmission.* International Organization for Standardization and International Electrotechnical Commission (1987).

ISO/IEC 7498-1 AD2. *Information Processing Systems—Open Systems Interconnection—Basic Reference Model Addendum 2: Multipeer Data Transmission.* International Organization for Standardization and International Electrotechnical Commission (1989).

ISO/IEC 7498-2 (=ITU-TS X.800). *Information Processing Systems—Open Systems Interconnection—Basic Reference Model—Part 2: Security Architecture.* International Organization for Standardization and International Electrotechnical Commission (1988).

ISO/IEC 7498-3 (=ITU-TS X.650). *Information Processing Systems—Open Systems Interconnection—Basic Reference Model—Part 3: Naming and Addressing.* International Organization for Standardization and International Electrotechnical Commission (1987).

ISO/IEC 7498-4 (=ITU-TS X.700). *Information Processing Systems—Open Systems Interconnection—Basic Reference Model—Part 4: Management Framework.* International Organization for Standardization and International Electrotechnical Commission (1989).

ISO/IEC 8208. *Information Technology—Data communications—X.25 Packet Layer Protocol for Data Terminal Equipment.* International Organization for Standardization and International Electrotechnical Commission (1995).

ISO/IEC 8571-1. *Open Systems Interconnection—File Transfer, Access and Management (FTAM)—Part 1: General Introduction.* International Organization for Standardization and International Electrotechnical Commission (1988).

ISO/IEC 8571-2. *Open Systems Interconnection—File Transfer, Access and Management (FTAM)—Part 2: Virtual Filestore Definition.* International Organization for Standardization and International Electrotechnical Commission (1988).

ISO/IEC 8571-3. *Open Systems Interconnection—File Transfer, access and Management (FTAM)—Part 3: The File Service Definition.* International Organization for Standardization and International Electrotechnical Commission (1988).

Appendix

ISO/IEC 8571-4. *Open Systems Interconnections—File Transfer, Access and Management (FTAM)—Part 4: The File Protocol Specification*. International Organization for Standardization and International Electrotechnical Commission (1988).

ISO/IEC 8613. *Information Technology—Open Document Architecture (ODA) and Interchange Format*. International Organization for Standardization and International Electrotechnical Commission (1994).

ISO/IEC 8730. *Banking—Requirements for Message Authentication (Wholesale)*. International Organization for Standardization and International Electrotechnical Commission (1990).

ISO/IEC 8732. *Banking—Key Management (Wholesale)*. International Organization for Standardization and International Electrotechnical Commission (1988).

ISO/IEC 8802-3 (=ANSI/IEEE Std 802.3). *Information Processing Systems—Local Area Networks—Part 3: Carrier Sense Multiple Access with Collision Detection*. International Organization for Standardization and International Electrotechnical Commission (1996).

ISO/IEC 8802-5 (=ANSI/IEEE Std 802.5). *Information Technology— Telecommunications and Information Exchange between Systems—Local and Metropolitan Area Networks—Specific Requirements—Part 5: Token Ring Access Method and Physical Layer Specifications*. International Organization for Standardization and International Electrotechnical Commission (1995).

ISO/IEC 8859. *Information Technology—8-Bit Single-Byte Coded Graphic Character Sets*. International Organization for Standardization and International Electrotechnical Commission (1992).

ISO/IEC 8879. *Telecommunications and Information Exchange between Systems— Use of X.25 to Provide the OSI Connection-mode Network Service*. International Organization for Standardization and International Electrotechnical Commission (1992).

ISO/IEC 9000-3. *Quality Management and Quality Assurance Standards—Part 3: Guidelines for the Application of ISO 9001 to the Development, Supply and Maintenance of Software*. International Organization for Standardization and International Electrotechnical Commission (1991).

ISO/IEC 9072-1 (=ITU-TS X.219). *Remote Operations—Part 1: Model, Notation and Service Definition*. International Organization for Standardization and International Electrotechnical Commission (1989).

ISO/IEC 9072-2 (=ITU-TS X.229). *Remote Operations—Part 2: Protocol Specification*. International Organization for Standardization and International Electrotechnical Commission (1989).

ISO/IEC 9075. *Information Technology—Database Languages—SQL.* International Organization for Standardization and International Electrotechnical Commission (1992).

ISO/IEC 9075-3. *Information Technology—Database Languages—SQL—Part 3: Call-Level Interface (SQL/CLI).* International Organization for Standardization and International Electrotechnical Commission (1995).

ISO/IEC 9075-4. *Information Technology—Database Languages—SQL—Part 4: Persistent Stored Modules (SQL/PSM).* International Organization for Standardization and International Electrotechnical Commission (to be published).

ISO/IEC 9314. *Information Processing Systems—Fibre Distributed Data Interface (FDDI).* International Organization for Standardization and International Electrotechnical Commission (1989).

ISO/IEC 9579-1. *Information Technology—Open Systems Interconnection—Remote Database Access.* International Organization for Standardization and International Electrotechnical Commission (1993).

ISO/IEC 9594-1 (=ITU-TS X.500). *Information Processing Systems—Open Systems Interconnection—The Directory—Part 1: Overview of Concepts, Models and Service.* International Organization for Standardization and International Electrotechnical Commission (1988).

ISO/IEC 9594-2 (=ITU-TS X.500). *Information Processing Systems—Open Systems Interconnection—The Directory—Part 2: Models.* International Organization for Standardization and International Electrotechnical Commission (1988).

ISO/IEC 9594-3 (=ITU-TS X.500). *Information Processing Systems—Open Systems Interconnection—The Directory—Part 3: Abstract Service Definition.* International Organization for Standardization and International Electrotechnical Commission (1988).

ISO/IEC 9594-4 (=ITU-TS X.500). *Information Processing Systems—Open Systems Interconnection—The Directory—Part 4: Procedures for Distributed Operations.* International Organization for Standardization and International Electrotechnical Commission (1988).

ISO/IEC 9594-5 (=ITU-TS X.500). *Information Processing Systems—Open Systems Interconnection—The Directory—Part 5: Protocol Specifications.* International Organization for Standardization and International Electrotechnical Commission (1988).

ISO/IEC 9594-6 (=ITU-TS X.500). *Information Processing Systems—Open Systems Interconnection—The Directory—Part 6: Selected Attribute Types.*

International Organization for Standardization and International Electrotechnical Commission (1988).

ISO/IEC 9594-7 (=ITU-TS X.500). *Information Processing Systems—Open Systems Interconnection—The Directory—Part 7: Selected Object Classes.* International Organization for Standardization and International Electrotechnical Commission (1988).

ISO/IEC 9594-8 (=ITU-TS X.500). *Information Processing Systems—Open Systems Interconnection—The Directory—Part 8: Authentication Framework.* International Organization for Standardization and International Electrotechnical Commission (1988).

ISO/IEC 9595 (=ITU-TS X.710) *Information Technology—Open Systems Interconnection—Common Management Information Service (CMIS).* International Organization for Standardization and International Electrotechnical Commission (1990).

ISO/IEC 9596. *Information Technology—Open Systems Interconnection—Common Management Information Protocol (CMIP).* International Organization for Standardization and International Electrotechnical Commission (1991).

ISO/IEC 9735. *Electronic Data Interchange for Administration, Commerce and Transport (EDIFACT)—Application Level Syntax Rules.* International Organization for Standardization and International Electrotechnical Commission (1990).

ISO/IEC 9945-1 (=IEEE 1003.1). *Information Technology—Portable Operating System Interface (POSIX)—Part 1: System Application Program Interface (API) [C Language].* International Organization for Standardization and International Electrotechnical Commission (1990).

ISO/IEC 9945-2 (=IEEE 1003.2). *Information Technology—Portable Operating System Interface (POSIX)—Part 2: Shell and Utilities.* International Organization for Standardization and International Electrotechnical Commission (1993).

ISO/IEC 10021-1. *Information Technology—Text Communication—Message-Oriented Text Interchange Systems (MOTIS)—Part 1: System and Service Overview.* International Organization for Standardization and International Electrotechnical Commission (1990).

ISO/IEC 10021-2. *Information Technology—Text Communication—Message-Oriented Text Interchange Systems (MOTIS)—Part 2: Overall Architecture.* International Organization for Standardization and International Electrotechnical Commission (1990).

ISO/IEC 10021-3. *Information Technology—Text Communication—Message-Oriented Text Interchange Systems (MOTIS)—Part 3: Abstract Service Definition Conventions.* International Organization for Standardization and International Electrotechnical Commission (1990).

ISO/IEC 10021-4. *Information Technology—Text Communication—Message-Oriented Text Interchange Systems (MOTIS)—Part 4: Message Transfer System: Abstract Service Definition and Procedures.* International Organization for Standardization and International Electrotechnical Commission (1990)

ISO/IEC 10021-5. *Information Technology—Message Handling Systems (MHS): Message Store: Abstract Service Definition.* International Organization for Standardization and International Electrotechnical Commission (1996).

ISO/IEC 10021-6. *Information Technology—Text Communication—Message-Oriented Text Interchange Systems (MOTIS)—Part 6: Protocol Specifications.* International Organization for Standardization and International Electrotechnical Commission (1990).

ISO/IEC 10021-7. *Information Technology—Text Communication—Message-Oriented Text Interchange Systems (MOTIS)—Part 7: Interpersonal Messaging System.* International Organization for Standardization and International Electrotechnical Commission (1990).

ISO/IEC 10021-8. *Information Technology—Message Handling Systems (MHS)—Part 8: Electronic Data Interchange Messaging Service.* International Organization for Standardization and International Electrotechnical Commission (1995).

ISO/IEC 10021-9. *Information Technology—Message Handling Systems (MHS)—Part 9: Electronic Data Interchange Messaging System.* International Organization for Standardization and International Electrotechnical Commission (1995).

ISO/IEC 10026-1. *Information Processing Systems—Open Systems Interconnection—Distributed Transaction Processing—Part 1: OSI TP Model.* International Organization for Standardization and International Electrotechnical Commission (1992).

ISO/IEC 10026-2. *Information Processing Systems—Open Systems Interconnection—Distributed Transaction Processing—Part 2: Service Definition.* International Organization for Standardization and International Electrotechnical Commission (1992).

ISO/IEC 10026-3. *Information Processing Systems—Open Systems Interconnection—Distributed Transaction Processing—Part 3: Protocol Specification.* International Organization for Standardization and International Electrotechnical Commission (1992).

Appendix

ISO/IEC 10040 (=ITU-TS X.701). *Information Technology—Open Systems Interconnection—Systems Management Overview.* International Organization for Standardization and International Electrotechnical Commission (1991).

ISO/IEC 10164-7 (=ITU-TS X.736). *Systems Management—Part 7: Security Alarm Reporting Function.* International Organization for Standardization and International Electrotechnical Commission (1992).

ISO/IEC 10164-8 (=ITU-TS X.740). *Systems Management—Part 8: Security Audit Trail Function.* International Organization for Standardization and International Electrotechnical Commission (1992).

ISO/IEC 10164-18 (=ITU-TS X.744). *Systems Management—Part 18: Software Management Function.* International Organization for Standardization and International Electrotechnical Commission (1996).

ISO/IEC 10165-1 (=ITU-TS X.720). *Management Information Standards—Structure of Management Information (SMI)—Part 1: Management Information Model (MIM).* International Organization for Standardization and International Electrotechnical Commission (1993).

ISO/IEC 10165-2 (=ITU-TS X.721). *Management Information Standards—Structure of Management Information (SMI)—Part 2: Definition of Management Information (DMI).* International Organization for Standardization and International Electrotechnical Commission (1992).

ISO/IEC 10165-4 (=ITU-TS X.722). *Management Information Standards—Structure of Management Information (SMI)—Part 4: Guidelines for the Definition of Managed Objects (GDMO).* International Organization for Standardization and International Electrotechnical Commission (1992).

ISO/IEC 10165-5 (=ITU-TS X.723). *Management Information Standards—Structure of Management Information (SMI)—Part 5: Generic Management Information (GMI).* International Organization for Standardization and International Electrotechnical Commission (1992).

ISO/IEC 10165-6 (=ITU-TS X.724). *Management Information Standards—Structure of Management Information (SMI)—Part 6: Requirements and Guidelines for Implementation Conformance Statement Proformas Associated with Management Information.* International Organization for Standardization and International Electrotechnical Commission (1991).

ISO/IEC 10165-7 (=ITU-TS X.725). *Management Information Standards—Structure of Management Information (SMI)—Part 7: General Relationship Model (GRM).* International Organization for Standardization and International Electrotechnical Commission (1993).

ISO/IEC 10166-1. *Information Technology—Document Filing and Retrieval (DFR)—Part 1: Abstract Service Definition and Procedures.* International Organization for Standardization and International Electrotechnical Commission (1989).

ISO/IEC 10166-2. *Information Technology—Document Filing and Retrieval (DFR)—Part 2: Protocol Specification.* International Organization for Standardization and International Electrotechnical Commission (1989).

ISO/IEC 10175-1. *Information Technology—Text and Office Systems—Document Printing Application (DPA)—Part 1: Abstract Service Definition and Procedures.* International Organization for Standardization and International Electrotechnical Commission (1996).

ISO/IEC 10175-2. *Information Technology—Text and Office Systems—Document Printing Application (DPA)—Part 2: Protocol Specification.* International Organization for Standardization and International Electrotechnical Commission (1996).

ISO/IEC 10181-1 (=ITU-TS X.810). *Open Systems Interconnection—Security Frameworks in Open Systems—Part 1: Overview.* International Organization for Standardization and International Electrotechnical Commission (1992).

ISO/IEC 10181-2 (=ITU-TS X.811). *Open Systems Interconnection—Security Frameworks in Open Systems—Part 2: Authentication Framework.* International Organization for Standardization and International Electrotechnical Commission (1993).

ISO/IEC 10181-3 (=ITU-TS X.812). *Open Systems Interconnection—Security Frameworks in Open Systems—Part 3: Access Control.* International Organization for Standardization and International Electrotechnical Commission (1992).

ISO/IEC 10181-4 (=ITU-TS X.813). *Open Systems Interconnection—Security Frameworks in Open Systems—Part 4: Non-repudiation.* International Organization for Standardization and International Electrotechnical Commission (1993).

ISO/IEC 10181-5 (=ITU-TS X.814). *Open Systems Interconnection—Security Frameworks in Open Systems—Part 5: Confidentiality.* International Organization for Standardization and International Electrotechnical Commission (1993).

ISO/IEC 10181-6 (=ITU-TS X.815). *Open Systems Interconnection—Security Frameworks in Open Systems—Part 6: Integrity.* International Organization for Standardization and International Electrotechnical Commission (1993).

ISO/IEC 10181-7 (=ITU-TS X.816). *Open Systems Interconnection—Security Frameworks in Open Systems—Part 7: Security Audit Framework.*

International Organization for Standardization and International Electrotechnical Commission (1993).

ISO/IEC 10181-8 (=ITU-TS X.817). *Open Systems Interconnection—Security Frameworks in Open Systems—Part 8: Confidentiality Framework.* International Organization for Standardization and International Electrotechnical Commission (1996).

ISO/IEC 10646-1. *Information Technology—Universal Multiple-Octet Coded Character Set (UCS)—Part 1: Architecture and Basic Multilingual Plane.* International Organization for Standardization and International Electrotechnical Commission (1993).

ISO/IEC 11586-1 (=ITU-TS X.830). *Open Systems Interconnection—Generic Upper Layers Security (GULS)—Part 1: Overview, Models and Notation.* International Organization for Standardization and International Electrotechnical Commission (1993).

ISO/IEC 11586-2 (=ITU-TS X.831). *Open Systems Interconnection—Generic Upper Layers Security (GULS)—Part 2: Security Exchange Service Element (SESE) Service Definition.* International Organization for Standardization and International Electrotechnical Commission (1993).

ISO/IEC 11586-3 (=ITU-TS X.832). *Open Systems Interconnection—Generic Upper Layers Security (GULS)—Part 3: Security Exchange Service Element (SESE) Protocol Specification.* International Organization for Standardization and International Electrotechnical Commission (1993).

ISO/IEC 11586-4 (=ITU-TS X.833). *Open Systems Interconnection—Generic Upper Layers Security (GULS)—Part 4: Protecting Transfer Syntax Specification.* International Organization for Standardization and International Electrotechnical Commission (1993).

ISO/IEC 11587 (=ITU-TS X.702). *Information Technology—Open Systems Interconnection—Application Context for Systems Management with Transaction Processing.* International Organization for Standardization and International Electrotechnical Commission (1994).

ISO/IEC 13208. *Message Handling Systems—Electronic Data Interchange Messaging System.* International Organization for Standardization and International Electrotechnical Commission (1992).

ISO/IEC 13209. *Text and Office Systems—Message Handling—Electronic Data Interchange Messaging Service.* International Organization for Standardization and International Electrotechnical Commission (1992).

ISO/IEC 13594. *Information Technology—Lower Layers Security.* International Organization for Standardization and International Electrotechnical Commission (1995).

ISO/IEC 14392. *Information Technology—Directory Services—Application Program Interface (API) [Language Independent].* International Organization for Standardization and International Electrotechnical Commission (1996).

ISO/IEC 14394. *Information Technology—Directory Services C Language Interfaces—Binding for Application Program Interface (API).* International Organization for Standardization and International Electrotechnical Commission (1996).

ISO/IEC 15802-1. *Information Technology—Telecommunications and Information Exchange between Systems—Local and Metropolitan Area Networks— Common Specifications—Part 1: Medium Access Control (MAC) Service Definition.* International Organization for Standardization and International Electrotechnical Commission (1993).

ISO/IEC 15802-2. *Information Technology—Telecommunications and Information Exchange between Systems—Local and Metropolitan Area Networks— Common Specifications—Part 2: LAN/MAN Management, Service and Protocol.* International Organization for Standardization and International Electrotechnical Commission (1994).

ISO/IEC 15802-3. *Information Technology—Telecommunications and Information Exchange between Systems—Local and Metropolitan Area Networks— Common Specifications—Part 3: System Load Protocol.* International Organization for Standardization and International Electrotechnical Commission (1994).

ITU-TS I.120. *Integrated Services Digital Networks (ISDNs).* International Telecommunication Union—Telecommunications Sector (March 1993).

ITU-TS I.361. *B-ISDN ATM Layer Specification.* International Telecommunication Union—Telecommunications Sector (November 1995).

ITU-TS X.36. *Interface between Data Terminal Equipment (DTE) and Data Circuit-Terminating Equipment (DCE) for Public Data Networks Providing Frame Relay Data Transmission Service by Dedicated Circuit.* International Telecommunication Union—Telecommunications Sector (April 1995).

ITU-TS X.76. *Network-to-Network Interface between Public Data Networks Providing the Frame Relay Data Transmission Service.* International Telecommunication Union—Telecommunications Sector (April 1995).

Johnson, Johna Till. "The Internet: Corporations Worldwide Make the Connection", *Data Communications International,* Vol. 23, No. 6, page 67 (April 1994).

Johnson, Johna Till. "Enterprise NOSs. Now's the Time". *Data Communications International,* Vol. 24, No. 7, page 40 (May 21, 1995).

Kennedy, Randall C. "The Elegant Kludge", *BYTE,* Vol. 20, No. 8, page 54 (August 1995).

King, Steven S. "After Downsizing: Overcoming Client-Server Chaos", *Data Communications International,* Vol. 23, No. 8, page 52 (May 21, 1994).

Klessig, Robert W., and Tesink, Kaj. *SMDS. Wide-Area Data Networking with Switched Multi-megabit Data Service.* Prentice-Hall, Englewood Cliffs, N.J. (1995).

Kosiur, Dave. "E-Mail Grows Up", *BYTE,* Vol. 21, No. 12, page 135 (December 1996).

Kuhn, Thomas S. *The Structure of Scientific Revolutions.* University of Chicago Press (1962), Second Edition (1970). Cited in Kuhn, Thomas S. *Die Entstehung des Neuen. Studien zur Struktur der Wissenschaftsgeschichte.* Suhrkamp, Frankfurt (1967), Third Edition (1976).

Langsford, Alwyn, and Moffett, Jonathan D. *Distributed Systems Management.* Addison-Wesley, Reading, Mass. (1993).

Lem, Stanislaw. *Solaris (*1961). 8. Auflage Deutscher Taschenbuch Verlag, München (1992). Movie by Andrei Tarkovsky (1971).

Lemay, Laura, and Perkins, Charles. *Teach Yourself Java in 21 Days.* Sams.net Publishing (1996). Excerpted in "Yes, Java's Secure. Here's Why", *Datamation,* Vol. 42, No. 5, pages 47–49 (March 1, 1996).

Lewis, Jamie. "LDAP Unites the Internet", *BYTE,* Vol. 21, No. 12, page 121 (December 1996).

McCarthy, Vance. "Performance Tools Kill the Gremlins on Your Net", *Datamation,* Vol. 42, No. 15, pages 88–91 (September 1996).

McLuhan, Marshall. *Understanding Media: The Extensions of Man.* Routledge, London (1964). Reprinted 1994.

Melatti, Lee. "Fast Ethernet: 100 Mbit/s Made Easy", *Data Communications International,* Vol. 23, No. 16, page 111 (November 1994).

Microsoft NT. *Windows NT Resource Kit.* Volume 1. Microsoft Press, Redmond, Wash. (1993).

Miller, Chris L. "Transborder Tips and Traps", *BYTE,* Vol. 19, No. 6, page 93 (June 1994).

Nadeau, Michael. "Vendors Work to Cure Incompatibility Blues", *BYTE,* Vol. 19, No. 6, page 32 (June 1994).

NMF Forum 24. *Application Services—Trouble Management Function. Issue 1.0.* Network Management Forum (August 1992)

NMF/OMNIPoint. *Network Management Forum. Discovering OMNIPoint.* Prentice-Hall, Englewood Cliffs, N.J. (1993).

OMG/CORBA. *The Common Object Request Broker: Architecture and Specification, Revision 1.2.* Object Management Group, Boulder, Colo. (1993).

OMG/OMTF. *The OMG Object Model V0.9.* Object Management Group/Object Model Task Force, Boulder, Colo. (1991).

Orfali, Robert, Harkey, Dan, and Edwards, Jeri. *Essential Client/Server Survival Guide.* John Wiley & Sons, New York (1994).

OSF. *Application Environment Specification (AES)/Distributed Computing.* Prentice-Hall, Englewood Cliffs, N.J. (1993).

OSF. *Introduction to OSF DCE.* Prentice-Hall, Englewood Cliffs, N.J. (1993).

OSF. *OSF DCE Administration Guide.* Prentice-Hall, Englewood Cliffs, N.J. (1993).

OSF. *OSF DCE Administration Reference.* Prentice-Hall, Englewood Cliffs, N.J. (1993).

OSF. *OSF DCE Application Development Reference.* Prentice-Hall, Englewood Cliffs, N.J. (1993).

OSF. *OSF DCE Porting and Testing Guide.* Prentice-Hall, Englewood Cliffs, N.J. (1993).

OSF. *OSF DCE Release Notes.* Prentice-Hall, Englewood Cliffs, N.J. (1993).

OSF. *OSF DCE Technical Supplement.* Prentice-Hall, Englewood Cliffs, N.J. (1993).

OSF. *OSF DCE User's Guide and Reference.* Prentice-Hall, Englewood Cliffs, N.J. (1993).

Parnas, David Lorge. "Software Aspects of Strategic Defense Systems", *Commun. ACM,* Vol. 28, No. 12, pages 1326–1335 (December 1985).

Petzold, Charles. *Programming the OS/2 Presentation Manager.* Microsoft Press/Penguin Books, Redmond, Wash. (1989).

Rauch, Peter, and Lawrence, Scott. "100VG-AnyLAN: The Other Fast Ethernet", *Data Communications International,* Vol. 24, No. 3, page 129 (March 1995).

Appendix

Redcom 6/96. "ActiveX: Microsoft's Internet Client Development Strategy", *Directions on Microsoft,* (June 1996). Redmond Communications, Inc., ISSN 1077–4394.

Reinhardt, Andy. "Managing Storage", *BYTE,* Vol. 19, No. 6, page 153 (June 1994).

Reinhardt, Andy. "The Network with Smarts", *BYTE,* Vol. 19, No. 10, page 51 (October 1994).

RFC 768. Postel, J. *User Datagram Protocol.* Internet Activities Board (1980).

RFC 783. Sollins, K. *TFTP Protocol (Revision 2).* Internet Activities Board (1981).

RFC 791. Postel, J. *Internet Protocol.* Internet Activities Board (1981).

RFC 792. Postel, J. *Internet Control Message Protocol.* Internet Activities Board (1981).

RFC 793. Postel, J. *Transmission Control Protocol.* Internet Activities Board (1981).

RFC 821. Postel, J. *Simple Mail Transfer Protocol.* Internet Activities Board (1982).

RFC 822. Crocker, D. *Standard for the Format of ARPA Internet Text Messages.* Internet Activities Board (1982).

RFC 827. Rosen, E. *Exterior Gateway Protocol (EGP).* Internet Activities Board (1982).

RFC 854. Postel, J., and Reynolds, J. *Telnet Protocol Specification.* Internet Activities Board (1983).

RFC 888. Seamonson, L., and Rosen, E. *STUB Exterior Gateway Protocol.* Internet Activities Board (1984).

RFC 904. Mills, D. *Exterior Gateway Protocol Formal Specification.* Internet Activities Board (1984).

RFC 950. Mogul, J., and Postel, J. *Internet Standard Subnetting Procedure.* Internet Activities Board (1985).

RFC 951. Croft, W., and Gilmore, J. *Bootstrap Protocol.* Internet Activities Board (1985).

RFC 959. Postel, J., and Reynolds, J. *File Transfer Protocol.* Internet Activities Board (1985).

RFC 1006. Rose, M., and Cass, D. *ISO Transport Services on Top of the TCP: Version 3.* Internet Activities Board (1987).

RFC 1014. Sun Microsystems, Inc. *XDR: External Data Representation Standard.* Internet Activities Board (1987).

RFC 1032. Stahl, M. *Domain Administrators Guide.* Internet Activities Board (1987).

RFC 1034. Mockapetris, P. *Domain Names—Concepts and Facilities.* Internet Activities Board (1987).

RFC 1035. Mockapetris, P. *Domain Names—Implementation and Specification.* Internet Activities Board (1987).

RFC 1055. Romkey, J. *Nonstandard for Transmission of IP Datagrams over Serial Lines: SLIP.* Internet Activities Board (1988).

RFC 1057. Sun Microsystems, Inc. *RPC: Remote Procedure Call Protocol Specification: Version 2.* Internet Activities Board (1988).

RFC 1058. Hedrick, C. *Routing Information Protocol.* Internet Activities Board (1988).

RFC 1094. Sun Microsystems, Inc. *NFS: Network File System Protocol Specification.* Internet Activities Board (1989).

RFC 1101. Mockapetris, P. *DNS Encoding of Network Names and Other Types.* Internet Activities Board (1989).

RFC 1108. Kent, S. *Security Options for the Internet Protocol.* Internet Activities Board (1991).

RFC 1112. Deering, S. *Host Extensions for IP Multicasting.* Internet Activities Board (1989).

RFC 1155. Rose, M., and McCloghrie, K. *Structure and Identification of Management Information for TCP/IP-based Internets.* Internet Activities Board (1990).

RFC 1157. Case, J., Fedor, M., Schoffstall, M., and Davin, C. *Simple Network Management Protocol (SNMP).* Internet Activities Board (1990).

RFC 1183. Everhart, C., Mamakos, L., Ullmann, R., and Mockapetris, P. *New DNS RR Definitions.* Internet Activities Board (1990).

RFC 1212. Rose, M., and McCloghrie, K., eds. *Concise MIB Definitions.* Internet Activities Board (1991).

RFC 1213. Rose, M., and McCloghrie, K., eds. *Management Information Base for Network Management of TCP/IP-based Internets: MIB-II.* Internet Activities Board (1991).

RFC 1348. Manning, B. *DNS NSAP RRs.* Internet Activities Board (1992).

RFC 1349. Almquist, P. *Type of Service in the Internet Protocol Suite.* Internet Activities Board (1992).

Appendix

RFC 1350. Sollins, K. *The TFTP Protocol (Revision 2)*. Internet Activities Board (1992).

RFC 1388. Malkin, G. *RIP Version 2—Carrying Additional Information*. Internet Activities Board (1993).

RFC 1421. Linn, J. *Privacy Enhancement for Internet Electronic Mail: Part I: Message Encryption and Authentication Procedures*. Internet Activities Board (1993).

RFC 1422. Kent, S. *Privacy Enhancement for Internet Electronic Mail: Part II: Certificate-Based Key Management*. Internet Activities Board (1993).

RFC 1423. Balenson, D. *Privacy Enhancement for Internet Electronic Mail: Part III: Algorithms, Modes, and Identifiers*. Internet Activities Board (1993).

RFC 1424. Kaliski, B. *Privacy Enhancement for Internet Electronic Mail: Part IV: Key Certification and Related Services*. Internet Activities Board (1993).

RFC 1508. Linn, J. *Generic Security Service Application Program Interface*. Internet Activities Board (1993).

RFC 1509. Wray, J. *Generic Security Service API: C-bindings*. Internet Activities Board (1993).

RFC 1510. Kohl, J., and Neuman, B. *The Kerberos Network Authentication Service (V5)*. Internet Activities Board (1993).

RFC 1513. Waldbusser, S. *Token Ring Extensions to the Remote Network Monitoring MIB*. Internet Activities Board (1993).

RFC 1533. Alexander, S., and Droms, R. *DHCP Options and BOOTP Vendor Extensions*. Internet Activities Board (1993).

RFC 1540. Postel, J., ed. *Internet Official Protocol Standards*. Internet Activities Board (1993).

RFC 1542. Wimer, W. *Clarifications and Extensions for the Bootstrap Protocol*. Internet Activities Board (1993).

RFC 1731. Myers, J. *IMAP4 Authentication Mechanisms*. Internet Activities Board (1994).

RFC 1777. Yeong, W., Howes, T., and and Kille, S. *Lightweight Directory Access Protocol*. Internet Activities Board (1995).

RFC 1778. Howes, T., Kille, S., Yeong, W., and Robbins, C. *The String Representation of Standard Attribute Syntaxes*. Internet Activities Board (1995).

RFC 1779. Kille, S. *A String Representation of Distinguished Names.* Internet Activities Board (1995).

RFC 1808. Fielding, R. *Relative Uniform Resource Locators.* Internet Activities Board (1995).

RFC 1823. Howes, T., and Smith, M. *The LDAP Application Program Interface.* Internet Activities Board (1995).

RFC 1866. Berners-Lee, T., and Connolly, D. *Hypertext Markup Language—2.0.* Internet Activities Board (1995).

RFC 1883. Deering, S., and Hinden, R. *Internet Protocol, Version 6 (IPv6) Specification.* Internet Activities Board (1996).

RFC 1884. Hinden, R., and Deering, S. *IP Version 6 Addressing Architecture.* Internet Activities Board (1996).

RFC 1885. Conta, A., and Deering, S. *Internet Control Message Protocol (ICMPv6) for the Internet Protocol Version 6 (IPv6).* Internet Activities Board (1996).

RFC 1886. Thomson, S., and Huitema, C. *DNS Extensions to support IP version 6.* Internet Activities Board (1996).

RFC 1887. Rekhter, Y., and Li, T. *An Architecture for IPv6 Unicast Address Allocation.* Internet Activities Board (1996).

RFC 1889. Schulzrinne, H., Casner, S., Frederick, R., and Jacobson, V. *RTP: A Transport Protocol for Real-Time Applications.* Internet Activities Board (1996).

RFC 1890. Schulzrinne, H. *RTP Profile for Audio and Video Conferences with Minimal Control.* Internet Activities Board (1996).

RFC 1939. Myers, J., and Rose, M. *Post Office Protocol—Version 3.* Internet Activities Board (1996).

RFC 1964. Linn, J. *The Kerberos Version 5 GSS-API Mechanism.* Internet Activities Board (1996).

RFC 2060. Crispin, M. *Internet Message Access Protocol—Version 4rev1.* Internet Activities Board (1996).

Richter, Jane. "ODBC 2.0 Further Establishes Cross-Product Data Sharing Standard", *BYTE,* Vol. 19, No. 11, page 52 (November 1994).

Rivest, R., Shamir A., and Adleman, L. *A Method for Obtaining Digital Signatures and Public-Key Cryptosystems.* MIT Laboratory for Computer Science, memo LCS/TM82 (1977).

Rose, Marshall. *Open Book: A Practical Perspective on OSI*. Prentice-Hall, Englewood Cliffs, N.J. (1990).

Russell, Deborah, and Gangemi, G. T. Sr. *Computer Security Basics*. O'Reilly & Associates, Sebastopol, Calif. (1991).

Saltzer, J. H., Reed, D. P., and Clark, D. D. "End-to-End Arguments in System Design", *ACM Transactions on Computer Systems*, Vol. 2, No. 4, pages 277–288 (November 1984).

Santifaller, Michael. *TCP/IP and ONC/NFS Internetworking in a UNIX Environment*. Addison-Wesley, Reading, Mass. (1994).

Sarna, David E., and Febish, George J. "Client/Server Scalability Myth", *Datamation*, Vol. 40, No. 18, pages 31–32 (September 15, 1994).

Semich, J. William. "Client/Server CASE: Oxymoron or Essential?" *Datamation*, Vol. 40, No. 17, pages 67–80 (September 1, 1994).

Semich, J. William. "Client/Server Unchained: Finally, Hardware Independence", *Datamation*, Vol. 41, No. 11, pages 40–45 (June 15, 1995).

Semich, J. William. "Manage Factory Production With CA-Unicenter", *Datamation*, Vol. 42, No. 8, pages 34–38 (April 15, 1996).

Semich, J. William and Fisco, David. "Java: Internet Toy or Enterprise Tool?" *Datamation*, Vol. 42, No. 5, pages 28–29 (March 1, 1996).

Sheldon, Tom. "MAPI Blooms in Chicago", *BYTE*, Vol. 19, No. 11, page 163 (November 1994).

Simpson, David. "The Java-based 'Internet PC'", *Datamation*, Vol. 42, No. 5, page 33 (March 1, 1996).

Simpson, David. "Will DMI Hold Down Desktop Costs?" *Datamation*, Vol. 42, No. 17, page 96 (November 1996).

Sokol, Phyllis K. *From EDI to Electronic Commerce: A Business Initiative*. McGraw-Hill, New York (1995). ISBN 0-07-059512-7.

Stallings, William. *SNMP, SNMPv2, and CMIP: The Practical Guide to Network Management Standards*. Addison-Wesley, Reading, Mass. (1993).

Stallings, William. "Kerberos Keeps the Enterprise Secure", *Data Communications International*, Vol. 23, No. 14, page 103 (October 1994).

Stallings, William. "Patching the Cracks in SNMP", *BYTE*, Vol. 21, No. 8, page 55 (August 1996).

Stallings, William. "The New and Improved Internet Protocol", *BYTE*, Vol. 21, No. 9, page 55 (September 1996).

Stallings, William. "Internet Armor", *BYTE*, Vol. 21, No. 12, page 127 (December 1996).

Stein, Richard Marlon. "Object Databases", *BYTE*, Vol. 19, No. 4, page 75 (April 1994).

Stix, Gary. "Domesticating Cyberspace", *Scientific American*, Vol. 269, No. 2, pages 84–92 (August 1993).

Tanenbaum, Andrew S. *Computer Networks*. Prentice-Hall, Englewood Cliffs, N.J. (1981).

Tanenbaum, Andrew S. *Distributed Operating Systems*. Prentice-Hall, Englewood Cliffs, N.J. (1995).

Tapscott, Don, and Caston, Art. *Paradigm Shift. The New Promise of Information Technology*. McGraw-Hill, New York (1993).

Thé, Lee. "Getting Into the Workflow", *Datamation*, Vol. 40, No. 19, pages 65–68 (October 1, 1994).

Thé, Lee. "Workflow Tackles the Productivity Paradox", *Datamation*, Vol. 41, No. 15, pages 65–73 (August 15, 1995).

Trammell, Kelly. "Under Construction", *BYTE*, Vol. 20, No. 8, pages 93–101 (August 1995).

Udell, Jon. "Special Report. Advanced Operating Systems. The Great OS Debate", *BYTE*, Vol. 19, No. 1, page 117 (January 1994).

Udell, Jon. "Componentware", *BYTE*, Vol. 19, No. 5, page 46 (May 1994).

van Hoff, Arthur, Shaio, Sami, and Starbuck, Orca. *Hooked on Java*. Addison-Wesley, Reading, Mass. (1995). Excerpted in "What is this Thing Called Java?", *Datamation*, Vol. 42, No. 5, pages 45–46 (March 1, 1996).

Varhol, Peter D. "Small Kernels Hit It Big", *BYTE*, Vol. 19, No. 1, page 119 (January 1994).

Varney, Sarah E. "Datawebs! Link the Web to Your Legacy Data and Apps", *Datamation*, Vol. 42, No. 7, pages 38–47 (April 1, 1996).

VITAL. *Introduction to VITAL. Designing Information Systems for the 1990s*. Apple Computer Inc., Cupertino, Calif. (1992).

Walton, Mary. *The Deming Management Method*. Perigee Books (Putnam), New York (1986).

Wayner, Peter. "Objects on the March", *BYTE*, Vol. 19, No. 1, page 139 (January 1994).

Wayner, Peter. "Agents Away", *BYTE,* Vol. 19, No. 5, page 113 (May 1994).

Wayner, Peter. "EDI Moves the Data", *BYTE,* Vol. 19, No. 10, page 121 (October 1994).

Wayner, Peter. "DragNET", *BYTE,* Vol. 20, No. 12, page 106 (December 1995).

Weinberg, Steven. *Dreams of a Final Theory.* Vintage, London (1993).

Wirth, Niklaus. "The Personal Computer Lilith", *Microcomputer Systems Design,* Lecture Notes in Computer Science No. 126, Springer-Verlag, Berlin (1981).

WOSA. *Windows Open Services Architecture Corporate Backgrounder.* Microsoft Corporation. Part Number 098-34801.

WOSA/XFS. *A Client-Server Architecture for Financial Enterprise Computing, Windows Open Services Architecture Extensions for Financial Services: Overview of Objectives, Architecture and Elements.* Banking Systems Vendor Council (April 1993).

X/Open C193. *X/Open CAE Specification C193. Distributed TP: The XA Specification.* X/Open Company Limited (1992). ISBN 872630-24-3.

X/Open C306. *X/Open CAE Specification C306. Systems Management: Management Protocols API (XMP).* X/Open Company Limited (1994). ISBN 1-85912-027-X.

X/Open C307. *X/Open CAE Specification C307. Data Management: SQL Remote Database Access.* X/Open Company Limited (1993). ISBN 872630-98-7.

X/Open C315. *X/Open CAE Specification C315. OSI-Abstract-Data Manipulation API (XOM).* X/Open Company Limited (1994). ISBN 1-85912-008-3.

X/Open C415. *X/Open CAE Specification C415. FTAM High-level API (XFTAM), Version 2.* X/Open Company Limited (1995). ISBN 1-85912-092-X.

X/Open C419. *X/Open CAE Specification C419. Distributed TP: CPI-C Specification, Version 2.* X/Open Company Limited (1995). ISBN 1-85912-135-7.

X/Open C434. *X/Open CAE Specification C434. System Interface Definitions, Issue 4, Version 2.* X/Open Company Limited (1994). ISBN 1-85912-036-9.

X/Open C435. *X/Open CAE Specification C435. System Interfaces and Headers, Issue 4, Version 2.* X/Open Company Limited (1994). ISBN 1-85912-037-7.

X/Open C436. *X/Open CAE Specification C436. Commands and Utilities, Issue 4, Version 2.* X/Open Company Limited (1994). ISBN 1-85912-034-2.

X/Open C438. *X/Open CAE Specification C438. Networking Services, Issue 4.* X/Open Company Limited (1994). ISBN 1-85912-049-0.

X/Open C451. *X/Open CAE Specification C451. Data Management: SQL Call Level Interface (CLI).* X/Open Company Limited (1995). ISBN 1-85912-081-4.

X/Open C505. *X/Open CAE Specification C505. Distributed TP: The TxRPC Specification.* X/Open Company Limited (1995). ISBN 1-85912-115-2.

X/Open C506. *X/Open CAE Specification C506. Distributed TP: The XATMI Specification.* X/Open Company Limited (1995). ISBN 1-85912-130-6.

X/Open C520. *X/Open CAE Specification C520. Multiprotocol Transport Networking (XMPTN): Address Mapper.* X/Open Company Limited (1996).

X/Open C521. *X/Open CAE Specification C521. Multiprotocol Transport Networking (XMPTN): Access Node.* X/Open Company Limited (1996).

X/Open C522. *X/Open CAE Specification C522. Multiprotocol Transport Networking (XMPTN): Data Formats.* X/Open Company Limited (1996).

X/Open C608. *X/Open CAE Specification C608. API to Directory Services (XDS), Issue 3.* X/Open Company Limited (1996). ISBN 1-85912-180-2.

X/Open C609. *X/Open CAE Specification C609. API to Electronic Mail (X.400), Issue 3.* X/Open Company Limited (1996). ISBN 1-85912-185-3.

X/Open C610. *X/Open CAE Specification C610. X/Open Curses, Issue 4, Version 2.* X/Open Company Limited (1996). ISBN 1-85912-171-3.

X/Open D010. *X/Open Developers' Specification D010. Indexed Sequential Access Method (ISAM).* X/Open Company Limited (1990). ISBN 1-872630-03-0.

X/Open G207. *X/Open Guide G207. Systems Management: Reference Model.* X/Open Company Limited (1993). ISBN 1-85912-005-9.

X/Open G504. *X/Open Guide G504. Distributed TP: Reference Model, Version 3.* X/Open Company Limited (1996). ISBN 1-85912-170-5.

X/Open G506. *X/Open Guide G506. Multiprotocol Transport Networking (MPTN) Architecture, Version 2.* X/Open Company Limited (1996).

X/Open G508. *X/Open Guide G508. Architecture Neutral Distribution Format (XANDF) Guide.* X/Open Company Limited (1996).

X/Open P527. *X/Open Preliminary Specification P527. Architecture Neutral Distribution Format (XANDF) Specification.* X/Open Company Limited (1996).

Yavin, David. "Replication's Fast Track", *BYTE,* Vol. 20, No. 8, pages 88A–90 (August 1995).

Index

Appendix

About the Author

Thomas S. Ligon has 18 years of experience in software development, including work on mainframes, minicomputers, and PCs, with a primary emphasis on data communications. His work has included maintenance, coding, design, project management, and general consulting for numerous clients in Germany and other parts of Europe. He received a bachelor's degree from the University of Richmond, Virginia, and a Dr. rer. nat. from the Ludwig-Maximilians Universität in Munich, Germany.

Dr. Ligon is currently a principal consultant for Microsoft in Germany, and previously held the position of project manager with Softlab, a German software company. This book was written while he was with Softlab, and published after he joined Microsoft. Any opinions expressed in the book are not necessarily those of either company.